VOLUME ONE
THE LIFE AND TEACHINGS
OF
JESUS CHRIST

FROM BETHLEHEM THROUGH THE SERMON ON THE MOUNT

VOLUME ONE

THE LIFE AND TEACHINGS
OF
JESUS CHRIST

FROM BETHLEHEM THROUGH THE SERMON ON THE MOUNT

EDITED BY
RICHARD NEITZEL HOLZAPFEL
& THOMAS A. WAYMENT

DESERET BOOK

SALT LAKE CITY, UTAH

© 2005 Richard Neitzel Holzapfel and Thomas A. Wayment

All rights reserved. No part of this book may be reproduced in any form or by any means without permission in writing from the publisher, Deseret Book Company, P. O. Box 30178, Salt Lake City, Utah 84130. This work is not an official publication of The Church of Jesus Christ of Latter-day Saints. The views expressed herein are the responsibility of the authors and do not necessarily represent the position of the Church or of Deseret Book Company.

DESERET BOOK is a registered trademark of Deseret Book Company.

Visit us at DeseretBook.com

Library of Congress Cataloging-in-Publication Data

The life and teachings of Jesus Christ : from Bethlehem through the Sermon on the mount / edited by Richard Neitzel Holzapfel, Thomas A. Wayment.
  p. cm.
  Includes bibliographical references and index.
  ISBN-10 1-59038-396-6 (alk. paper)
  ISBN-13 978-1-59038-396-4 (alk. paper)
  1. Jesus Christ—Biography. I. Holzapfel, Richard Neitzel. II. Wayment, Thomas A.
BT301.3.L54 2005
232.9'01—dc22   2004025652

Printed in the United States of America
R. R. Donnelley and Sons, Crawfordsville, IN
10 9 8 7 6 5 4 3

To Ted D. Stoddard, editor, mentor, and friend
To Mary Stoddard, counselor, supporter, and friend
— *Richard Neitzel Holzapfel*

For my father, Lowell Tomas Wayment, a true disciple and scholar
— *Thomas A. Wayment*

CONTENTS

Key to Abbreviations ... ix

Acknowledgments ... xi

Introduction: The World of the New Testament ... xiii
   Richard Neitzel Holzapfel and Thomas A. Wayment

Part 1: Historical Setting

1. Foretelling the Coming of Jesus ... 3
   Kent P. Jackson

2. The Story of the New Testament ... 21
   Thomas A. Wayment

3. The Jerusalem Temple, the Sadducees, and the Opposition to Jesus ... 48
   Jeffrey R. Chadwick

Part 2: Beginnings

4. Zacharias and Elisabeth, Joseph and Mary ... 91
   S. Kent Brown

5. From the Annunciation through the Young Adulthood of the Lord ... 121
   Richard D. Draper

6. Jesus in the Wilderness: Baptism, Fasting, and Temptations ... 160
   Richard Neitzel Holzapfel

Part 3: The Ministry Commences

7. Jesus' Early Ministry in Judea and Jerusalem *Thomas A. Wayment*	195
8. Galilee and the Call of the Twelve Apostles *Eric D. Huntsman*	213
9. Jesus Teaches at Jacob's Well *Gaye Strathearn*	247
10. Early Galilean Ministry and Miracles *Cecilia M. Peek*	269
11. The Setting of the Sermon on the Mount *Frank F. Judd Jr.*	306
12. A Reading of the Sermon on the Mount: A Restoration Perspective *Andrew C. Skinner*	330
13. The Sermon on the Plain *Thomas A. Wayment*	355
Conclusion: A Journey through a Sacred Story *Richard Neitzel Holzapfel and Thomas A. Wayment*	379
Appendix: The Birth and Death Dates of Jesus Christ *Thomas A. Wayment*	383
Contributors	395
Scripture Index	397
Subject Index	409

KEY TO ABBREVIATIONS

BOOKS

ABD   David Noel Freedman, ed., *The Anchor Bible Dictionary*, 6 vols. (New York: Doubleday, 1992).

AJ   Josephus, *Antiquities of the Jews*, trans. Ralph Marcus, Loeb Classical Library (Cambridge, Massachusetts: Harvard University Press, 1943).

BM   Raymond E. Brown, *The Birth of the Messiah* (New York: Doubleday, 1993).

DNTC   Bruce R. McConkie, *Doctrinal New Testament Commentary*, 3 vols. (Salt Lake City: Deseret Book, 1965–73).

GEL   William F. Arndt and F. Wilbur Gingrich, *A Greek-English Lexicon of the New Testament and Other Early Christian Literature*, ed. Frederick W. Danker, 3d. ed. (Chicago: University of Chicago Press, 2000).

JD   *Journal of Discourses*, 26 vols. (London: Latter-day Saints' Book Depot, 1954–86).

JTC   James E. Talmage, *Jesus the Christ: A Study of the Messiah and His Mission according to Holy Scriptures both Ancient and Modern* (Salt Lake City: Deseret Book, 1988).

JW   Josephus, *The Jewish War*, trans. H. St. Thackeray, Loeb Classical Library (Cambridge, Massachusetts: Harvard University Press, 1927–28).

MM	Bruce R. McConkie, *The Mortal Messiah: From Bethlehem to Calvary*, 4 vols. (Salt Lake City: Deseret Book, 1981).
TDNT	Gerhard Kittel and Gerhard Friedrich, eds., *Theological Dictionary of the New Testament*, ed. and trans. Geoffrey W. Bromiley, 10 vols. (Grand Rapids, Michigan: William B. Eerdmans, 1964–99).
TPJS	Joseph Smith Jr., *Teachings of the Prophet Joseph Smith*, comp. Joseph Fielding Smith (Salt Lake City: Deseret Book, 1976).

BIBLE VERSIONS AND STUDY AIDS

NAV	New Authorized Version
NIV	New International Version
NRSV	New Revised Standard Version
NJB	New Jerusalem Bible
KJV	King James Version
BD	Bible Dictionary
LXX	Septuagint
MT	Masoretic Hebrew
JST	Joseph Smith Translation

ACKNOWLEDGMENTS

We thank Cory Maxwell, our publisher; Jack Lyon, our editor; and Shauna Gibby, our designer, for their efforts in bringing the volume to fruition.

We thank Ted D. Stoddard for his sleepless nights and long days at the end of our efforts to finish editing this book. His good humor, inquisitive nature, and ability to make us look good are appreciated and acknowledged.

Several Brigham Young University student research assistants helped us along the way: Jamie Karpowitz and Rex Price, who helped with the source editing, and W. Kenneth Hamblin, Adrianne Gardner Malan, and Jon Rainey, who helped track down articles and books and performed other duties that greatly facilitated the completion of this project.

We have benefited greatly from the collaboration between the faculty of Religious Education and the Department of Classics at Brigham Young University. Their contributions, presented in this volume, will make a lasting impression on our understanding of the New Testament.

Last, but certainly not least, we thank our wives, Jeni and Brandi, for their support, insights, and patience.

INTRODUCTION

THE WORLD OF THE NEW TESTAMENT

RICHARD NEITZEL HOLZAPFEL AND THOMAS A. WAYMENT

As John finished his Gospel narrative, he reflected, "These [things] are written, that ye might believe that Jesus is the Christ, the son of God; and that believing ye might have life through his name" (John 20:31), thus revealing his own personal reasons for retelling the story of Jesus of Nazareth.

Anyone who has studied the life of Jesus has felt a compelling desire to learn more about Him from the earliest witnesses of His life. *From Bethlehem through the Sermon on the Mount*, the second book (although volume 1) in the series dealing with the life and ministry of Jesus Christ, is a result of our passionate interest in the greatest of all lives.[1] Like our earlier volume, this compilation takes advantage of the most recent developments and advances in New Testament studies, as viewed through the lenses of faith and the Restoration by some of the best New Testament scholars in The Church of Jesus Christ of Latter-day Saints. Their efforts provide context to the story that was "published throughout all Judea, and began from Galilee, after the baptism which John preached; how God anointed Jesus of

---

[1] Richard Neitzel Holzapfel and Thomas A. Wayment, eds., *From the Last Supper through the Resurrection: The Savior's Final Hours* (Salt Lake City: Deseret Book, 2003).

Nazareth with the Holy Ghost and with power: who went about doing good" (Acts 10:37–38).

Like other Deseret Book publications, and even the study helps published in the current LDS edition of the scriptures themselves, *From Bethlehem through the Sermon on the Mount* is not intended to be "an official or revealed endorsement of the Church of the doctrinal, historical, cultural and other matters set forth." Rather, it is based on the "best available scholarship of the world and [is] subject to reevaluation based on new research and discoveries or on new revelation."[2] The final word on doctrinal interpretation will always rest with the First Presidency and the Quorum of the Twelve Apostles, those called and chosen to provide authoritative doctrinal insights for the Church.

Even with this important limitation, we hope to provide deeper insight into the culture, language, and history of the New Testament. Ultimately, we want the book to help believers come closer to the historical setting of Jesus' own world so they will figuratively begin a sacred journey along the dusty paths and roads, through the valleys and wilderness, and into the villages and towns of first-century Jewish Palestine—a land made holy by the presence of God's own Son. We hope this journey will help the reader not only to realize the value of mentally walking where Jesus walked but also, as our friend and colleague D. Kelly Ogden so poignantly expressed a number of years ago, to realize "the importance of walking as Jesus walked."[3]

Reconstructing the Past

Many questions are of interest to New Testament students today—questions that simply never dawned on the original authors of the books of the New Testament when they took stylus and papyri in hand to record their witnesses of Christ for a specific audience in a specific geographic setting and at a specific time in history.

---

[2] The Bible Dictionary, "Introduction."
[3] D. Kelly Ogden, *Where Jesus Walked: The Land and Culture of New Testament Times* (Salt Lake City: Deseret Book, 1991), viii.

INTRODUCTION: THE WORLD OF THE NEW TESTAMENT

As a result, for example, we can look in vain to find solid information that would help identify, without question, who the *Herodians* are as mentioned in the Gospels (see Matthew 22:16) or that would give us such things as a physical description of Jesus of Nazareth or of the other disciples who followed Him.

The New Testament witnesses presupposed that certain parts of their culture would be assumed by the readers who lived in their day. The writers probably did not envision readers thousands of years in the future asking of them (through their texts) questions about people, places, events, and practices of the day.[4] We cannot imagine that Mark, Luke, Matthew, or John ever thought that readers at the beginning of the twenty-first century would say, "I wish you had told me Jesus' height, the length of His hair, the color of His eyes, and the color of His beard, if He even had one." They probably never thought about such issues or about sharing with modern readers the myriad of other linguistic, cultural, and historical clues that would have illuminated the story for those living beyond (both in time and place) their days.

When the original authors wrote the stories preserved in the four Gospels, they wrote in the common language of the eastern Roman Empire, Koine Greek (meaning "common [dialect]").[5] Written Greek is significantly more concise than English, resulting in verbal constructions and implied pronouns that cannot be reproduced in English without the addition of explanatory words or phrases.

Translators of the New Testament faced the daunting task of reproducing the nuance and intent of the Greek text in addition to translating accurately the precise meaning of the original words. One

---

[4] They were sensitive to the fact that some of their readers were not Jews, were unacquainted with Jewish practice, or did not speak Hebrew or Aramaic (see, for example, Mark 14:36 and John 2:6).

[5] New Testament Greek diverges from the rest of Koine in that New Testament Greek preserves traces of Semitic tone and flavor by adopting Semitic modes of speech and reflecting Semitic interference in grammar. Additionally, New Testament Greek has some distinct vocabulary—coining new words to express biblical concepts and investing older words with distinctly Christian meaning.

INTRODUCTION: THE WORLD OF THE NEW TESTAMENT

convention that developed in the Middle Ages was to place in italics all additional words used by the translators to make sense of difficult Greek idioms, implied subjects, or pronouns.

Additionally, the authors wrote without punctuation, without chapters and verses (even without paragraphing), and without spaces between words. Our modern English translation provides much more than a rendering of two-thousand-year-old Greek words into English; it involves a whole system of verses and chapters, giving us an easy way to access the text—helpful tools and context not envisioned by the original authors themselves.

Today, we have spaces between English words, breaks in sentences, punctuation, capitalization, versification of content, and chapter divisions in our New Testament—making the text grammatically easier to read but simultaneously corrupting some of the original meanings and thus creating the need for interpretation. *From Bethlehem through the Sermon on the Mount* attempts to identify some of those corruptions and confusions by reexamining the early New Testament stories that deal with Jesus' birth and that continue through the Sermon on the Mount.

Between the Testaments

Even the most casual reader of the Bible senses vast differences in the tone, texture, and doctrines of the Old and New Testaments. After reading Malachi and then turning to Matthew's Gospel, a reader may feel that more than unspoiled time has passed lazily between the end of the Old Testament period and the beginning of the New Testament. The nearly five centuries that separate the two parts of the Bible represent far more than a mere chronological divide. They also represent a hefty cultural gap.

By almost any account, an entirely new group of people seemingly rises into view within the pages of the New Testament in contrast to the group portrayed in the Old. Certainly the people, one group in the Old Testament and another in the New, inhabited the same geographical area, shared a basic religious point of view, and were of

INTRODUCTION: THE WORLD OF THE NEW TESTAMENT

the same families and clans. Yet these two chronologically separate peoples seem deeply dissimilar in significant ways.

For example, one obvious example of differences that a reader encounters between the Old and New Testaments appears in common personal names. In the Old Testament, a reader becomes familiar with the names Jacob, Joshua, Miriam, Hannah, and Elijah. In the New Testament, we read regularly of James, Jesus, Mary, Anna, and Elias. In actuality, the New Testament names James, Jesus, Mary, Anna, and Elias are the Greek equivalents of the same names found in the Hebrew Old Testament—Jacob, Joshua, Miriam, Hannah, and Elijah. The case is much like the names of Paul and Pablo. They are the same name, but one is English and the other is Spanish.

However, we would be irresponsible if we led readers to suppose that the major differences between the Old and New Testaments lie simply in language. The Old Testament has come down to us in Hebrew, with a few Aramaic sections, and the New Testament comes to us in Greek. Though this observation is true, the central difference between the peoples who lived at the end of the Old Testament period and those at the beginning of the New was the ever-shaping, ever-renewing passage of time.

Those nearly five centuries brimmed with far-reaching changes that included periods of crippling crisis, brilliant inventiveness, cautious adaptation, and painful transition. By all odds, the major influence in that era arose from Hellenization. By definition, Hellenization sought to repackage the world as Greek. Making its relentless influence felt initially with the coming of Alexander the Great into the Near East in the late fourth century B.C., Hellenization affected people in profound ways and explains many of the differences in tone and texture between the Old and New Testaments.

Politically, the tides of history continued to sweep across the land so that by the time Gabriel appeared to Zacharias in the temple (see Luke 1:5–25), Herod the Great ruled the land of Israel, from Judea and Idumea north to Galilee and the Golan, as a client-king of the

INTRODUCTION: THE WORLD OF THE NEW TESTAMENT

Roman Empire. The political, economic, and religious center of the Jewish world remained at Jerusalem. However, it was a large and spacious site within the city that was the very heartbeat of Judaism. Known as the "Mountain of the House [of the Lord]," the enormous, raised platform was the largest in the Roman Empire. On this splendid, raised site was the jewel of Jerusalem—the holy temple.

The Jewish religious world focused on the temple at Jerusalem, but the daily life of most Jews of the first century revolved around work, family, and worship in a local synagogue. Their beliefs determined what they ate, what they did on the seventh day of the week, and how they treated their neighbors and provided an interpretive framework for them about their place in the world.

The land of Israel experienced great changes after the death of Herod in 4 B.C. when it was divided into differing political jurisdictions by Rome. Eventually, Judea was governed by a Roman prefect and a high priest who was personally appointed by the prefect. Herod's son Antipas ruled the Galilee in the way his father had ruled the entire region—the façade of the Jewish world overlaid with a Greco-Roman veneer. Greco-Roman culture, the fusing of Greek philosophy, language, and art with Roman ideals and political structures, was now the major influence of the period. Its pervasive influence was felt in almost every aspect of Jewish life in the land of Israel and throughout the Mediterranean. Nevertheless, the Jews of the first century were bound together by their loyalty to God, the law of Moses, the temple at Jerusalem, and their holy land. Roman infringements on Jewish religious practice helped Jews overlook their differences and unite under the name of God.

The New Testament opens dramatically when the heavens open again and God, through His angels, speaks to men and women of goodwill (see Matthew 1 and Luke 1). Then, suddenly and radically, John the Baptist alters the social, political, and religious landscape of first-century Judaism when he announces that the coming of the "one mightier" than any prophet has finally and at long last arrived. The time period is one of transition for the Jews, who had been without a prophet for hundreds of years.[6] Without warning, but not anticipated, God intervened dramatically and decisively in their history once again—with far-reaching consequences when, as prophesied in the Old Testament, His messenger suddenly appears: "Behold, I send my messenger before thy face, which shall prepare thy way before thee" (Mark 1:2; compare LXX Exodus 23:20; Malachi 3:1).

John the Baptist entered the stage of human history at a decisive moment, ending a nearly five-hundred-year silence since the close of the Old Testament period and baptizing and preaching the "baptism of repentance for the remission of sins" (Mark 1:4).

Contributions of LDS New Testament Studies

We asked some of our colleagues at Brigham Young University, those trained in the various disciplines relating to New Testament studies (ancient history, Greek and Latin, textual criticism, Roman civilization, and geography), to reexamine the sources, including the New Testament text itself. Their efforts were also to focus on what had already been said on the subject by faithful Latter-day Saints through the years—to see what we could discern today because of new discoveries and new scholarly discussions that we could not have known earlier because of the fragmentary nature of the evidence.[7]

---

[6] For a fuller discussion of this important transitional period, see S. Kent Brown and Richard Neitzel Holzapfel, *Between the Testaments: From Malachi to Matthew* (Salt Lake City: Deseret Book, 2002).

[7] This is not an effort to supplant the fine and faithful work by an earlier generation of LDS scholars or of past General Authorities who have written so faithfully and passionately and provided us some of the best additional witnesses to the most important events in human history. We are building upon the sure foundation they erected. Elder James E. Talmage, whose language and sensitivity in describing the life of Jesus the Christ may never be surpassed, did not have access to the Joseph Smith Translation or to the Dead Sea Scrolls, both of which open new windows of understanding on the world of the first century and on the Prophet Joseph Smith's doctrinal contributions about the text itself. If Elder Talmage were alive today and had an opportunity to update his marvelous prose, most likely (based on the fact that he carefully studied and quoted from non–Latter-day Saints of his day before writing his masterpiece) he would take advantage of the additional "light and knowledge" God has revealed through various means, including remarkable discoveries dealing directly with the New Testament text and the world of Jesus (see Articles of Faith 1:9).

INTRODUCTION: THE WORLD OF THE NEW TESTAMENT

The witness that Jesus is the Christ, the Son of God, has been firmly and irrevocably planted by the original Apostles, prophets, and Gospel authors; yet the multiple and important nuances of the story, based on archaeological discoveries and advances in linguistic and textual studies, provide us another opportunity to reconsider and reinforce that original witness found in the New Testament while we take time to discover a most remarkable period and place when God demonstrated His love by giving us His "only begotten Son, that whosoever believeth in him should not perish, but have everlasting life" (John 3:16).

Kent P. Jackson begins this book by providing a thoughtful review of the Old Testament prophecy concerning the coming of the Savior. Thomas A. Wayment outlines the development of the New Testament text and how it was initially gathered, written down, translated, and passed on to us. Jeffery R. Chadwick, based on decades of living, working, and teaching in the Holy Land, provides a word picture of Jerusalem at the time of Jesus' life and ministry, allowing us to understand better the physical and social setting of the stories we encounter in the Gospels.

Following the completion of his book-length study of Mary and Elisabeth, S. Kent Brown adds to his previous discussion about Mary and Elisabeth an examination of the lives of Zacharias and Joseph—giving us an opportunity to consider carefully these first four actors in the story.[8] Richard D. Draper meticulously leads us through the narratives of the birth and early years of Jesus as found in Matthew and Luke.

Richard Neitzel Holzapfel provides a review of Jesus' wilderness experience by comparing the individual texts that preserve material about His baptism, fasting, and temptations—the immediate preludes to Jesus' public ministry.

Thomas A. Wayment then sets the stage for what is often called the "early Judean ministry," in which Jesus identifies His earliest

---

[8] S. Kent Brown, *Mary and Elisabeth: Noble Daughters of God* (Salt Lake City: Covenant Communication, 2002).

disciples and continues to glean disciples in the regions where John the Baptist taught. The "Galilee and the Call of the Twelve Apostles" chapter reveals the careful attention that Eric D. Huntsman brings to his study of the New Testament. He deftly deals with linguistic nuances for such terms as *disciple*, *apostle*, and the more important word in the New Testament, the Twelve.

Gaye Strathearn examines the story of the woman at the well by providing a detailed discussion of Jesus' encounter in Samaria with the unnamed woman who came there to obtain water but went away with something significantly more important. The next important period in Jesus' public ministry is known as the "early Galilean ministry," and Cecilia M. Peek wades through the scholarly discussions to provide the reader with important insights that will enrich their understanding of the earliest teachings and miracles of Jesus through the discerning and careful pen of a faithful LDS scholar.

The climax of *From Bethlehem through the Sermon on the Mount* is the Sermon on the Mount itself. Frank F. Judd first examines the social setting of this important and well-known sermon with the care and insight he has become known for in his classes on the campus of Brigham Young University. Andrew C. Skinner then reviews and provides insights into the actual teachings of the Sermon on the Mount—supplying us with real-life applications that Jesus intended when He first sat with His disciples in Galilee so many years ago. Finally, Thomas A. Wayment looks at the lesser-known Sermon on the Plain, recorded by Luke, and establishes its relationship to the Sermon on the Mount.

In this book, we examine the first chapters in the four Gospels: Matthew, Mark, Luke, and John. Although they do not represent the earliest New Testament documents to have survived from antiquity, they are the only ones that provide a detailed review of some of the important events, teachings, and activities of Jesus of Nazareth.[9]

---

[9] See Richard Neitzel Holzapfel, "Early Accounts of the Story," in Richard Neitzel Holzapfel and Thomas A. Wayment, eds., *From the Last Supper through the Resurrection: The Savior's Final Hours* (Salt Lake City: Deseret Book, 2003), 401–21.

The New Testament Canon

The Gospels are part of a larger collection of early Christian documents that are known today as the New Testament, which consists of twenty-seven books.[10] Of course, the word *testament* has several distinct meanings in English; but in this context, it means *covenant*. The Old Testament (or the old covenant) represents the covenant instituted with Abraham (Genesis 17) but renewed and expanded at Mount Sinai (Exodus 19). The New Testament (or the new covenant) represents the covenant Jesus instituted on the fateful and faithful last night (see Matthew 26:26–28). Of course, this new covenant was not unanticipated (see Jeremiah 31:31).

Even the Gospels themselves can be and often are divided into two separate and distinct sections: the synoptic Gospels (Matthew, Mark, and Luke) and the fourth Gospel (John). *Synoptic* means "look alike"; a careful examination of these three Gospels makes it clear why they are identified as such: they have many similarities, whereas John is markedly different. For example, the synoptics share a remarkable amount of language and highlight similar stories.

One problem that plagues scholars is how to explain the material that Matthew and Luke share in common but that is not found in Mark, as scholars typically assume that both Matthew and Luke used Mark as their common source (see discussion below). The simplest explanation seems to suggest that both Matthew and Luke used Mark as an important source. They also used a common "oral source," revealing another independent relationship to one another.

Following the four Gospels, our current arrangement in the New Testament, originating in the fourth century, is the book of Acts.[11]

---

[10] The English word *canon* derives from a Greek term that originally meant "ruler" or "measuring rod."

[11] The definitive form and order of the New Testament can be traced to Athanasius's thirty-ninth festal letter (A.D. 367). Although Athanasius was the first to provide a list of accepted books in the same order as our modern New Testament, the canonizing of individual books took place as early as the second century. As early as the turn of the first century, Christian authors relied on the authority of the Gospels and of the Pauline epistles to establish doctrine for the Church. Athanasius's festal letter, therefore, should

INTRODUCTION: THE WORLD OF THE NEW TESTAMENT

Originally, Luke and Acts were read together. They were both written by the same author, at the same time, and to the same audience (see Luke 1:1–4 and Acts 1:1–3). In some ways, unfortunately, our current New Testament separates these two works from each other, even though they were intended to be read together.

The next division within the New Testament is the epistles or letters section. It is divided into two separate groupings: the letters of Paul and the general Epistles. The Pauline letters (epistles of Paul) are located in the third section or division of the New Testament canon. They are basically arranged by length (longest to the shortest), a convention followed in many ancient collections, including the Old Testament prophetic section. Addressed to specific congregations ("to the Romans") or to specific individuals ("to Timothy"), they represent some of the earliest New Testament documents to have survived the ravages of time. Thessalonians and even Galatians may be the oldest documents in the New Testament, composed in the late 40s or early 50s, a decade before the Gospels were written.

Hebrews, though significantly longer than the last book in the Pauline letters, Philemon, was placed after Philemon because the early Church was unsure about the authorship of this important book. Whether Paul wrote the text with the help of someone else (which would explain the non-Pauline elements found in the book) or whether someone else like Apollos, a co-laborer of Paul, wrote it alone (which would explain the Pauline elements found in the book) may never be discovered—unless we find the original autograph or get a distinct revelation through the president of the Church. What is important is the fact that it was preserved and accepted as authoritative and, therefore, deemed worthy of our study.[12]

---

be viewed as a later statement of earlier discussions and decisions.

[12] Although Latter-day Saints generally accept Pauline authorship of Hebrews, the Church has no official position on the matter—other than that Hebrews constitutes one of the books of scripture in the New Testament canon and therefore stands with the other scriptures accepted by the Church. Joseph Smith himself assumed Pauline authorship, as most Protestants of his day did, and quoted from it often; but we have no indication that he ever sought a specific revelation on the subject. Asking about

INTRODUCTION: THE WORLD OF THE NEW TESTAMENT

The general Epistles, sometimes identified as "catholic" (meaning "universal"), follow Hebrews. The letters of James, Peter, John, and Jude represent counsel and direction to the Church during a critical period and are usually addressed to more than one person or congregation—hence the title "general."

Finally, the New Testament ends with the awe-inspiring vision, "the Revelation of Jesus Christ, which God gave unto him, to shew unto his servants things which must shortly come to pass; and he sent and signified it by his angel unto his servant John" (Revelation 1:1).

Writing the Story Down

When we pick up our modern, rather inexpensive New Testament and compare it to the cost of producing the original text, we might not appreciate the costly and laborious process of producing the text in the first place. The very process of recording the words and deeds of Jesus is a remarkable story, as is its transmission into the modern day. Certainly, the earliest stories and recollections of Jesus' life were passed along in the oral culture of the day. Soon, however, they began to be written down—to be preserved and codified.

The authors accessed the tools of the writer's trade. Pen, ink, and papyrus or parchment were the essential prerequisites for any written document. Without these, their records could have been written only as inscriptions on stone or buildings. The rather primitive nature of the components, however, meant that the writers of antiquity needed a surprising amount of equipment. The writing utensils included reeds (which served as pens for writing on papyrus); sharp knives (used to shape one end of a section of the reed to a point and split it); and stone (which served as an abrasive to rub off the superfluous fibers of a frayed pen—the nib). Ink was made from oils and/or water and lamp black. The writing material was papyrus or parchment.

---

authorship for Hebrews may simply never have crossed his mind because the accepted, conventional religious wisdom at the time was the assignation of Paul as the author. In the end, moreover, the authorship of Hebrews makes no difference for our use (see TPJS, 59).

INTRODUCTION: THE WORLD OF THE NEW TESTAMENT

The English word *paper* is derived via Old French from the Latin *papyrus*, itself simply the transcription of the Greek *papyros*, which was the name of a plant (*Cyperus papyrus*) that grew in the swamps of Egypt or in shallow, stagnant pools left by the fall of the Nile after the flood season. Why papyrus was selected as the medium of choice is seen in its characteristics, which included a fineness, stoutness, whiteness, and smoothness that were hard to duplicate. Variation in characteristics gave rise to different qualities of paper, each associated with a different width. The best paper was thirteen Roman inches wide (9.75 modern inches; the current American standard is 8.5 inches).

This was not all; the writer needed a piece of ivory or shell to smooth the papyrus or parchment and prepare it for writing. The writer also needed a fine knife to mark the margins, leaving a faint but unambiguous trace; the knife also served to rule the lines on which the letters stood. Finally, he required a sponge. Using a damp sponge made it possible to erase a mistake before the ink dried; the sponge also served to clean the pen after writing.

Authorship, Dating, and Audience

The book of Mark, likely the earliest written Gospel, was probably composed in Rome for a Roman audience sometime between A.D. 60 and 70. This Gospel has repeatedly been identified as "Peter's memoirs" since the earliest times. In a discourse in the book of Acts (see Acts 10:37–43), Peter begins the story of Jesus by referring to His baptism by John the Baptist, the same as Mark's Gospel begins, which seems to confirm that Mark preserves Peter's method of introducing the "good news" of Jesus Christ, the Son of God (Mark 1:1–15). John Mark (see Acts 12:12) was the secretary to Peter (1 Peter 5:13) and former traveling companion to Barnabas and Paul (see Acts 12:25). Matthew, most likely the second Gospel to have been written and preserved, was composed, as one tradition holds, in Syrian Antioch for a Jewish audience sometime between a.d. 60 and 80.

Matthew is identified with Levi, the tax collector whom Jesus called in Capernaum (Mark 2:14; Matthew 9:9) and who was also a member of the Twelve (Mark 3:18). At first, we may think it unnatural for Matthew, a member of the Twelve, to rely on Mark for Matthew's basic story line because Mark was neither a disciple of Jesus during the public ministry nor a member of the Twelve later in life. However, because Mark's Gospel is best understood as Peter's memoirs, we can see the natural rationale for Matthew to use Mark because Peter was acquainted with Jesus earlier than Matthew and also because Peter was a member of the inner circle of disciples (along with James and John).

Luke, third among the synoptic Gospels, was probably composed as a missionary tract for the Gentile mission in western Turkey and Greece. It is addressed to one person, Theophilus (a Greek name, "beloved of God"), possibly the patron who paid to have the text written in the first place. Composed about the same time as Matthew or a little later (A.D. 70–80), Luke acknowledges that "many have taken in hand to set forth" the story of Jesus, but he indicates that he wanted to present an updated or corrected version of the story because he had interviewed eyewitnesses (see Luke 1:1–4). Additionally, Luke continued his story by composing a second book, Acts (see below). Luke himself was sometimes the traveling companion of Paul (beginning in Acts 16:10) and may be the "beloved physician" referred to in one of Paul's own letters (Colossians 4:14).

John's Gospel was most likely composed in Ephesus during an earlier period than is generally acknowledged, likely contemporary with Mark in the decade from A.D. 60 to 70. Generally, the later dating to the end of the first century, the early or late 90s, has been preferred among Latter-day Saints for polemical usage against those attacking the acceptance of additional scriptures beyond the Bible. The malediction found in Revelation 22:18–19 has often caused the faithful to search for a way to undermine the claims of non-Latter-day Saints who use the passage as a means of attacking the validity of our additional scriptures. If the Gospel of John were written late, possibly even later than the book of Revelation, then the claim that the canon was already closed is thereby nullified.

As young missionaries in Italy, we were sometimes confronted with this particular text, which was used to disavow the possibility of additional scripture beyond the Bible. Our standard response was to invoke the generally accepted scholarly proposition for a late dating, suggesting to our inquisitors that if we were to take these verses in Revelation at face value, we would have to rip the Gospel of John from our Bible because, as we argued, the fourth Gospel was written *after* the book of Revelation was composed.[13]

The problem with this argument is that we allow a scholarly bias to date the Gospel of John late because the late dating helps us defend our acceptance of additional scripture beyond the New Testament canon. Generally, the main reason for dating the fourth Gospel so late is a scholarly theory that John's Gospel represents an evolutionary development about Jesus that is not found in the earliest Gospels.

Scholars typically feel that Mark's Gospel is the most historically accurate account of Jesus' life because it does not recount the virgin birth, which in their minds is a fiction developed in the early Church. If this argument were to hold true, then John's account, which spans back into the preexistence, would also be a product of the early Church rather than the account of an eyewitness.

Certainly, unlike Mark, John begins his Gospel story about Jesus before His baptism. Also, unlike Matthew and Luke, John begins his Gospel story about Jesus before His birth. John, of course, starts, "In the beginning was the Word, and the Word was with God, and the Word was God" (John 1:1). Yet all the elements of John's high Christology, the term used in scholarly and popular print to describe his so-called developed theology, can be found in earlier stories about Jesus that even predate Paul's writings, which are considered the earliest documents in the New Testament. For example, the pre-Pauline hymns found in Philippians (see Philippians 2:5–11) and

---

[13] The context of the passage in Revelation is the book itself, the book of Revelation. The twenty-seven-book canon had not been developed when John wrote Revelation; therefore, it is historically impossible for him to have conceived of his statement as a warning to those who would add to our present canonized New Testament. A similar injunction is found in the book of Deuteronomy (see Deuteronomy 4:2–3).

INTRODUCTION: THE WORLD OF THE NEW TESTAMENT

Colossians (see Colossians 1:15–20) demonstrate that the early Christians did not have to wait until the early or late 90s to have something like the prologue found in the first chapter of John, which proclaims the descent and exaltation of God Himself in the form of His Son (see John 1:1–18).

The fourth Gospel, however, does stand apart from the synoptic Gospels. Even a cursory reading reveals that about 80 to 90 percent of John is unique material. In many places, unlike the synoptic Gospels, John may have provided us the only firsthand account of several important stories because he was part of Jesus' inner circle (Peter, James, and John) and was intimately present.

John is known as John the Beloved, the Apostle John, John the Evangelist, and John the Revelator, all preserving some clue to his activities as a disciple of Jesus. He, along with his brother, was a fisherman at the Sea of Galilee with their father. They were associated with John the Baptist before Jesus called them to follow Him.

Any scholar who believes himself or herself to be free of bias is certainly more biased than those who openly profess their biases. We openly accept a bias in presenting this volume. This study is a product of believing scholars who want to share their experiences in journeying side by side with the Savior and His Apostles during His mortal ministry. We have sought to accept knowingly our bias and present the most historically accurate picture of the life of Jesus that can be reconstructed today. Scholarship can never replace faith, but our faith has been greatly informed through our appreciation of the historical setting and circumstances of Jesus' mortal ministry (Doctrine and Covenants 88:118; 90:15).

Jesus' story will be the greatest told in our dispensation, and hopefully each generation of believers will seek to understand everything possible about Him. Future studies will be written on the life of Jesus; but, as John declared, "There are also many other things which Jesus did, the which, if they should be written every one, I suppose that even the world itself could not contain the books that should be written" (John 21:25). This volume is our attempt to understand the

One who was greater than even a prophet (Mark 1:7)—greater than anyone else who has ever lived, is living, or will yet live on our planet, even Jesus Christ.

PART 1

HISTORICAL SETTING

I.
FORETELLING THE COMING OF JESUS

KENT P. JACKSON

Behold, the time cometh, and is not far distant, that with power, the Lord Omnipotent who reigneth, who was, and is from all eternity to all eternity, shall come down from heaven among the children of men, and shall dwell in a tabernacle of clay.

MOSIAH 3:5

The Old Testament prophet Amos taught a vital doctrine when he said, "Surely the Lord God will do nothing, but he revealeth his secret unto his servants the prophets" (Amos 3:7). If this principle is true for anything, it certainly was true for the all-important topic of the earthly mission of Jesus Christ—the most significant event that would ever take place on this earth. The atoning work of the Savior was of such importance that it required both declaration and preparation. Thus, "the Lord God hath sent his holy prophets among all the children of men, to declare these things to every kindred, nation, and tongue, that thereby whosoever should believe that Christ should come, the same might receive remission of their sins, and rejoice with exceedingly great joy, even as though he had already come among them" (Mosiah 3:13).

Redemption through the atoning blood of Jesus Christ is the ultimate message of all revelation and, therefore, also of the prophetic words in the Old Testament and the Book of Mormon. But the Lord adapts His teaching to the spiritual maturity of His audience. In His wisdom, He gives people "all that he seeth fit that they should have" (Alma 29:8), "according to the heed and diligence which they give unto him" (Alma 12:9). For that reason, Book of Mormon prophecies of Christ are very different from those in the Old Testament. In the Book of Mormon, those prophecies are presented in "plainness" (2 Nephi 25:4, 7)—in clear and direct words with a full understanding of Jesus' mission. In contrast, the Old Testament prophets ministered among those who are described in the scriptures as rebellious and unworthy, and thus their prophecies of Jesus' coming are generally veiled in symbols and images—in what the Book of Mormon calls "types" and "shadows" (Mosiah 3:15).

In this chapter, we will review some Book of Mormon prophecies of Christ and then see how the message of His coming is expressed in the Old Testament. We will examine selected Old Testament passages that teach of Jesus, and we will be reminded—as we always should be when we study the Bible—how indispensable modern revelation is for our understanding of the Lord and His work.

Prophecies of Jesus in the Book of Mormon

Early in the Book of Mormon, we are told how Lehi and his children learned about Jesus and His coming ministry. Lehi first saw in vision "One descending out of the midst of heaven" (1 Nephi 1:9). Then, from reading a book given him in a vision, he preached to the people of Jerusalem concerning "the coming of a Messiah, and also the redemption of the world" (1 Nephi 1:19). Further information came in later revelations. Nephi reported that "six hundred years from the time that my father left Jerusalem, a prophet would the Lord God raise up among the Jews—even a Messiah, or, in other words, a Savior of the world" (1 Nephi 10:4). The power of Christ's atonement was made known to them: "Wherefore, all mankind were in a lost and in a fallen state, and ever would be save they should rely on this Redeemer" (1 Nephi 10:6). Nephi's language, here and elsewhere, suggests that in the early years of the Book of Mormon experience, Lehi and his children were learning many details of the fullness of the gospel for the first time.[1]

Away from their homeland and the limitations imposed on the Israelites because of their general rebelliousness, the family of Lehi was taught the mission of Christ in the plainness that would characterize the words of the Book of Mormon. Nephi reported his father's teachings about the Savior's earthly experiences, beginning with the mission of John the Baptist (1 Nephi 10:7–9). Jesus would preach the gospel and be killed, after which He would rise from the dead (1 Nephi 10:11). Jesus would be "their Lord" (1 Nephi 10:14) and "the Son of God" (1 Nephi 10:17). Jacob learned from an angel that the Savior would be called Christ (2 Nephi 10:3), and Nephi learned that His name would be Jesus. Nephi wrote, "According to the words of the prophets, and also the word of the angel of God, his name shall be Jesus Christ" (2 Nephi 25:19).

Beginning with these early references, clear teaching of the earthly mission of Jesus appears throughout the Book of Mormon, and in every way it becomes a Christian book, very different from the Old Testament. Consider the words of King Benjamin with which the present chapter begins: "The Lord Omnipotent . . . shall come down from heaven among the children of men, and shall dwell in a tabernacle of clay" (Mosiah 3:5). Benjamin went on to teach that Jesus would go among the people doing great miracles, "healing the sick, raising the dead, causing the lame to walk, the blind to receive their sight, and the deaf to hear," "curing all manner of diseases," and casting out devils (Mosiah 3:5–6). However, Jesus' earthly ministry would entail much more than doing good works and alleviating the

---

[1] See the discussions in Kent P. Jackson, "The Beginnings of Christianity in the Book of Mormon," in *The Book of Mormon: The Keystone Scripture*, ed. Paul R. Cheesman (Provo, Utah: Religious Studies Center, Brigham Young University, 1988), 91–99, and "One Family's Testimony of Christ," *Ensign* (February 2000): 23–27.

discomforts of mortal men and women: "He shall suffer temptations, and pain of body, hunger, thirst, and fatigue, even more than man can suffer, except it be unto death; for behold, blood cometh from every pore, so great shall be his anguish for the wickedness and the abominations of his people" (Mosiah 3:7). "He cometh unto his own, that salvation might come unto the children of men even through faith on his name" (Mosiah 3:9). Yet they would scourge and crucify him (Mosiah 3:9). Benjamin taught further that Jesus would rise from the dead and judge the world (Mosiah 3:10).

Other Book of Mormon prophets spoke similarly of Christ's coming. Abinadi taught, "God himself shall come down among the children of men, and shall redeem his people" (Mosiah 15:1). Jesus would suffer temptation but would not yield. He would be "mocked, and scourged, and cast out, and disowned by his people" (Mosiah 15:5). He would be "crucified" and killed. He would break the "bands of death," "make intercession for the children of men," and take upon Himself "their iniquity and their transgressions" (Mosiah 15:7–9). Jesus would also rise from the dead, and in doing so He would conquer death for others as well (Mosiah 16:7). Amulek affirmed that "Christ shall come among the children of men, to take upon him the transgressions of his people"; "he shall atone for the sins of the world" (Alma 34:8). Alma added that Jesus "surely shall come to take away the sins of the world; yea, he cometh to declare glad tidings of salvation unto his people" (Alma 39:15).

In addition to these references to Jesus' ministry on earth, the Book of Mormon contains many other passages that teach the doctrine of the Savior and the power of His atoning work. Indeed, the message of Christ is the central theme of the Book of Mormon—before His coming as well as after. Thus, those among the Nephites and Lamanites who knew and loved the revelations of their prophets looked forward with great anticipation to Jesus' earthly ministry. And they were prepared to receive Him at His coming.

Prophecies of Jesus in the Old Testament

Like all our standard works, the Old Testament teaches us of God and our relationship to Him. Authors of historical books do that by recording His interaction with His people and the work He does through historical events to bring about their well-being. The God of the Old Testament is a faithful friend who stands with those who honor Him. He protects them, leads them, and delivers them. Through the words of the prophets, we witness His pleading for His children to change their hearts, to conduct their lives in a way that would lead to their happiness, and to come unto Him and find salvation.

These are also the very things that we see exemplified in the words and actions of Jesus Christ in the New Testament. The Old Testament also teaches us of God by preserving psalms, poems, hymns, stories, and sayings that describe, praise, and typify His divine character. Through these means, it teaches us of the Lord Jehovah, bears testimony of Him, and brings glory to His name.

We see the awesome character of Jehovah throughout the Old Testament, but it is from modern revelation that we learn who He is and the full nature of His work. In the Book of Mormon passages cited above, we learn that He would be born into the world as Jesus Christ. The knowledge that Jesus is the God of ancient Israel helps us understand the Old Testament in ways that would not be possible otherwise. We understand, for example, that Jehovah's mighty acts of deliverance anciently were types of, and bore testimony to, His ultimate act of deliverance—the Atonement. All of Israel's religion, law, history, and daily experience bore testimony of this greatest act of salvation.

The Old Testament is thus, indeed, a testament of Jesus Christ, although it presents special challenges for its readers. Because of the imperfect transmission of the record and the all-too-frequent apostasy of the Israelites, its message of Christ is not as visible as it is in our other scriptures. According to the prophets, the Israelites were unable even to live up to the moral requirements of the law of Moses, let alone to receive the higher law of the gospel.[2] The limitations of their faith are reflected in the nature of the Old Testament. For the most part, it is a book directed to, and recorded for, the Israelite nation in general—not the worthy Saints who may have been among them. The words of the prophets in it are their public pronouncements to their wayward society, not their private teachings to those who had risen above the sins of their generation. This explains the heavy emphasis on judgment and punishment, and it explains also why celestial things, "the solemnities of eternity" (Doctrine and Covenants 43:34), are not as apparent.[3]

The law of Moses, revealed when the people were found unworthy and unwilling to receive greater things (Doctrine and Covenants 84:23–27), was "a very strict law" for a "stiffnecked people" (Mosiah 13:29). Still, it bore a forceful testimony of the Atonement by means of symbolic representations, primarily through the teaching power of ordinances. At its roots and even in its details, the law of Moses was a grand prophecy of the atoning mission of Jesus Christ, and thus it is primarily in the law that the types and shadows of Christ and His gospel are seen.[4] "This is the whole meaning of the law," Amulek said, "every whit pointing to that great and last sacrifice; and that great and last sacrifice will be the Son of God, yea, infinite and eternal" (Alma 34:14). Jacob wrote, "My soul delighteth in proving unto my people the truth of the coming of Christ; for, for this end hath the law of Moses been given; and all things which have been given of God from the beginning of the world, unto man, are the typifying of him" (2 Nephi 11:4).

One way in which Old Testament prophets foretold the earthly ministry of Jesus was to foretell Jehovah's coming in glory. The vast

---

[2] For example, see JST Psalm 14:2–3; Isaiah 1:4–5; Jeremiah 6:6–7; Ezekiel 22:2–4, 8–13; Hosea 4:1–2, 11–18; Amos 2:4, 6–8; Micah 6:10–13, 16; Habakkuk 1:2–4; Zephaniah 1:4–6.

[3] For an extended discussion of these issues, see Kent P. Jackson, *The Restored Gospel and Ancient Israel* (Salt Lake City: Deseret Book, 2005), chapters 1–3.

[4] John provides a telling example in the Passover feast (John 19:36). See also Exodus 12:46; Numbers 9:12; 1 Corinthians 5:7; 1 Peter 1:19.

majority of the prophecies of Christ in the Old Testament are prophecies of the Second Coming, not of Jesus' earthly mission. Prophecies of His coming in glory bear testimony that Israel's God, Jehovah, is a God of salvation, who at the end of time will free the world from sorrow and injustice.

At His coming in power, He will deliver His people from all temporal enemies—from foreign rulers and oppressors, from exile, from drought, from famine, and from persecution. "I the Lord am thy Saviour and thy Redeemer," Jehovah said, "and beside me there is no saviour" (Isaiah 60:16; 43:11).

Temporal salvation points to the greater salvation over sin and death. Thus, all prophecies of end-time deliverance from earthly enemies also foretell deliverance from spiritual enemies. All the prophets who testified of Jehovah's work, of His mercy, and of His power to save were also testifying of the atoning mission of Jesus Christ—because Jehovah is Christ and because His work is one.

Some Latter-day Saints, from our Christian vantage point, wrongly fault the Jews of Jesus' time for not understanding the prophecies or for confusing those of His Second Coming with those of His first coming. But we should remember that they had the same Old Testament we have today, and in its writings, prophecies of the Lord's coming in glory are abundant, whereas those of His mortal ministry are relatively few.[5]

As we will see in the examples that follow, messianic prophecies were generally written in such a way that their meaning relative to Christ's earthly mission is not apparent on the surface. In general, only those who know the plan of salvation or are familiar with the events of Jesus' mortal ministry can understand them. Thus, given the evidence we have in the Old Testament itself, we would not

---

[5] Our Old Testament was the Bible of common Judaism in Jesus' day, as is seen in the numerous references to its content in the New Testament and early Jewish literature. The many biblical fragments preserved among the Dead Sea Scrolls, essentially contemporary with Jesus, also show the existence and canonicity of what we call the Old Testament. The texts preserved show only minor and, for the most part, insignificant differences from the text in modern Bibles.

expect that the Jews of Jesus' time—without additional revelation—would be looking forward to the coming of the Messiah with the same understanding that we have today.

Selected Messianic Prophecies

Two events from the Old Testament are worth noting under the category of messianic prophecies and serve as examples of how historical events often point to the mission of Jesus Christ. They are not technically prophecies, but they nonetheless serve a prophetic function by foreshadowing Jesus and His earthly work.

The first is the binding and near sacrifice of Isaac in Genesis 22:1–18. Paul seemed to be borrowing language from that Genesis story when he wrote that God the Father "spared not his own Son, but delivered him up for us all" (Romans 8:32; compare Genesis 22:2, 12). Jacob in the Book of Mormon called the event "a similitude of God and his Only Begotten Son" (Jacob 4:5).

The second event is when Moses made an image of a "fiery serpent" and set it on a pole so "every one that is bitten, when he looketh upon it, shall live" (Numbers 21:8). In the Gospel of John, Jesus taught, "As Moses lifted up the serpent in the wilderness, even so must the Son of man be lifted up: that whosoever believeth in him should not perish, but have eternal life" (John 3:14–15).

Nephi son of Helaman in the Book of Mormon taught, "Did [Moses] not bear record that the Son of God should come? And as he lifted up the brazen serpent in the wilderness, even so shall he be lifted up who should come. And as many as should look upon that serpent should live, even so as many as should look upon the Son of God with faith, having a contrite spirit, might live, even unto that life which is eternal" (Helaman 8:14–15). Latter-day Saints can see and understand these meanings, but in neither case would that be possible without knowing beforehand the mission of Jesus and understanding His gospel.

The following examples are among the most well known of Old Testament passages that foretell or reflect on Jesus' mortal ministry, including some that are presented by New Testament writers as prophecies of Him. These do not include all the passages that have been identified either in antiquity or in modern times as looking forward to Christ, but they illustrate well the unique qualities of this kind of scripture.[6] Perhaps as much as anything else, they highlight how dependent we are on the New Testament and on modern revelation to understand the words of the Old Testament.

"The Lord thy God will raise up unto thee a Prophet from the midst of thee, of thy brethren, like unto me; unto him ye shall hearken. . . . I will raise them up a Prophet from among their brethren, like unto thee, and will put my words in his mouth; and he shall speak unto them all that I shall command him" (Deuteronomy 18:15, 18).

Moses foretold the coming of a great prophet who, like Moses, would speak the words of God. That prophet was Jesus Christ, but the identification is not made clear in Moses' words. By the days of Jesus, the prophet had become an object of hope and expectation, and his coming was anticipated alongside that of Elijah and the Messiah, though the Jews were uncertain about the relationship among the three (Mark 6:15; John 1:25). Some who witnessed Jesus' ministry recognized Him as that prophet (John 6:14), and John the Baptist and Peter made the identification explicit (JST John 1:20–29; Acts 3:22–24). Modern revelation removes all doubt (1 Nephi 22:21; 3 Nephi 20:23; Joseph Smith—History 1:40; Doctrine and Covenants 133:63).

"The Lord hath said unto me, Thou art my Son; this day have I begotten thee" (Psalm 2:7).

Hebrews twice cites this passage as a prophecy of Jesus (Hebrews 1:5; 5:5), and Paul did the same in his sermon at Antioch in Pisidia (Acts 13:33). Psalm 2 is an enthronement poem in which the king is invested by God with power over the nations. Although it may have been applied to earthly kings in ancient Israel or Judah, its ultimate

---

[6] See the list in the Topical Guide in the English LDS edition of the Bible, under "Jesus Christ, Prophecies about." The selection presented here represents the most significant passages listed there.

context is surely heavenly and universal, with God's millennial King receiving the government over the earth.

"My God, my God, why hast thou forsaken me? . . . All they that see me laugh me to scorn: they shoot out the lip, they shake the head, saying, He trusted on the Lord that he would deliver him: let him deliver him, seeing he delighted in him. . . . They part my garments among them, and cast lots upon my vesture" (Psalm 22:1, 7–8, 18).

Psalm 22 is a poem in which the speaker suffers abuse at the hands of tormenters and yet remains true to the God of Israel. Some New Testament scholars believe that the Gospel writers, in varying ways, crafted their accounts of Jesus' crucifixion to build the narrative around some of the language in the psalm (with other psalms as well).[7] In its present form, the poem itself does not seem to be the account of Jesus' sufferings, yet there is no question that some of the events of the Savior's last hours are reflected in it, including the dividing of Jesus' clothing (Psalm 22:18; John 19:24), the piercing of His hands and feet (Psalm 22:16; Luke 24:39), the mocking and derision (Psalm 22:6–8; Matthew 27:39–43), and Jesus' crying out to the Father with a feeling of abandonment (Psalm 22:1; Matthew 27:46). Both Matthew and John saw the events on the cross as the fulfillment of prophecy in the psalm (Matthew 27:35; John 19:24).

New Testament speakers and writers used Old Testament language and quoted Old Testament passages frequently—and for a variety of purposes.[8] That does not necessarily mean that the original context foretold a New Testament event. There is a difference between applying a passage and identifying the fulfillment anticipated by the original author. But, in some instances, the New Testament writers or speakers stated that the Old Testament words were fulfilled in New Testament events, even when a connection may not seem apparent, or

---

[7] See the discussions in John Dominic Crossan, *Who Killed Jesus?* (San Francisco: HarperSanFrancisco, 1995), 133–59, and Raymond E. Brown, *The Death of the Messiah: From Gethsemane to the Grave*, 2 vols. (New York: Doubleday, 1994), 1455–67.

[8] For what is intended to be a comprehensive list, see Robert G. Bratcher, ed., *Old Testament Quotations in the New Testament*, rev. ed. (London: United Bible Societies, 1961).

even possible, to modern readers. That is particularly true with the Psalms. In using the Old Testament in that way, the writers and speakers were illustrating their belief that the message of Christ is so central to the Old Testament that its words—from any context— can be used to prefigure Jesus and events in His life and mission.[9]

"*Behold, a virgin shall conceive, and bear a son, and shall call his name Immanuel. . . . For before the child shall know to refuse the evil, and choose the good, the land that thou abhorest shall be forsaken of both her kings*" (Isaiah 7:14, 16).

This prophecy, spanning Isaiah chapters 7, 8, and part of 9, uses a current event as a type to teach of Christ and His salvation. It foretells deliverance from a contemporary enemy in the eighth century B.C. The enemy, an alliance of Israel and Syria, threatened the existence of the kingdom of Judah, the nation in which Isaiah lived. It was a profound threat with life-and-death consequences. The sign of deliverance that God provided would be the birth of a son, whose coming would signify that God was with Judah to deliver its people. The son was probably Isaiah's own child, as Isaiah 8:1–4 and 18 suggest.[10]

But the sign was also intended to point to an even greater act of deliverance, the birth of the Son of God, whose coming would signify God's act of deliverance not only from temporal foes but also from the

---

[9] An example might include Peter's citing of Psalm 69:25 in Acts 1:20. Similarly, Matthew cited Hosea 11:1 ("When Israel was a child, then I loved him, and called my son out of Egypt"; Matthew 2:15: "Out of Egypt have I called my son") as being fulfilled when the baby Jesus was brought by Joseph and Mary out of Egypt. In the Hosea passage, the Lord chastises His people by telling how He brought the Israelites from Egyptian bondage into the promised land, where they nonetheless rebelled against Him and acted wickedly (see Hosea 11:1–12). But Matthew saw Jesus as the very embodiment and fulfillment of the history of Israel, and thus Hosea's words regarding ancient Israel were appropriated to Jesus, even if the original context is not parallel.

[10] The Hebrew that underlies "a virgin" in the King James translation, *hā'almâ*, actually says "the young woman," meaning a specified woman of marriageable or childbearing age without reference to sexual experience. Matthew 1:23, following the Greek Septuagint translation, uses *parthenos*, a word that can mean either "a virgin" or "a marriageable young woman," in paraphrasing Isaiah 7:14. The King James translators chose to recast Isaiah 7:14 to match the New Testament reference instead of following Isaiah's Hebrew word. See Arndt and Gingrich, GEL, "*parthenos*."

ultimate enemies—sin, death, and hell. Thus, this messianic prophecy foretells Christ's eternal salvation by means of a prophecy of temporal salvation for Isaiah's own time; the contemporary deliverance was a type of the greater deliverance to come. Although this prophecy seems clear to those who know Jesus, it is not difficult to see that few in the generations of Isaiah and Jesus would have understood it beyond its contemporary application.[11] For those who know the Savior and His gospel, studying it carefully in its context (Isaiah 7–8) is a revelation itself, which shows how all things point to Christ.[12]

"Unto us a child is born, unto us a son is given: and the government shall be upon his shoulder: and his name shall be called Wonderful, Counsellor, The mighty God, The everlasting Father, The Prince of Peace. Of the increase of his government and peace there shall be no end, upon the throne of David, and upon his kingdom, to order it, and to establish it with judgment and with justice from henceforth even for ever" (Isaiah 9:6–7).

This prophecy speaks of Christ's first coming within the larger context of His entire ministry (Isaiah 9:1–7). Verse 6 continues the news of salvation presented in Isaiah 7–8, announcing again the birth of a son whose coming would symbolize deliverance. But whereas Christ's birth was an event of His mortal ministry, the rest of the prophecy points to millennial things: "government," "Prince of Peace," and "throne of David." This is a case where a prophecy of Jesus' earthly mission is found within a passage that is primarily millennial. Although we can understand this prophecy, it is not known to what extent people in the days of Jesus could or did understand it. Handel's *Messiah* has associated it permanently with the Christmas story, but it is never mentioned in the New Testament as a prophecy of Christ.

"The voice of him that crieth in the wilderness, Prepare ye the way of the Lord, make straight in the desert a highway for our God" (Isaiah 40:3).

---

[11] Nephi copied these Isaiah chapters in their entirety from the plates of brass (see 2 Nephi 17–19). Yet he did not comment on the Immanuel prophecy, nor did he suggest a connection with the coming of Jesus.

[12] See Keith A. Meservy, "God Is with Us," in *Studies in Scripture, Vol. 4: 1 Kings to Malachi*, ed. Kent P. Jackson (Salt Lake City: Deseret Book, 1993), 95–98.

This prophecy is also millennial, with applications in other settings.[13] It speaks of the time in which the Lord will restore His people in peace and forgiveness, the earth will be transformed, and the glory of the Lord will be revealed to all flesh (Isaiah 40:1–5). Because the end-of-the-world context is clear in Isaiah's prophecy and because the messenger sent to prepare Christ's way belongs ultimately in that setting, how do we explain the fact that all three synoptic Gospels identified the event with the ministry of John the Baptist, the messenger sent to prepare the way for Christ's coming in mortality? (Matthew 3:3; Mark 1:2–3; Luke 3:4–6). The answer is simple, and it teaches us much about the objectives of the Gospel writers. They were not citing the passage to teach us who John was but to teach us who Jesus was. Matthew, Mark, and Luke were taking a prophecy of Jehovah's rule in the Millennium and bringing it to bear on the earthly ministry of Jesus of Nazareth, thereby teaching us that Jesus is God.

"Behold my servant, whom I uphold; mine elect, in whom my soul delighteth; I have put my spirit upon him: he shall bring forth judgment to the Gentiles. . . . I the Lord have called thee in righteousness, and will hold thine hand, and will keep thee, and give thee for a covenant of the people, for a light of the Gentiles; to open the blind eyes, to bring out the prisoners from the prison, and them that sit in darkness out of the prison house" (Isaiah 42:1, 6–7).

The magnificent revelation in Isaiah 42:1–7 is a prophecy of the work of the Lord's Servant, a theme that runs through several of the chapters in Isaiah. Matthew saw its fulfillment in Christ (Matthew 12:17–21). Its message pertains to the Savior in both His mortal and postmortal roles. In all meekness, He will bring justice (KJV "judgment") to the world (Isaiah 42:1–4), and He will be both a covenant and a light (Isaiah 42:6). His mission will include giving sight to blind eyes and bringing out "the prisoners from the prison, and them that sit in darkness out of the prison house" (Isaiah 42:7). Reference to

---

[13] See Kent P. Jackson, "Comfort My People," in Jackson, *Studies in Scripture, Vol. 4*, 134–35, and "The Appearance of Moroni to Joseph Smith," in *Studies in Scripture, Vol. 2: The Pearl of Great Price* (Salt Lake City: Randall Book, 1985), 348–49, and footnote 25.

the deliverance of those in prison brings to mind Jesus' postmortal mission to the spirits of the dead (Doctrine and Covenants 138). Yet His entire mission—before, during, and after His ministry in the flesh—is one of liberating His disciples from the bondage of spiritual impairment and the prison of sin.

"He is despised and rejected of men. . . . Surely he hath borne our griefs, and carried our sorrows. . . . He was wounded for our transgressions, he was bruised for our iniquities: . . . and with his stripes we are healed" (Isaiah 53:3–5).

The prophecy of Christ in Isaiah 53 as the Suffering Servant is the most revealing of the messianic prophecies in the Old Testament. It summarizes Jesus' mortal ministry, His suffering, His bearing of our grief and our sins, His atoning intercession, and His death. Its importance as a prophecy of the Messiah is attested in the fact that it is cited so frequently in the New Testament as referring to Christ.[14] It is difficult to imagine how anyone since Jesus' day could interpret this passage as something other than a prophecy of Christ. And it is difficult to imagine that anyone in ancient Judah could have read it without understanding that one individual would bear the sins of the whole nation, suffering and dying for them.

Yet, because the identity of the Servant is not explained in the revelation and no context for fully understanding it is provided, its meaning was beyond the grasp of most of Isaiah's countrymen and of the Jews in Jesus' day, just as its messianic purpose is not accepted by Jews today and even (remarkably) by some Christians. We can be most thankful that New Testament writers made the prophecy's meaning clear, and in modern revelation, we have Abinadi's explanation of it (Mosiah 14–16).[15]

"The Spirit of the Lord God is upon me; because the Lord hath anointed me to preach good tidings unto the meek; he hath sent me to bind up the brokenhearted, to proclaim liberty to the captives, and the opening of the prison

---

[14] See Matthew 8:17; Luke 22:37; John 12:38; Acts 8:32–33; Hebrews 9:28; 1 Peter 2:22, 24–25.

[15] See David R. Seely, "The Lord Will Bring Salvation," in Jackson, *Studies in Scripture, Vol. 4*, 151–54.

to them that are bound; to proclaim the acceptable year of the Lord" (Isaiah 61:1–2).

Jesus Himself taught that He was the fulfillment of this prophecy. In the synagogue in Nazareth, He announced, "This day is this scripture fulfilled in your ears" (Luke 4:21; see 4:16–22). The specific verses He read (Isaiah 61:1–2), which foretell His mortal work, can also be understood as belonging to His millennial work. As with the examples from Isaiah 9, 40, and 42, the larger context of this prophecy is millennial (Isaiah 61:1–11). In this case, it is clear that Jesus' audience understood correctly that the prophecy foretells the work of the Messiah, which explains their reaction when He identified Himself as the subject of the revelation (Luke 4:28–30).[16]

"But thou, Beth-lehem Ephratah, though thou be little among the thousands of Judah, yet out of thee shall he come forth unto me that is to be ruler in Israel; whose goings forth have been from of old, from everlasting" (Micah 5:2).

This prophecy foretells the birthplace of the Messiah, and it was recognized as such not only by Matthew but also by the chief priests and scribes whom Herod assembled to find where the promised child would be born (Matthew 2:1–8). Bethlehem was also the hometown of King David, who preceded Jesus by a thousand years. Obviously, it was not a coincidence that the prototype king came from the very town in which the true King would later be born, reminding us that earthly things point to things that are heavenly.

"Rejoice greatly, O daughter of Zion; shout, O daughter of Jerusalem: behold, thy King cometh unto thee: he is just, and having salvation; lowly, and riding upon an ass, and upon a colt the foal of an ass" (Zechariah 9:9).

This prophecy is very instructive, as it provides an intersection, like some of the others above, between Jesus' mortal and millennial ministries. The overall setting of the revelation is millennial. As we read in verse 10, it plays out in the day in which the Lord will destroy the military armaments of men (the chariot, the horse, and the battle bow). He will announce peace to the nations, and He will rule from

---

[16] See Seely, "The Lord Will Bring Salvation," 160–61.

sea to sea, meaning the entire earth. It will be in that day that those who are in prison will be freed through "the blood of thy covenant" (Zechariah 9:11).

The ultimate fulfillment of Zechariah's prophecy is thus the Second Coming of Jesus and events associated with it. But this prophecy was also fulfilled during His earthly ministry—in an anticipatory event that shows us that Jesus was the promised Messiah whose first coming foreshadows His coming at the end of the world. At His triumphal entry into Jerusalem, Jesus rode a young donkey over the Mount of Olives and into the city. It is obvious from the record in the Gospels that He planned the event carefully; all things needed to be in order as a means of teaching the people who He was. The Savior rode a donkey because in biblical times, a horse was primarily military equipment, and He was coming as the Prince of Peace. People on the streets shouted "Hosanna to the Son of David: Blessed is he that cometh in the name of the Lord; Hosanna in the highest" (Matthew 21:9). Matthew recognized the event as fulfilling Zechariah's words (Matthew 21:4–5). But, significantly, John tells us that it was only after Jesus' ascension—after the Apostles had received the Holy Ghost—that they understood what had happened (John 12:16).

Jehovah Is Salvation

When Philip asked the Ethiopian reading Isaiah 53, "Understandest thou what thou readest?" the Ethiopian responded, "How can I, except some man should guide me?" (Acts 8:30–31). Philip then "began at the same scripture, and preached unto him Jesus" (Acts 8:35). Likewise, Paul, teaching in the Thessalonian synagogue, "as his manner was, ... reasoned with them out of the scriptures, opening and alleging, that Christ must needs have suffered, and risen again from the dead" (Acts 17:2–3). And Jesus, resurrected and walking with disciples on the road to Emmaus, also taught from the Old Testament: "Beginning at Moses and all the prophets, he expounded unto them in all the scriptures the things concerning himself" (Luke 24:27). Then, meeting with His Apostles, he said, "These are the words which I spake unto you, while I was yet with you, that all things must be fulfilled, which were written in the law of Moses, and in the prophets, and in the psalms, concerning me." "Then opened he their understanding, that they might understand the scriptures" (Luke 24:44–45).

We, too, need revelation and explanation to open our understanding to the prophecies of the Old Testament. As can be seen from the passages discussed above, Old Testament prophecies concerning Jesus do not stand on their own as witnesses of the Savior's coming. All of them require explanation based on a knowledge of the events of Jesus' ministry or on an understanding of the Atonement. The Jews in Jesus' day had neither of those sources. Thus, God gave them John the Baptist, Jesus Himself, Apostles, and other witnesses to explain to them the meaning of the veiled words in their own scriptures. To us, He has given the gift of the Holy Ghost and modern revelation, particularly the Book of Mormon.

From the examples of some of the scriptures discussed above, we are reminded that Christ's eternal ministry is one great work. Passages in which prophecies of His first coming are contained within broader prophecies of His Second Coming and the Millennium show that they are two aspects of the same ministry to provide salvation. From those prophecies, we see that Christ's earlier coming, for which He set aside His glory and descended below all things, was presented in Old Testament revelations with great caution and reserve. The transcendent sanctity of the Atonement led the prophets to foretell it in ways that required greater humility and faith on the part of readers and additional revelation and explanation from the Lord's servants. It was this first coming that the Israelites from Moses to Jesus needed most but understood least.

By means of truth revealed through the Prophet Joseph Smith, we learn that worshipers of ancient Israel's God, Jehovah, were worshipers of Jesus Christ, even if they did not know Him by that name and in that role. The many good people who looked forward to the coming of the Messiah were looking forward to the coming of Jesus, even though they did not know who He was and what He would do.

HISTORICAL SETTING

Perhaps those who could see beyond the symbols would have seen Jehovah Himself as the fulfillment of the law of Moses. Perhaps they would have seen, as did John the Baptist, that Jesus of Nazareth was the promised Deliverer: "Behold the Lamb of God, which taketh away the sin of the world" (John 1:29).

All the prophets testified of Christ and foretold His acts of redeeming mercy (Acts 3:18, 24; 3 Nephi 20:24).[17] Some, such as Nephi, Jacob, and Benjamin, spoke directly and explicitly of Jesus' ministry, and their words are preserved in "plainness" for us today. Others, such as Isaiah and his brethren of the Old Testament prophets, taught the message of Christ's coming in ways that require the enlightenment of the gospel and the Holy Ghost to be understood. When we know that Jesus is Jehovah, we can see the words of His gospel written on every page of the Old Testament. Every ordinance of cleansing, every exclamation of praise, every hymn of thanks, and every prophecy of redemption bears testimony to Him and His work. Together, they proclaim that salvation is to be found only in Jesus Christ.

---

[17] See also Jacob 4:4; Mosiah 13:33; Helaman 8:16, 18.

II.

THE STORY OF THE NEW TESTAMENT

THOMAS A. WAYMENT

These [things] are written, that ye might believe that Jesus is the Christ, the Son of God; and that believing ye might have life through his name.

JOHN 20:31

The rich history of the New Testament text provides a fascinating glimpse into the process of keeping the stories and teachings of Jesus alive among believers in the decades and centuries after Jesus' death. Additionally, the story of the transmission of the New Testament text opens to us a window into the traditions and beliefs of Christians during a period that witnessed intense persecution from without and extensive challenges from within postapostolic Christianity.

How the scribes, early postapostolic church leaders, and others treated the text of the individual books of the New Testament during the second century and later reveals much about their beliefs and concerns for doctrine and also provides clues as to when the text of the New Testament began to suffer corruption. When we open the pages of the 1979 LDS edition of the King James Version, we often fail to recognize the complexities associated with providing an accurate and complete English translation.

By all accounts, Jesus spoke Aramaic as His native language and was possibly familiar with written Hebrew and travelers' Greek.[1] Hebrew was the primary language of Israel before the rise of the neo-Assyrian Empire (eighth century B.C.) and later when the Aramaic dialect was spread throughout the eastern Mediterranean, partially as a result of relocation of Aramaic peoples and partially as a result of Aramaic's becoming the recognized language of diplomacy (2 Kings 18:26).[2]

Aramaic was widely spoken in the Galilee as a result of the Assyrian expansion and also because of its affinity with indigenous Canaanite languages.[3] Therefore, Jesus' upbringing in Nazareth and His ministry in Galilee both strongly suggest that Jesus and His Galilean disciples would naturally speak Aramaic. Additionally, as noted below, the Gospels preserve several Aramaic words coming from Jesus' lips, suggesting that He spoke Aramaic as His primary language.

Unfortunately, if any original manuscripts, texts, or accounts of Jesus' ministry were written in Aramaic, none of them survived past the first century. What this means is that the earliest manuscripts of the New Testament, written exclusively in Greek, are translations of what Jesus taught and said in His native tongue. This situation holds

---

[1] Eric M. Meyers, ed., *Galilee through the Centuries: Confluence of Cultures* (Winona Lake, Indiana: Eisenbrauns, 1999). The close proximity of Sepphoris and Nazareth is a strong argument that Jesus would have been familiar with spoken Greek. Jesus' knowledge of written Hebrew or Aramaic is implied on several occasions in the New Testament. In several instances, Jesus read directly from Old Testament scrolls. Although these scrolls may have been the popular Targums (Aramaic Bible translations that came into being sometime after the Jews returned from Babylonian exile and, in some cases, not put into final form until the fourth or fifth century A.D.), they may also have been written in Hebrew (see Luke 4:17–22; 24:27; John 7:15). John records an instance where Jesus read publicly (John 7:15). John's account of this event records the surprise of those present because Jesus could do what only those with a formal education could do—namely, read biblical scrolls.

[2] The text of 2 Kings 18:26 reads, "Speak ... to thy servants in the Syrian language; for we understand it: and talk not with us in the Jews' language." The term *Syrian* refers to the language of the Syrians—that is, Aramaic. The implications are that the leaders of the people spoke the language of diplomacy, Aramaic, whereas the people spoke Hebrew.

[3] See Stephen A. Kaufman, "Languages (Aramaic)," in *ABD*, 4:173–78.

true for the teachings of the early Apostles, who were Galileans and whose command of Greek was likely quite limited.

Therefore, in the New Testament, preciously few words that Jesus actually spoke have not been translated into a secondary language before being passed down to us. This fact of history does not mean that Jesus did not speak the sayings attributed to Him in the New Testament but instead recognizes that what we have in the New Testament is a translation of what Jesus taught in Aramaic. A few Aramaic terms and phrases that have not been translated into Greek have been passed on to us by the evangelists and Paul. Those words are "Raca" (Matthew 5:22); "Abba" (Mark 14:36); "Talitha cumi" (Mark 5:41); "Ephphatha" (Mark 7:34); "Eloi, Eloi lama sabachthani" (Mark 15:34); and "Amen" (for example, Matthew 5:18, 26; 6:2). Everything else has been passed on in translation.[4]

The Manuscripts of the New Testament

The earliest manuscripts of the New Testament can be dated to a hundred years and later after the death of Jesus. The earliest fragment of a New Testament text is papyrus 52 (designated p52 and containing John 18:31–33, 37–38), which dates to circa A.D. 125. Before the fourth century (the most important three centuries of textual development), forty-three manuscripts of the New Testament exist, whereas by the sixteenth century, more than fifty-three hundred New Testament manuscripts are in existence.[5] These manuscripts are written exclusively in Koine Greek and are often very fragmentary for the first few centuries A.D. The manuscripts are written on papyrus, parchment (goat skin), and vellum (calf skin) and, in the

---

[4] For reasons unclear to us, Mark chose to preserve only a few of Jesus' words in Aramaic. Jesus' use of the term "Abba" to invoke the Father warranted attention and preservation rather than a simple translation. Paul also used the term to invoke the Father, teaching his audience that we now have a special relationship with the Father recognizable by the ability to use this private invocation with God Himself. See Morna D. Hooker, *The Gospel According to Mark*, ed. Henry Chadwick, *Black's New Testament Commentaries Series* (London: A & C Black, 1991), 348–49.

[5] Kurt Aland and Barbara Aland, *The Text of the New Testament*, trans. Erroll F. Rhodes (Grand Rapids: Eerdmans, 1989), 78–96.

first two centuries, generally contained only one book of the New Testament per manuscript.[6] Scribes decorated some of the manuscripts (*deluxe* or *illuminated*), and others simply contain text. By the beginning of the fifth century onward, several complete Bibles have survived, each containing the twenty-seven books of the New Testament along with various collections of apocryphal books. These manuscripts are often referred to as *codices*.

By the fourth and fifth centuries A.D., a fairly significant body exists of complete manuscripts in Greek (beginning in the late first century), Latin (beginning in the second century), and Coptic (beginning of the third century). By the fifth century onward, the list of manuscripts includes translations from Greek into Syriac (evident by the beginning of the third century but texts only from the fifth century and later), Armenian (evident only in a ninth-century manuscript and later), and Georgian (ninth century). The importance of these early versions for the study of the New Testament text is often overlooked, but these secondary translations offer independent witness to the transmission of the text and the willingness of Church leaders to translate the text into the common languages of the empire for missionary needs. The text of the New Testament was sacred, but the translation was not. Early members and missionaries freely translated the books of the New Testament into a variety of languages.

These translations are known together as the "versions" because none of the manuscripts used in the translation process are available or known. Therefore, we have the translation but no means of checking the accuracy of that translation because the primary documents are not extant. The versions offer an independent witness to the text of the New Testament and are not simply translations of texts now available to us.

---

[6] The two most notable exceptions are manuscripts p45, containing portions of all four Gospels and Acts, and p46, containing Romans, 1 and 2 Corinthians, Galatians, Ephesians, Philippians, Colossians, 1 and 2 Thessalonians, and Hebrews.

The Translation of Jesus' Words into Greek

What is problematic in the history of the text of the New Testament is determining who was responsible for these early translations and who translated Jesus' words and teachings from Aramaic to Greek and then subsequently into other languages such as Latin, Coptic, and so forth. We do not know whether these early translations, especially the Greek, were undertaken by inspired men, church leaders, or others. Because Jesus and His Apostles spoke primarily, if not exclusively, Aramaic, Matthew and John, who wrote the traditional eyewitness accounts, must have relied on a translator or translation of sources to compose their accounts. Both Matthew and John appear to have been composed in Greek, using Aramaic sources. They both reveal traits of Aramaic phraseology in their compositions. Mark and Luke, both second-generation Christians, had the ability to write in Greek and therefore could have been involved in the earliest translations of Jesus' words into Greek.[7] The accounts of Jesus' ministry and teachings might already have been translated into Greek, and Mark and Luke made use of what was already available to them.

Most scholars today suggest that Mark and Luke had access to records that were already translated into Greek before their time of writing. The issue is important because if Mark and Luke already had access to a Greek translation, then an authoritative translation was likely in existence before or contemporary with their conversions. If Mark and Luke relied on a common source, then relatively strong evidence suggests they both accepted a single source as authoritative. Their quiet approval of such an early source indicates that it carried

---

[7] Mark may have been acquainted with Jesus during His last week in Jerusalem (he is sometimes identified as the "young man" mentioned in Mark 14:51–52), but he was not among the Twelve during the mortal ministry of Jesus. He is mentioned directly for the first time in the book of Acts (see Acts 12:12). Luke was most likely a convert who joined the Church following Jesus' resurrection. He is mentioned indirectly for the first time in the book of Acts (see Acts 16:10; the beginning of the "we" passages). There is a late tradition, identifying him with the unnamed disciple on the road to Emmaus, but internal evidence and early tradition do not confirm this later identification.

some weight among Christians; but, at the same time, it needed either expansion or addition of other materials. On the other hand, if Mark and Luke made or were involved in those translations, then the issue arises of what Aramaic records were available to these authors in the earliest period.

These questions cannot be answered with complete confidence; however, internal evidence suggests that the authors of the Gospels made use of outside sources and of one another in writing their accounts.[8] Matthew, Mark, and Luke almost certainly made use of one another when they wrote their Gospel accounts. Internal evidence strongly suggests that Mark wrote the earliest of the synoptic Gospels. Matthew and Luke then made use of Mark's Gospel and possibly other earlier sources lost to us today.[9] In all probability, Mark was written first, followed by Matthew. Subsequently, Luke made use of Mark and Matthew and other traditions that were then available.[10] If all this is correct, then what does it tell us about the accurate transmission of the words of Jesus?

The Earliest Gospel Sources

If Mark wrote the earliest Gospel and if subsequent authors relied so heavily on his account, then significant reasons must have existed for relying on the work of a second-generation Christian and not on an eyewitness apostolic account. Early Church tradition of the fourth century likely provides the clue to answering this puzzle. An early Church bishop involved in the Council of Nicea (A.D. 325) records that Mark made use of Peter's memoirs when writing his account.[11]

---

[8] The Gospel of John is excluded from this discussion because its text is textually independent from the three synoptic Gospels (Matthew, Mark, and Luke).

[9] Robert H. Stein, *The Synoptic Problem: An Introduction* (Grand Rapids: Baker, 1987).

[10] Luke 1:1–3 suggests that the author of Luke had access to traditions that he felt were important for understanding the ministry of Christ. This suggestion reveals the author's open reliance upon sources and his interest in correcting earlier traditions.

[11] Eusebius quotes an otherwise unknown Christian, Papias, of the second century, who reported that Mark used Peter's memoirs in composing Mark's Gospel (*Church History* 3.39). Irenaeus also had access to the writings of Papias and passed on the same tradition as Eusebius (*Against Heresies* 3.1.1). Justin Martyr, a third-century Christian

We have no evidence that later editors tried to correct or alter the tradition that the second Gospel was written by a second-generation Christian rather than an Apostle, thus suggesting a consistent tradition that Mark was both early and authoritative for the Christian Church. Therefore, we have today a significant clue as to how Jesus' words came to be translated into Greek and subsequently passed down to us.

The writing of Mark's Gospel can be dated accurately to the decade or two before the fall of Jerusalem in A.D. 70. Mark was written at a time when the growing needs of gentile converts were being felt by Aramaic-speaking Church leaders in Jerusalem and Palestine. Early Church leaders must have realized that the early Christian Church could not continue to rely solely on the Old Testament and the relatively uncirculated accounts of Jesus' words in Aramaic.[12] A far-reaching Greek translation was necessary if the Church was going to continue expanding among the gentile population of the eastern Roman Empire. According to our best understanding, Mark's Gospel was the first attempt to remedy this growing need in the Church.

What may be surprising to many today is that Mark's Gospel, though useful in this respect, had several shortcomings in the eyes of early Church members. Its Greek was by no means polished, and many members felt that it placed several events out of their proper historical order, in some cases, did not use pronouns precisely, and so forth. The Gospels of Matthew and Luke were almost certainly a response to this problem.[13] Matthew and Luke bear strong witness

---

author, offers independent confirmation to this tradition (*Dialogue with Trypho* 106.3). Scholarly attempts to distance the relationship between Mark and Peter have proved largely unsuccessful. See Helmut Koester, *History and Literature of Early Christianity* (New York and Berlin: Walter DeGruyter, 1987), 160–77.

[12] Craig Evans, "Introduction," in Matthew Black, *An Aramaic Approach to the Gospels and Acts*, 3d ed. (Peabody, Massachusetts: Hendrickson, 1967), v–xxv.

[13] See Papias, as cited by Eusebius, "This, too, the presbyter used to say. 'Mark, who had been Peter's interpreter, wrote down carefully, *but not in order*, all that he remembered of the Lord's sayings and doings. For he had not heard the Lord or been one of his followers, but later, as I said, one of Peter's. Peter used to adapt his teachings to the occasion, without making a systematic arrangement of the Lord's sayings, so that Mark

that Mark's Greek needed correction, and both authors sought to clarify some of the grammatical problems of Mark.[14] Matthew and Luke reflected an overt concern to correct the order of events in Mark's Gospel, likely relying on the traditional eyewitness authority of Matthew or of Luke's association with Paul, who bore clear witness to many of the major events from the life of Jesus.[15] For the earliest period of New Testament history, we can discover that the Gospel accounts, especially those of Matthew, Mark, and Luke, were written in response to the growing needs of Greek speakers within the Church. By the time these authors wrote, the story of Jesus' life was three decades in the past. The authors made use of what was most readily available to them—the memoirs of Peter, the leading member of the Quorum of Twelve Apostles, and other available accounts of Jesus' words. This information supports the thinking that the earliest translation was carried out under the direction of Church leaders in an effort to respond to the need in the Church for Greek speakers to have a scriptural account of Jesus' life.

The Gospel of John offers a surprisingly less complex picture of how it was passed on in the earliest period. Most scholars today

---

was quite justified in writing down some things just as he remembered them. For he had one purpose only—to leave out nothing that he heard, and to make no misstatement about it" (Eusebius, *The History of the Church from Christ to Constantine*, ed. Andrew Louth, trans. G. A. Williamson [London: Penguin, 1989], 103–4; emphasis added).

[14] Two examples of the process demonstrate this point. First, Mark writes that Jesus "*could not* do any mighty work there . . . and he marveled because of their unbelief" (Mark 6:5–6; emphasis added; author's translation). Matthew apparently tidies it up when he writes that Jesus "*did not* do any mighty works there because of their unbelief" (Matthew 13:58; emphasis added; author's translation). Second, Matthew seems to clarify Mark with minor additions and omissions when dealing with the episode in Gethsemane. For example, when we compare Mark 14:32 and Matthew 26:36, Mark seems to be vague when he writes, "And they came to a place which was called Gethsemane," whereas Matthew writes, "Then cometh Jesus with them unto a place called Gethsemane." Apparently, Matthew wanted to clarify for his readers that Jesus was present, although He is never explicitly mentioned in this episode from Mark.

[15] See Richard Neitzel Holzapfel, "Early Accounts of the Story," in Richard Neitzel Holzapfel and Thomas A. Wayment, eds., *From the Last Supper through the Resurrection: The Savior's Final Hours* (Salt Lake City: Deseret Book, 2003), 401–21, and Martin Hengel and Anna Maria Schwemer, *Paul between Damascus and Antioch: The Unknown Years* (Louisville: Westminster/John Knox, 1997), 1–21.

question whether the Apostle John wrote or had anything to do directly with the Gospel of John; instead, they maintain that John was written by a second- or third-generation follower.[16] The burden of proof for this view comes from the dating of the Gospel of John, which most scholars believe was written in the last decade of the first century A.D. Because John was possibly written nearly sixty years after Jesus' death, scholars face the impossibility of believing that John, Jesus' Apostle, could have been alive and writing. The same argument holds true of the epistles of John and the book of Revelation. This problem, however, is not insuperable for Latter-day Saint scholars because both the Book of Mormon and the Doctrine and Covenants teach that John never tasted death but was instead granted the privilege of continuing his ministry until Jesus came again (3 Nephi 28:6–7; Doctrine and Covenants 7:1–8). The Gospel of John, therefore, could easily have been written by John even after the other Apostles had died.

Other more subtle reasons exist to show why scholars suggest such a late date for the writing of the Gospel of John. However, they are not based on external historical criteria but rely entirely on assumptions about the doctrine, teachings, and setting of the Gospel of John. In fact, until quite recently, scholars held that the Gospel of John may have been written as late as A.D. 125, but that opinion collapsed after the discovery of a papyrus fragment containing a portion of the Gospel of John that could be dated through handwriting analysis to A.D. 100–125.[17]

What this means is that the Gospel of John could be closer to being an eyewitness account of Jesus' life than any other New Testament writing—when we understand that the synoptic Gospels also contain historically accurate information that can be traced back through Peter and Mark to Jesus. Despite the objections of scholars,

---

[16] R. Allen Culpepper, *John, the Son of Zebedee: The Life of a Legend* (Minneapolis: Fortress Press, 2000), 72–85.

[17] The papyrus fragment is catalogued as p52 and contains John 18:31–33, 37–38. See also Koester, *History and Literature*, 181–83.

the Gospel of John does not appear to be based on other sources but is built upon what Jesus' disciple, John the Beloved, experienced firsthand.[18]

The late dating for the Gospel of John has become an almost consensus position in New Testament scholarship. Few scholars today question the dating of A.D. 90; however, the reasons for the late dating are suspect. What is at stake is the value of the Gospel of John in helping us understand the ministry of Jesus of Nazareth. If, as scholars contend, the Gospel of John is a late composition of the final decade of the first century, then its accounts have little historical value.

A result of the late dating of John is that very few scholars consider it an accurate source of Jesus' life. This position has often been unwittingly defended in the recent past by those who hope for a late dating for the Gospel of John, a position that justifies the claim that the author of Revelation continued to write even after he had included the famous warning, "If any man shall take away from the words of the book of this prophecy, God shall take away his part out of the book of life" (Revelation 22:19). If John had written his Gospel after he wrote Revelation, then clearly he could not have meant to apply this statement to all future revelations. Unfortunately, the late dating of the Gospel of John also weakens its validity as a historical source.

The New Testament epistles offer a different vantage point on the life of Jesus. All the epistles from Romans to Jude, with the possible exception of Hebrews, are personal correspondence written or dictated by Church leaders. They were not meant to include a history of what Jesus did or said; but they do reflect how the author understood the problem at hand and how the teachings of Jesus helped offer a solution. For that reason, they are invaluable documents on Church practice and belief, but they tell little about what Jesus said

---

[18] Representative of this view is Robert Fortna, *The Gospel of Signs: A Reconstruction of the Narrative Source Underlying the Fourth Gospel*, Society for New Testament Studies Monograph Series, 11 (London: Cambridge University Press, 1970).

and did. Unfortunately, the epistles of Paul, Peter, John, James, and Jude contain only brief glimpses into the life history of Jesus.[19]

The New Testament after the Death of the Apostles

In many respects, the history of the New Testament following Jesus' death leaves the impression that the story of His life is in question. From the few records we do have, we see a surprising degree of agreement on the essential facts of His mortal ministry.[20] By the last two decades of the first century A.D., all the men who are called Apostles in the New Testament had passed away with the exception of John the Revelator, who continued to minister as a transfigured being.[21] Unfortunately, we have no early manuscripts for the majority of New Testament books until the third century; and for others, we have no manuscripts until the fifth century A.D.[22] That leaves a window of 125 to 325 years where the accuracy of the New Testament text cannot be verified. This period of textual uncertainty is most likely the origin of major textual changes to the text of the New Testament. In other words, the period from A.D. 100 to A.D. 300 is the likely origin for the corruption of the New Testament text.

New Testament scholars state the problem differently but arrive at the same conclusion. They point to the second century as the most important decade of "textual development" for the text of the New Testament.[23] The manuscripts that exist from the eighth century onward are, in most particulars, identical to the text of our modern New Testament. Many minor differences exist in the manuscripts

---

[19] Important references to what Jesus did historically can be found in Romans 4:25; 5:8–10; 6:3–4; 8:15; 15:3; 1 Corinthians 1:23; 2:8; 5:7; 11:23–26; 15:3–4; 2 Corinthians 13:4; Galatians 1:15–16; 2:20; 3:1, 13; 4:6; Philippians 2:8; 3:10; Colossians 2:14; 1 Thessalonians 2:15; 4:14; 5:10; 1 Timothy 6:13; James 2:8; 2 Peter 1:17–18.

[20] Richard Neitzel Holzapfel, "Early Accounts of the Story," 403–5.

[21] See 3 Nephi 28:6–12.

[22] The two most notable exceptions are 1 and 2 Timothy, whose first manuscript attestation is codex Sinaiticus (circa A.D. 400).

[23] Larry Hurtado, "Beyond the Interlude? Developments and Directions in New Testament Textual Criticism," in *Studies in the Early Text of the Gospels and Acts*, ed. D. G. K. Taylor (Atlanta: Society of Biblical Literature, 1999), 26–48.

from the Middle Ages, a major reason why so many different English translations exist today. As we move backward in time, the manuscripts contain more variant readings and alternate wordings. As a general rule, the earlier the manuscript, the more variation that will exist in its text. Scholars have identified the second century A.D. as the most important century for New Testament textual alteration. Latter-day Saints generally use the more theologically implicit term "apostasy" to describe this period, whereas scholars speak of revisions, alterations, and adaptation to describe the same occurrence.

An important issue for Latter-day Saints is the question of how the textual corruption of the New Testament text corresponds to the apostasy. Was the apostasy partially a result of altered sacred texts, or was the alteration of the texts simultaneous with the beginning of the apostasy? In other words, was the apostasy the result of corrupted texts, or was it the cause of corrupted texts? Because we can accurately provide a date for the period when the text of the New Testament was corrupted, we should also be able to provide a comparative date for the beginnings of the great apostasy.

The age of apostasy is readily recognizable through the prophecies found in the New Testament. In their sermons and teachings, Peter, Luke, Paul, and others testified of an impending apostasy of authority and doctrine.[24] They reflect a definite sense of nearness in their teachings, and the influences of the apostasy were already being felt among the Christian churches.

Based on the writings of the New Testament, the force of the apostasy apparently was already felt in the apostolic age. And given the heretics' aberrant views, we can logically suppose that a concerted effort was made to change the doctrines of the New Testament shortly after the deaths of the first Apostles.[25]

---

[24] See Matthew 24:5–11 (Joseph Smith—Matthew 1:1–18), Acts 20:29–31, and 2 Thessalonians 2:1–12.

[25] Compare Kent P. Jackson, "'Watch and Remember': The New Testament and the Great Apostasy," in *By Study and Also by Faith: Essays in Honor of Hugh W. Nibley*, ed. John M. Lundquist and Stephen D. Ricks (Salt Lake City and Provo: Deseret Book and Foundation for Ancient Research and Mormon Studies, 1990), 81–117; Kent P.

New Testament Textual Variants

Understanding how textual variants arose and how they function in the text provides a clear picture into the origins of the New Testament. Although many of the earliest manuscripts contain significant variants, they are usually limited to single words or short phrases. Rarely does a variant reading extend beyond a single verse or two.

As mentioned, in general, the earlier the New Testament manuscript, the greater the number of variant readings; however, those variant readings often do not add significant amounts of text but generally alter the meaning of only a single verse or two. The most significant corruption of the New Testament and other early documents from the apostolic era can be most accurately traced to the period prior to the Council of Nicea (A.D. 325) and after the death of the Apostles in the latter half of the first century A.D. For this roughly 250-year period, the text of several books of the New Testament cannot be documented with certainty.

Inadvertent Scribal Errors

Early manuscripts are written in a style known as running script (a script written without word divisions or grammatical breaks), differentiated by whether the text is written in all capitals (uncial or majuscule) or in lower case cursive (miniscule). The two types of manuscripts can be dated broadly because most early manuscripts were written in uncial script and later manuscripts were written in minuscule. This statement should not be taken as a definite rule, but it holds true for the majority of manuscripts.

All these manuscripts were written with little punctuation, and because writing materials were expensive, scribes employed different conventions. Manuscripts were almost always written without spacing between words. In fact, at first glance, an entire book from the New Testament would appear to be a single sentence. Later, textual signs were developed to divide the text into sense lines and

---

Jackson, *From Apostasy to Restoration* (Salt Lake City: Deseret Book, 1996), 8–18.

short sections that facilitated comparison, but these were external to the writing. So, for example, 2 Peter 2:13 would read as follows:

ANDSHALLRECEIVETHEREWARDOFUNRIGHTEOUSNESSA
STHEYTHATCOUNTITPLEASURETORIOTINTHEDAYTIMES
POTSTHEYAREANDBLEMISHESSPORTINGTHEMSELVESWI
THTHEIROWNDECEIVINGSWHILETHEYFEASTWITHYOU

This type of writing gave rise to a significant number of variants that sought to clarify how the text should be divided. Although not evident in the English translation, the phrase "sporting themselves with their own deceivings" contains an alternate textual tradition that reads, "sporting themselves in their (during the) sacrament" (author's translation). The problem is that the word for "deceivings" (*apatais*) can be easily confused with the word for the "sacrament" (*agapais*) in Greek. A scribe's farsightedness or an inadvertent, quick glance at the manuscript from which he was copying could easily confuse the two words, with both making good sense. The New Testament contains numerous examples in which the difficulty of copying and transmitting texts has given rise to variant textual traditions.[26] Variants also arose as a result of scribes not hearing the text pronounced correctly. As we move toward the Middle Ages, we see a greater tendency for scribes and copyists to be less familiar with original pronunciations of words from New Testament times. So, for example, a scribe might hear the word "conflict" (*neikos*) pronounced when the text actually read "victory" (*nikos*). These misunderstandings gave rise to interesting textual variations, such as "Death is swallowed up in conflict," when it should read, "Death is swallowed up in victory" (1 Corinthians 15:54).[27] This type of variant is typically quite easy to detect because it occurs when the translation involves a synonym or similarly pronounced word.

---

[26] For an excellent introduction to this subject, see Bruce M. Metzger, *The Text of the New Testament: Its Transmission, Corruption and Restoration*, 2d ed. (New York and Oxford: Oxford University Press, 1968), 186–206.

[27] The example is taken from Metzger, *The Text of the New Testament*, 191.

A third type of textual error can be categorized as inadvertent scribal error. The ways in which scribes could inadvertently alter the text are too numerous to list but are generally quite easy to detect. Some of the most common occurrences involve a scribe's reading the last word of a line and then, in scanning across the page to copy the following line, inadvertently starting to copy again several lines lower (homoeoteleuton or homoeoarcton). Scribes also commonly skipped over words or repeated short phrases as their eyes glanced back and forth between manuscripts.[28] In the vast majority of these instances, the variant in question obviously arose out of a scribal error rather than as a result of textual tampering.

Intentional Scribal Alterations of the Text

Intentional alterations by scribes is the most important text variant because the alterations reveal something of the scribe who made the alteration and of the text in question.[29] Often, scribes attempted to "correct" texts they felt were open to misinterpretation, were prone to misuse, or contained contradictory doctrine and teachings. A classic example of this textual variant occurs in Mark 1:2 where the author, combining a quotation from Malachi 3:1 and Isaiah 40:3, makes the statement, "as it is written in the prophet Isaiah." The statement is clearly an error on the part of the original author who inadvertently did not identify that the quotation came from Malachi and Isaiah. However, scribes who recognized this slight error could not restrain themselves from correcting it.[30]

Scribes had to exercise great control in leaving contradictions intact in the text they were copying. Many scholars today have

---

[28] See Metzger, *The Text of the New Testament*, 186–95.

[29] We now have a famous statement by one Church father, Jerome, who, speaking of scribes, said that "they do not write down what they find, but what they think it means; and while they seek to correct the errors of others, they reveal their own" (Epistula ad Lucinum 61.5; author's translation).

[30] This reading is found in Sinaiticus (fourth century), Vaticanus (fourth century), and Bezae Catabrigiensis (fifth century), among others. Other scribes corrected it to read "as written in the prophets," the reading of Alexandrinus (fifth century), Freer (fifth century), and Byzantine manuscripts of the sixth century onward.

sensed the perplexing problem of why certain events in the New Testament are told more than once and why the wording is not identical. For example, the two versions of the Lord's Prayer do not contain the same wording (Matthew 6:9–13; Luke 11:2–4). Scholars have put forward theories from almost every conceivable vantage point in attempting to explain this. Scribes were not immune to this sentiment, and one particular scribe of the fifth century openly harmonized the two prayers along with a number of other seemingly contradictory passages.[31] Our modern King James Version contains much of the harmonized text instead of what is likely the original text. This variation results because the King James Version used a Greek text known as the *Textus Receptus*, prepared by Erasmus in the early sixteenth century. The *Textus Receptus* is a Greek compilation based on several older manuscripts of the New Testament. The quality of the manuscripts used by Erasmus, when judged by the standards of today's manuscript collections, is rather limited. The *Textus Receptus* contains almost all the harmonized readings because it is based almost entirely on late Byzantine manuscripts.[32]

Had the text of the Lord's Prayer not been harmonized by later scribes, it would read, "Father, hallowed be thy name, thy kingdom come. Give us each day our bread for tomorrow. And forgive us our sins, even as we forgive everyone indebted to us. And do not bring us into trial" (author's translation).[33] The simple fact is that the Lord could easily have given both versions of the prayers, but Christians were susceptible to attack by those who pointed out contradictions in the texts. Scribes were often prone to correcting and harmonizing these apparently contradictory accounts to undermine the positions of their opponents who saw the differences as signs of a Christian cover-up.[34]

---

[31] See Bezae Catabrigiensis and the miniscules 162 and 700.

[32] Bruce M. Metzger, *The Bible in Translation: Ancient and English Versions* (Grand Rapids: Baker, 2001), 70–80; Koester, *History and Literature*, 35–39.

[33] This earlier version of the prayer can be found in p75, a third-century A.D. papyrus manuscript, and in codex Sinaiticus (fourth century), among others.

[34] Metzger, *Text of the New Testament*, 201–3, reaches a similar conclusion based on

A few brief examples of textual variants may suffice to demonstrate how the text of the New Testament was changed by insiders to respond to the questions of those outside the faith. Changing the text of any sacred scripture is no easy task, as the altered text will often be readily identifiable by those of faith. Those passages used by heretics or those called into question by heretics are difficult to change because the argument often focuses narrowly on a defined subject. If either party changed the text in the midst of a controversy, the resulting change would be too obvious and would hold little, if any, credence. Therefore, those who wished to alter the text of sacred scripture were forced to come up with a means of altering text without being easily detected. Either they had to change it in all copies, produce a more authoritative text, or convince their audience that the altered text was somehow more correct than the previously used text.

This type of textual maneuvering gave rise to numerous variant readings. The first example was born out of the anti-Adoptionist controversies of the second and third centuries. The Adoptionists held that Christ was divine, but unlike other Christian believers, they held that He had been given that status as a result of His inherent goodness. Christ, in their view, was wholly human and was made of flesh and blood like any other mortal, but He became a God when the Father adopted Him as His Only Begotten Son. This viewpoint quickly came under suspicion by other Christians, and a series of councils were held to repress this growing doctrinal scandal.[35] We are certain that those who held Adoptionist beliefs were unable to alter the text of the New Testament, partly because they were under suspicion and partly because the scriptures they used to defend their positions were already well known and established. For those on the

---

the numerous variants that appear aimed at undermining the positions of those outside the Church.

[35] For example, the Council of Antioch (A.D. 268) convened to respond to this growing issue in the Church. This council, however, does not mark the beginnings of Adoptionist thinking but instead represents the latter end of it. Adoptionist beliefs can be traced to the beginnings of Christianity.

inside, being in the position of orthodoxy permitted greater access to the texts of sacred scripture.

One of the primary confusions of the biblical text is the issue of Jesus' parentage. As the stories clearly state, Jesus' true father was the Father, yet several ambiguous statements, primarily in Luke, provide wiggle room for pro-Adoptionist believers. One of the passages in question states, "When they had completed those days, as they returned, the boy Jesus remained in Jerusalem, but his parents did not know it" (Luke 2:43; author's translation).[36] The statement "his parents" can give rise to the conclusion that Joseph and Mary were His parents, a position that is obviously contradicted in the birth stories but is nonetheless open to Adoptionist interpretation.[37] Scribes of more orthodox extraction took upon themselves the duty of countering the claims through the alteration of the New Testament text. A number of Greek witnesses from the fifth century onward corrected the passage to read, "Joseph and his mother knew it not" (KJV Luke 2:43).[38] Although this slight change effected no great alteration of text, it did successfully end any slight confusion over Jesus' parents. Joseph was not Jesus' literal father, a claim made popular as early as the first century.

Other important examples can be found in John 1:27, Luke 1:3, and Matthew 4:1. In each of these instances, we have evidence of an overt scribal correction of a presumed doctrinal problem or inconsistency. In the example from John, a scribe added an endorsement by John of Jesus' baptism by fire and the Holy Ghost in an effort to clarify

---

[36] The KJV text does not follow the earliest manuscript witnesses but follows a later variant text under discussion here and therefore confuses the issue. It reads, "Joseph and his mother knew not of it" (Luke 2:43).

[37] See Bart D. Ehrman, *The Orthodox Corruption of Scripture: The Effect of Early Christological Controversies on the Text of the New Testament* (New York and Oxford: Oxford University Press, 1993), 47–118.

[38] The most important witnesses are Alexandrinus (fifth century) and Codex Ephraemi Rescriptus (fifth century). The reading became so popular after the ninth century that the majority of later manuscripts contain it. Earlier manuscripts such as Sinaiticus (fourth century) contain the more ambiguous reading.

that John truly did believe in Jesus.[39] The issue of whether all of John's followers had converted to Jesus was a thorny one for the Church, and several instances in the New Testament reveal that not all of John's followers left John to follow Jesus (Matthew 11:1–6; Luke 7:19–23; Acts 18:24–28; 19:1–6).[40] The problem appears to have been especially acute in Ephesus, the likely location where the Gospel of John was written, and therefore an addition to the Gospel of John would have some ability to undermine the position of those who believed in John but did not convert to Jesus.

In Luke 1:3, the author states, "It seemed good to me also, having had perfect understanding of all things from the very first, to write unto thee in order, most excellent Theophilus." We might question Luke's statement "It seemed good to me" and ask whether it was an inspired decision to write. Was he directed to write a Gospel by Church leaders or by an Apostle, or was the decision to do so one he made on his own? Several Latin copyists realized this potential issue and corrected it by adding, "It seemed good to me and the Holy Spirit" (author's translation).[41]

A third example comes from Matthew 4:1, where the text states, "Then was Jesus led up of the Spirit into the wilderness to be tempted of the devil." We can readily see that a doctrinal issue is raised when the Spirit leads the Savior so He can be tempted.[42] Scribes also recognized the problem, and beginning with the fourth century, a concerted effort was made to correct the doctrinal issue raised in this

---

[39] The text adds at the end of John 1:27, "He will baptize you with the Holy Spirit and fire" (author's translation). The reading can be traced back to Codex N (Greek; sixth century).

[40] The Pseudo Clementine Recognitions, which taught that he was the Messiah, claim to reproduce a scandalous belief by followers of John the Baptist. The tradition is questionable but likely reveals some of the friction between Christians and later followers of John (*Recognitions*, 1.54, 60).

[41] This example was taken from Metzger, *The Text of the New Testament*, 201–2. This reading can be found in the old Latin codices b, q, and in the majority of Vulgate manuscripts.

[42] The JST also corrects this passage to read, "Then was Jesus led up of the Spirit into the wilderness to be with God" (JST Matthew 4:1).

verse.[43] Scribes of diverse backgrounds and traditions sought to remove the ambiguity, including one scribe who completely removed the phrase "of the devil."[44]

More obvious tampering with the text of the New Testament can be seen in 1 John 5:7 ("For there are three that bear record in heaven, the Father, the Word, and the Holy Ghost: and these three are one"), a passage that has been titled the Comma Johanneum (the Johannine Comma). This passage, known for its open endorsement of the doctrine of the Trinity, does not appear in any ancient Greek manuscript. However, it appears in our King James Version because Erasmus included it in his Greek collation (*Textus Receptus*), a text that was later used by the KJV translators. Erasmus informed the local bishop that 1 John 5:7 was not present in his Greek manuscripts. Whether under direction of the bishop or someone close to him, a manuscript was forged that included this spurious passage. The forgery is known as Manuscript 61, sometimes referred to as the Leicester Codex, and is now housed at Trinity College, Dublin.[45]

The origin of the insertion can be dated to the fourth century Latin treatise, the *Liber Apologeticus*, authored by someone close to Priscillian.[46] Because of Priscillian's heretical leanings, the marginal note that would become 1 John 5:7 was viewed with suspicion until the eighth century, where it begins to appear in Latin manuscripts of the New Testament. The verse was accepted as part of the canon in the 1592 Clementine Latin Vulgate and was later sanctioned by Pope Leo XIII in the late nineteenth century.[47] The importance of this addition is its clear demonstration that scribes were willing to insert materials they felt clarified doctrine or strengthened their own positions.

---

[43] The first attempt to correct this reading can be dated to Codex Sinaiticus (fourth century).

[44] The changes to this verse can be traced in the Latin and Syriac translations. The scribe of miniscule 713 (twelfth century) removed the phrase, "of the devil."

[45] Metzger, *The Text of the New Testament*, 62, 101–2.

[46] Metzger, *The Text of the New Testament*, 101–2.

[47] Metzger, *The Text of the New Testament*, 102.

The Development of the Canon of the New Testament

The development and canonization of the books of the New Testament were complicated processes that were driven externally by heretics and internally by perception and local sentiment. The idea that early Church bishops met to discuss, exclude, accept, and then ratify the twenty-seven books that would become the New Testament is not historically accurate. The process of developing a canon and the arguments used both to exclude and include certain books into the canon of the New Testament are detailed and complex. A brief sketch of the most important influences will help demonstrate the complexity of the issue.

The creation of a book had something to do with the development of the idea of canon because it provided a logical framework for considering what should be included between the covers of the book and what should be excluded. In the apostolic era, New Testament writings, like other writings from antiquity, were written on papyrus and parchment scrolls. Scrolls like Luke-Acts were viewed as a unit, but the concept did not exist of a book into which an author intended his work to be placed. He could write in anticipation of his work being accepted as authoritative as other works, but the idea that it would be included as a chapter in a larger work is a modern concept.

The chief influences bearing on the development of the canon in the first two centuries can be described primarily as heretical. Under the pressure of Gnostics, who had both developed their own canon and were questioning the authenticity of several books now included in the New Testament, the early Christians began to consider how their powerful influence could be thwarted.[48]

Marcion's influence on the development of the New Testament canon cannot be overlooked either. In the mid-second century,

---

[48] Gnostic influence is evident already in the later writings of the New Testament—for example, 1 Timothy 6:20. The phrase "science falsely so called" is, in Greek, "gnosis so called falsely." For an introduction into the complexities of Gnostic origins and thought, see Kurt Rudolph, *Gnosis: The Nature and History of Gnosis*, trans. Robert McL. Wilson, P. W. Coxon, and K. H. Kuhn (New York: HarperSanFrancisco, 1987).

Marcion was excommunicated from the Church in Rome for heretical ideas. His expulsion from the Church seems to have ignited something within himself, and he immediately began a concerted effort to gain followers and tear down what he viewed to be false teachings.

Marcion rejected the Old Testament outright, but he felt that Paul was the true voice of Christianity. He accepted a collection of ten epistles of Paul and emphasized that the Gospel of Luke was more correct than the other New Testament Gospels.[49] Marcion's "canon" of the New Testament is the first verifiable written canon; however, it should not be understood to have defined the Christian canon. At most, it hastened the development of a more widely recognized canon instead of following local preferences and customs. Marcion's canon obviously drew from those books that were already accepted as canonical, but it negatively defined what was not canonical, a position that makes sense if other authoritative books were already being used by Christians.

One of the other major influences bearing on the development of the Christian canon was the influence of the Montanists, a late second-century heretical sect whose adherents believed strongly in the inspiration of the Holy Spirit. The Montanists claimed to receive new revelations under the direction of the Spirit, many of which had a strong apocalyptic outlook. The influence of the Montanists was twofold: they created a general suspicion of apocalyptic works like the book of Revelation, and they forced other Christians to consider whether new works could be added to the body of already accepted works.[50] Christians were now forced to consider closing the canon and to define exactly what constituted acceptable scripture, a movement accelerated earlier by Marcion and now brought into the light by Montanus and his followers.

---

[49] Marcion accepted the epistles from Romans to 2 Thessalonians, following our modern canonical order, and the epistle to Philemon, but he rejected 1 and 2 Timothy, Titus, and Hebrews.

[50] Bruce M. Metzger, *The Canon of the New Testament: Its Origin, Development, and Significance* (Oxford: Clarendon Press, 1997), 99–106.

As external forces continued to put pressure on the Church to formulate a distinct canon of accepted books, internal struggles also shaped which books would be included and which would be excluded. The majority of our information comes from early Christian leaders who were seeking to define the parameters of the New Testament in light of pointed questioning. One of the first to define clearly the canon in a general epistle, Origen (A.D. 185–254), wrote in his *Expositions on the Gospel According to John* that 2 Peter was of questionable authenticity, as also were 2 and 3 John, although he accepted the other books of our New Testament as canonical.[51] Writing nearly a generation later, Eusebius (A.D. 265–340) also questioned 2 Peter and 2 and 3 John but also openly questioned the authenticity of the epistles of Jude and James. The wrangling over the contents of the New Testament continued until the close of the fifth century when a stamp of approval was placed on the twenty-seven-book canon by the Third Synod of Carthage (a.d. 497).[52]

The debates over the canon did not take place in a single weekend session but instead represent more than three hundred years of development. By the early second century, a belief was already evident that certain scriptural books had greater value than others. As heretics questioned the doctrines of the early Christians, decisions began to be made concerning what books would be used to establish doctrine and correct practice. As the writings of the New Testament Apostles and missionaries began to supplant the Old Testament in Christian worship services, an acceptable body of approved texts was also developed. Although some disputes arose over the authenticity of some texts (2 Peter and 1 and 2 John especially) and the value of some books (Revelation), the books that would become officially recognized as the canon of the New Testament were always considered important. Certainly, many books were excluded—some that

---

[51] Discussed in Metzger, *The Canon of the New Testament*, 308.

[52] Athanasius's 39th Festal Letter is the first to include all the books of the New Testament in their canonical order. His encyclical letter represents Alexandrian church tradition in Egypt and later became the position of the western church. See Metzger, *The Canon of the New Testament*, 312–15.

have been lost and others that are currently available. The canonization of the New Testament, however, reveals a need within the early Church for a body of material that would prove useful in establishing practice and at the same time in helping undermine the position of the heretics.

Summary

A discussion of textual variants and canonization of the New Testament is an important part of understanding how the New Testament can be used in understanding Jesus' life and ministry and the history of the first-century Church.

We often labor under the impression that large amounts of material have been removed from the New Testament and that new textual discoveries will yield significant lost truths. This stance may prove true in the future, but of the fifty-three hundred fragmentary and complete manuscripts available to us today, very few add significant amounts of material to the text of the New Testament. They are part of a larger Christian dialogue where scribes and Church leaders used the text of the New Testament to correct and clarify the doctrine of the Church. Most of the new information gleaned from the manuscripts of the New Testament comes in the form of a few new words here and there—not lost chapters or stories.

Certainly, early books have been lost and destroyed, and we can only lament their loss; but they cannot inform our understanding of the New Testament until they are rediscovered. When we seek to understand how the New Testament was put together and altered over the centuries, we must understand that changes did occur. Changes often had to be slight so as not to be detected by outsiders. An unbeliever could not simply alter the text of the New Testament and expect anyone to believe the result.

The many variants in the New Testament tell us more about the difficulties faced by early Christians than about the doctrines of the New Testament. The stories of Jesus' life and the activities of the Apostles are largely unassailable. The major details of His life are not textually in question. The New Testament Gospels appear to be complete documents without major gaps or interpolations.[53] Although literally hundreds of thousands of variants of the New Testament text are known, they offer only minor alterations to the existing texts.[54] The attacks on Christianity have come most recently not from the inside over disputed texts but largely from an understanding of what sources the evangelists used in writing their accounts and what documents constitute the earliest texts of Christianity.

A New Age of Inquiry

Today, the quest to understand who Jesus was has become an issue based not so much on the complete canonical Gospels as they appear in our King James Version but instead on the sources behind those accounts. Theoretically, if we could prove that the authors of the Gospels used a source to compile their accounts, then at the same time we would have identified a document that had greater intrinsic value than the texts now available to us. They would be closer in time to Jesus and would reflect a greater likelihood that they were written by someone who knew Jesus personally. Scholars have proposed that such sources did exist and were used extensively by the authors of Matthew, Luke, and possibly John.

Today, many scholars assume without further consideration that Matthew and Luke had recourse to an earlier Gospel now referred to as Q, from the German word *quelle* for "source."[55] This document is a

---

[53] Several proposals have been made for possible large-scale corruption such as that evident in John 6:1, which states that Jesus "went over the sea of Galilee." However, in the preceding verse of John 5, Jesus is in Jerusalem (see John 5:1). In the transition between the two chapters, Jesus has traveled well over a hundred miles, a possible indication that some text has been removed.

[54] Current thinking on the number of New Testament textual variants puts the number somewhere between 250,000 and 300,000. See Kurt and Barbara Aland, *The Text of the New Testament*, 48–71.

[55] The most important work to date on the subject is John S. Kloppenborg Verbin, *Excavating Q: The History and Setting of the Sayings Gospel* (Minneapolis: Fortress Press, 2000). See also Robert Stein, *The Synoptic Problem: An Introduction*, for a beginner's introduction. For an opposing view, see Mark Goodacre, *The Case Against Q* (Harrisburg, Pennsylvania: Trinity Press, 2002).

literary hypothesis and is not manifest in any manuscript tradition. Scholars reconstructed it by excerpting those passages that Matthew and Luke have in common—but for which there is no parallel in Mark. The theory is that Matthew and Luke used Mark as a source but that they also had recourse to an unknown Gospel (Q), which they both accepted as authoritative. Therefore, if we take out those passages for which Matthew and Luke share a verbatim parallel, then we are able to define what was likely in Q. One of the many difficulties with the theory is that if only one author quoted from this hypothetical source, then it would not appear in our reconstructions. Therefore, the entire hypothesis is prone to making arguments from silence.

These documents that scholars speak of are purely imaginary creations; they have never actually been seen or spoken of by anyone in the ancient world. Using these hypothetical literary sources, scholars are painting a radically different view of early Christianity, proposing such things as the belief that a divine Jesus was a late Christian legend, that His earliest disciples were confused by His death, or that Jesus was simply a Galilean prophet who died tragically and suddenly.[56] The fact that we have no physical evidence of the existence of Q has not stopped scholarly discussion and publication. This reconstruction of early Christian origins, based on the modern creation of a source, is undermining the faith of many New Testament readers and seeks to propose a very different picture of who Jesus was and what He taught than is found in the New Testament.

The impression has been given by scholars who argue for the existence of Q, as well as by popular media outlets, that this new picture of early Christianity has been built upon new textual discoveries such as the Dead Sea scrolls or the Nag Hammadi documents.[57] This

---

[56] For the most recent and comprehensive treatment of this issue, see Verbin, *Excavating Q*, 409–46.

[57] Most recently, Dan Brown has popularized many of the conclusions developed through the Q hypothesis. See *The Da Vinci Code* (New York: Doubleday, 2003). See also the ABC special aired by Peter Jennings entitled "The Search for Jesus" (June 1999), where the life of Jesus was reconstructed using the model developed by Q scholars.

stance is not legitimate.[58] In reality, these new "discoveries" have been based solely on literary hypotheses of the New Testament. Some scholars see a growing need to respond to these proposals before more plain and precious truths become lost or confused in the polemics of our dispensation.

The New Testament offers a sound witness that Jesus was the Son of God, Messiah, and Savior of the world and that those who knew Him personally remembered that He taught them these very truths. The historical reality is that Jesus lived and that the New Testament, including its shortcomings, testifies that He was the Christ. The result presents itself as a united voice. It is the modern world that has turned against itself and questioned motives and sources. The author of the Gospel of John may have summarized it best when he said that "these [things] are written that ye might believe that Jesus is the Christ, the Son of God; and that believing ye might have life through his name" (John 20:31).

---

[58] See Philip Jenkins, *Hidden Gospels: How the Search for Jesus Lost Its Way* (Oxford and New York: Oxford University Press, 2001).

III.

THE JERUSALEM TEMPLE, THE SADDUCEES, AND THE OPPOSITION TO JESUS

JEFFREY R. CHADWICK

In that same hour said Jesus to the multitudes, Are ye come out as against a thief with swords and staves for to take me? I sat daily with you teaching in the temple, and ye laid no hold on me.

MATTHEW 26:55

The Talmud records the awe and adoration of the Jewish people for their temple at the time of Christ with the exclamation "Whoever has not seen the temple of Herod has never seen a beautiful building!"[1] But it was at Jerusalem, within the management of that very temple, that the plot to kill Jesus of Nazareth was conceived and carried out.

Jesus Himself revered the temple of Herod. He went to extraordinary lengths to demonstrate the importance of keeping its precincts sacred, casting out merchants and money changers at two different Passover festivals. The first cleansing occurred at the beginning of His ministry (see John 2:13–17), and the second cleansing at the end

---

[1] The Babylonian Talmud passage is Baba Batra 4a (author's translation). Although written down centuries after Christ, it represents the memory and oral transmission of Jewish adoration of the temple of Herod in the first century A.D.

(see Matthew 21:12–16), thus framing the public ministry.² Added to cessation of profane trafficking in the sacred precincts, even for a few hours on each occasion, was Jesus' singular claim that the temple was "my Father's house" and even "My house" (John 2:16; Matthew 21:13). Jesus' actions and speech naturally infuriated the corrupt managing directors of the temple, the chief priests of Jerusalem, and their allies, the clan of the Sadducees. They claimed special privilege and jealously protected their power and source of wealth—the priestcraft they exercised in their control of the temple. Jesus' actions at the beginning of the public ministry directly challenged the wicked "husbandman" whose anger at the loss of immorally high profits was channeled into a concrete conspiracy to kill the Lord of the vineyard's own Son, the "heir," during the Savior's final visit to the temple (see Matthew 21:33–46).

The Chief Priests and the Sadducees

The Sadducees, and particularly their leaders, the chief priests and elders of Jerusalem, were Jesus' real enemies. They were the only organized Jewish group who represented a significant and imminent threat to Jesus' life or liberty. Though certain Pharisees opposed Jesus on some matters (Sabbath healing), the Pharisees were generally benign regarding Him. But the chief priests and Sadducees despised Him and felt threatened by Him for reasons that were doctrinal, economic, and political. These are the men who conceived and carried out the plot that led to Jesus' death.

Origin of the Sadducees. At the time of Jesus, the Sadducees were the elite priestly party of Jerusalem. They had been so for centuries.³

---

² Although some scholars suggest that each is a retelling of the same event, there is clear evidence that the cleansings were independent and thus frame the public ministry; see Richard D. Draper, "Jesus' Prophecies of His Death and Resurrection," in Richard Neitzel Holzapfel and Thomas A. Wayment, eds., *From the Last Supper through the Resurrection: The Savior's Final Hours* (Salt Lake City: Deseret Book, 2003), 7–10.

³ For a review of this important period between the close of the Old Testament and beginning of the New Testament eras, see S. Kent Brown and Richard Neitzel Holzapfel, *Between the Testaments: From Malachi to Matthew* (Salt Lake City: Deseret Book, 2002).

As we read it in English, the Greek term *Sadducee* most likely represents the Hebrew word *tzaddoki*, or Zadokite. The Sadducees were Zadokites. But who were the Zadokites? During the tenth century B.C., Zadok was the Aaronic priest loyal to both David and Solomon, appointed by Solomon to be the high priest at the Jerusalem temple (1 Kings 2:35). The family of Zadok became the clan of Aaronic priests who, generation after generation, perpetually managed the temple in Jerusalem.

As a result, the Zadokite clan based itself in and around Jerusalem, and over time Zadokite priests were not found in other areas of the land of Israel. Early in the second century B.C., the Zadokites began to become corrupted by Hellenistic and pagan influences, especially during the years when the Greco-Syrian king Antiochus IV ruled over Judea. Following the Hasmonean revolt (167–142 B.C.) and during the decades of Judean independence that followed (141–63 B.C.), high priests began to be appointed from outside the Zadokite clan,[4] primarily from the priestly Hasmonean family that also assumed the kingship.[5] During this time, Hellenistic influence did not diminish but rather increased, and the Greek term *Sadducee* became common.

Some of the Sadducees became estranged from the Hasmonean leadership of Judea, feeling that the high priest's office had been improperly usurped. Certain of these left the country for Egypt.[6] Others stayed in Judea but stood in opposition to the Hasmonean

---

[4] The first of these was Alcimus, who was an Aaronic priest but not of the line of Zadok. He was appointed about 161 B.C. See 1 Maccabees 7:5, 9.

[5] Jonathan, brother of Judah Maccabee (the Hasmonean who led the revolt against Syria), was appointed to be high priest in 152 B.C. He also assumed the political leadership of Judea. See 1 Maccabees 10:18.

[6] Onias IV, a Zadokite priest, moved to Egypt with a faction of his clan at this time and received permission from Ptolemy VI to build a Jewish temple at Leontopolis. He and his successors conducted Levitical sacrifice there until the Emperor Vespasian forbade their operations and closed their temple shortly after A.D. 70. See Josephus, *War*, 1.1.1, 7.10.3–4, and *AJ*, 13.3.1–3. Onias IV was a son of Onias III, a Zadokite who was high priest in Jerusalem until 174 B.C. when he was deposed by the new Syrian monarch Antiochus IV.

high priests (these became the Essenes, who will be discussed below). But the majority of Sadducees stayed in Jerusalem and remained active in the day-to-day practical management of the temple under the Hasmonean high priests. Also during this time, the views of the Pharisees (discussed below) became popular among the vast majority of the Jewish population. As a result, the high priests and the Sadducees found themselves compelled by consensus to perform procedures of the temple ritual in accordance with Pharisee views.

In spite of all these events, the Sadducees patiently continued in their managerial appointments. When the Romans invaded the land of Israel in 63 B.C., the Sadducees' position as the bureaucracy of the temple was still unquestioned. They had essentially reconciled themselves to serving under high priests who were not genealogically Zadokite. On the other hand, the high priests began to be considered, and also began to consider themselves, as part of the Sadducee clan, which lent a measure of legitimacy to their own positions.

During the reign of Herod the Great (38–4 B.C.), Hasmoneans were no longer appointed to the high priest's office, and priests of other Aaronic lineage were installed by Herod and the Roman governors who succeeded him. Any man who became high priest obtained the position by paying the king or governor a huge fee, essentially purchasing the office. By the time Jesus was an adult, the Sadducee party of Jerusalem included both the high priestly elite, who also ran political affairs in Judea as subordinates of the Roman governor, and the genealogical Zadokites, who were the bureaucratic management of the temple under the chief priests.

Other Aaronic Priests. Other than the Sadducees, twenty-four courses or clans of Aaronic priests served at the temple. These are all listed by their family name in 1 Chronicles 24. Of those clans, sixteen courses descended from Aaron's son Eleazar, and eight courses descended from Aaron's son Ithamar. Hundreds of years after Chronicles was written, the same twenty-four priestly courses were still serving at the Jerusalem temple. Their service was unpaid, and other than receiving portions of certain sacrifices, they gained no wealth from their temple activity. All of these clans were required to serve at the Jerusalem temple during the weeks of the major festivals: Passover, Weeks (*Shavuot*), Rosh HaShanna, Tabernacles (*Sukkot*), and Hanuka. Additionally, each of the twenty-four courses served another week every sixth months, which kept the temple staffed all year long. For each clan, this meant voluntary service of at least six weeks a year, spread over the whole calendar.

An example of this service is recorded in Luke 1, where Zacharias, an Aaronic priest of the course of Abia (the eighth course), was serving a week at the Jerusalem temple when the angel appeared to him at the altar of incense to announce that John would be born.

The service of the twenty-four courses of Aaronic priests was strictly voluntary and honorable. Many of those priests were offended by the corruption of the chief priests and Sadducees. Some of the ordinary priests were themselves Pharisees (cf. John 1:19, 24). Luke noted that a great number of those ordinary priests even joined the church (Acts 6:7).

Sadducee Priestcraft. In contrast to the volunteer priests, the Sadducees made their living at the management of the temple and the industries associated with its rituals and purity. The chief priests controlled the franchises for merchants who traded in goods used at the temple, for those who sold sacrificial animals and birds, and for money changers who provided coinage acceptable for donation at the temple treasury. When Jesus cast out money changers and animal sellers from the temple courts during His first visit to the temple at the beginning of His public ministry (see John 2:15), He was not only challenging the authority of the chief priests but also interfering with their sources of income.

The chief priests also controlled the management of the *miqva'ot* (ritual immersion pools) outside the southern gates of the temple. Industries related to Mosaic law cleanliness, such as the production of stone vessels for pure water (cf. John 2:6) and temple implements of metal or other materials, were all under the shadow of Sadducean bureaucracy. Even the construction activities that were constantly going on at the thirty-six-acre temple complex were under their control. The Sadducees in general, and their chief priests in particular, had their fingers in every temple-related operation that occurred in Jerusalem and all of Judea, and they enriched themselves significantly from temple proceeds. If priestcraft is defined as the exercise of priesthood for the purpose of getting gain, then the Sadducean chief priests were the very personification of priestcraft. In this regard, it is telling that the Book of Mormon prophet Jacob specifically pointed to "priestcrafts and iniquities at Jerusalem" as the reason that Jesus would be crucified (2 Nephi 10:5).

The office of high priest was a political appointment in Jesus' day. This was historically the case, as it was King Solomon who had appointed Zadok nearly a thousand years previously. But since Hellenistic times, as already mentioned, the office had often been bought from whatever monarch or governor happened to be ruling. Most of the high priests of the first century were from one of four Sadducean families (who were not necessarily genealogically Zadokite): the house of Boethus, the house of Annas, the house of Kathros, and the house of Ishmael ben Phiabi. Joseph Caiaphas, who was high priest during Jesus' adulthood, was of the house of Annas, being the son-in-law of Annas, who had himself been high priest from A.D. 6 to 15. (The name *Annas* is Greek in form—the actual Hebrew name was *Hanan*.) Caiaphas paid the Roman governor Valerius Gratus a large fee to obtain the office in A.D. 18 and continued to pay to remain in the position when Pontius Pilate became governor in A.D. 26.[7]

The relationship of Caiaphas and the other chief priests and Sadducees to the Roman governor was essentially that of collaborator to occupier. This arrangement worked well for both Rome and the chief priests and Sadducees. The local government functions of Jerusalem and Judea, from legislation and taxation to police control, were under the control of the chief priests as executives and certain "elders" or

---

[7] F. F. Bruce, *New Testament History* (New York: Doubleday Galilee, 1969), 64–65. Both Caiaphas and Pilate were deposed from their offices in A.D. 36.

aldermen appointed by them. The high priest himself reported directly to the Roman governor, who exercised overall executive discretion for security, military control, and capital punishment.

Thus, Caiaphas could order the arrest of Jesus and preside over a trial to convict Him of a crime for which execution was the punishment, but only Pontius Pilate could mandate that Roman soldiers be present at the arrest and carry out a capital sentence (John 18:3).[8] Still, by any measure, the chief priests, elders, and Sadducees in general were allies of the Roman occupiers of Judea. They were resented by a great many of the common Jews of the country as well as by the other Aaronic priests who served at the Jerusalem temple. In this regard, however, we should remember that Pilate and Caiaphas did not govern the Galilee or the Transjordanian territory of Perea (which Herod Antipas ruled as tetrarch) or the Golan (which Herod Philip ruled as tetrarch). Nor did the Sadducees have any influence in Perea, Galilee, or the Golan. Thus, Jesus was in danger of the ire of His real enemies, the Sadduceans, only when He was in Judea.

The Sanhedrin. The only place where the chief priests and the Sadducean bureaucracy shared their control of Judea was in the Judean senate, or Sanhedrin. This was an assembly of seventy Jewish "elders" or alderman, based on the biblical reference to seventy elders of Israel who assisted Moses and Aaron (Exodus 24:1; Numbers 11:16). The Sanhedrin was presided over by the high priest, bringing the total number of senate seats to seventy-one. It was initiated early in the second temple period, after the return to Jerusalem from Babylon, and operated as a local governing assembly for Judea successively under Persian, Hellenistic, and Hasmonean control.

Positions on the Sanhedrin were allotted by monarchs or governors, after which they were often hereditary. During the reign of the Hasmonean queen Salome Alexandra, Pharisees were appointed in

---

[8] John 18:3 records that *"speiran,"* that is, Roman officers, were also present at the arrest. The term translated as "officers" is the typical Greek rendering of the Latin *cohort.* See S. Kent Brown, "The Arrest," in Holzapfel and Wayment, *From the Last Supper through the Resurrection,* 191–92.

great numbers to the Sanhedrin, and thereafter they constituted a majority vote in the body.

At the time of Herod the Great, the Sanhedrin was largely inactive because of his mistrust of all parties on it. But it was revived in practice and importance after A.D. 6, when Roman governors began ruling Judea.

When Jesus began His public ministry, Joseph Caiaphas presided over the Sanhedrin because he was high priest. The Sadducees held a minority of seats on the body, but only a minimum quorum of twenty-three members (known as a "small Sanhedrin") was required to conduct business. Because the high priest controlled the agenda and the apparatus to summon the body, he and his associate chief priests and Sadducees could dictate the decision making of the Sanhedrin by conducting sessions where only their own allies were in attendance. Rarely, however, was a major or controversial action taken by the Sanhedrin without the consensus that a larger quorum or the whole senate itself provided.

But Jesus' popularity among the Jewish masses, as well as His open opposition to the authority of the chief priests and Sadducees and their ministry of the temple and Jerusalem, represented such a threat to their political power and income that they were willing to take desperate measures to be rid of Him. The majority of Pharisees, on the other hand, would most likely never have participated in a plot to take Jesus' life.[9] Jesus' trial was probably conducted before a "small Sanhedrin" numbering not many more than the twenty-three minimum votes necessary to conduct business and packed (except for Joseph of Arimathea) almost solely with Caiaphas's Sadducean allies. A guilty verdict against Jesus was virtually guaranteed.

Sadducee Doctrine. We know of no religious documents written by the Sadducees. Perhaps they created some, but if any survived the

---

[9] This was also true of Pharisee relations to the Twelve Apostles. When they were on trial before the complete Sanhedrin, the majority vote of the Pharisees, inspired by Gamaliel's noble address, led to their acquittal and a directive forbidding harassment against them (Acts 5:27–39).

Jewish war with Rome, none has been discovered. The information we know about them is derived from sources that were hostile to them—namely the New Testament, the Talmud (which preserves Pharisee points of view), the Dead Sea Scrolls (which preserve Essene points of view), and the Jewish historian Josephus. What Sadducees said about themselves would surely have taken a different tone than these sources.[10] For example, whereas Josephus describes the Pharisees as friendly and having the public's best interest at heart, his summary of the Sadducees is that they were boorish and rude to their fellow Jews, regarding them little better than Gentiles.[11] A Talmud passage remembers the dread of the Jewish populace toward the chief priestly cliques and their subordinate thugs who controlled life in Jerusalem and Judea at the time of Jesus:

> Woe is me because of the house of Boethus—Woe is me because of their clubs.
>
> Woe is me because of the house of Annas—Woe is me because of their conspiracies.[12]
>
> Woe is me because of the house of Kathros—Woe is me because of their quill.[13]
>
> Woe is me because of the house of Ishmael ben Phiabi—Woe is me because of their fist.
>
> They are the high priests, and their sons are the treasurers,
>
> Their sons in law are the officers, and their servants beat the people with staves.[14]

---

[10] Lee I. A. Levine, "Hellenism and the Hasmoneans," in *Ancient Israel*, ed. Hershel Shanks (Washington: Biblical Archaeology Society, 1999), 256.

[11] Josephus, *War*, 2.8.14.

[12] The text reads *Hanan* rather than the Greek Annas, but this is the Annas of John 18:24, who had been high priest prior to his son-in-law Caiaphas. The word *laheshatan* is literally "whisperings" but is rendered "conspiracies" because it refers to "secret conclaves to devise oppressive measures" (note 13 to this verse in Soncino Talmud, English version).

[13] The term "quill" here is a writing instrument, "with which they write evil decrees" (note 14 to this verse in the Soncino Talmud, English version).

[14] Pesahim 57a, author's translation.

The New Testament relates that Sadducees denied the doctrine of resurrection (Matthew 22:23; Mark 12:18; Luke 20:27). Josephus concurred, maintaining that they denied the continuation of the soul after death, rewards in heaven, and penalties in hell. He also recorded that Sadducees thought God was not interested in whether men acted for good or for evil and that people could freely choose good or evil without the expectation of divine reward or punishment.[15] Essentially, Sadducees minimized God's role in human destiny and emphasized man's own choices as the sole movers in history.[16] We know clearly from the New Testament that Sadducees had no qualms about the use of crucifixion as a capital punishment (Matthew 27:20–22; Mark 15:11–13; Luke 23:13–23; John 19:6). This had probably been a Sadducee position for at least two centuries, as it was apparently also the position of the breakaway Saducean sect known as the Essenes. According to the Essene Temple Scroll, the "hang him on a tree" passage of Deuteronomy 21:22 justified crucifixion as a punishment for certain crimes.[17] That passage was interpreted in just the opposite manner, however, by the Pharisees, whose doctrinal positions forbade crucifixion, as recalled in the Talmud.[18]

Sadducees also appear to have been very strict about what was considered improper on the Sabbath. They were extremely annoyed with Jesus for healing a crippled man on a festival Sabbath—the "feast of the Jews" mentioned in John 5, which was probably Rosh HaShanna (John 5:1–16). As with other passages in John where "the Jews" are noted as Jesus' detractors, these were probably the Saducean temple and municipal bureaucracy. (Pharisees are not mentioned at all in the John 5 episode—as will be discussed below.)

The Sadducean establishment was apparently still angry with Jesus for that Sabbath breach a full year after it happened (see John

---

[15] Josephus, *War*, 2.8.14.
[16] David Flusser, "The Sadducees and Menander," in *Judaism and the Origins of Christianity*, ed. David Flusser (Jerusalem: Magnes Press/Hebrew University, 1988), 612.
[17] Yigael Yadin, *The Temple Scroll* (New York: Random House, 1985), 204–8.
[18] Sanhedrin 46b. See also the explanation of Yadin, in *The Temple Scroll*, 205.

7:1, 11, 13, 19, 21, 25). Josephus mentioned that the Essenes were particularly fanatic about Sabbath observance (see below), and this may have been something they shared with their Jerusalem Saducee rivals.

One area where the Sadducees appear to have had a unique view was in regard to the coming of a messiah, an "anointed one" of the house of David, to rule as king over Israel. The Pharisees and the Essenes, though different in doctrine on so many counts, both anticipated the coming of a Davidic messiah, in addition to a priestly messiah and even an Ephraimite messiah.[19] But the Sadducees seem to have moved away from any messianic hopes. This belief may seem odd in view of the fact that it was the Davidic dynasty who had favored Zadok's lineage in Old Testament times.

But this particular doctrinal drift may have been recent, originating only with the rise of Hasmonean and Herodian kings who required Sadducee allegiance and continuing into the first century A.D. when the Roman Caesars and governors demanded the same. The Sadducees and their chief priests were not merely collaborators with the Romans; they were also their allies, and thus the notion of a messianic "king of the Jews" was inherently threatening to Saducean interests. Jesus implicitly indicated at every juncture that He was the promised messiah, the son of David; and both the Pharisees and the Jewish public, in general, were fascinated with Him in this regard. Knowing that "whoever maketh himself a king speaketh against Caesar," it is little wonder that the chief priests denounced Jesus with the antimessianic affirmation "We have no king but Caesar" (John 19:12, 15).

The Pharisees—Jesus' Rabbinical Admirers

In stark contrast to the priestcraft of the chief priests and Sadducees stood the students of the scriptures known as the Pharisees. When the information available about them from the New Testa-

---

[19] Harris Lenowitz, *The Jewish Messiahs* (New York: Oxford University Press, 1998), 31–34.

ment and other sources is carefully considered, we see clearly that many Pharisees were either respectfully benign or enthusiastically supportive in their attitudes and actions toward Jesus. It is unfortunate that the Pharisees have been so maligned in Christian commentary and conversation over the centuries. Too often, Christians have laid blame at the door of the Pharisees for events that were actually the doings of the Sadducees.[20]

Certainly, it cannot be said that there were no Pharisees who opposed Jesus, for there were some. But the Pharisees were not a monolithic movement, and they held different and often quite contradictory religious views even among themselves.

The term *Pharisees* comes from the Greek form of the Hebrew word *perushim*, which can be translated somewhat loosely as "separatists." It also carried the connotation of being holy and can therefore be rendered as "saints."[21] The Pharisees are seen emerging in Jewish history in the second century B.C., during the Hasmonean period, as opponents of the trend toward Hellenistic interpretation and influence in Jewish religious and social life.

They advocated that the Jewish people should remain holy by keeping themselves apart from corrupting Gentile influences, which they believed had been the case during the centuries before the Hasmonean revolt. As the Sadducees moved increasingly in the direction of Greco-Roman philosophy and religion (such as denying the physical resurrection), the Pharisees became strong advocates for the traditional, biblical teachings and practices that had prevailed in the centuries after the return from Babylon. These were the "traditions of the elders" that the Pharisees wished to preserve, including

---

[20] An increasing alienation developed between the heirs of the Pharisees, the rabbis of the late first and second centuries, and the Christian community. This sharp division most likely colored early Christian attitudes about Jews in general and the Pharisees specifically, since only the Pharisees and their heirs survived as a recognizable and cohesive body following the devastating events of the Jewish war (A.D. 66–70); see Lawrence H. Schiffman, *Who Was a Jew?* (Hoboken, New Jersey: KTAV, 1985), 51–67.

[21] Leo Baeck, "The Pharisees," in *The Pharisees and Other Essays*, ed. Leo Baeck (New York: Schocken, 1966), 5–9.

the notion that many of the traditions were actually an "oral law" given by God to supplement the "written law" received by Moses on Mount Sinai. Interestingly, however, Pharisees did not always agree on just which tradition or "oral law" was actually correct.

In the years before Jesus' birth, two scholars came to prominence among the Pharisees. These were Hillel and Shammai. Hillel was originally from Babylon but had moved to Jerusalem during the reign of Herod the Great. He became the most revered teacher of his time, recognized by consensus as *nasi* (president) of the diverse community of Pharisee scholars. Hillel is said to have been active in his teaching from around 30 B.C. to A.D. 10.[22] Shammai was probably younger than Hillel and became the *av bet din* (chief of court, essentially a vice president) by consensus. However, Shammai stood in opposition to Hillel on many questions of interpretation and procedure about the Mosaic law. The impression of Shammai and his disciples recalled in the Talmud and other early Jewish sources is that they represented only a minority of Pharisee opinion, were less concerned for average citizens than they were for the rich, and were more extreme in their interpretations of the law of Moses than Hillel and his supporters.[23]

The most famous story told about Hillel and Shammai concerned a Gentile who sought their teachings as he considered conversion to Judaism. The Gentile came to Shammai saying, "I will become a proselyte if you will expound the entire law (of Moses) while I stand upon one foot"—a request for a summary statement of scriptural teaching that was short and concise. Shammai drove the Gentile away with a builder's cubit. The Gentile then came to Hillel with his request and was received as a proselyte. Hillel taught him, "Whatever is hateful to yourself, do to no other person—this is the whole Law, the rest is but commentary. Now go and do it."[24]

Hillel's "golden rule" was well known among Jews during Jesus'

---

[22] Yitzhak Buxbaum, *The Life and Teachings of Hillel* (Northvale, New Jersey: Jason Aronson, 1994), 43–45.

[23] Buxbaum, *The Life and Teachings of Hillel*, 50–51, 58–59.

[24] Shabbat 31a.

lifetime and was even rephrased in the positive by Jesus himself: "Whatsoever ye would that men should do to you, do ye even so to them: for this is the law and the prophets" (Matthew 7:12). If Jesus' golden rule was a pure twenty-four carats, Hillel's earlier version was at least eighteen carats. We can safely assume that Jesus, having grown up during the very time Hillel was teaching, must have been influenced by him.[25]

Hillel and Shammai established academies in Jerusalem where Pharisees and others could study scripture and the oral law (or traditions of the elders). The Hebrew names for these schools were *beyt Hillel* and *beyt Shammai*. It is entirely possible that Jesus, as a boy visiting Jerusalem, heard Hillel teach—perhaps on the temple mount at Passover when He was twelve (Luke 2:46). Even if this was not the case, however, Jesus would have been aware, like most Jews in His day, of the teachings of Hillel, for they had influenced everything from the way in which temple sacrifices were carried out to the matters of everyday life in the villages of Galilee.

One difference of opinion between *beyt Hillel* and *beyt Shammai* was in regard to permissible activities on the Sabbath. For example, *beyt Shammai* ruled that practicing the healing arts was not permitted on either the weekly Sabbath or the festival Sabbaths. *Beyt Hillel*, however, took the more pragmatic view that danger to life or health suspends the prohibitions of the Sabbath and that healing arts were, therefore, permissible. Hillel himself had received medical care on the Sabbath, when as a young man he had nearly frozen to death.[26]

The difference between Hillel and Shammai on Sabbath healing was at play all through Jesus' ministry, even though most readers of the Gospels are not aware of it. With one exception, every time Jesus came into conflict with Pharisees, it was on the issue of the Sabbath, and all but one of those instances were about His having healed on

---

[25] David Flusser, "Hillel's Self Awareness and Jesus," in *Judaism and the Origins of Christianity*, ed. David Flusser (Jerusalem: Magnes Press/Hebrew University, 1988), 35.

[26] Yoma 35b.

the Sabbath.[27] In each case, however, Jesus' healings would have been entirely consistent with Hillel's own pragmatic Sabbath views, which were popular among both Pharisees and Jews in general.

The Hillel-Shammai division on Sabbath healing is evident in the John 9 story of Jesus and the man born blind. Having brought the blind man sight, Jesus was criticized by some Pharisees (undoubtedly of *beyt Shammai*) for breaking the Sabbath but was praised by others of the Pharisees (most likely of *beyt Hillel*) who found no fault with his Sabbath miracle: "Therefore said some of the Pharisees, This man is not of God, because he keepeth not the sabbath day. Others said, How can a man that is a sinner do such miracles? And there was a division among them" (John 9:16). Throughout the four Gospels, the Pharisees we see in opposition to Jesus were almost always the more extreme, but less numerous or popular, "Shammaite zealots."[28]

Many Pharisees, like the majority of the Jewish populace in general, seem to have admired Jesus greatly. Pharisees followed Jesus all around Galilee and Judea, asking Him His points of view on many of the critical issues they did not agree on themselves. Nicodemus, a prominent Pharisee member of the Sanhedrin, not only was an example of this but was also a representative of others. When he came to Jesus, he was probably representing a group of like-minded Pharisees when he said, "Rabbi, we know that thou art a teacher come from God" (John 3:2). The tired idea that he came by night to hide his support for Jesus might not be correct, as he was also seen later boldly defending Jesus before the assembled Sanhedrin (John 7:50–51).[29]

---

[27] The single non-Sabbath incident was on the question of ritual hand washing (Matthew 15:1–6 and Mark 7:1–13), and the one Sabbath incident that was not a healing occurred when Jesus' disciples rubbed ears of grain in their hands (Matthew 12:1–8; Luke 6:1–5).

[28] The term "Shammaite zealots" is not my own but is borrowed from Buxbaum, *The Life and Teachings of Hillel*, 217.

[29] As a member of the Sanhedrin, Nicodemus would have had a busy daily schedule. Jesus Himself was busy with the festival crowds at the temple during the day. The only opportunity for a private visit was during the evening hours. Commentaries suggesting that there was something amiss in Nicodemus's night visit seem to forget that many of

Nicodemus and his associates were likely associated with *beyt Hillel*, which, during Jesus' adulthood, was led by Hillel's own grandson, Gamaliel. Neither Shammai, Hillel, nor Gamaliel is mentioned in the four Gospels, but Gamaliel is mentioned by name in the dramatic Acts 5 account of the trial of the Twelve Apostles. There, the high priest and Sadducees had arrested the Apostles and put them in prison (Acts 5:17–18). The entire Sanhedrin was called into session to try them (Acts 5:21). When it became obvious that the intent of the high priestly party was to have the Apostles put to death, Gamaliel (who had become *nasi*, like his grandfather Hillel before him) called upon the Sanhedrin to release the Apostles and leave them alone, suggesting that their work might be of God (Acts 5:33–40).

Clearly, the Pharisees of *beyt Hillel* were not the enemies of Jesus and His Apostles; in fact, they appear to have been to some degree allies. It is for this reason that we can surmise with a high degree of certainty that Gamaliel, Nicodemus, and their Pharisee fellows were not called to the "small Sanhedrin" that tried and convicted Jesus.

Pharisee Doctrine. The theology of the Pharisees cannot have suddenly emerged in full form in the Hasmonean period; it must have been forming earlier, but how much earlier is difficult to say.[30] The New Testament portrays Pharisees as believing in the coming of a messiah, as do numerous Talmud passages. Pharisees also believed in divine atonement, redemption, and resurrection from the dead, according to the Talmud, Josephus, and the New Testament (Acts 23:8).[31] Because Jesus taught these same concepts, Pharisees were naturally interested in His messianic allusions and teachings about eternal life—in contrast to the Sadducees, who rejected them outright. Pharisees derived many of their beliefs from the oral law they believed Moses received and to the "traditions of the elders" that had accumulated in the intervening centuries. It is sometimes

---

our own interviews with bishops and stake presidents are also held in the evening.

[30] Lawrence H. Schiffman, "Jewish Sectarianism in Second Temple Times," in *Great Schisms in Jewish History*, ed. Raphael Jospe and Stanley M. Wagner (New York: KTAV, 1981), 14.

[31] Josephus, *War*, 2.8.14; *AJ*, 18.1.3.

claimed that Jesus opposed all of the Pharisees' traditions, but this was not so.

On one occasion when Jesus was asked why His disciples did not adhere to the "traditions of the elders" by ritually washing their hands before eating, He did offer criticism in return (Matthew 15:1–6; Mark 7:1–13). What is interesting in that episode is that He did not use ritual hand washing as an example of manmade commandments—it was, after all, based on a legitimate passage in the law of Moses (Leviticus 15:11). Instead, clearly irritated by the extremist Pharisees who had confronted Him, Jesus criticized an odd and obscure misuse of Corban procedure—laws initially designed to protect dedicated temple donations (Mark 7:11). Had Jesus been against all Pharisee tradition (as is often erroneously suggested by modern commentaries), He would presumably have condemned the washing traditions that were the extremists' original complaint. Instead, without denigrating the notion of ritual washing, He ruled that to eat without such washings did not render a person impure (Matthew 15:20).

On another occasion in Matthew 23, where Jesus was openly critical of hypocrisy practiced by some Jerusalem Pharisees, He actually commanded His own disciples, and all Jews in general, to strictly adhere to Pharisee teachings: "Then spake Jesus to the multitude, and to his disciples, Saying, The scribes and the Pharisees sit in Moses' seat: All therefore whatsoever they bid you observe, that observe and do" (Matthew 23:1–3).

It is notable that on Jesus' final visit to Jerusalem, indeed on the very day He chastised some Pharisees for hypocrisy, He was not verbally opposed by any Pharisees whatsoever. It was the chief priests and Sadducees who openly opposed Him and challenged Him, seeking to catch Him in His words. Pharisees were not really even involved in the question of tribute to Caesar (see below).

The doctrine of the Pharisees rejected crucifixion as a violation of the law of Moses. The Gospel of John does record that at least some Pharisees—likely Shammaites—were involved in ordering the arrest of Jesus (John 18:3).[32] However, in all four Gospels, there is not a single mention of the word *Pharisee* in any passage dealing with the trial before the chief priests and elders, the sentencing interviews with Pilate, and the carrying out of the crucifixion. It was the Sadducees who conceived and carried out the plot. The Pharisees simply drop off the radar screen in the accounts of Jesus' trial and death.

The Herodians and the Essenes

The sect known in the New Testament as the Herodians was involved in two brief but significant episodes in the account of Jesus' ministry. A third reference to the group was directly connected to the Saducean intrigues against Jesus at Jerusalem. Various commentaries have offered differing theories about the Herodians, but best evidence suggests they are to be identified with the sect Josephus called the Essenes. General consensus also points to the Dead Sea Scrolls as having been produced by certain of the Essenes. But the Dead Sea Scrolls have also been convincingly connected to an aberrant sect of Sadducees. The approach I prefer accommodates all of these views.

During the 1980s, Israeli archaeologist and biblical scholar Yigael Yadin published evidence he discovered suggesting that the New Testament term "Herodians" was an alternative name for the Essenes. Based on clues he found in the famous Temple Scroll of the Dead Sea Scrolls, he identified "the leaven of the Herodians" (Mark 8:15) as a reference to Essene doctrine.[33] Yadin also noted that other scholars had proposed the Herodians as Essene based on a report of Josephus. Herod the Great proffered special kindness and protection to the Essene sect, according to Josephus, because when Herod was young, an Essene prophet named Menalaus had predicted that Herod would become king and enjoy a long reign. When Herod ascended

---

[32] Sanhedrin 46b. See also Yadin, *The Temple Scroll*, 204–5.
[33] Yadin, *The Temple Scroll*, 80–84. Yadin also points out that whereas some New Testament manuscripts of Mark 8:15 read "the leaven of Herod," others read "the leaven of the Herodians." See also footnote 35 below.

the throne, he therefore showed favor to all the Essenes.[34] Josephus also mentioned that the Essenes did not confine themselves to one location (such as Jerusalem) but lived in significant numbers in every town of the land of Israel.[35] Herodians were specifically noted by Mark as present in the Galilee (Mark 3:6). In Yadin's model, the Herodians in Galilee were most likely Galilean Essenes.

More recently, biblical scholar Lawrence Schiffman demonstrated that sectarian documents among the Dead Sea Scrolls were produced by an aberrant group of Zadokites—that is, Sadducees.[36] As pointed out earlier, during the Jewish revolt of the second century B.C. and the rise of the independent Hasmonean monarchy, the Sadducees had lost control of the high priest's office to the priests of the Hasmonean clan. Nevertheless, most Sadducees remained in Jerusalem, and the main line of their movement remained active in the management of the temple. Still, the aberrant movement of nonmainline Sadducees who produced the Dead Sea Scrolls resented the mainline Sadducees of Jerusalem and rejected both their authority and their apostate tendencies. The aberrant Sadducees were opposed to Greco-Roman influence and control, which the Jerusalem Sadducees embraced, as well as the Jerusalem Sadducees' capitulation to perform temple rituals according to Pharisee interpretations.[37]

In view of all available data, a simple synthesis of the evidence offered by both Yadin and Schiffman seems to offer the best understanding of these matters. It is that the Dead Sea Scrolls were produced by these aberrant, out-of-power Sadducees and that they were called Essenes by Josephus but Herodians (perhaps an unflattering term) by Mark in the New Testament. If so, then a New Testament enigma that appears a single time in Matthew can be solved.

---

[34] Josephus, AJ, 15.10.4–5.

[35] Josephus, War, 2.8.4.

[36] Lawrence H. Schiffman, *Reclaiming the Dead Sea Scrolls* (New York: Doubleday, 1995).

[37] Lawrence H. Schiffman, "The Sadducean Origins of the Dead Sea Scroll Sect," in *Understanding the Dead Sea Scrolls*, ed. Hershel Shanks (New York: Random House/Biblical Archaeology Society, 1992), 41.

Matthew 16 records that while Jesus was in Galilee, certain Pharisees and Sadducees approached Him, requesting a sign from heaven. Jesus dismissed the request with His allusion to the sign of the prophet Jonas and afterward warned His disciples to beware of the leaven (or doctrine) of the Pharisees and the Sadducees (see Matthew 16:1–12). The enigma in this story is that it portrays Sadducees as coming to Jesus in the Galilee in company with Pharisees. Our understanding of mainline Sadducees is that they had virtually no base or population outside of Judea, and they would have been highly unlikely to join Pharisees in seeking messianic signs from Jesus or any other source. However, if Matthew 16 is referring not to mainline Jerusalem Sadducees but to a group of the aberrant, out-of-power Sadducees (Essenes/Herodians) who lived in the Galilee and who had messianic expectations, then the enigma is solved.

Support for this solution is found in Mark's account of this same event (see Mark 8:11–15). In Mark, only Pharisees are mentioned as seeking the sign; but afterward, Jesus, as noted above, warns His disciples against both "the leaven of the Pharisees and the leaven of Herodians."[38] That Matthew uses the term *Sadducees* to describe the men whom Mark calls Herodians, both in a Galilean setting, suggests that the identification of the Essenes/Herodians as aberrant Sadducees is likely correct. It may also have been that the Sadducees of Matthew 3:7, who went with Pharisees to inquire of John the Baptist, were, in fact, such Essenes/Herodians, for it is clear that the Jerusalem Sadducees rejected John outright (Matthew 21:23–25).

Mark also recorded another event in the Galilee where Herodians and Pharisees interacted with Jesus. On a Sabbath day in the synagogue of an unnamed northern town, Jesus healed a man's withered hand. After this, "the Pharisees went forth, and straightway took counsel with the Herodians against him" (Mark 3:6).

---

[38] The King James Version simply reads "the leaven of Herod" (Mark 8:15), but some alternative Greek texts read "Herodians," which makes more sense in terms of the warning about religious doctrine and in view of the New Testament passages that mention the "Herodians." See text footnotes for Mark 8:15 in *Novum Testamentum, Graece et Latine*, ed. Eberhard Nestle (London: United Bible Societies, 1998).

As already pointed out, the Pharisees who opposed Jesus' healing on the Sabbath would likely have been adherents of Shammai's restrictive views, not students of the more practical Hillel and Gamaliel, who considered Sabbath-day healing a worthy endeavor. The students of Shammai were predictably upset with Jesus. But why would the Essenes/Herodians have been upset? Josephus offers an answer. He recorded that the Essenes were "stricter than all Jews in abstaining from work on the seventh day," so much so that they refrained even from relieving their bowels on Saturday![39] Thus, the Herodians could have been more extreme in their opposition of Jesus' healings on the Sabbath, which they regarded as labor, than were even the Pharisee students of Shammai who sought them out.

The most remarkable incident involving reference to the Herodians, however, took place in Jerusalem, at the temple mount, on the final day that Jesus taught in public. The incident is alluded to in all three of the synoptic Gospels and is one where information from each of those Gospels is vital to understanding what exactly happened. The incident occurred right after Jesus' clash with the Saducean chief priests and elders on the issue of authority. Matthew reports, "Then went the Pharisees, and took counsel how they might entangle him in his talk. And they sent out unto him their disciples with the Herodians, saying . . . Is it lawful to give tribute unto Caesar, or not?" (Matthew 22:15–17).

The Matthew account seems straightforward—because the Sadducees failed to defeat Jesus verbally, the Pharisees and Herodians took up the challenge. But there is more to the story—elements that Matthew fails to tell us. According to Mark, it was actually the chief priests and elders who sent Pharisees and Herodians to ask Jesus about Caesar's tribute! Though Mark 12:13 simply reads, "They send unto him certain of the Pharisees and of the Herodians, to catch him in his words," a careful reading of the verses leading up to this statement clearly reveals that the antecedent of "they" was, in fact, the chief priests of Mark 11:27. So it was really the Sadducean elite who,

---

[39] Josephus, *War*, 2.8.9.

having been defeated by Jesus on the question of their authority, tried to "catch Jesus in his words" by sending men who asked Jesus, "Is it lawful to give tribute to Caesar, or not?" (Mark 12:14).

In Luke's account, the questioners are not even real Pharisees or Herodians but "spies" pretending to be "just men!" After the authority debacle, Luke 20 relates the tribute event this way: "And the chief priests and the scribes the same hour sought to lay hands on him; and they feared the people: for they perceived that he had spoken this parable against them. And they watched him, and sent forth spies, which should feign themselves just men, that they might take hold of his words, that so they might deliver him unto the power and authority of the governor. And they asked him, saying . . . Is it lawful for us to give tribute unto Caesar, or no?" (Luke 20:19–22).

Given the animosity that existed between the Sadducees and the Pharisees and also between those same Sadducees and the Essenes/Herodians, it was most unlikely that any real Pharisees or Herodians would have deigned to do the chief priest's dirty work. But it appears, based on Luke's report, that the Sadducean leadership employed imposters to play the role of Pharisees and Herodians trying to entrap Jesus on the question of Roman tribute, and this for the specific purpose of turning Him over to Pilate on charges of rebellion and tax evasion. In this episode, then, it becomes clear that the opposition to Jesus was not primarily a Pharisee phenomenon, or even an Essenes/Herodian product, but a deliberate conspiracy of Jerusalem's ruling Sadducean priestcraft, directed by Joseph Caiaphas and his fellow chief priests!

Exploring the Temple of Herod

Jerusalem's temple mount was called *har habayit* by the Jewish population of the land of Israel in Jesus' day. They used this biblical Hebrew term as a part of their regular spoken Aramaic language. *Har habayit* literally means "the mountain of the house" and was the abbreviated way of expressing the biblical phrase found in Isaiah 2:2:

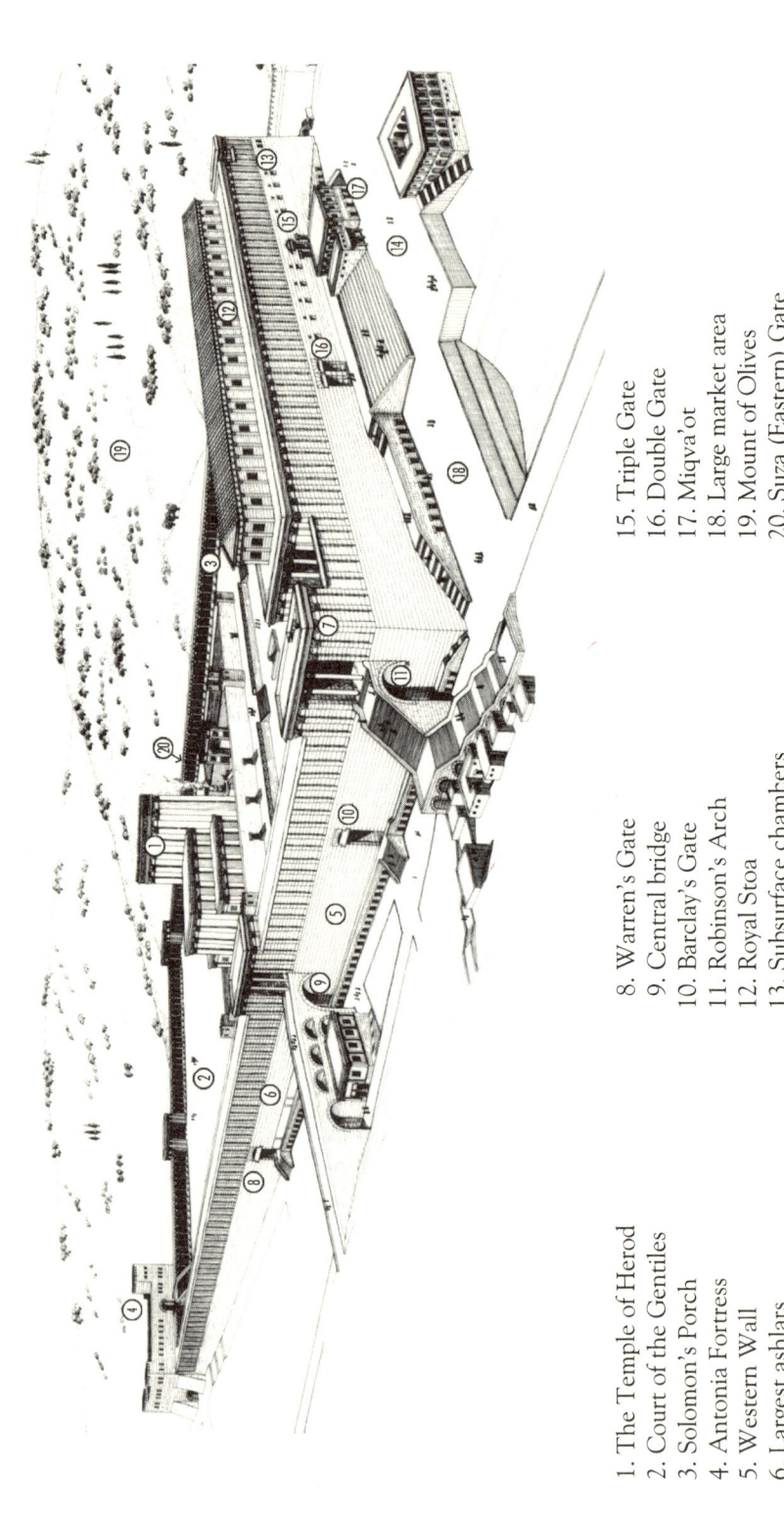

1. The Temple of Herod
2. Court of the Gentiles
3. Solomon's Porch
4. Antonia Fortress
5. Western Wall
6. Largest ashlars
7. Pinnacle of the Temple
8. Warren's Gate
9. Central bridge
10. Barclay's Gate
11. Robinson's Arch
12. Royal Stoa
13. Subsurface chambers
14. Stairway
15. Triple Gate
16. Double Gate
17. Miqva'ot
18. Large market area
19. Mount of Olives
20. Suza (Eastern) Gate

"the mountain of the house of the Lord."[40] This Jerusalem hilltop where the temple stood was also known in the Bible as "mount Moriah" (2 Chronicles 3:1) and was believed to be the site where Abraham had bound his son Isaac (Genesis 22:1–10). Solomon constructed the first temple on Mount Moriah in approximately 950 B.C. That edifice, often called the temple of Solomon, was destroyed, along with Jerusalem itself, by the Babylonians in 586 B.C. The Jewish nation, which returned to Jerusalem from captivity in Babylon, built a second temple, often called the temple of Zerubbabel, in 520 B.C. on the very site of the first temple. A more modest structure than Solomon's, that second edifice stood for five hundred years.

In 20 B.C., Herod the Great, whom the emperor and senate of Rome had appointed king over the land of Israel, set out to replace the temple of Zerubbabel. After five centuries, the old structure was in poor repair, and its outer courts were too small for the Jewish crowds at festival times. Since Aaronic priests were the only Jews who could tread on the ground of the temple's holy place, Herod had a thousand priests trained as stonemasons. In an eighteen-month period, those priests reverently disassembled Zerubbabel's structure and built a new, larger, more spectacular temple building (see illustration, item 1). During that time, however, the daily animal sacrifice was never halted, even though the large altar of sacrifice was completely refurbished. Jewish tradition also asserts that during the construction of the new temple structure, rain fell only at night, so not a day's labor was lost. This was considered a miracle and a sign that the work had divine approval.

The interior of the new temple structure featured the same dimensions as the two earlier temples—interior floor surface of the holy place and holy of holies combined was 20 cubits by 60 cubits (about 33 by 99 feet), and the interior height was 45 cubits (about 66 feet).

---

[40] In the King James Version of the Bible, this phrase in Isaiah 2:2 is rendered "the mountain of the Lord's house," using an apostrophe possessive instead of the more literal construct case for "the house of the Lord." But the construct English form "the house of the Lord" is found elsewhere throughout the King James Version (cf. 1 Kings 7:51).

But the exterior of Herod's new temple was greatly expanded—the exterior length was 172 feet and the width was 123 feet. A second story was added atop the entire building, and the enclosed porch on the east end of the building was enlarged to a width of 173 feet, with its facade reaching an unprecedented height of some 162 feet.[41] Because only the Aaronic priests could enter this temple building, most Jews were familiar only with its gorgeous exterior. The first-century Jewish historian Josephus recorded, "To approaching strangers [Herod's temple] appeared from a distance like a snow-clad mountain; for all that was not overlaid with gold was of purest white."[42] The whole structure was built of local Jerusalem limestone, which was mostly brilliant white. When visitors entered the temple mount complex, however, a richer variety of hues was evident: some Jerusalem limestone featured rose-colored marbling. The Talmud records that other colored stones, as well as genuine marble (which had to be imported), were incorporated into the exterior facing of the structure: "And of what was it built? Rabba saith of stones marble and green—there are others which say of stones blue, marble and green."[43] The opulent marble and cool facing stone colors of green and blue contrasted handsomely with the white- and rose-accented limestone blocks.

As Josephus mentioned, gold was used richly in the exterior design of Herod's temple, causing the building to gleam in the Mediterranean sunlight. Gold-capped crenellations lined the roof edges of the temple and its massive porch, and gold leaf was applied to the porch's 150-foot-high pilasters. Additionally, floral and geometric carvings graced many of the upper courses of the temple's stone

---

[41] By comparison, the Muslim shrine known as the Dome of the Rock, which presently stands on the temple site, is 104 feet high—much shorter than the 162-foot-high facade of Herod's temple.

[42] Josephus, *War*, 5.5.6.

[43] Baba Batra 4a (author's translation). A similar passage in Sukkah 51b reads, "Whoever has not seen the temple in its construction has never seen a building of beauty. And which was this? . . . This was the temple of Herod. And of what was it built? Rabba says of stones marble and green. Others say of stones marble, blue, and green" (author's translation).

blocks. The details of these border carvings were painted in multicolored motifs of blue, red, and yellow, as were the Corinthian capitals of the limestone, marble, and colored granite pillars that held up the porticos surrounding the temple (the granite was imported from Sinai and Egypt). Some of the pillar capitals were also decorated in gold-colored paint mixed with gold leaf. The gleaming gold details and the colorful border accessories in the masonry of both the temple and its outer courts made the Herodian complex a spectacular feast for the eyes of all who visited Jerusalem.

Because the main temple building was so tall, it loomed high over the separation walls that kept Jewish women and Gentiles from entering the inner court of Israel, where only men were allowed to witness the activities at the outdoor altar of animal sacrifice. To the east of the court of Israel was the court of women, about 180 feet square, with its massive semicircular stairway leading up to the bronze gates of Nicanor—the monumental western entry to the court of Israel and the temple itself. From the court of women, just east of the court of Israel, and even from the exterior court of the Gentiles, the rich and colorful decor of the tall and splendid temple was both easily viewed and awe inspiring. But the temple building itself occupied only the central area of the temple mount. The holy building itself, the court of Israel, and the court of women, all of which were open only to Jews, were surrounded by a barrier fence called the *soyag*.

Outside this barrier fence was the much larger court of the Gentiles (see illustration, item 2), surrounding the restricted area on all sides. Signs in Greek posted along the *soreg* informed Gentile visitors to the temple mount that they could not proceed into the restricted courts on pain of death. The court of Gentiles was huge, however, and afforded plenty of room for both Jewish and Gentile visitors alike.

The Eastern Wall and Solomon's Porch. (See illustration, item 3.) Herod had expanded the large outer court of the temple mount from its modest earlier dimensions by constructing new retaining walls to the west of the temple along the central valley ridge and to the south of the temple down the Ophel slope. This project doubled the size of the temple mount courts from what had existed before. But the centuries-old eastern wall of the temple mount, which bordered the Kidron Valley, was left intact. The pillared portico along this ancient eastern wall was known as Solomon's Porch. Jesus and his Apostles were known to preach there (John 10:23; Acts 3:11; 5:12). Josephus described it thus: "This portico was part of the outer temple, and was situated in a deep ravine [the Kidron]. It had walls four hundred cubits long and was constructed of square stones, completely white, each stone being twenty cubits long and six high. This was the work of King Solomon, who was the first to build the whole temple."[44]

The only alterations Herod made in the eastern wall was to extend its length southward by 105 feet, so that the total length of the eastern rampart was 1,536 feet. The single gate entering the complex through the eastern wall (from the Kidron Valley) was probably the gate through which Jesus triumphantly rode a few days before His crucifixion (Matthew 20:1–12). It was known as the Shushan gate,[45] and its construction may have dated from Persian times.

The north side of the temple mount was a utilitarian area. Outside the northern wall were artificial pools (reservoirs) that stored large amounts of water for the washing and cleaning activities at the temple itself. One of these was called the pool of Israel, and another, the double pool of Bethesda (with its five porches), was where Jesus performed a miraculous healing (John 5:2–9).

A purely functional supposition is that a gate must have existed in the northern wall, facilitating the transfer of water, and perhaps sacrificial animals from the pens outside the city, onto the temple mount. But the location or even the name of such a gate is not

---

[44] Josephus, AJ, 20.9.7.
[45] Today, the so-called "golden gate" of the temple mount sits above the area where the ancient Shushan gate was located. The name "Shushan" is a reference to Susa, in Persia (Iran), and was probably given to that eastern gate because of the portrayal of the Shushan palace upon the gate (Mishna, Midot 1:3). It may have been built during the time that Judea was under Persian dominion (537–332 B.C.) because the second temple had been built early in that period (520 B.C.).

recorded. The so-called Tadi gate referred to in Midot 1:3 of the Mishna was closed and "not used at all."

On the northwest corner of the temple mount, incorporated into the northern wall, a massive fortress stood. Called the Antonia (honoring Herod's late Roman comrade Mark Anthony), the fortress featured four high towers and direct access to the court of the Gentiles via a steep stairway. The Antonia fortress (see illustration, item 4) loomed 112 feet above the north court of the temple mount, allowing soldiers a clear view of the Jewish crowds at the temple and facilitating security and crowd control at busy festival times. Jesus may have been sentenced and beaten in the Antonia, prior to carrying His cross outside the city. And the Apostles, including Paul, seem to have been incarcerated there for short periods (Acts 4:3; 5:18; 22:24). Paul even spoke from the stairway (Acts 21:37–40).

The Western Wall and the Pinnacle. A new western retaining wall was built by Herod's architects along the central valley west of the temple mount. It was a magnificent architectural and engineering feat—Josephus called it "the most prodigious work that was ever heard of by man."[46] The western wall (see illustration, item 5) stretched 1,590 feet from north to south. At its south end (the temple mount's southwest corner), the wall stood more than 150 feet above the bedrock on which it was founded.

Very large and handsomely cut stone blocks, called ashlars, were used to build this wall. They were often huge, sometimes 30 feet long or more, and weighed over 100 tons. One single stone in the lower course of the western wall (see illustration, item 6) was 46 feet long and weighed an estimated 570 tons.[47] The visible face of each stone was decorated with an incised rectangular margin, about three inches wide, around the face of the ashlar.[48] After new sewers and paving

---

[46] Josephus, *AJ*, 5.11.13.

[47] Eilat Mazar, *The Complete Guide to the Temple Mount Excavations* (Jerusalem: Shoham Academic and Research Publication, 2002), 32.

[48] Today, portions of the lower courses of this retaining wall are visible at Jerusalem. One segment, which has been visible for centuries, is the familiar Jewish prayer area that has long been called the Western Wall (the term Wailing Wall is somewhat disparaging

were laid along the western wall, it still rose more than 100 feet above the level of the street at the southwest corner, or pinnacle, of the temple mount.

The pinnacle of the temple was located atop the tower at the south end of the temple mount's western wall (see illustration, item 7). This tower stood 104 feet high from the street below and overlooked the main market area of Jerusalem.[49] From a small niche on the tower's open roof, a trumpet was sounded by a priest to mark the onset of Sabbath each Friday at sunset. Festival Sabbaths, such as Passover, were also heralded by a trumpet blast from this pinnacle. It was to this high station on the southwest tower, overlooking the busy market of the holy city, that Jesus came just prior to the start of His ministry (Matthew 4:5–7).

Josephus said there were four gates that entered the temple mount along the western wall.[50] The northernmost of these, today known as Warren's Gate,[51] was approached by a single stairway from the valley street and entered the temple mount through a high, monumental door, where a tunnel stairway led to the temple mount platform just west of the temple itself (see illustration, item 8). This was the quickest way for people living in Jerusalem's northern quarters to enter the temple complex. Farther south, an elevated bridge (see illustration, item 9), which spanned the valley on a series of tall arches, led from the western upper city of Jerusalem to an ornate gate high in the western wall that opened onto the temple mount platform just south of the temple.[52] This bridge and gate afforded easy access to the temple mount from the area of Herod's palace on the western

---

and ought not be used).

[49] The height was 32 meters as measured metrically. Meir Ben-Dov, *In the Shadow of the Temple* (Jerusalem: Keter, 1985), 92.

[50] Josephus, AJ, 15.11.5.

[51] Warren's Gate is a modern name, not the ancient name. Charles Warren discovered the gate during his explorations in Jerusalem in 1867. The gate may be seen by visitors today in the Kotel Tunnel (Western Wall tunnel), north of the Western Wall plaza in Jerusalem.

[52] The arches north of today's Western Wall plaza, notably Wilson's Arch, recall the location of the Herodian arched bridge and gate at this location.

edge of the city and was used by many of the Jerusalem elite from the wealthier neighborhoods on the city's western hills.

Farther south, a third gate led up into the temple mount from the street level of the valley (see illustration, item 10). Known today as Barclay's Gate,[53] it was probably the gate of Coponius mentioned in Midot 1:3 of the Mishna.[54] It stood 36 feet 6 inches tall, was 18 feet 3 inches wide, and was approached from the market street by a thirteen-foot-high stairway and led to another tunnel stairway that opened onto the temple platform above. People living in the city center of Jerusalem could use Barclay's/Coponius's Gate, or they could use the spectacular multiflight stairway that sat atop Robinson's Arch[55] to enter the royal stoa at the south end of the western wall, just under the pinnacle tower (see illustration, item 11).

The Southern Wall and the Royal Stoa. The royal stoa was a large pillared basilica (see illustration, item 12) that Herod had his architects add to the southern end of the temple mount. (The Greek term for *pillar* is "stoa.") The temple platform was extended southward by an additional 105 feet, and the long basilica was constructed atop the addition. To accommodate the Ophel slope, a series of support arches were erected to form the framework around which the southern wall was built, after which a pavement was laid atop the framework and the royal stoa atop that pavement. The result was that the area inside the southern wall was hollow (see illustration, item 13), particularly at the southeastern corner.[56]

The royal stoa itself was a grand structure. Not since Solomon had built his royal palace just south of the first temple had such a beautiful

---

[53] Named after J. T. Barclay, who explored Jerusalem in the 1860s and recognized the massive lintel of the huge gate. The lintel may be seen today at the south end of the women's section of the Western Wall prayer area. The threshold of the gate lies 20 feet below the lintel.

[54] Ben-Dov, *In the Shadow of the Temple*, 140–42.

[55] Named after the American explorer Edward Robinson, who identified the spring of the arch during his 1839 visit to Jerusalem.

[56] Today, this hollow area is known as Solomon's Stables. Long an undeveloped subterranean vault, Solomon's Stables were refitted into a Muslim prayer hall during the 1990s.

building stood near the temple on the temple mount. Josephus said of the royal stoa, "This cloister deserves to be mentioned better than any under the sun."[57] The long building stretched from west to east along the entire 912-foot length of the southern temple mount wall (that is, atop Herod's southern extension of the temple mount platform). Towers on the eastern and western ends were accessed from outside the temple mount by huge, multiple-flight stairways (on the west, this was the stairway over Robinson's Arch). The basilica featured a vaulted ceiling and clerestory windows, all supported by a series of 160 pillars divided into four long rows of 40 pillars each. The interior was richly decorated in gold and other multicolored carvings of the same type as on the exterior of the temple. Along its north side, the royal stoa opened onto the temple mount platform.

The function of the building was to provide a center for government and public commerce at the temple mount—but one that did not actually sit upon the holy ground of Moriah's summit (this was made possible because the Herodian extension sat upon arch-supported vaults). Around A.D. 30 (forty years before the temple was destroyed), the Sanhedrin moved its offices into the royal stoa.[58] Part of the structure was the scene of money exchange and the sale of sacrificial birds and animals, as licensed by the managing priests of the temple. These were necessary services, inseparably connected with the rituals of the temple itself. Jesus' casting out of certain money changers and animal sellers was probably at or near the royal stoa (John 2:15; Matthew 21:12).[59] Events such as Nicodemus's defense of Jesus (John 7:45–52) and the decision to seek Jesus' arrest (John 11:47–57) probably occurred in the Sanhedrin offices there.[60]

---

[57] Josephus, AJ, 15.11.5.

[58] Mazar, The Complete Guide to the Temple Mount Excavations, 34.

[59] Leen Ritmeyer and Kathleen Ritmeyer, Secrets of Jerusalem's Temple Mount (Washington, D.C.: Biblical Archeological Society, 1998), 20. Mazar, The Complete Guide to the Temple Mount Excavations, 34. My own view is that Jesus would not have objected to commercial activity at the stoa itself but to any activity that had proceeded north outside the stoa into the court of the temple mount proper.

[60] The trial of Jesus, however, seems to have been held before a minimum quorum of the Sanhedrin (twenty-three members or more) convened at the home of the high priest

The "treasury of the temple" where Jesus preached on one occasion (John 8:20) may also have been at the royal stoa.

Beneath the royal stoa, along the exterior of the temple mount's southern wall, a monumental staircase 215 feet in length facilitated the movement of large crowds into and out of the temple mount complex (see illustration, item 14). The steps of this staircase were alternatingly wide and narrow, allowing a comfortable ascent up the Ophel ridge to the "house of the Lord." Two gateways accessed the temple mount platform from this stairway via long tunnels that ran underneath the royal stoa. The eastern gate and tunnel complex, often called the triple gate (see illustration, item 15) because of its three doorways, was for people entering the temple mount. The western gate and tunnel complex, usually referred to as the double gate (see illustration, item 16), were for people exiting the temple mount. (It may have been outside this double gate that Jesus met a man born blind, as recorded in John 9:1–7, and anointed his eyes with clay.)

At the base of the monumental stairway were a number of ritual immersion pools (*miqva'ot*, singular *miqve*) where Jewish worshipers could purify themselves before entering the temple mount (see illustration, item 17). A large market area (see illustration, item 18) was located near the stairway, extending west toward the pinnacle of the temple and the valley street where much of Jerusalem's traffic flowed. Many who came to Jerusalem as visitors to the Jewish festivals, such as Passover or the Feast of Tabernacles, would have visited the markets and ascended to the temple mount via the triple gate and tunnel in the southern wall.

Having taken, as it were, a tour of the Herodian temple mount and the walls and gates that surrounded it, we may now summarize the known visits of Jesus to the temple and recall His interaction there with the Jewish crowds who adored Him as well as with the Sadducean chief priests who despised Him.

---

himself, not at the royal stoa. That quorum would have been almost totally dominated by chief priests and Sadducees.

Jesus at the Temple of Herod

The four Gospels record Jesus' visits to the temple of Herod on eight different journeys to Jerusalem. The first two, recorded in the second chapter of Luke, took place during His infancy and childhood and involved no recorded difficulties with the chief priests or Sadducees. The third was the temptation of Jesus at the temple pinnacle, where no incident involving other people was recorded. The other five events were part of Jesus' active ministry and were highly charged with friction between Jesus and the Sadducean priestcraft. Each of these events will be briefly outlined here.

The Infant Jesus at the Temple. At the age of eight days, Jesus was circumcised and given His name, according to the law of Moses and Jewish custom (Luke 2:21). Forty days after His birth, He was taken by Joseph and Mary from Bethlehem to the temple of Herod at Jerusalem, where two sacrifices were made, according to the instructions in Leviticus 12. They would have purchased two doves in a small wicker cage from one of the merchants in the market near the temple for a price of about one silver sheqel for the pair. This was about a day's wage for a laborer. Mary would then have immersed herself in one of the *miqva'ot* (ritual immersion pools) located just south of the gates to the temple mount. This purification would have cost a couple of *prutot* (small bronze coins worth about a dollar each).

After the immersion, Mary and Joseph would have entered the temple compound through the eastern tunnel of the southern gates. Whether the large southern stoa basilica atop the tunnels was yet complete at the time Jesus was born is unknown, but it would certainly have at least been under construction. Proceeding with the baby past the *soreg* barrier, the couple would have come to one of the south gates leading to the priestly court. Mary could not have entered the court of sacrifice, but she would have been met at the gate by a priest (probably one of the volunteer priests of the twenty-four courses), who would have briefly examined the baby to assure its gender and circumcision and then accepted from her hand the wicker cage with the two doves, one for the burnt offering and one for the sin offering (Leviticus 12:8). Both birds would have been slain and burned completely by the priests on the large altar. After this ordinance, as Joseph and Mary walked in the court of women, or even through the court of the Gentiles, they were met by Simeon and Anna, who delivered prophecies concerning the recently born Messiah (Luke 2:25–38).

At Passover During Jesus' Thirteenth Year. The Passover event happened after Jesus had turned twelve years old. He was in his thirteenth year and had probably become *bar mitzvah* in his hometown of Nazareth.[61] This practice meant that He was accepted as a young man in His community, old enough to put on *tefillin* (phylacteries) for morning prayer, old enough to participate as a full partner in a *minyan* of ten men required for a public prayer service, old enough to perform Torah readings from the books of Moses or *Haftarah* readings from the prophets during the synagogue service, and old enough to discuss and expound the scriptures with the elders of Israel.

Having come to Jerusalem with Joseph, Mary, and a larger traveling party from Nazareth, Jesus might have gone to the expansive temple mount on the afternoon before Passover to witness the slaughter of the lamb that His parents and travel party would roast in a large mud-brick oven that afternoon. Thousands of lambs were slaughtered by hundreds of volunteer Aaronic priests at the temple on the day of Passover eve each spring. The roasted lambs would be eaten after sundown that evening with the *matzot* (unleavened bread), *maror* (bitter herbs), and other foods that had been prepared for the feast.

As early as the second day after Passover, Joseph, Mary, and their party could have commenced their five-day walk back to Nazareth. But after a day's journey, discovering that Jesus was not with the other youths in the party, Joseph and Mary returned to Jerusalem. Three days after arriving back at the capital, and a total of five days since they had started back to Nazareth, Joseph and Mary finally found Jesus at the temple mount. Perhaps it was in the venerated

---

[61] McConkie, MM, 377, "son of the law."

eastern portico, Solomon's Porch, or perhaps in the court of women—both were locations where Jewish audiences gathered to hear the discussions of the era's scholars. Jesus had taken upon Himself, as a new *bar mitzvah*, the privilege no ordinary boy his age would assume—that of discussing and expounding the scriptures with the great sages (undoubtedly Pharisees) of His age. It is possible that Hillel himself was present when "they found him in the temple, sitting in the midst of the doctors, both hearing them, and asking them questions. And all that heard him were astonished at his understanding and answers" (Luke 2:46–47).

At the Pinnacle of the Temple. The first record of Jesus visiting the temple mount as an adult is in connection with His temptation at the pinnacle. He had surely been to Jerusalem and the temple numerous times between age twelve and age thirty, but of that period the scriptures are silent. It is proper to observe that while Jesus may have inherited some Aaronic lineage from His mother Mary's family (Luke 1:36 notes that she was kin to Elizabeth, whom Luke 1:5 lists as a "daughter of Aaron"), He is more frequently noted as a "son of David," and there is no evidence in the New Testament texts that He was, or ever officiated as, an Aaronic priest. This being the case, He probably never entered the court of sacrifice in front of the temple proper, nor did He enter the temple's holy place in mortality. Like other nonpriests, He would have restricted Himself to the court of men, where He could observe the animal sacrifices on the great bronze altar, and to the other outer courts of the temple mount.

The textual notion that "the devil taketh him up into the holy city, and setteth him on a pinnacle of the temple" is realistically unsupportable (Matthew 4:5; see also Luke 4:9). Joseph Smith's rendering of the passage to read "the Spirit setteth him on the pinnacle of the temple" (JST Matthew 4:5) is more in keeping with how Jesus operated. Whether this means that Jesus was actually transported by the Holy Spirit or whether it means that Jesus was led by the Spirit to climb the steps to the temple pinnacle Himself, the result was the same.

There is no hint in the text that temple authorities hindered Jesus as He stood at the very top of the southwest tower, perhaps in the very niche that was "the place of trumpeting," looking at a thousand Jerusalemites in the bustling market square more than a hundred feet below. Perhaps pondering how He would commence His public ministry, He was there tempted by the devil to jump from the pinnacle to the market below, with an allusion to Psalm 91 that angels would safely conduct Him downward so that He would not so much as injure His foot on the stone pavement (Matthew 4:5–7; Luke 4:9–12). Though it would have been a spectacular way to call attention to Himself as the Messiah of God, Jesus rejected the temptation and commenced His ministry in another fashion.

At Passover—John 2. Jesus opened His public teaching ministry just before Passover at Jerusalem when He drove out the animal vendors and money changers from the temple courts, exclaiming, "Take these things hence; make not my Father's house an house of merchandise" (John 2:16). No Pharisees are mentioned in connection with this event (either by name or by implication). The "Jews" who challenged Jesus' actions (John 2:18, 20) were not Pharisees, or we could expect John to call them such. Instead, the "Jews" who challenged Jesus at the temple in this and other chapters of John were surely, in the context of their actions, Sadducees.

John is the only Gospel that does not mention the Sadducees by name. Instead, John alludes to them by describing their pervasive presence and control at the temple mount and their opposition there to Jesus' miracles and doctrines. Jesus' statement about raising up "this temple" in three days (John 2:19) was not understood by those Sadducees, or they would have been even more offended because of Jesus' allusion to the doctrine of resurrection, which they rejected. In contrast to the "Jews" of John 2 (the Greek term could legitimately be translated "Judeans" and have reference to the Sadducees as the bureaucrats of Judea), the common Jewish people visiting Jerusalem at that Passover were impressed by Jesus' miracles, and "many believed in his name" (John 2:23).

HISTORICAL SETTING

It was during this same visit to the capital that Jesus met with the high-ranking Pharisee Nicodemus, who, representing other Pharisees (probably of *beyt Hillel*), confessed, "Rabbi, we know thou art a teacher come from God" (John 3:1). It appears that in Jesus' first preaching and ministering visit to the Jerusalem temple, it was only the Sadduceans who took offense at him.

At Rosh HaShanna—John 5. The "feast of the Jews" that Jesus attended at Jerusalem in John 5 was likely the new-year festival that was already by this time called Rosh HaShanna ("head of the year") by the Jewish community. The doctrinal discussion (dispute!) Jesus had with the "Jews" at the temple on that occasion featured all the themes associated with Rosh HaShanna and the "days of awe" that followed, culminating at Yom Kippur (the Day of Atonement) ten days later. Judgment, resurrection, witnesses of one's works (good or evil), and the yearly recommencement of Torah readings (that is—reading the law of Moses again beginning at Genesis) were all themes of Jewish discussion at the High Holy Days, not the spring Passover festival.[62]

Rosh HaShanna was a Sabbath day because it was a high festival day. Even if it had not been Saturday, for Jesus to heal on this "feast of the Jews" would have been considered a Sabbath breach. After raising up a man who had been crippled thirty-eight years, Jesus was accosted by the "Jews" at the temple "because he had done these things on the sabbath day" (John 5:16). The same "Jews" wished further to kill Him for perceived blasphemy because He "said also that God was his Father, making himself equal with God" (John 5:18). Again, these "Jews" must contextually be understood as the Sadducees—Pharisees are nowhere mentioned as opposing Jesus here. The Sadducee intransigence with regard to Sabbath activity explains their rage at Jesus on this occasion. In the days preceding

---

[62] The LDS Bible footnote to John 5:1, suggesting that "feast of the Jews" was a Passover, is difficult to defend in the context of John 5 and is most likely incorrect. See the discussion of Thomas A. Wayment, "Jesus' Early Ministry in Judea and Jerusalem," in this volume.

Passover, He had merely cast out merchants, but at this festival, He had violated a Sabbath, at least according to their interpretation. This would not be forgotten, for a full year later, at the John 7 Feast of Tabernacles, the issue of the John 5 Sabbath healing would resurface.

Additionally, Jesus' references to sin, atonement, judgment, and resurrection were doctrinally offensive to the Sadducean "Jews" and would have occasioned even more of their animosity toward Him. Jesus' own testimony of "the resurrection of life" versus "the resurrection of damnation," doubly offensive to Sadducees for judgmental and afterlife implications, was remarkably paralleled by Pharisee teachings connected with Rosh HaShanna. The Talmud tractate Rosh HaShanna recalls Pharisee teachings concerning judgment that closely parallel Latter-day Saint understanding of Jesus' references (in John 5:28–29) to differing degrees of resurrection: "Three books are opened (in heaven) on Rosh HaShanna: the book of life of the wicked, the book of life of the righteous, and the book of life of those in between" (author's translation).[63]

At the Feast of Tabernacles—John 7. For about a year, Jesus did not travel to Jerusalem for festivals. "He would not walk in Jewry [that is, Judea], because the Jews sought to kill him" (John 7:1). In this passage, "the Jews" (which can also be rendered "Judeans") again likely refers to the Sadducees of Jerusalem. But in the middle of the autumn Feast of Tabernacles (the Jewish *Sukkot* festival), Jesus arrived at Jerusalem incognito (John 7:10) and, having made His way unmolested to the temple mount, began teaching openly among the Jewish crowds He knew would protect Him from Sadducean mischief (John 7:14, 31–32). He publicly announced that the local authorities wished Him dead (John 7:19), and even though the non-Judean Jews visiting for the festival thought He was exaggerating (John 7:20), the locals of Jerusalem knew very well that the Sadducean leadership sought His death (John 7:25).

Jesus referred to His raising of the crippled man on Rosh HaShanna of the previous autumn (John 7:21) and suggested that His

---

[63] Rosh HaShanna 16b.

healing on the Sabbath was consistent with the practice of circumcision on the Sabbath (John 7:22–24), a position that was accepted by Pharisees of *beyt Hillel*. Later, it is reported that certain Pharisees (likely "Shammaite zealots") joined with the chief priests (a Sanhedrin quorum) in issuing an arrest warrant for Jesus (John 7:32). Days later, the temple police still had not arrested Jesus, and they were criticized by the same Saducean priests and Shammaite Pharisees for the failure (John 7:45), in spite of Nicodemus's encouragement to them to actually listen to Jesus' teachings and give Him a fair hearing (John 7:50–51).

The vehement exchange over the subject of "Abraham's seed" that occurred on the day after *Sukkot* (John 8:33–58) was, again, probably a clash between Jesus and the Sadduceans. No Pharisees are mentioned, and the "Jews" who insulted Him (John 8:48) were clearly also opposed to the notion of an afterlife and the potential for resurrection of Abraham and the prophets (John 8:52–53). Those Sadducees' attempt to stone Jesus there on the temple platform was averted only by Jesus' quick exit from the holy compound (John 8:59), probably through the double gate tunnel on the south side of the temple mount.

Jesus' ability to exit safely may have been the result of a divided temple crowd; some actively sought his death while others accepted Him as a prophet or even the Messiah. As Jesus quickly exited the temple, he encountered a man sitting on the steps who was "blind from his birth" (John 9:1). Having anointed his eyes with mud made from His spittle, Jesus sent the man away from the temple to wash at the pool of Siloam (John 9:6–7).

The day was another festival Sabbath (*Shemini Atzeret*, the single-day holiday after the end of *Sukkot*); thus, this was another Sabbath healing, which was subsequently argued, for both good and evil, by Pharisees of the persuasions of Hillel and Shammai (John 9:14–16).

The Saducean "Jews" also visited the newly seeing young man at his parents' home (John 9:18), and whereas his parents had not expressed fear in the presence of the Pharisees, they did fear the negative reactions of the Sadducees (John 9:22), who apparently exercised considerable power over their Jerusalem synagogue. Having been offended by the young man's testimony of Jesus, they excommunicated him. Later, when the Sadducees were no longer a threat on the scene, Jesus, with Pharisees in stride, sought the young man out and comforted him (John 9:35–41).

At Hanuka—The Feast of Dedication—John 10. Jesus' winter visit to Jerusalem at the Feast of Dedication (that is, *Hanuka*) several weeks later was also an occasion to teach at the temple (John 10:22–23). Standing under the eastern portico called Solomon's Porch, safe from the threat of winter rain, Jesus again taught of His divine identity as the shepherd of Israel, an allusion His listeners would recognize from Psalm 23—"The Lord is my shepherd." Again at this festival, John records no Pharisee interference or opposition to Jesus, but he does record that the "Jews" (contextually, the Saducean temple management) again opposed Him and again attempted to stone Him (John 10:31). Every appearance of Jesus at the temple of Herod brought the ire of the Sadducees and their chief priests.

Jesus' Final Passover—John 12. Four months later, Jesus made His final journey to Jerusalem and His final visits to the spectacular temple of Herod. The events are well known to students of the Gospels, so it is necessary only to list them.

1. Jesus entered Jerusalem in a messianic parade, accompanied by numerous of His Jewish disciples, and received the eager acceptance of large multitudes in the city and the temple (Matthew 21:1–11; Mark 11:1–11; Luke 19:29–44; John 12:12–50).

2. He again cast out the money changers and animal vendors, directly challenging the corruption and authority of the chief priests and the Sadducees (Matthew 21:12–17; Mark 11:15–19; Luke 19:45–48).

3. His authority to act in such a manner at the temple was, in turn, challenged by the chief priests and Sadducees, but they were confounded by His answers (Matthew 21:23–27; Mark 11:17–33; Luke 20:1–8).

4. The chief priests sent men posing as Pharisees and Herodians to try to entrap Jesus in His teachings—this was the "tribute to Caesar" question (Matthew 22:15–25; Mark 12:13–17; Luke 20:20–26).

5. The Sadducees attempted one last time to entrap Jesus themselves, asking about marriage in the resurrection (Matthew 22:23–33; Mark 12:18–27; Luke 20:27–39).

6. Jesus commended a faithful Pharisee scribe for asking about the "greatest commandment" (Matthew 22:34–40; Mark 12:28–34).

7. Jesus confirmed the Pharisee status as teachers of the law but condemned hypocrisy among them (Matthew 23:1–39; Mark 12:38–40; Luke 20:45–47).

Jesus then left the temple mount for the last time in mortality. As He exited, His disciples commented to Him on the superb architecture and artisanship of the temple He loved: "Master, see what manner of stones and what buildings are here!" (Mark 13:1). Jesus sadly prophesied that not a single stone of those spectacular buildings would remain standing upon another, so great would be the destruction that was coming to the temple mount (Matthew 24:1; Mark 13:2)—a prediction that came to pass a mere forty years later.

PART 2

BEGINNINGS

IV.
ZACHARIAS AND ELISABETH, JOSEPH AND MARY

S. KENT BROWN

They were both righteous before God, walking in all the commandments and ordinances of the Lord blameless.

LUKE 1:6

Zacharias and Elisabeth, Joseph and Mary—ordinary people. But events would show them to be extraordinary. The Lord God drew four ordinary-appearing people to the center of His redemptive work and entrusted to two of them—women—the secret of the ages: who the long–awaited Messiah was to be. None of these individuals could have anticipated the stunning, radiant experiences that washed over them and changed their lives forever. These experiences came one after another, unbidden by them, yet divinely orchestrated, touching their lives and those about them.[1]

In fact, the era was one of difficulty for inhabitants of ancient Palestine. The aging and sick King Herod was nearing the end of his sometimes tumultuous reign. Although he had brought order to the

---

[1] Most of what we know about these four people in the months and years surrounding the births of John and Jesus comes from the Gospel of Luke, with some details from the Gospel of Matthew. The approach in this chapter assumes that they are generally reliable as historical records.

country, through both threat and generosity, his successor had not been clearly identified, and whether the struggle over succession would lead to deadly civil conflict had not been determined. Various groups in the region—Pharisees, Sadducees, Zealots, and Essenes— were engaged in the contest for men's souls. The chief priests, the most influential persons in the society because of their control of the temple, were on a tight leash from Herod. Moreover, the presence of five hundred or more auxiliary Roman soldiers in the capital city— mostly the hated Samaritans—stood as a constant reminder to citizens that they served a distant political master.[2] Into this circumstance, which led many to look for a deliverer, came an angel whose message changed everything.

Zacharias

According to Luke's Gospel, the celestial events that touched these individuals and their children fittingly began in the sanctuary of the temple, one of the most sacred spots on earth.[3] Here the angel Gabriel found Zacharias as he performed the task of lighting the incense, an assignment that came to a priest only once in his lifetime (see Luke 1:9, 11).[4] The piece of the angel's message that caught in Zacharias's mind was the surprising news that his "wife Elisabeth [would] bear . . . a son" (Luke 1:13). Zacharias greeted this news with an objection, "Whereby shall I know this? for I am an old man, and my wife well stricken in years" (Luke 1:18). From this rather sturdy response arise two important points. First, Zacharias possessed a character that exhibits a quiet yet firm confidence in the presence of the Divine. In this dimension of his personality, he joins a select group of persons, including Enoch, Moses, Jeremiah, and, as we will

---

[2] See Emil Schürer, *The History of the Jewish People in the Age of Jesus Christ*, rev. ed. by Geza Vermes, Fergus Millar, and Matthew Black, 3 vols. (Edinburgh: T&T Clark, 1973–87), 1:362–67.

[3] In that era, at least two other temple sanctuaries were functioning, both in the Americas, one in Zarahemla and one in Bountiful (see Mosiah 2:1, 6; 3 Nephi 11:1).

[4] Mishnah, *Tamid* 5.2 holds that a priest offers incense only once.

see, Mary.⁵ Second, Zacharias personifies the most influential persons in his society because he was a priest who enjoyed access to the holy temple. In the continuation of the story, he represents other priests who held enormous power to influence other people.

Zacharias was apparently not among the leaders of the priesthood. At the head of all priestly officials stood the high priest, who, until a few generations before Zacharias, had descended from Zadok, the high priest of King Solomon's day.⁶ The high priest at the time of Zacharias's ministry in the sanctuary was Simon, son of Boethus (c. 22–5 B.C.). Beneath him served a group of chief priests who dealt with the daily and seasonal sacrifices, temple finances, and crowd control. This latter person bore the title "captain of the temple," a title known from the New Testament (Acts 4:1; 5:24). Beyond these men were the seven thousand or so priests who assisted at the temple for one week twice a year. Zacharias was one of these priests. Others who helped at the temple were the Levites, descendants of the tribe of Levi.⁷

Zacharias was a member of the Abia course of priests, the eighth of twenty-four, as they were numbered anciently.⁸ Hence, he was officiating either during the eighth week after the New Year, which fell in the autumn, or during the thirty-second week, which occurred in the spring. How do we know which? A simple set of calculations reveals that the angel came to him during the eighth week, in the

---

⁵ On the questioning by Enoch, Moses, and Jeremiah, see Moses 6:31; Exodus 3:11, 13; 4:1; Jeremiah 1:6. Consult also Talmage, *JTC*, 80–81.

⁶ See the brief history of priests in S. Kent Brown and Richard Neitzel Holzapfel, *Between the Testaments: From Malachi to Matthew* (Salt Lake City: Deseret Book, 2002), 159–71.

⁷ See Joachim Jeremias, *Jerusalem in the Time of Jesus* (Philadelphia: Fortress Press, 1969), 147–221, 377–78.

⁸ The priestly order of Abia or Abijah was the eighth of twenty-four orders (see 1 Chronicles 24:7–19), and its time for temple service was presumably during the eighth and thirty-second weeks of the year, the former coming two months after the new year. There were evidently two calendars within Jewish life in this era, one that started in the spring and one that started in the fall. The latter—New Year in the fall—was apparently the older system. I adopt it for this study. See Schürer, *The History of the Jewish People in the Age of Jesus Christ*, 1:18–19, 587–601.

autumn. We count backward from Mary's delivery in the spring, for she gave birth when shepherds, rather than their children, were "abiding in the field, keeping watch over their flock by night" because it was the lambing season (Luke 2:8). Otherwise, the owner's children typically spent the nights with the sheep.[9] We also calculate that Mary became pregnant when Elisabeth was about five and a half months along (see Luke 1:36). Both women, we assume, carried their infants to term, nine months. Because Mary gave birth in early April,[10] we calculate that she conceived her son the prior July. Elisabeth, therefore, would have conceived her baby in or about January, after Zacharias had returned home from his autumn duties at the temple. These calculations mean that Elisabeth gave birth to John approximately in October. The year of Zacharias's ministering was either 7 or 6 B.C., a date arrived at by noting Herod's death in March or April 4 B.C.[11]

We are also drawn to the question of whether Zacharias was ministering in the sanctuary during a festival, thus increasing the impact of his experience on the large gathering, "the whole multitude of the people" who "marvelled that he tarried so long in the temple" (Luke 1:10, 21). The answer is, probably not. The closest autumn festival times to Zacharias's ministering—the New Year, Day of Atonement, and Feast of Tabernacles—all occurred too early for the eighth week when Zacharias was ministering. Hanukkah season comes too late, by about twenty-three days, beginning the twenty-fifth day of the month of Chislev.[12] Hence, the large crowd, "the whole multitude," may

---

[9] The youthful David, for example, was the family member who "keepeth the sheep" (1 Samuel 16:11).

[10] A possible pointer to the spring is the date of April 6, noted in Doctrine and Covenants 20:1. See John F. Hall, "April 6," in *Encyclopedia of Mormonism*, Daniel H. Ludlow et al., eds. (New York: Macmillan, 1992), 61–62.

[11] On the year, see S. Kent Brown, C. Wilfred Griggs, and H. Kimball Hansen, review essay on *April Sixth*, by John C. Lefgren (Salt Lake City: Deseret Book, 1980), in *BYU Studies* 22 (summer 1982): 375–83, and "Afterwords," *BYU Studies* 23 (spring 1983): 252–55.

[12] On the date for Hannukah, see Schürer, *The History of the Jewish People in the Age of Jesus Christ*, 162–63.

have gathered not because of a holiday but because Zacharias was lighting the incense just before the Sabbath, on Friday afternoon, when large numbers would have gathered at the temple to welcome the Sabbath.[13]

Zacharias must have returned home a penitent man. The angel had abruptly taken away his ability to speak and, as we learn from a later scene, his ability to hear because he was unable to hear the question about the name of his new son (see Luke 1:20, 22, 62).

Zacharias's penitence would naturally have led him to intense efforts to regain God's favor. Entombed within the silence of his mind, he was left to rethink events at the temple and, more important, his status before God. We know he succeeded because of events on the day that his infant son received circumcision and a name.[14] On that happy day, the friends and relatives who gathered in the home of Zacharias and Elisabeth expressed doubt when she claimed that their son was to be named John. As they mused aloud that "none of thy kindred . . . is called by this name [John]," they turned to Zacharias and "made signs . . . how he would have him called." When the aged priest wrote that "His name is John," repeating the angel's name for the infant, it was as if a power outside Zacharias took hold of his face and "his mouth was opened . . . and he spake, and praised God" (Luke 1:61–64).

Zacharias probably delivered the glowing prophecy about his son and the coming Messiah on the same day and in the presence of the same guests (see Luke 1:67–79). If so, the day of John's naming brimmed brightly with manifestations of spiritual power. And it all occurred in the home of Zacharias and Elisabeth. On this occasion, "Zacharias was filled with the Holy Ghost, and prophesied" that his tiny son would "be called the prophet of the Highest" and, in Isaiah's language, would "go before the face of the Lord to prepare his ways."

---

[13] On the morning and evening sacrifices and the accompanying incense offerings, see Alfred Edersheim, *The Temple: Its Ministry and Services*, repr. (Grand Rapids: William B. Eerdmans, 1983), 152–73.

[14] The events narrated in Luke 1:57–79 stand as proof that circumcision and naming of a male child occurred on the same day.

Moreover, this child would "give knowledge of salvation unto his people by the remission of their sins," thus making concrete "the tender mercy of our God" in their lives. As a result, those who "sit in darkness and in the shadow of death" would find their feet lifted onto and then guided in "the way of peace" (Luke 1:67, 76–79). In a word, redemption was at hand. And its radiant, promise-filled manifestation lay in the home of a priest.

We must add a final pair of observations about traditions associated with Zacharias, both having to do with his death. First, although an early Christian text dating to about A.D. 150 claims that Zacharias was killed in the area of the temple because he refused to disclose the whereabouts of his son to authorities, the tradition is unreliable. Second, this tradition does not really illuminate Jesus' sad saying about "the [martyrs'] blood of Abel unto the blood of Zacharias, which perished between the altar and the temple" (Luke 11:51; see also Matthew 23:35).

The reference to the death of Zacharias, father of John, by execution at the temple arises in a document more than a hundred years after any such event might have occurred, raising questions about its veracity. A reliable estimate for the composition of the document in question, the *Protevangelium of James*, is about A.D. 150.[15] A question arises because of an editorial that ran in the *Times and Seasons* in Nauvoo, Illinois, on September 1, 1842, which plainly refers to information in the *Protevangelium* and claims that the martyred Zacharias of Luke 11:51 was John's father. At issue is whether Joseph Smith wrote that editorial. If he did, he would have put his prophetic stamp on the notion that the Zacharias noted in Luke 11:51 was John the Baptist's father. As a matter of fact, the evidence stands against Joseph Smith's authoring the editorial in the *Times and Seasons*. Instead, the author was likely W. W. Phelps.[16]

---

[15] Edgar Hennecke and Wilhelm Schneemelcher, eds., *New Testament Apocrypha*, 2 vols. (Philadelphia: Westminster Press, 1963–64), 1:372.

[16] The editorial is reprinted in *TPJS*, 260–61, and connects Luke 11:51 and the *Protevangelium of James*, 23–24. Four compelling circumstantial reasons stand against crediting the editorial to Joseph Smith. (1) The editorial was unsigned. Joseph Smith

In the case of Jesus' words about Zacharias, Matthew's report clarifies that Jesus was pointing to an Old Testament prophet of the same name (see Matthew 23:35). Moreover, people of Jesus' day were aware of martyrs whose fates stood chronicled in the Old Testament, beginning with Abel's martyrdom in the book of Genesis, the first book in the Bible. In the next generation, the last book in the Hebrew Bible was fixed to be the second book of Chronicles, an arrangement of the Old Testament that rested on a precedent evident before Jesus' day.[17] Why is this important? Because the last-mentioned martyr in the Hebrew Bible was a certain Zacharias, son of Jehoiada, whom people in Jerusalem stoned about 840 B.C. for denouncing them (see 2 Chronicles 24:20–22). In this light, when drawing attention to Abel and Zacharias, Jesus is pointing to the first martyr in scripture—and to the last. Hence, we see the Old Testament Zacharias, not the Baptist's father, in Jesus' words recorded in Luke 11:51.

Elisabeth

Little is preserved about Elisabeth. She appears in the record, apparently, because of her role as mother of John the Baptist. And the recorded events take place during a few brief months. Even so, enough peeks through our sources to let us see a genuinely gracious and spiritual woman. Her youth stands beyond our gaze, of course.

---

typically signed his letters and editorials, as in Doctrine and Covenants 127 and 128, which he wrote in the early days of September 1842. (2) The editorial appears in third person, not first person, which was Joseph Smith's preferred style. Again, Doctrine and Covenants 127 and 128 serve as comparisons. (3) During August 1842, Joseph Smith was moving from house to house among members of the Church to avoid arrest. Although evidence exists that he was hiding in Nauvoo during August, as well as in outlying communities, he would have enjoyed little peace to pen a long editorial. (4) The writing style of the editorial matches most closely that of W. W. Phelps, not the Prophet Joseph. These four observations rest on those of my colleague Richard L. Anderson. See S. Kent Brown, *Mary and Elisabeth: Noble Daughters of God* (American Fork, Utah: Covenant Communications, 2002), 94–95.

[17] The final order of scriptural books was set at the end of the first century A.D. in Yavneh under Yohanan ben Zakkai and his fellow scholars, an order that seemingly rests on earlier precedents, as hinted in the prologue of the book of Jesus ben Sirach. See Schürer, *The History of the Jewish People in the Age of Jesus Christ*, 2:316–19.

She probably grew up without being able to read and write.[18] But we can imagine that, as one "of the daughters of Aaron," she had a deep respect for the life of priests, the life of service to God (Luke 1:5).

When she married Zacharias, she and her acquaintances must have seen her union as one bursting with promise. But no children came, no tiny voices, no renewal of life. As time wore on, people wondered why she did not become a mother. In one of the few quoted lines from her, she refers to her "reproach among men" (Luke 1:25). Her society measured God's approval of women by their children. She did not know, nor did others, that God had chosen her for an important role: to be the mother of the Messiah's forerunner.[19]

In her earliest appearance in scripture, Elisabeth is the object of a prophecy on the lips of the angel Gabriel, who visited Zacharias in the temple: "Thy wife Elisabeth shall bear thee a son" (Luke 1:13). Elisabeth's special child was to "be filled with the Holy Ghost, even from his mother's womb" (Luke 1:15; see also Doctrine and Covenants 84:27). Elisabeth would become a mother, even though she was past childbearing—"well stricken in years" (Luke 1:7, 18). In a measure, this miracle would come because of her righteous life, for scripture calls her both "righteous" and "blameless" (Luke 1:6).

The warming companionship of the Holy Ghost from before her son's birth points convincingly to the uprightness of her personal life. In contrast to her husband, Elisabeth likely did not express doubt when she finally learned of the angel's prophecy. Even after all those years, she must still have been praying with her husband for a child—"thy prayer is heard," said the angel to Zacharias (Luke 1:13).[20] As an illustration of her closeness to God, she intoned, "Thus hath *the Lord dealt with me*" (Luke 1:25; emphasis added).

---

[18] Jeremias, *Jerusalem in the Time of Jesus*, 363, 373.

[19] For a general treatment of Elisabeth, see Brown, *Mary and Elisabeth*, 19–33.

[20] Leon Morris raises the question of whether Zacharias's prayer might have been formal and liturgical rather than a personal prayer for a child (*Luke: An Introduction and Commentary*, rev. ed. [Grand Rapids: William B. Eerdmans, 1988], 76). Although this is possible, the angel's words seem to point to a more personal prayer. Certainly, Zacharias's objections in Luke 1:18 make better sense if we accept this latter view.

God's miracles soon began to grace her life. We sense that a divine sequence began when "Elisabeth conceived" (Luke 1:24), the first in a series of miracles that would become almost commonplace over a brief period of time. Less certain is the full meaning of the expression that Elisabeth "hid herself five months" (Luke 1:24). Why hide herself? The account does not tell us. And such an act is not known as a custom. Perhaps she did not want to risk displeasing heaven, perhaps she did not want to draw public attention to herself, or perhaps she wanted to cherish the miracle of her coming child with just her husband for a time.

Later, when Mary visited her home, the Spirit of God came almost visibly upon Elisabeth (see Luke 1:41). On that occasion, she said respectfully to Mary, "Blessed art thou among women, and blessed is the fruit of thy womb. And whence is this to me, that the mother of my Lord should come to me?" (Luke 1:42–43). As her words disclose, here she became a prophetess, effectively playing the role that her unborn son would eventually play—announcing the coming Messiah. Hence, Elisabeth stood as a prophetic herald, both receiving impressions from God's Spirit about Mary's special child and then declaring them. Significantly, Elisabeth did not know about Mary and her expected child before Mary arrived at Elisabeth's home. In receiving God's gracious revelation of who the Messiah's mother was to be, Elisabeth became one of only two persons who knew Mary's sacred secret. As seems apparent, Mary had told no one else about her pregnancy and expected child.

Elisabeth also became the first witness to the virgin birth.[21] Under inspiration, Elisabeth prophesied, "Blessed is she [Mary] that believed: for there shall be a performance of those things which were told her from the Lord" (Luke 1:45). We ask, What were "those things which were told her from the Lord?" In brief, they were that Mary would "conceive in [her] womb, and bring forth a son" who would "be called the Son of the Highest" (Luke 1:31–32). Moreover, "those things" included the angel's revelation to Mary: "The power of

---

[21] On Elisabeth as a witness for the virgin birth, see Brown, BM, 301.

the Highest shall overshadow thee: therefore also that holy thing which shall be born of thee shall be called the Son of God" (Luke 1:35). Thus, besides learning through the Spirit who the mother of the Messiah was to be, Elisabeth came to understand that Mary's pregnancy was miraculous, as was her own.

We learn another dimension of Elisabeth's personality from Mary's visit: her evident lack of jealousy. Many people become envious when an honor comes to another, especially to a younger person, but Elisabeth did not. As a gracious hostess, she put the younger woman at the center of attention: "Blessed art thou among women, and blessed is the fruit of thy womb" (Luke 1:42). Except for Elisabeth's statement about "the babe" that "leaped in [her] womb for joy" (Luke 1:44), all her attention rested on Mary. Clearly, therefore, Elisabeth was one who put the interests of others first. In this light, the command that Mary felt in the angel's words about visiting Elisabeth was apparently meant to send Mary to the one person whom God had prepared to assist her in surmounting the challenges and fears that she surely would have experienced following the angel's announcement (see Luke 1:36). Elisabeth was that person.

In a different vein, we note that the exact family relationship between Elisabeth and Mary remains unknown. The word translated "cousin" (Greek *syngenis*—Luke 1:36) is a general term for a relative. Even so, they may have been first or second cousins.[22] Their ancestral link was close enough that Mary felt comfortable traveling to the distant home of Elisabeth for the first months of Mary's pregnancy. Moreover, because the two women recognized one another when they met, they apparently had spent time together in the past. Such contacts would not likely occur between people who were only distantly related and who lived more than one hundred miles apart.[23]

---

[22] The law governing a priest marrying a wife does not prohibit him from marrying outside his own tribe, that of Levi (see Leviticus 21:13–14). On this matter, consult the observations of Morris, *Luke: An Introduction and Commentary*, 75, and Schürer, *The History of the Jewish People in the Age of Jesus Christ*, 2:240–42.

[23] Based on the approximate distance from Nazareth to Bethlehem if traveling through the Jordan Valley via Beth Shean and Jericho (210 km. or 130 miles).

Hence, even though they lived an almost prohibitive distance from each other, the warm relationship between them seems to arise from an affectionate and apparently regular association.[24]

In this connection, we assume that Elisabeth's home was within a reasonable distance of Jerusalem. Why? Because she was both an Aaronite and a relative of Mary who was descended from the family of David (see Luke 1:5, 36; Romans 1:3). To grasp how these two women of different lineages would be related to one another, we must identify a likely place where their common ancestors met. One of the few places where the families of priests and the families descended from King David would readily mix and marry was the general region between Jerusalem and Bethlehem. There priests' families resided close to the temple, and families with genealogical ties to David still held property in and around David's hometown of Bethlehem. Because married couples typically remained within the same general area as their parents, we can therefore believe that Elisabeth and Zacharias had not moved from the Jerusalem-Bethlehem corridor.

Joseph

As with Zacharias and Elisabeth, our sources for Joseph are quite meager. Most focus on his early association with Mary. Before turning to them, we must answer the question, Why were children of families from the Bethlehem area, Joseph and Mary, living in Galilee, far to the north? We know from Joseph's trip to Bethlehem to register for the tax that his ancestral home was there. Also, Mary descended from King David, whose family had come from this town (see 1 Samuel 16; Romans 1:3). To frame an answer, we must sketch some background.

---

[24] A number of hypotheses about Elisabeth seem wrongheaded. First, some writers have pointed to the fact that she bears the name of Aaron's wife (see Exodus 6:23) and that Mary bears the name of Aaron's sister Miriam (see Exodus 15:20–21). These writers suggest that these names were part of a divine design. Second, a number of scholars hold that Elisabeth was the real singer of the Magnificat, the song or poem that Mary recites, beginning with the words, "My soul doth magnify the Lord" (see Luke 1:46–55). For a critique of these views, see Brown, *BM*, 266, and Brown, *Mary and Elisabeth*, 26–27.

In 104, Aristobulus, the Hasmonean king of Jerusalem, sent his armies to conquer Galilee and thereby to enfold people there, both Jews and non-Jews, into his kingdom. After taking control of Galilee, he sent government functionaries to keep order in the society so that people would pay taxes and, in the words of Josephus, follow "the law of the Judeans," which included submitting to circumcision and the payment of tithes to the temple and its priests.[25] Some of the government agents from the south settled in Galilee, sinking roots into its soil and garnishing their lives with its opportunities and pleasant climate. The ancestors of Mary and Joseph may have been among these southern officials. Or they may have migrated because of opportunities for a good livelihood that arose after Aristobulus's conquest. Or, more darkly, those who claimed descent from David—such as the ancestors of Joseph and Mary—may have moved northward because they sensed that the Hasmonean rulers, who were not of David's line, saw them through suspicious eyes as silent yet looming threats.[26]

Later Christian tradition portrays Joseph as an older man and the father of several children when he marries Mary.[27] However, no early source, including the New Testament, presents this view. Customarily, a groom was a few years older than his bride, as we can observe in

---

[25] Josephus, AJ, 13.9.1 (§257), repeats the expression. On the migration of southerners to the north, see Richard A. Horsley, *Archaeology, History and Society in Galilee: The Social Context of Jesus and the Rabbis* (Valley Forge, Pennsylvania: Trinity Press, 1996), 25–28; also consult Schürer, *The History of the Jewish People in the Age of Jesus Christ*, 1:217–18; Aryeh Kasher, *Jews, Idumaeans, and Ancient Arabs* (Tübingen: J. C. B. Mohr, 1988), 80–83.

[26] Talmage hints at the possibility that Joseph's family had fled Jerusalem because of their possible connection to the Judean throne (JTC, 87; also 89–90). On the priestly origin of the Hasmonean family, see 1 Maccabees 2:1–30.

[27] This viewpoint about Joseph meshes with the later Christian doctrine that Mary remained a virgin throughout her life and thus was not the mother of Jesus' brothers and sisters noted in the New Testament. These children, the tradition claims, were those of Joseph and his first wife. Consult *Protevangelium of James* 9.2; it is a fourth-century text that initially exhibits most of these characteristics for Joseph: *The Death of Joseph*, 2–3, in Forbes Robinson, *Coptic Apocryphal Gospels, Texts and Studies*, vol. 4 (Cambridge: Cambridge University Press, 1967), 131–32; also Montague Rhodes James, *The Apocryphal New Testament* (Oxford: Oxford University Press, 1924), 42.

the Near East today. Because a young woman could become betrothed between twelve and twelve and one-half years of age, followed by marriage about a year later, the prospective groom was to be at least thirteen and usually no older than eighteen.[28] Hence, we can reasonably believe that Joseph was in his mid or late teens when Mary was betrothed to him.

Her considerable inner qualities had probably begun to shine out to those who were paying attention. We do not know whether Mary had other suitors for her hand, but somehow Joseph and his parents endeared themselves to Mary's parents, who would make the decision about their daughter.

In mentioning Mary's parents, we can probably assume safely that they were still living. This point seems reasonable, especially if Mary was no older than thirteen when betrothed. Her mother would likely not yet have reached her thirtieth birthday. If Mary's father and mother were already dead, then we would have to build a case for a male relative overseeing the betrothal process, an unwarranted reconstruction in light of Mary's return to Nazareth following the visit to Elisabeth. The trip to Elisabeth's home clearly implies that Mary had traveled there in her recent memory, most likely in the company of her father. If Mary's trip is seen as a "flight," why did she not stay with Elisabeth until Mary's delivery? Moreover, early Christian tradition mentions parents who are still living during her youth.[29]

---

[28] On the age of a bride, see Herbert Danby, *The Mishnah* (Oxford: Oxford University Press, 1972), notes on *Ketuboth* 3.1, 8 and *Kiddushin* 1.2 (248–49, 321); also Jeremias, *Jerusalem in the Time of Jesus*, 363–66; on the minimum age for a bridegroom, see Roland De Vaux, *Ancient Israel*, repr. (Grand Rapids: William B. Eerdmans, 1997), 2 vols. (New York: McGraw-Hill Book Company, 1961), 1:29; on the customary maximum age for a bridegroom, see William Rosenau, *Jewish Ceremonial Institutions and Customs*, 3d ed. (Detroit: Singing Tree Press, 1925, Reprint 1971), 151, who cites the Mishnah tractate *Pirke Aboth* 5.24. For a visual sense of these ages, see the photograph of the newly married Moroccan Jewish couple, with the bride at thirteen and the groom at about twenty, in Hayyim Schneid, *Marriage* (Philadelphia: Jewish Publication Society of America, 1973), 94. For a summary of the betrothal process, see Brown, *Mary and Elisabeth*, 41–43, 101–2.

[29] On Mary's parents in the *Protevangelium of James*, see James, *The Apocryphal New Testament*, 39–44.

The betrothal process began with the prospective groom's father approaching the bride's parents, perhaps through a mutual acquaintance. The initiative lay on the groom's side. But the bride's parents held all the power because they could refuse even to meet with the father of the groom. To be sure, the prospective bride and groom might be related, though not always.[30] But the families of Joseph and Mary were likely related to one another. Besides, they all lived in the same small town, Nazareth, so that each set of parents, if related, knew the child in the other family.

If Mary's parents were favorably disposed to an opening contact with Joseph's father, he would have visited Mary's father in her parents' home, where together they would have discussed arrangements, such as the terms of the betrothal and the bride price. Above all, this visit would have signaled the willingness of her mother and father to consider an offer of marriage from Joseph's father. If all went well, the young woman would be married in the presence of her family, particularly her father, as custom required.[31]

The bride price, the sum of money the groom paid to the bride's father as compensation for her loss to her family, had to be fixed. The bride's price was called *mohar*, and the groom or his father typically paid this sum at the time of betrothal. If the parties reached agreement and if at least two witnesses were present, the betrothal might begin as soon as the father of the groom met with the father of the bride.[32] The date of the marriage was also a matter for discussion; it was usually set for a Wednesday.[33] The betrothal lasted from one

---

[30] De Vaux, *Ancient Israel*, 1:29–31; Jeremias, *Jerusalem in the Time of Jesus*, 363–66.

[31] The important connection between father and daughter, particularly in matters of marriage and the making of vows, appears in Exodus 22:16–17; Numbers 30:3–5, 16; Deuteronomy 21:10–13; 22:15. For comment, see David Daube, *The Exodus Pattern in the Bible* (London: Faber and Faber, 1963), 65–66; Phyllis A. Bird, "Women: Old Testament," in Freedman, *ABD*, 6:956; also Jeremias, *Jerusalem in the Time of Jesus*, 363–66.

[32] De Vaux, *Ancient Israel*, 1:26–27, 33; Alan Coates Bouquet, *Everyday Life in New Testament Times* (New York: Charles Scribner's Sons, 1953), 147.

[33] Wednesday is the day on which a virgin is to be married, according to later tradition. Widows remarry on Thursdays (see Mishna *Ketuvoth* 1:1). In an interesting twist, the JST reads "third day of the week" in John 2:1, evidently Tuesday for the marriage at

month to one year, with the normal length being a year. Following betrothal, the families considered the couple to be married, though the bride and groom did not live together and the husband did not yet support his wife.[34] In the case of Joseph and Mary, their betrothal lasted at least several months because Mary was able to visit Elisabeth for "about three months" and, upon Mary's return home, their marriage was still in the future (Luke 1:56; see also Matthew 1:18–19). As we shall see, before their betrothal ran its natural course, an angel changed everything.

The King James Version calls Joseph a carpenter, an occupation that he probably learned from his father and certainly passed on to Jesus (see Matthew 13:55; Mark 6:3). The Greek term (*tektoän*) denotes any artisan, a person skilled with the hands. Although Joseph would not have found much work in Nazareth because the village consisted of only a few homes in his youth,[35] he and others like him may have found work in Sepphoris, the most important city in Galilee. Sepphoris lay just over the hill, three miles northwest of Nazareth. The city was the administrative center in Galilee; presumably, the demand for skilled craftsmen during Joseph's youth would have been high. Then, in 4 B.C., upon the death of Herod the Great, perhaps while Joseph and Mary were in Egypt (see Matthew 2:14–15), the town revolted against Roman rule. In response, the military forces of Varus, the Roman governor of Syria, sacked Sepphoris, burning it to the ground and enslaving its inhabitants.

Cana, although Wednesday cannot be ruled out. If Tuesday is the correct day, it would be perhaps an unusual day for a marriage.

[34] See Rosenau, *Jewish Ceremonial Institutions and Customs*, 154; Schneid, *Marriage*, 10. Even the angel who appeared to Joseph in a dream during the betrothal period called Mary "thy [Joseph's] wife" (Matthew 1:20), thus respecting the custom.

[35] Alfred Edersheim tries to make a case for Nazareth as a town on a trade route (*The Life and Times of Jesus the Messiah*, 2 vols. [Grand Rapids: William B. Eerdmans, 1962], 1:147). But this view is untenable in the light of modern research and archaeological investigation. See Bellarmino Bagatti, *Excavations in Nazareth*, Studium Biblicum Franciscanum, 17 (Jerusalem: Franciscan Printing Press, 1969), and David F. Graf, Benjamin Isaac, and Israel Roll, "Roads and Highways (Roman)," Freedman, *ABD*, 5:782–87.

When Herod Antipas, son of Herod the Great, inherited Sepphoris and the surrounding territory in the same year, he immediately initiated a major rebuilding program of both the town and its walls.[36] Thus, after Joseph returned from Egypt with his family (see Matthew 2:19–23), it was likely attractive for him to resettle in Nazareth, where life was quiet and he could find work at a good wage in nearby Sepphoris. If anything, Joseph was a person of high, noble character. In a brief review, we notice first that he was responsive to duty. We have only to read of his willingness to pay the redemption price for the newly born Jesus at the temple—five shekels in his day, a hefty sum,[37] though he was poor—and of his willingness to help his wife meet her sacrificial obligation after she had given birth (see Luke 2:22–24). Moreover, though he was not the biological father of the infant Jesus, he seems to have filled that role honorably when naming and circumcising Mary's baby (see Luke 2:21).[38] In addition, Luke writes that Joseph and Mary "went to Jerusalem every year at the feast of the passover," filling an obligation that lay upon every Israelite, particularly men (Luke 2:41; see also Exodus 23:14–17).

Second, on no fewer than two occasions he received visitations from angels. To be sure, the angels' messages had to do with Mary's coming child and the safety of the infant Jesus, both celestial concerns (see Matthew 1:20–21; 2:13). But another source tells us that angels communicate with "the chosen vessels of the Lord" (Moroni 7:31). Joseph evidently fit into this category of "chosen vessels."

---

[36] For a brief history of Sepphoris, see James F. Strange, "Sepphoris," in Freedman, *ABD*, 5:1090–93, and Eric M. Meyers, ed., *Galilee through the Centuries* (Winona Lake, Indiana: Eisenbrauns, 1999). For the essential pieces of the history of the town in Josephus, see *AJ*, 14.15.4 (§414); 17.10.9 (§289); 18.2.1 (§27); *War*, 1.16.2 (§304); 2.5.1 (§68). In his last will, Herod named his son Herod Antipas as tetrarch of Galilee (see Josephus, *AJ*, 17.8.1 [§188]).

[37] Though Luke does not say that Joseph paid the five shekels, he intimates it (see Luke 2:23). The five shekels were Tyrian shekels, used in temple matters, and would have been equivalent to twenty denarii or wages for twenty days' work. See Schürer, *The History of the Jewish People in the Age of Jesus Christ*, 2:62–67.

[38] On these obligations, including naming, circumcising, and sacrificing, see Brown, *Mary and Elisabeth*, 30, 49–50, 56–57.

Third, his response to the news of Mary's pregnancy is expected and yet exemplary. When he finally learned that she was "with child," the news must have been devastating for him. Even so, to his everlasting credit, he was "not willing to make her a publick example" but rather sought a way to break off the betrothal quietly (Matthew 1:18–19). We suspect that, in a country town like Nazareth, there may have been those who would want to exact the maximum punishment on Mary—execution by stoning (see Deuteronomy 22:21). Joseph's attempt to keep Mary out of the public eye points firmly to a merciful strand in his character. We sense that in Joseph we meet a truly forgiving young man.

We do not know when Joseph died. Because he does not appear in any of the Gospel accounts that rehearse moments from Jesus' ministry, we might safely conclude that Mary was already a widow. If Joseph married when he was in his mid to late teens, as seems likely, he would have been less than fifty when he died because Jesus began His ministry when He was "about thirty years of age" (Luke 3:23). We do know that Joseph lived long enough to see Jesus' twelfth birthday (see Luke 2:41–51). In any event, Mary seems to have outlived Joseph by a number of years.[39] Perhaps the most enduring legacy that Joseph bequeathed to anyone he bequeathed to Jesus, for in Jesus we find Joseph's name living on: "Jesus of Nazareth, the son of Joseph" (John 1:45).

Mary

Of the four individuals treated in this chapter, Mary is the most anticipated person in prophecy.[40] Not only was she known by name among Book of Mormon prophets (see Mosiah 3:8; Alma 7:10) but she was also the subject of two prophecies many centuries before her birth. In the only Old Testament prophecy, received by Isaiah in the

---

[39] On what Mary may have witnessed in the growing church after the death of Jesus, see Brown, *Mary and Elisabeth*, 79–81.

[40] For a general treatment of the youthful Mary, see Brown, *Mary and Elisabeth*, 35–62.

eighth century B.C., we read, "Behold, a virgin shall conceive, and bear a son, and shall call his name Immanuel" (Isaiah 7:14). As we might guess, a good deal of discussion has arisen about this passage. Most scholars believe that the expected woman was Isaiah's own wife, partly because, in their view, a person cannot possibly see far into the future and partly because the Hebrew term translated "virgin" ('almah) can be rendered "a young woman" who is married.[41] In fact, Isaiah says of the child that "butter and honey shall he eat" (Isaiah 7:15), a possible reference to the return to normal times and to the end of the siege that Jerusalem was enduring when Isaiah uttered his prophecy.[42] This part of Isaiah's prophecy may have pointed to his own day. But the reference to the "virgin" and to the name Immanuel appears to envision an era far from that of Isaiah. In this connection, the Jewish translator of this passage into Greek in the third century B.C. rendered the Hebrew term 'almah with the Greek word for virgin, *parthenos*, which almost always means a woman who is unmarried and has known no man. Hence, in one of the earliest interpretations of Isaiah's words, the mother-to-be was evidently thought of as a virgin, not a young married woman, even though the Hebrew term allows this meaning. Further, when the inspired Matthew quoted Isaiah's words "Behold, a virgin" (Matthew 1:23) and applied them to Mary, he was certifying that Isaiah's prophecy pointed to her.

The name of the coming infant, Immanuel, also points to Mary's child. As we learn from Matthew, the name means "God with us"

---

[41] The Hebrew term is 'almah (Isaiah 7:14). For a summary of the usual views that deny the tie between Isaiah's prophecy and Mary, see R. B. Y. Scott and G. D. Kilpatrick, *The Book of Isaiah*, *The Interpreter's Bible*, vol. 5 (Nashville: Abingdon, 1956), 218–20, and Gerhard Delling, "parthenos," in Kittell and Friedrich, *TDNT*, 5:831–33. A more positive assessment is that of Ceslas Spicq, *Theological Lexicon of the New Testament*, 3 vols. (Peabody, Massachusetts: Hendrickson Publishers, 1994), 3:44–49.

[42] In addition, "before the child shall know to refuse the evil, and choose the good, the land that thou [King Ahaz of Judah] abhorest shall be forsaken of both her kings" (Isaiah 7:16). That is, before the promised infant grows old enough to discern between good and evil, the two enemy kings conducting the siege would be dead, which happened within a short time (see 2 Kings 15:30; 16:9).

(Matthew 1:23). This Immanuel would serve as "a sign" from "the Lord himself" (Isaiah 7:11, 14). The question is, "a sign" for what purpose? In answer, the promised child would come to "a virgin" and would literally be Immanuel—not in some abstract sense that God's influence would extend over His people but in a more concrete sense that God Himself would actually live among His people, prompting us to recall that "the Word [Christ] was made flesh, and *dwelt among us*" (John 1:14; emphasis added).

To Isaiah's prophecy we add the vision of Nephi almost six hundred years before Mary's infancy. At the beginning of Nephi's vision, he saw "in the city of Nazareth . . . a virgin" who was exceedingly "fair above all other virgins" (1 Nephi 11:13, 15).[43] Although we do not learn the name of this young woman, Nephi writes that she later appeared "bearing a child in her arms." The guiding angel called this child "the Son of the Eternal Father" (1 Nephi 11:20–21), plainly pointing to Mary as the mother.

Though we know nothing of Mary's birth and earliest years or of events that may have left their mark, we assume that the most important influence on her came from her mother, who must have lived into Mary's youth as early Christian tradition affirms.[44] From her, Mary would have learned homemaking arts and nurturing skills, as well as remedies for illnesses and wounds. With her mother, she

---

[43] Nephi would have known her status either from the veil of a virgin, as Rebekah (see Genesis 24:65), or from the double sash of a virgin, as Aseneth. See the document *Joseph and Aseneth*, 14:14–15 in James H. Charlesworth, ed., *The Old Testament Pseudepigrapha*, 2 vols. (New York: Doubleday, 1983, 1985), 2:225; also Douglas R. Edwards, "Dress and Ornamentation," in Freedman, *ABD*, 2:235, 237.

[44] Christian tradition has given names to Mary's parents, Joachim and Anna, and holds that following Mary's stay at Elisabeth's home, she returned to "her house," implying that her parents were still alive. The earliest source for these features is the *Protevangelium of James*, whose composition may date as early as A.D. 150, perhaps within one hundred years of Mary's death. However, there is no evidence that the *Protevangelium* preserves the real names of Mary's parents. Moreover, the *Protevangelium* exhibits no connections to the genealogies preserved by Matthew and Luke. Consult *Protevangelium of James* 1.1–2.1; 4.1; 7.2; on the dating, see Hennecke and Schneemelcher, *New Testament Apocrypha*, 1:372. On the uncertain origin of the names of Mary's parents, consult Brown, *BM*, 288.

would have learned to work in field and orchard. Through her mother, she would have come to understand holiness and appreciate the sanctifying effects of devotion. In her mother, Mary would have seen an example of how she would raise children and be a wife.

Her father's influence would carry a different tone, especially because she would have spent less time with him. In our mind's eye, we see him putting his phylacteries on his arm and on his forehead while Mary watches his every move. She would have seen him raise his prayer shawl to cover his head as he began to pray. She would have witnessed his respect for the Sabbath as he welcomed it by song and prayer. She would have smelled the outdoors in his clothing. She would have traveled with him to Jerusalem for festivals, as her acquaintance with Elisabeth illustrates. She would have seen him depart for worship at the synagogue.[45] She would have known his expectation that she keep herself pure so that she could marry properly. In all, we judge that her childhood was not unusual and that she grew up in a normal home. These things would have served her well when unusual events came upon her.

Although the scripture accounts do not record Mary's age at betrothal, we assume that her parents would look for a young man's parents to approach soon after her twelfth birthday, or perhaps earlier. In reality, she would have been young when she became betrothed to Joseph, in her early teens at a minimum.[46] Because she spent "about three months" in the home of Elisabeth (Luke 1:56), we surmise that the angel came early in her betrothal—which normally lasted a year—rather than later. His appearance changed everything.

The angel's greeting hints at Mary's high status long before this astonishing moment: "Hail, thou that art highly favoured, the Lord is with thee: blessed art thou among women" (Luke 1:28). Some scholars have suggested that God's choice of Mary to be the mother

---

[45] A synagogue stood in Nazareth when Jesus was an adult (see Luke 4:16). Presumably, this building, or its predecessor, was standing when Mary was a child.

[46] Bruce R. McConkie judges that Mary would have married in her early teens; see MM, 1:223.

of His Son was an act of grace, a pure gift to her.[47] But scripture reveals her to have been a noble daughter of God long before her mortal birth. Both the prophecy of Isaiah and the vision of Nephi point to God's long acquaintance with Mary (see Isaiah 7:14–16; 1 Nephi 11:13–21). Other prophecies, all from the Book of Mormon, buttress this observation.

The most noteworthy comes on the lips of an angel who appeared to King Benjamin about 125 B.C. His gracious words disclose the names of the coming Savior and His mother: "He shall be called Jesus Christ, the Son of God . . . and his mother shall be called Mary" (Mosiah 3:8). Forty or so years after the angel appeared to Benjamin, Alma the Younger said of the coming Messiah, "He shall be born of Mary . . . she being a virgin, a precious and chosen vessel" (Alma 7:10). Hence, we can clearly see that God knew Mary's name as well as her exceptional character. Plainly, a growing aggregate of prophecies about this young woman existed, becoming ever more specific about her as a person.[48] Because all these details became known before Mary's birth, God's choice of her was not unexpected.

Her personality appears initially in her response to the angel. She was not a shy, retiring youth. Of course, she was frightened at first, as the angel's words reveal: "Fear not, Mary" (Luke 1:30). She was also "troubled" at his greeting (Luke 1:29).[49] But Mary seems soon to have recovered her bearings, for after the angel announced that she would "conceive in [her] womb, and bring forth a son," she asked, "How shall this be, seeing I know not a man?" (Luke 1:31, 34). From this question, we can surmise that she did not suffer from self-doubt. As with Enoch and Moses and Jeremiah before her, she possessed the

---

[47] On God's choice of Mary more or less out of the blue, see Beverly Roberts Gaventa, *Mary: Glimpses of the Mother of Jesus* (Minneapolis: Fortress Press, 1999), 16, 18; also Joel B. Green, *The Gospel of Luke* (Grand Rapids: William B. Eerdmans, 1997), 86–87.

[48] Another prophecy comes from King Lamoni. He says that the Savior will "be born of a woman" (Alma 19:13).

[49] A related term appears for Zacharias at the appearance of the angel: "he was troubled" (Luke 1:12). The two related words tie the experiences together, as does the fact that the same angel came to both.

pluck and the presence of mind to ask a difficult question on the occasion of the announcement of the ages, who the Messiah was to be. Her question, "How shall this be . . . ?" does not intimate that she did not believe. She was asking the question *how* rather than *if* the angel's promise would come to pass. Moreover, her question shows that she instinctively understood the personal costs of her becoming pregnant.[50]

Whether Mary shared her astonishing news with anyone in her home is unknown. As Luke recounts events, she apparently left almost immediately for Elisabeth's home. The trek was a daunting experience for a young woman, barely out of her girlhood, during July, one of the hottest months in the Jordan Valley, the likely route of her walk.[51] She must have gone in the company of other travelers, something that her family would have insisted on. What is remarkable is that she sensed in the angel's words a divine directive that she visit Elisabeth: "Thy cousin Elisabeth . . . hath also conceived a son in her old age" (Luke 1:36). From what we have seen of Elisabeth, she was the perfect person to take her young cousin under her wing during the first weeks of pregnancy while Mary was still trying to absorb all that the angel had told her.

It seems only natural to speculate about how Mary became pregnant. Four passages of scripture bear on any answer. Significantly, all four reveal little about the process. The first comes from Nephi, who wrote that he had seen in his vision "the mother of the Son of God . . . carried away in the Spirit for the space of a time." He next "beheld the virgin . . . bearing a child in her arms" (1 Nephi 11:18–20). From this description, we learn only that the Spirit was an aid in the conception. The words of Alma the Younger disclose the same. He prophesied that "Mary . . . shall be overshadowed and conceive by the

---

[50] Thomas Cahill notices Mary's willingness to raise questions in his *Desire of the Everlasting Hills: The World before and after Jesus* (New York: Doubleday, 1999), 95. On the questioning by Enoch, Moses, and Jeremiah, see Moses 6:31; Exodus 3:11, 13; 4:1; Jeremiah 1:6. Consult also Talmage, *JTC*, 80–81.

[51] That Mary left in July is evident from the spring birth of Jesus, during the lambing season (see Luke 2:8).

power of the Holy Ghost" (Alma 7:10). A third instance is very similar. To the youthful Joseph, an angel declared, "Fear not to take . . . Mary [as] thy wife: for that which is conceived in her is of the Holy Ghost" (Matthew 1:20). The fourth passage consists of words from the angel to Mary: "The Holy Ghost shall come upon thee, and the power of the Highest shall overshadow thee" (Luke 1:35). In summary, the four passages—taken individually or together—do not reveal how Mary conceived. It seems best to follow the cautioning words of President Harold B. Lee, who said, "You asked about . . . the birth of the Savior. . . . If teachers were wise in speaking of this matter about which the Lord has said but very little, they would rest their discussion on this subject with merely the words which are recorded on this subject in Luke 1:34–35. . . . Remember that the being who was brought about by [Mary's] conception was a divine personage. We need not question His [God's] method to accomplish His purposes."[52]

It may have been after Mary's return to Nazareth that she first shared her secret with her family and Joseph, leading Matthew to write that "she was found with child," as if that were a discovery (Matthew 1:18). Although she was legally bound to Joseph and although later Jewish law would see a child conceived by her before the end of her betrothal as legitimate,[53] Joseph sought "to put her away privily," likely because of growing public resentment (Matthew 1:19). Joseph's actions brought the angelic response: "Joseph, thou son of David, fear not to take unto thee Mary thy wife." Why not? Because "that which is conceived in her is of the Holy Ghost" (Matthew 1:20). It is evident that Mary would need someone to stand by her during the coming years. That need is highlighted by the long-lived perception, which followed her Son into His adulthood, that people believed her to have conceived Him illegitimately. On

---

[52] Clyde J. Williams, ed., *The Teachings of Harold B. Lee* (Salt Lake City: Bookcraft, 1996), 13–14.

[53] Henri Daniel-Rops, *Daily Life in the Time of Jesus*, trans. Patrick O'Brian (New York: Hawthorn Books, 1962), 142.

one occasion some huffy Pharisees said accusingly to Jesus, "We be not born of fornication," implying that He had (John 8:41).[54] Such an understanding would have reflected badly on Mary as long as she lived.

The marriage festivities for Mary would not have turned out as she had hoped. The night before a marriage brought women of both families together for a celebration at the bride's home. The following day, an escort of friends and family would accompany the bride to the home of her groom.[55] Certainly, Mary experienced none of these happy, treasured moments. She and Joseph probably thought it wise that she take her place in his home out of the sight of townspeople.[56]

Luke's notice that the tax enrollment drew Joseph and Mary to Bethlehem may be only part of the story. When they left Nazareth, they may have traveled with others who were going to Jerusalem for the Passover feast, for their journey was in the springtime, as verified by the shepherds spending nights with their ewes and the observation that sleeping accommodations in Bethlehem were already full, apparently with Passover visitors (see Luke 2:7–8; JST Luke 2:7).[57]

Although Mary and Joseph later stayed in a "house" in Bethlehem, hinting at the possibility of nearby relatives and properties (Matthew 2:11), they at first sought lodging in an "inn" (Luke 2:7). The term translated "inn" presents several possible meanings. In the sense that tradition preserves, an inn would have offered rooms to guests. Each room faced a central courtyard that was open to the sky.

---

[54] Compare the smug question from these same Pharisees: "Where is thy Father?" (John 8:19).

[55] On the bridal party and the procession, see Schneid, *Marriage*, 1–17; Daniel-Rops, *Daily Life in the Time of Jesus*, 144; "Marriage," *Encyclopedia Judaica*, 11:1032–34; on the bride's jewelry, consult De Vaux, *Ancient Israel*, 1:33, and Bouquet, *Everyday Life in New Testament Times*, 148.

[56] On fasting as an act of penitence at marriage, consult Rosenau, *Jewish Ceremonial Institutions and Customs*, 154; on seeking atonement at the time of marriage, see Schneid, *Marriage*, 18.

[57] Bethlehem lay on a major trade route that connected Jerusalem with northwest Arabia and the Red Sea. But it is unlikely that the visitors who filled the inns of Bethlehem were traders because a day's journey southward from Jerusalem would have taken them much farther than the mere five miles separating Jerusalem and Bethlehem.

Travelers' animals stayed in the courtyard if there was risk in leaving them outside. Because of the evident poverty of Mary and Joseph, we might consider other possible meanings for the word "inn."

Another meaning is "guest room," normally an extra room within a reasonably well-to-do home such as the chamber where Jesus and His Apostles spent the Last Supper (see Luke 22:11).[58] This sense raises the possibility that Mary and Joseph went to the home of relatives. Naturally, relatives would expect Mary and Joseph to call on them even if other guests were already in the home. If the guest room was already occupied—"there was no room for them" (Luke 2:7)—the relatives would have tried to make Mary and Joseph comfortable in other quarters. Domesticated animals—sheep, cows, donkeys—typically were kept on the first floor, and the family occupied the home's upper levels. On this view, Mary and Joseph could have been offered a place to stay on the ground floor near the animals. Although Luke's report mentions only Mary and Joseph, his silence may not exclude helpful, attentive relatives.[59]

According to tradition, Mary gave birth in a cave, which may be true. Plainly, Mary gave birth in a place for animals because she "laid [Jesus] in a manger," a trough where animals ate (Luke 2:7). In the Near East, poorer people often lived in caves with their animals because caves were warm in the winter and cool in the summer. Caves were also less expensive to maintain than a constructed home because caves required little upkeep. On a different view, people

---

[58] The word rendered "inn" at Luke 2:7 (*katalyma*) is the same as the "guestchamber" in Luke 22:11. Luke's narrative mentions "the inn"; the Joseph Smith Translation reads "the inns" (JST Luke 2:7). There is a large literature on the term translated "inn" and what it might reveal about the circumstances that brought Mary and Joseph into a place with animals. Here is only a sample: Gustaf Dalman, *Sacred Sites and Ways* (New York: MacMillan, 1935), 41–43; Brown, BM, 399–401; Kenneth E. Bailey, "The Manger and the Inn: The Cultural Background of Luke 2:7," *Theological Review* 2 (1979): 33–44; Joseph A. Fitzmyer, *The Gospel According to Luke*, The Anchor Bible, 2 vols. (New York: Doubleday, 1981, 1985), 1:408.

[59] According to the *Protevangelium of James* 18.1–19.1, just before Mary gave birth, Joseph found a midwife. But this detail cannot be verified. See Hennecke and Schneemelcher, *New Testament Apocrypha*, 1:383–84.

occasionally built their homes over caves because caves served as places to keep animals or for storage. In either case, it is not beyond possibility to think of Mary giving birth in a cave. How she and Joseph might have come to such a spot we do not know. But in a cave, the cool air of springtime would not have chilled Mary and her new baby.

Scripture does offer clues about how Mary coped physically. Luke writes that "she brought forth her firstborn son, and wrapped him in swaddling clothes,[60] and laid him in a manger" (Luke 2:7). All the verbs in this passage describe actions of Mary. She gave birth and then found enough strength to wrap her newborn and lay Him in a manger. Is it not likely that she felt God's Spirit lending her strength and calming her fears? She was giving birth to God's own Son. He must have been watching over her as she welcomed her firstborn child into the world.

Mary's delivery brought religious obligations that she readily filled. Eighteen months after the angel appeared to Zacharias, Mary and Joseph entered the temple to take care of two requirements "according to the law of Moses" (Luke 2:22). In Luke's words, "when the days of [Mary's] purification according to the law . . . were accomplished, they brought [the infant Jesus] to Jerusalem, to present him to the Lord" (Luke 2:22).

In the eyes of the law of Moses, childbirth renders a woman unclean in a ritual sense. To rid herself of uncleanness, a woman waited forty days after the birth of a male child—eighty in the case of a female—and then offered sacrifices for her purification. The sacrifices consisted of a lamb and either a young pigeon or a turtledove. For the poor, the law allowed sacrifices of either two pigeons or two turtledoves (see Leviticus 12:2–8). Because Mary and Joseph offered either two turtledoves or two pigeons, it is evident that they were poor (see Luke 2:24). In their offering, Mary and Joseph demonstrated both their general respect for law and custom as well as their reverence for the Mosaic law as a collection of directives from God.

---

[60] The expression "swaddling clothes" refers to bands of cloth that a mother wrapped around a baby rather than to a blanket.

Mary's other task was to redeem her firstborn son. By law, the firstborn child in an Israelite family, or the firstborn of any animal, belonged to God. In the case of animals, an owner sacrificed this firstborn with the firm expectation that God would consequently increase the owner's flocks and herds. In the case of children, as we have seen, parents redeemed the firstborn child in Mary's era by bringing a five-shekel payment to the priests as a redemption price (see Numbers 18:15–16).[61] This act was part of presenting the infant "to the Lord" (Luke 2:22–23).

When Mary and Joseph had taken care of their obligations at the temple—and Luke emphasizes their obedience—they were approached by persons named Simeon and Anna. Simeon spoke directly to Mary. His tone was melancholy, almost fearful: "Yea, a sword shall pierce through thy own soul" (Luke 2:35). These words, almost as an aside, look to Mary's heartache at how her people would mistreat her divine Son.

Mary and her family evidently returned to Bethlehem after their experience in the temple. Luke, of course, records that "when [Mary and Joseph] had performed all things . . . they returned . . . to their own city Nazareth" (Luke 2:39). But Luke's account seemingly skips over certain events. According to Matthew's record, Mary and Joseph and their baby were forced to flee to Egypt (see Matthew 2:13–15). It is immaterial whether, as some scholars hold, Luke purposely passed over such events or, as others believe, he did not know of them.[62] However, it is important for filling out our picture of Mary to take up the reports in Matthew's Gospel, including the deaths of the children in Bethlehem and the flight to Egypt.

---

[61] In the earliest form of this law, parents evidently offered an animal as a vicarious sacrifice in the place of the child (see Exodus 13:2, 11–15; 34:19–20). As these passages illustrate, the only exception to sacrificing the firstborn among animals was the firstborn donkey.

[62] Brown, for example, believes that the information in Matthew about the visit of the wise men and the trip to Egypt is unhistorical (*BM*, 188–90, 203, 225–28). Morris, on the other hand, writes that "there is no way of knowing whether he [Luke] knew" of the flight to Egypt (*Luke: An Introduction and Commentary*, 99).

Though Mary and Joseph were poor, they had stayed on in Bethlehem at least six weeks to meet the Mosaic requirement for ritually purifying a new mother at the temple. By then, Mary and Joseph possibly found lodging in the home of a relative in or near Bethlehem—"the house" (Matthew 2:11). Apparently, Mary and Joseph settled into life there almost as if they were making it their permanent home. Such a view of events allows us to understand, at least in a measure, the occurrences in Bethlehem that Matthew reports.

The family may have lived in Bethlehem for a year or more. This length of time makes sense of Herod's vicious order to kill children there "from two years old and under" (Matthew 2:16).[63] Perhaps Jesus had reached His first birthday.

For centuries, Herod has been vilified for his horrific act. Happily for Mary and Joseph, and for us, God was watching over His Son. Hence, anticipating Herod's deadly outburst, "the angel of the Lord appeareth to Joseph in a dream, saying, Arise, and take the young child and his mother, and flee into Egypt, and be thou there until I bring thee word" (Matthew 2:13).

Mary's little family found safety in Egypt, as had many others before.[64] How much of an impact her time in Egypt exerted on her we cannot know. Flight is never easy, even if a person has time to prepare. Correctly, art has attempted to portray this event in generally

---

[63] Some critics dismiss the historicity of the story of Herod murdering the children in Bethlehem (see Matthew 2:16). But Herod's act of ordering the deaths of the children is completely in keeping with his character. He was murderous, even within his own family, killing off sons and a wife. His bloodthirsty paranoia, chronicled by Josephus, became terrifyingly rampant in his later years. Hence, it seems that a critic—anyone who wants to discount any part of the scriptural record about events that affected Mary and Joseph in Bethlehem—must start with Matthew's accuracy in depicting what is known about Herod's character. Much of what we know about ancient history has come down to us in only one written source. For these events, Matthew is the source. Handy sketches of Herod's life appear in F. F. Bruce, *New Testament History* (Garden City, New York: Anchor Books, 1972), 20–24, and Richard Neitzel Holzapfel, "King Herod," in *Masada and the World of the New Testament*, ed. John F. Hall and John W. Welch (Provo, Utah: BYU Studies, 1997), 35–67.

[64] See the discussion, for instance, in S. Kent Brown, "Biblical Egypt: Land of Refuge, Land of Bondage," *Ensign* 10 (September 1980): 44–50.

arduous tones. For its part, Egyptian Christian tradition has sketched the journey in rich hues, though much of this tradition is legendary. If Mary and Joseph owned a donkey or a mule, it had to serve the needs of three persons. The weather was probably hot during their trek, and they would have lived in poverty while there.[65]

Their stay in Egypt ended when "an angel of the Lord appeareth in a dream to Joseph in Egypt" and instructed him to "take the young child and his mother, and go into the land of Israel." So they happily returned because "Herod was dead" and also—significantly—"they . . . which sought the young child's life" (Matthew 2:19–20). It seems natural that God would wait until after Herod's death to send these instructions through His angel. But scripture adds forebodingly that unnamed others had joined in seeking "the young child's life."

Such a scheme to destroy young Jesus explains two aspects of the larger story. First, tradition holds that Mary and her family stayed in Egypt almost four years, a seemingly excessive claim until we notice that, besides Herod, who was near the end of his life, others "sought the young child's life." Their deaths would have occurred over an extended period. Hence, God kept the family safe in Egypt. Second, the widening impact of God's witnesses who spoke of amazing events surrounding Jesus' birth became visible. Over time, stories and rumors from priests and shepherds and temple worshipers reached persons who viewed such reports not only with disdain but also with evident hostility. But because Mary and her family spent these years first in Egypt and then in Nazareth, far from Jerusalem and the centers of power, the opposition to Mary's son, which had begun to flare, died down, giving her an opportunity to raise her son and other children out of the gaze of powerful and hateful eyes.

If nothing else, our review of Mary's youth as a betrothed girl and young mother has shown a thread of severe difficulties that must

---

[65] Consult the review of the Egyptian traditions in Otto Meinardus, *Christian Egypt: Ancient and Modern* (Cairo: The American University in Cairo Press, 1977), 275–79, 601–49. See also Aziz S. Atiya et al., eds., *The Coptic Encyclopedia*, 8 vols. (New York: Macmillan, 1991), s.v. "Flight into Egypt," 4:1117–18.

have shaped her adult life. The news from the angel, though it bore the fulfillment of celestial hopes, also carried a threat to her as an honorable person. Then, the fact that she became pregnant out of wedlock would have colored other people's perceptions of her ever after. Following that, she gave birth to her firstborn in Bethlehem, far from her Galilean home in Nazareth. Then, coping with her new, strange Bethlehem environment as a thirteen- or fourteen-year-old mother would have challenged her abilities. After that, Herod's murderous threat against her child would have both frightened and unnerved her. Finally, the sudden flight to Egypt and her residence in a foreign environment in her early teens, where few if any could speak her language, Aramaic, would have daunted most youths. Such challenges, all possibly coming before her fifteenth birthday, would have tested her mettle and, as she learned to deal with them, imparted strength to her. It is to her credit that when we next see her in the pages of the Gospels—the marriage at Cana (see John 2:1–10)—experience has plainly honed her personality in all the right ways.[66]

Conclusion

The divinely orchestrated events that rushed upon Zacharias and Elisabeth, Joseph and Mary, at first surprised them and those who were close to them. But after the initial surprises, these people seem to have settled into a pattern of life that allowed them to wait upon the Lord and be ready to do His bidding. The accounts of Luke and Matthew disclose the remarkable abilities of these seemingly ordinary people. Along the way, the Lord shaped Joseph and Mary into the parents who would spiritually and properly influence their remarkable sons.

---

[66] Consult Brown, *Mary and Elisabeth*, 63–85.

V.

FROM THE ANNUNCIATION THROUGH THE YOUNG ADULTHOOD OF THE LORD

RICHARD D. DRAPER

And he received not of the fullness at first, but continued from grace to grace, until he received a fullness.
DOCTRINE AND COVENANTS 93:13

The threat of death filled the air. In some it created fear; in others, bloodlust. Unless something happened shortly, hundreds, if not thousands, of innocent people would die. The Church of Christ needed a miracle, literally. In desperation, its leader, Nephi, son of Nephi and grandson of Helaman, "cried mightily unto his God in behalf of his people, yea, those who were about to be destroyed because of their faith in the traditions of their fathers" (3 Nephi 1:11).

The plan leading to this moment of prayer was to execute all who believed the prophet Samuel's prophecy: "Five years more cometh, and behold, then cometh the Son of God to redeem all those who shall believe on his name. And behold, this will I give unto you for a sign at the time of his coming; for behold, there shall be great lights in heaven, insomuch that in the night before he cometh there shall be no darkness, insomuch that it shall appear unto man as if it was day" (Helaman 14:2–3).

For reasons not explained in the text, the sign did not appear when many felt it should. Indeed, months passed and still it did not come. As a result, many began to doubt, feeling "very sorrowful, lest by any means those things which had been spoken might not come to pass" (3 Nephi 1:7).

The Church's enemies took full advantage of the possibility, "rejoicing over their brethren, saying: Behold the time is past, and the words of Samuel are not fulfilled" (3 Nephi 1:6). Over the next while, agitators began an aggressive anti-Christian campaign, and their uproar was successful. With their continued misunderstanding about the date of the appearance of the sign, the wicked were able to rally an ever-growing segment of the population against their hated brethren. When the agitators gained enough backing, they set an execution date for any who continued to wait for the birth of Christ.

In faith and loving concern for his people, Nephi raised his voice in prayer. "He cried mightily to the Lord all that day," maybe because there would be no tomorrow (3 Nephi 1:12). The Lord responded, "Lift up your head and be of good cheer; for . . . on this night shall the sign be given, and on the morrow come I into the world" (3 Nephi 1:13). Sure enough, "at the going down of the sun there was no darkness; and the people began to be astonished because there was no darkness when the night came" (3 Nephi 1:15). Among those who plotted the death of the Christians, some "fell to the earth and became as if they were dead, for they knew that the great plan of destruction which they had laid for those who believed in the words of the prophets had been frustrated" (3 Nephi 1:16). Further, "they began to fear because of their iniquity and their unbelief," and some repented of their sins (3 Nephi 1:18). Samuel was not, however, the first Nephite to know by revelation of the Lord's birth. Centuries earlier, Israel's God had opened a vision to Nephi, son of Lehi.

Nephi's Vision of the Birth of the Savior

The vision took Nephi back to Jerusalem, the city he had left only days before. The city he saw, however, was not his but one that would exist six hundred years in the future. The scene swept across other cities and towns to stop at a small hamlet that did not actually exist yet, eighty miles to the north. It would be called Nazareth. There he "beheld a virgin, . . . exceedingly fair and white" (1 Nephi 11:13).

The scene served as the stage for Nephi's angel guide to ask him a penetrating question: "Knowest thou the condescension of God?" (1 Nephi 11:16). *Condescension*—a powerful word. It describes, in this case, the voluntary waiving of dignity and suppression of power on the part of the exalted Messiah for the purpose of creating free interaction between Him and His Father's other children. Love drove the condescension. Gracious love allowed Him to overlook rank, unworthiness, social walls, and religious boundaries.[1]

The angel's question, as it was designed to, puts the story of the nativity in perspective. The event shows the condescension of a God. The Father apparently designed it to help Nephi and us understand this important aspect of the Lord's mission. That lens, as this chapter will show, helps us see better the Lord's life from conception to young adulthood.

The Witness of the Gospels

Other writers also told the story of the divine birth and youth of the Lord from a historical rather than prophetic viewpoint. These were Matthew and Luke, who saw in history the fulfillment of prophecy. Both writers drew upon already existent materials.[2] Luke tells us he had access to a number of accounts that came from eyewitnesses "even as they delivered them unto us" (Luke 1:1–2). The commonality of both records confirms the idea that the Church already possessed core information. The two accounts, however, are not identical. The differences show us that the Christian community did not yet possess a canonized account of the Lord's life.[3]

---

[1] *Merriam Webster's Dictionary of Synonyms* (Springfield, Massachusetts: Merriam Webster, 1984), s.v., "stoop."
[2] Brown, *BM*, 109–10.
[3] Brown, *BM*, 34. The Church never did receive a canonized account. From the days

One important piece they preserved was the story of the Lord's nativity. Although neither John nor Mark contains such an account, it was obviously important for Matthew's and Luke's purposes to include it.[4]

The story of the nativity not only supplied a defense against malicious accusation that Jesus was born illegitimately but also provided the early believers and those who would listen to the proclamation of the good news an important understanding of who and what Jesus was. For example, Matthew, who apparently wrote to Jews, viewed Jesus as the new Moses, whose life paralleled that of the great prophet. For him, the Lord's infancy and youth were as integral to Jesus' story as that of Moses' story, a position that may originate with the prophecy of a new prophet like Moses in the latter days.[5] Also, Matthew stressed Jesus' mission to Israel, but aspects of his witness show he was conscious of its outreach to the Gentiles. By citing Genesis 12:3 in his genealogy, Matthew was able to show that all nations are blessed through Abraham and his heirs, Jesus being the most important.[6]

Luke, who apparently wrote to Gentiles, emphasized the salvation that comes through Christ. Salvation took place, he believed, because Jesus was the Son of God as well as the Son of woman; therefore, salvation was universal. The Gentiles, therefore, had place

---

of the heretic Marcion to the present, a host of people have put together harmonies. Though they do bring details together, they also highlight the discrepancies among the texts and show that more information is yet needed.

[4] Imaginative writers in later centuries created stories to meet curiosity about this period. See Oscar Cullmann, "Infancy Gospels," in New Testament Apocrypha, ed. Wilhelm Schneemelcher, trans. R. McL. Wilson, 2 vols. (Philadelphia: Westminster/John Knox Press, 1963), 1:414–69. There may also be a subtle suggestion that Matthew and Luke were writing in a period when Christians had a greater interest in this subject, unlike an earlier period when Mark wrote his Gospel.

[5] The Gospel of Matthew is replete with parallels between Moses and Jesus. They both gave a new covenant, gathered the faithful, sought the redemption of Israel, and so forth. Many Christians saw in Jesus the fulfillment of Moses' prophecy of a future prophet. See John 1:21; Deuteronomy 18:15–18; 1 Nephi 22:20–21; Exodus 1–6.

[6] W. F. Albright and C. S. Mann, The Anchor Bible: Matthew (New York: Doubleday, 1971), 2–3.

among the Father's children.⁷ For that reason, Luke took pains to place his story in the context of world history as well as to trace the Lord's genealogy back to Adam, the father of all.

Both writers saw in Jesus the fulfillment of prophecy handed down by the Jews in their sacred writings, known today as the Old Testament. Matthew, however, focusing on the Jewish segment of the Christian community, used its witness to full advantage.⁸

The Genealogies and Their Significance

Both writers, as noted above, include the Lord's genealogy in their account. Genealogical records were important to many Jews. Among others, the Sanhedrin kept such records, mostly to assure the purity and, thus, the legitimacy of the priesthood.⁹ Luke and Matthew may have also used them in this same way—to legitimize the Lord's authority, message, and ministry.

On the surface, we might expect the genealogies to be identical. It takes only a brief comparison to find out they are not.¹⁰ This discrepancy is not surprising because each writer used the genealogy to stress his particular message. Since early times, to reconcile the differences, some scholars have postulated that Matthew recorded Joseph's

---

⁷ I. Howard Marshall, "Luke," in Freedman, ABD, 4:402–3.

⁸ The Christians used the Old Testament as a proof text for their beliefs, but Matthew standardized the way prophetic fulfillment was understood. "In finding this fulfillment, Mathew makes no attempt to interpret what we might consider the full or contextual meaning of the OT text that he cites; rather he concentrates on features of the text wherein there is a resemblance to Jesus or the NT event" (Brown, BM, 97). Thus, Matthew apparently saw in the Old Testament passages more than incidental agreement between Jesus and the Old Testament. They supported Matthew's thesis of the unity of God's plan for His children. A strong tie is evident between Jesus and Moses (Brown, BM, 104, 115). The biblical quotations in Matthew appear to be from a Palestinian recension of the Old Testament that differed slightly from both the LXX and MT, though some of the names follow the LXX. See Albright and Mann, Matthew, 3.

⁹ Robert H. Mounce, New International Commentary: Matthew (Peabody, Massachusetts: Hendrickson, 1991), 7.

¹⁰ Matthew's and Luke's genealogies have a number of discrepancies. Luke lists forty-one generations, which he traces through Nathan, and Matthew has twenty-six traced through Solomon. For a good discussion, see Mounce, Matthew, 7–8.

genealogy, whereas Luke's was actually that of Mary.[11] These have not taken into account the fact that genealogies of the period, being patriarchal, always traced male lines. That being the case, both belong to Joseph.[12] Because he took Mary as his bride, he became the legal, adopted father of the Lord. Thus, the Jews would have recognized Jesus' genealogy to be the same as Joseph's. Paul, however, records that "Jesus Christ our Lord . . . was made of the seed of David according to the flesh" (Romans 1:3). If Paul is to be taken literally, that may mean that Mary was also of Davidic descent, even if Luke does not record her ancestry.[13] Even so, we would expect to see closer agreement between the two than we see. From late antiquity, some scholars have tried to account for the discrepancies. Most feel that Matthew traced the royal lineage through Solomon, whereas Luke traced it through Solomon's half brother Nathan. What seems to have taken place is that Matthew gave the legal descent through the kingly line, which established the Lord's heirship to the throne of David.[14] Luke gave the natural or literal descent.[15]

---

[11] The point of Luke's genealogy was to show that Joseph was a descendant of Adam. His text says nothing about Mary. Apparently, Origen is the one who thought that Luke's genealogy belonged to Mary. He felt that the phrase "house of David" in Luke 1:27 modified "virgin," and thus he determined that Mary was a descendent of David. On this, see Brown, *BM*, 287. The *Protevangelium of James*, 10.1; Ignatius, *Ephesians* 18.2, and Justin Martyr, *Dialogue* 45.4 also make a similar Davidic claim. Thus, we see that later Christians of gentile extraction, not understanding Jewish law and ways, determined that Mary was Davidic. The *Protevangelium of James* 2.1 also gives Mary's parents as Anne and Joachim, but the document is not reliable. See Brown, *BM*, 287–88. The text does give Mary a tribe, however. She was a Levite (Luke 1:5, 36). See Joseph A. Fitzmyer, *The Gospel According to Luke I-IX* (New York: Doubleday, 1970), 344. If we do not follow Origen and if we assume Paul's statement in Romans 1:3 referred to Jesus' adoption by Joseph, then we have no evidence that Mary was a descendant of David. Brown, *BM*, 287–88.

[12] Donald A. Hagner, *World Biblical Commentary: Matthew 1–13*, 2 vols. (Dallas: World Books, 1993), 1:8.

[13] S. Kent Brown, *Mary and Elisabeth: Noble Daughters of God* (American Fork, Utah: Covenant Communications, 2002), 39.

[14] Matthew uses the word *egennēsen*, "to beget," which can also denote legal inheritance rather than physical descent. Matthew's point is that Jesus is the legal son of Joseph and of the line of David. Albright and Mann, *Matthew*, 9.

[15] Judah was promised the scepter (Genesis 49:10). David's house became the heir.

Both Luke and Matthew are really doing the same thing. They have preserved two strands of the Lord's genealogy. "Both establish him as a Son of David and, therefore, legal inheritor of the throne."[16] One reason they were motivated to do this seems to be that many of the early sources stressed the connection between the Messiah and the house of David (see Matthew 1:20 and Luke 1:32).[17]

When Matthew pointed out that Jesus was the son of Abraham, the son of David, he was doing more than highlighting the Lord's most prominent ancestors. The phrase "Son of David" had been interpreted by the Jews as a title for the messianic deliverer who would bring to Israel and the world the eternal and perfect kingdom of God.[18] Matthew was helping his readers make the connection.

Matthew introduced the Lord through His genealogy. Placing it at the beginning of his account, Matthew helped the reader understand who Jesus was (the Son of Abraham and the Son of David) and how that came to be (through Joseph, a descendent of David, accepting the child conceived under the power of the Holy Spirit). Though Matthew stressed Jesus' mission to Israel, like Luke he was conscious of its wider reach and so applied the promise of all nations being blessed through Abraham to the coming of the Messiah (Genesis 12:3). We should not be surprised, therefore, that Matthew preserved the intriguing story of the coming of the Magi. Their homage

---

So the first section of the genealogy comes to a close with David as king who supplanted Saul. In the second section, Matthew lists Davidic kings who reigned in Jerusalem, ending with Jeconiah, who, even with the Babylonian exile, had a son allowing the Davidic line to continue. Verse 17 in 1 Chronicles 3 mentions only the birth of Salathiel, but rabbis preserved the marvel of Jechoniah's begetting a son in captivity. The last section connects the end of the monarchy with the coming of the Messiah, thus linking the whole. See Brown, *BM*, 69, note 15.

[16] As quoted in Talmage, *JTC*, 89.

[17] Brown, *BM*, 159.

[18] As in 2 Samuel 7:4–17. See Hagner, *Matthew*, 9. Matthew's emphasis on the title "Son of David" is unique among the Gospel writers. The title stems from 2 Samuel 7:12, where God promised David that He would raise up one of David's offspring to succeed him and that through this one, God would establish His kingdom. The Jews saw in these verses a prophecy of the coming Messiah, and the title "Son of David" continued to carry strong messianic overtones. See Mounce, *Matthew*, 7.

demonstrated that righteous Gentiles recognized the seed of Abraham as a blessing to both them and the Jews.[19]

The Story Begins

Matthew tells us that Mary is both a virgin and engaged. The English word, however, hardly does justice to her actual condition. According to both Luke and Matthew, she is *mnêsteuô*—that is, betrothed (see Matthew 1:18; Luke 1:27). In Jewish culture, betrothal was a binding agreement. It was the beginning of the marriage and could be broken off only with a bill of divorce.[20]

Joseph and Mary were both young and full of hope as they entered into a one-year or perhaps a two-year period of engagement before the actual marriage—which consisted of leading the bride into the house of the bridegroom where certain formalities took place, including vows of fidelity and the bestowal of the dowry. Marriages of maidens usually took place on Wednesday, and marriages could not be celebrated on the Sabbath, the day before, or the day after, so that th e Sabbath rest would not be endangered.[21]

The Annunciation of Jesus' Birth

As the angel showed Nephi, the condescension would begin in the small hamlet of Nazareth. The town would actually not be established until the first century before the Lord's birth. Even then, it would be but a village for a long time, occupied by less than five hundred people when the Savior lived there.[22]

To a young woman named Mary (or as she pronounced it, Miriam), Gabriel came.[23] She was a lovely, virtuous woman whose

---

[19] Brown, *BM*, 53, 67–68.
[20] See S. Kent Brown, "Zacharias and Elisabeth, Joseph and Mary," in this volume.
[21] Alfred Edersheim, *Sketches of Jewish Social Life* (Peabody, Massachusetts: Hendrickson, 1994), 139, 140.
[22] Bellarmino Bagattti, *Excavations in Nazareth*, Studium Biblicum Fanciscanum 17 (Jerusalem: Franciscan Press, 1969). Though Bagatti found remains dating to the early Bronze Age, the Jewish village of Mary dates only to the first century B.C.
[23] Some scholars have questioned the virgin conception of the Lord. For a detailed

fidelity was so trusted by the Divine that her name was revealed to the American prophet King Benjamin.[24] Alma also knew of her purity and called her "precious and chosen" (Alma 7:10). Nephi understood in vision that her qualities would enable her to be the "mother of the Son of God" (1 Nephi 11:18). These qualities did not develop only in mortality; she was righteous and noble even before she was born, and, like Abraham, she seemingly stood among the great and noble spirits in the premortal world (see Abraham 3:22–23).[25] Her title, *virgin*, underscores her purity as well as the miracle of her conception.[26]

The angel Gabriel's announcement, "Hail, thou that art highly favored, the Lord is with thee: blessed art thou among women," signaled the beginning of the condescension of God (Luke 1:28).[27]

Mary was, naturally, "troubled at his saying" (Luke 1:29). The King James rendition does not do justice to her feelings. Luke chose the word *diatarassomai*, meaning to "thoroughly upset, confuse" or

---

discussion of the virgin conception, see Gerhard Delling, *TDNT*, 5:831–33. The Book of Mormon is very clear that Mary was a virgin and remained so until after the birth of her firstborn son. The Bible is also clear on the subject. See Matthew 1:18, which notes that the couple had no sexual relations until after the child was born. Of note, a minor Latin manuscript (K) and Sinaitic Syriac manuscripts (sy^s) of the New Testament change the reading of Matthew 1:25 to remove the statement that Joseph "knew" Mary. This change was likely influenced by the late doctrine of the perpetual virginity of Mary.

[24] A century and a quarter before Mary was born, an angel proclaimed to the Nephite King Benjamin that her name would be Mary. See Mosiah 3:8.

[25] Brown, *Mary*, 4.

[26] In Luke 1:27, we see an instance of Luke's carefulness in crafting his language. He does not call Mary *pais*, "girl," *paidiskē*, "little girl, or maid," or *korasion*, "maiden," but rather *parthenos*, "virgin or a young woman of marriageable age." This and the following phrase, "espoused to a man," prepare the reader for Luke 1:34. See Fitzmyer, *Gospel*, 343. Both Matthew and Luke affirm Mary's virginity at the time, though Luke's description is far closer to Deuteronomy 22:23 than Isaiah 7:14.

[27] The phrase "and when she saw him" is found in a number of ancient manuscripts but is absent in the majority of modern translations (Luke 1:29). Because the phrase is absent in the earliest manuscripts, some scholars deem it to be an interpolation. The reading is found in Codex Alexandrinus (A; fifth century), Codex Ephraemi Rescriptus (C; fifth century), and Codex Coridethianus (Q; ninth century), among others. Its absence in Codex Sinaiticus (ℵ fourth century) and Codex Vaticanus (B; fourth century) is compelling evidence for its being an interpolation.

"perplex greatly." She was a poor, if beautiful, peasant girl; yet an angel addressed her as one highly favored, one over whom the Lord watched, and one who had been singled out from all women for divine blessing. The words perplexed her, and she wondered what they could possibly mean.

The angel reassured her, saying that she had "found favour with God" (Luke 1:30). As a consequence, she would conceive and "bring forth a son" whom she was to name Jesus (Luke 1:31). He went on to tell her (and us) that her Son would be extraordinary. He would be the "Son of the Highest," inherit the "throne of his father David" (Luke 1:32), and rule over Israel forever (Luke 1:33). These attributes pointed in only one direction—Mary was going to be the mother of the Messiah.[28]

Although Mary accepted the idea that the Messiah would be born and even that she could be His mother, she wondered how that could be, "seeing I know not a man" (Luke 1:34). In response to Mary's "how" question, Gabriel gives us insight into the child's identity: He is holy, the Son of God. Though the first Christians saw much about their Messiah in Jewish terms, His conception broke with that tradition. Nowhere did the Jews understand their Messiah to be the literal Son of God.[29] This message is central to the nativity account and one of the insights that make it so precious.

Mary struggled to understand the "how," not the "if." The angel explained how the marvelous thing would be done: "The Holy Ghost shall come upon thee, and the power of the Highest shall overshadow thee: therefore also that holy thing which shall be born of thee shall be called the Son of God" (Luke 1:35). The angel's words

---

[28] Fitzmyer, *Gospel*, 337. The phrase "Of his kingdom there shall be no end" alludes to Isaiah 9:6 in the Greek Septuagint and Daniel 7:14. Fitzmyer, *Gospel*, 348. Luke 1:32–33 is a free interpretation of 2 Samuel 7:8–16. Here we find the promise of Nathan the prophet to David, which became the foundation of messianic expectation. Brown, *BM*, 310.

[29] See Richard Neitzel Holzapfel, "The Hidden Messiah," in *A Witness of Jesus Christ: The 1989 Sperry Symposium on the Old Testament*, ed. Richard Draper (Salt Lake City: Deseret Book, 1990), 80–95.

point to the divine intervention that would be required for her to conceive the Son of God. The Book of Mormon prophet Alma noted that Mary would be "overshadowed and conceive by the power of the Holy Ghost, and bring forth a son, yea, even the Son of God" (Alma 7:10). Nephi saw that "she was carried away in the Spirit," which resulted in the divine conception (1 Nephi 11:19).

The use of the term "Holy Ghost" has caused some confusion as to who the Father of Jesus was. As used by Luke and Matthew, the term "Holy Ghost" does not refer to the third member of the Godhead. The Gospel writers use the term here to describe the transforming power of God—or, as we might say, the Holy Spirit that would overshadow Mary and cause conception. That is the point of both Gospel writers—Jesus was miraculously conceived. His conception came though the interaction of divine power upon Mary.

Gabriel stressed to her the importance of the miraculous intervention. For this reason, the child that would be born of Mary would "be called the Son of God" (Luke 1:35).[30] Of note, the words Luke chose (*epeleusetai*, "to come upon," and *episkiasei*, "overshadow, cast a shadow over") hold no sexual connotations or nuances. Rather, they express the miraculous intervention on the part of God that would inaugurate Jesus' Davidic role and divine filiations.[31] Paul knew a similar tradition, stating that Jesus "was *born* after the Spirit" (Galatians 4:29; emphasis added). Luke's point is that Jesus was always the Son of God. Neither baptism nor resurrection would give Him new

---

[30] Fitzmyer, *Gospel*, 340.

[31] Some scholars have suggested that it was used as a euphemism for a quasisexual union, a sacred marriage (*hieros gamos*), as early as the sixteenth century (see Brown, *BM*, 290). Even some Latter-day Saints have speculated regarding "how" (see Joseph F. Smith, *Box Elder News*, Thursday, January 28, 1915, 3–4, as cited in *Messages of the First Presidency* and Bruce R. McConkie, *DNTC*, 1:83. Harold B. Lee, however, provides some caution on such speculation, demonstrating that no official LDS position has been taken on the subject (see Harold B. Lee, *Teachings of Harold B. Lee* [Salt Lake City: Bookcraft, 1996], 13–14). In this chapter, I have chosen to follow the theme developed in the scriptures, which emphasizes the miraculous and spiritual nature of the conception.

status.[32] Those events merely revealed to the more general Christian audience what was already known in the inner circle.

The angel also shared with Mary wonderful news; another miracle had taken place: "Thy cousin Elisabeth, she hath also conceived a son in her old age" (Luke 1:36).[33] Within a short time, Mary made the trip south to find her cousin. Additional confirmations were given (see Luke 1:40–45).

Joseph's Reaction to Mary's Pregnancy

For three months, Mary stayed with Elisabeth, making the life of the older woman easier with both physical and spiritual support; but Mary's stay had to end. Very likely, she stayed until John was born, though Luke does not so state.

As she traveled toward Nazareth, concerns must have flooded her mind. At the home of her relatives, there had been complete understanding. Indeed, Mary had had to explain nothing because of the sign and revelation God had given Elisabeth (see Luke 1:44). There, "her condition had served to confirm the testimony of Zacharias and Elisabeth; but how would her word be received at her own home"—and especially by Joseph?[34]

The text, albeit indirectly, gives the answer: Joseph did not "buy it."—As faithful and believing as he was, her story was just too much. The only rational explanation was that she had either been raped or committed adultery, making divorce an option to keep his family's honor intact.[35] We can imagine the heartache both must have

---

[32] See Richard Neitzel Holzapfel, "Jesus in the Wilderness: Baptism, Fasting, and Temptations," in this volume.

[33] The word in the text does not actually state the nature of the kinship. "Cousin" is *anepsios*; Luke uses *syggenis*, which means "kinswoman." See Fitzmyer, *Gospel*, 352. Wycliff's translation of the New Testament is the one that popularized the idea that they were cousins. See Brown, *Mary*, 31.

[34] Talmage, *JTC*, 84.

[35] Fitzmyer, *Gospel*, 344. Because the Mishnah was composed in the third century B.C., we must be cautious in applying too much of its teachings to the period of the Lord. Nonetheless, because it does reflect earlier ages, it is one of our best sources for the life and times of the Lord. See Herbert Danby, *The Mishnah* (London: Oxford University

experienced at the time. She had such wonderful news, but he would not hear her. He had loved and trusted her, and he felt she had betrayed him.

Rumor must have whispered in the lanes of this small village and hissed in the homes of this tight-knit community.[36] Some neighbors may have guessed that the child was Joseph's, and others probably suggested worse things. In Judea, custom allowed some latitude in the area of intimacy between the betrothed, and should the bride become pregnant, the baby was considered legitimate.[37] But conservative Galilee was not Judea. Here such things were frowned upon. Making the situation worse for Mary, the families would have known that the child was not Joseph's. We might wonder if the fathers spoke and if they discussed the law dealing with such a condition.[38] Joseph's father may have insisted that Mary's father was under obligation to deliver "a maid," a virgin, and it seemed he could not.[39] The irony of the situation was that he could, but who could understand the miracle that made that possible? Hurt feelings, disappointment, and perhaps even anger may have dominated the moment.

Joseph still had his option. A strict reading of the law demanded that Mary be stoned. The legal system, however, had grown ever less severe; and the scribes took the phrase in the law, "put away evil from Israel," as allowing for divorce (Deuteronomy 22:22). Joseph, a practicing Jew, was compelled to do something. Though unwilling to expose her to death or even open disgrace, he felt that divorce was necessary.[40] His struggle reveals both his upright and merciful nature.

Press, 1933), Ketuboth 4:4-5.

[36] The text suggests that others became aware as well, for "she was found with child" (Matthew 1:18).

[37] Henri Daniel-Rops, *Daily Life in the Time of Jesus*, trans. Patrick O'Brian (New York: Hawthorn Books, 1962), 142.

[38] Deuteronomy 22:13–21 discusses the penalty for loss of a woman's virtue and also the penalty if she was falsely accused.

[39] Brown, *Mary*, 47–48.

[40] Joseph was a righteous man; therefore, he followed the law (Matthew 1:19). Yet he did not want to publicly shame Mary. The Greek word *deigmatizō* meant "to expose" or "to humiliate in public," from *deigma* "specimen" or "example." He decided to break

Yielding to these, he decided to proceed—but without accusation of serious crime, which was his right. He would "put her away privily"—that is, quietly (Matthew 1:19).[41] Being divorced quietly, however, does not mean secretly, even though the English word "privily" means that.[42] To become engaged to Mary publicly and then divorce her secretly would have left her in horrible circumstances. It would have deprived her, among other things, of ever being able to marry again. No, Joseph decided he would not make a public example of her. In the quiet of her home and before two witnesses, he would hand her a writ of divorcement. Then, the deed would be done.

If gracious, Joseph was nonetheless determined. Seemingly, only angelic administration changed his mind. The words of the angel were most reassuring: "Joseph, thou son of David, fear not to take unto thee Mary thy wife" (Matthew 1:20). They reveal that heaven recognized Mary as Joseph's wife. Further, they gave assurance that the law had not been broken. Through the power of the Holy Spirit, she had conceived while keeping her virginity intact.[43] Finally, the salutation, "Joseph, thou son of David" (Matthew 1:20), meant to Joseph that, though he was of kingly lineage, marriage with Mary would cast no shadow upon his family status."[44]

The angel's words revealed another fact—not about Joseph or Mary but the child Mary would bear. The angel told Joseph to call the child "Jesus," explaining, "He shall save his people from their sins" (Matthew 1:21). We use an anglicized version of the Greek *Iēsous*. The name is a shortened form of the Hebrew meaning "Jehovah helps." However, popular etymology at the time connected the name to a root that meant "to save." The angel gave it this nuance.[45]

---

off the marriage the easiest way the law allowed—before two witnesses and without pressing charges. See Danby, *The Mishnah*, Sotah 1.5, and Mounce, *Matthew*, 10.

[41] The Greek word *lathra* means "secretly," but it is often translated "quietly."
[42] See Brown, *Mary*, 128.
[43] Brown, *BM*, 127.
[44] Talmage, *JTC*, 85.
[45] The name is a shortened form (yēšûaʿ) of the name Joshua (yᵉhôšûaʿ) from the root yšʿ, "to save. See Brown, *BM*, 131.

Matthew, following his pattern, commented on the prophetic nature of the event, quoting Isaiah 7:14. In that scripture, the child born of the virgin is called "Immanuel"—that is, "God with us." Jesus was not called by that name, but Matthew saw not so much a literal naming as what the child represented and the role He would play in the salvation of God's people. In other words, the Messiah was both Immanuel and Jesus; He embodied both God's presence and God's saving power.[46]

We can only imagine Joseph's relief when he understood that his bride-to-be had told the truth. Perhaps he also felt sorrow for not believing her. One thing is for sure—hearts were mended as he took her and her child to be his own. By taking Mary into his home, when or wherever that was, he assumed public responsibility for the mother and child. Later, in Bethlehem, by naming the child, Joseph formally acknowledged his role as the Savior's adopted father.[47]

Though Joseph willingly accepted Mary, the circumstances meant that she was deprived of the delights usually accompanying a marriage: the party the night before, the large escort the next day that accompanied the bride to the groom's home, and the excitement of being, even if for just a few hours, treated as a queen.[48] Instead, Mary probably waited in seclusion for the time of her quiet wedding to take place.[49]

The wedding may never have happened in Nazareth. If we take Luke at his word, she was still betrothed when the couple came to Bethlehem (Luke 2:5).[50] The reason Joseph did not yet take her into his house before the babe was born may have been, paradoxically, to safeguard the fact of Mary's virginity, an important witness that Jesus was the Son of God.

---

[46] Hagner, *Matthew*, 22.
[47] See Danby, *The Mishnah*, Baba Barha 8:6, and Brown, *BM*, 139.
[48] Ralph Gower, *The New Manners and Customs of Bible Times* (Chicago: Moody Press, 1987), 64.
[49] Brown, *Mary*, 48–49.
[50] At that point in the record, Luke still refers to her as "betrothed" (Greek *en-mésteumené*).

Filthy rumor, however, must have spread, putting its own ugly but believable spin on Mary's circumstances. The air would have reeked with its stench. Years later, the smell still clung to Jesus' ministry (see John 8:19, 41).[51] Perhaps, then, the announcement commanding Jewish males to return to their tribal headquarters came as a relief. It gave reason for Joseph and Mary to leave Nazareth.

Bethlehem

Eighty-five miles south of Nazareth and five more from Jerusalem sits Bethlehem along the way of the patriarchs.[52] The small village had an illustrious reputation. There Rachel died (Genesis 48:7); there Ruth lived with Naomi and married Boaz (Ruth 1:22); there David was born; and there, in the seventh century B.C., Chinham built an inn (that is, a khan) for weary travelers (Jeremiah 41:17). Many Jews believed, correctly, that the Messiah would come from that city.

Luke tells us that Rome ordered a general census that included Palestine. The Jewish Sanhedrin took the occasion to number the members of the tribes by having each family head return to the capital of his tribe. Thus, Joseph left Nazareth just at the time Mary was about due to deliver her child.

The enrollment likely did not force Mary to go to Bethlehem. As noted, more likely the many wicked tongues of rumor did it. Under such circumstances, she would not want to be far from him with whom she shared the divine truths.[53]

The couple would have traveled with a group for protection. However, with Mary being so close to delivery, they may have had to

---

[51] The early Christian father Origen (A.D. 185–232) preserves a long-persistent rumor that Jesus was the illegitimate son of a Roman soldier named Pantera. See Origen, *Against Celsus* 1.32, 33. The discovery of a first-century tombstone at Bingerbruck, Germany, fueled the same fire during the twentieth century. The inscription reads in translation, "Tiberius Julius Abdes Pantera, an archer, native of Sidon, Phoenicia, who in A.D. 9 was transferred to service in Germany."

[52] A principal north/south road that went from the Negev to Galilee along the ridge of the mountains.

[53] Talmage, JTC, 104.

move more slowly than the group. For that reason, they were perhaps among the last to arrive in Bethlehem. Joseph sought suitable housing but could find none. That is not to say that every nook in every place was already filled. The caravansary (Greek *pandocheion*), as crowded as it was, would likely have had room. Joseph was not looking for one of these overly public places to stay. Luke, careful with words, states that Joseph was looking for a *kataluma*—that is, an upper room in a private home.[54] Having ties to Bethlehem, Joseph may have been hoping to stay with relatives, but he arrived after their rooms were already full. He needed privacy and, because of the hospitable nature of the times, relatives may have suggested he use their stable. People in that culture lived close to their animals, some even using the ground floor to house them at night. Therefore, to have Mary use such a place as lodging would not have seemed an odd suggestion.

Later tradition speaks of Jesus being born in a cave.[55] The tradition may be right, as people during this period often exploited such opportunities to expand their living quarters and storage area by including caves as a part of the home.[56] Bethlehem had a number of limestone caves that people used for barns, storage, and, in some cases, lodging.

In privacy, but also in the humblest of circumstances, the Savior of the world and the king of the Jews was born. In His veins ran the blood of prophets, priests, and kings. Both Moses and David were His ancestors. His lot, however, was not to be born in the halls of the high priest or the palace of a prince. His condescension meant He would take up His abode with the common, the humble, the '*Am Ha-'aretz*—

---

[54] The Septuagint uses *kataluma* for five different Hebrew words, and "caravansary" is one. However, Luke seems to have chosen his words well. He knew the difference between a *pandocheion*, "caravansary" (see Luke 10:34) and a *kataluma*, "a guest room" (see Luke 22:11).

[55] Justin Martyr stated that Jesus was born in a cave (*Dialogue with Trypho*, 78), and Origen notes that one had become a tourist site by his time (*Against Celsus* 1.51).

[56] Jerome Murphy-O'Connor, *The Holy Land: An Oxford Archaeological Guide from Earliest Times to 1700* (Oxford: Oxford University Press, 1998), 374–75.

the people of the land. So it was that in a stable, Mary brought forth her "firstborn" son.

Luke mentions no one else being present, but we can wonder whether the local midwife may not have been called, with the woman of the household assisting as women have done over the ages, or whether family members who lived in Bethlehem may have assisted during this tender time. With Joseph, alone or with a few others, Jesus came into the world. He was the firstborn, not "the only born," as later tradition tried to render the phrase.[57] Thus, he was entitled to all the rights of the eldest son under the Mosaic law.[58]

Mary wrapped her Son, as was common, in long cloth strips (see Luke 2:7). These she had likely brought with her so she could comfort and protect Him. Then, she put Him to rest in a manger-cradle.

Angelic Visitation to the Shepherds

Sometime during the evening, in the grazing pastures not far away, near one of the sheep cotes, a group of shepherds lay resting when the "angel of the Lord came upon them" (Luke 2:9). Just how the angel did that, the record does not say, but the visitation was accompanied with such glory that it frightened the men. Quickly, the angel reassured them to "fear not" and explained that he brought "tidings of great joy, which shall be to all people" (Luke 2:10). The angel's words emphasize the universal nature of the joyful message. It was not just Bethlehem or Judea or even Jewry that would find joy in the tidings—but "all people."

The angel then gave them the news: "Unto you is born this day in the city of David a Saviour, which is Christ the Lord" (Luke 2:11). It was no longer just the glory that was startling but also the message. The angel proclaimed that the babe was "Savior," the term suggesting not only His duty but also his name. Further, this Savior was also the

---

[57] *Prōtotokos* is sometimes used as a synonym for *monogenēs*, "only begotten," but it also means "firstborn among many." In light of Mark 6:3, the latter is probably preferred.
[58] Brown, BM, 398.

long-awaited Messiah, who was also Lord.[59] That last word, "Lord" (Greek *kurios*), echoes the Hebrew *adonai*, the name used as a substitute for Jehovah. If that is true, then the shepherds understood that the Babe was not only Savior, the Messiah, but also their God and King, Jehovah. Little wonder they found the message startling.

If that was not enough, the shepherds immediately found themselves before a multitude of angels praising God and singing, "Glory to God in the highest, and on earth peace, good will toward men" (Luke 2:14).[60]

The shepherds, in their excitement, decided not to wait until morning to seek the infant but to go immediately to "see this thing which is come to pass" (Luke 2:15). The King James Version misses an important nuance in the shepherds' words found in the Greek. The men did not say, "Let us see this thing" but rather "Let us see this deed." The Greek *rēma* means "word" but also "deed." It is the "deed" that speaks volumes here.[61]

Interestingly, the angel did not give them directions to the Babe but rather told them what to look for.[62] First, the child would be a newborn, a baby just days, if not hours, old.[63] Second, the child would be found in a manger. Those two clues narrowed the shepherds' search. They knew that the child's parents must be visiting because he was in a stable, and they knew the birth had taken place within a

---

[59] Precisely what the angel said about Jesus, because of an ambiguity in the Greek, is not clear. He is definitely Savior, but because a definite article is not used before the word "Lord" (*kurios*), the angel may have referred to Him as the anointed Lord. Whatever the case, the shepherds must have understood the whole as an announcement that the long-awaited Deliverer had arrived.

[60] Because of an ambiguity in the Greek, we have a difficult time knowing just whom the blessing of peace includes. A single letter in one word of the angels' song changes the meaning considerably. Some manuscripts have *eudokia*, "good will to men," giving the cast a universal nature, whereas others have *eudokias*, "men characterized by goodwill," giving a selective cast. Based on Luke 2:10, the former seems to be the better reading.

[61] Brown, BM, 405.

[62] Though the KJV states that the angel gave them "a sign" (Luke 2:12), the JST mentions none. Rather, it reads, "And this is the way you shall find the babe, he is wrapped in swaddling clothes, and is lying in a manger." See JST Luke 2:12 in *The Holy Scriptures: Inspired Version* (Independence, Missouri: Herald Publishing House, 1974).

[63] Luke has the angel use the word *brephos*, meaning a newborn.

day or so. It may have been morning before they could find help for their search. They probably checked with midwives and asked around and, before long, found success. They found the child secure with His parents and worshiped Him. We can imagine how they shared with Joseph and Mary the experience of the night before and of the wonder of the angel's message.

The shepherds returned to their flocks—but only after sharing the news with others. The impact of their testimonies was tremendous, for "all they that heard wondered at those things that were told them" (Luke 2:18). The nuance of the Greek *thaumazō*, "wondered," is to marvel or be astonished, but if the shepherds shared with others what they themselves knew by direct revelation, we should not be surprised that the people were astonished. The Messiah had come, and though it was unheard of, He was Jehovah.

Once the shepherds gave their witness, they seem to have done little more, perhaps because they were not supposed to. They acted as witnesses, which began the song of praise on the earth that echoed the song of the heavenly hosts.[64] That was enough for now.

What they could not know was that to the east, certain wise men saw a star and, in excitement, prepared to take a journey to find the king of the Jews. And further east, half a world away, Saints prayed out their thanks to God for a night in which there was no darkness and in which their lives were spared.

The joyful and mind-boggling events, however, as thrilling as they were, could not get in the way of obedience to the law of Moses. So when Jesus was eight days old, the couple took Him to be named and circumcised.

The Circumcision and Naming of the Lord

If they had not done so before, the couple must have married shortly after the Lord's birth for, at the circumcision, Joseph acted as husband and father. He followed the instructions of the angel to have

---

[64] Brown, BM, 429.

the child named Jesus. Luke does not follow Matthew in defining the name. For him, what is important is that the couple obeyed the angel's instructions and God's written word.[65]

That Jesus was not exempt from the law is important to the Gospel writers. He was born under the law, submitted to the law, and fulfilled the law. His mission was to move humankind from the lesser to the greater law. But before He could do that, He had to come under the law Himself. His circumcision showed that He did.

How different His circumcision ceremony was from that of His relative John. The latter was celebrated with friends and family and much rejoicing. Joseph and Mary, being far from those closest to them, likely had few family and friends, if any, to celebrate the Child's coming under the law and being given His heavenly invoked name.[66]

The Presentation at the Temple

Luke tells us that when the time came for Mary's purification, she and Joseph traveled to Jerusalem. Women remained ceremonially unclean for a period of forty days after the birth of a boy, eighty after a girl (Leviticus 12:2–8). The law also stated that birth, not conception, rendered a woman unclean; therefore, even the virginal conception of the Lord did not spare Mary from having to become ritually pure.[67] Now the time was up, and she could enter the temple and make the prescribed offerings: a burnt offering of a lamb and a sin offering of a dove. If the offerer was poor, the law allowed a dove to replace the lamb (see Leviticus 1:14; 4:7).

That Mary used two turtledoves for her offering indicates the family's lowly circumstance, but that does not mean they belonged to the abject poor. Most people at that time would have had a difficult time sacrificing a lamb.[68] Though the young couple went to the temple in

---

[65] Brown, BM, 433.
[66] Plummer, *An Exegetical Commentary on the Gospel According to Saint Matthew* (London: E. Stock, 1909), 62.
[67] Brown, BM, 436.
[68] Plummer, *Commentary*, 65.

compliance with the law, the Father took the occasion to further bless them and spread the word about His Son.

The temple complex was colossal, almost a quarter of a mile in length. Though the family was likely in the court of women, a much smaller area, it was still about eight acres in size and was often thronged with busy people.[69] There the Spirit drew two aged souls, Simeon and Anna. The spiritual workings show the importance of witnesses who could counteract rumor and their potential damage.

Simeon was "just," "devout," and, according to Luke, "waiting for the consolation of Israel"—that is to say, for the coming of the Messiah (Luke 2:25).[70] His expectation was sure because the Holy Ghost had revealed to him "that he should not see death, before he had seen the Lord's Christ" (Luke 2:26).

We see prophecy flowing in the controlled rapture of Simeon's psalm, its beauty equaling some of David's best.[71] In ecstasy he exclaimed, "Lord, now lettest thou thy servant depart in peace" (Luke 2:29). Simeon's words repeat those of a slave requesting freedom either from a hard and arduous task or from slavery itself. For Simeon, death was release. He could go peacefully, knowing that the Messiah had come and that all would be well with Israel.[72]

Simeon's words leave no room for any political agenda, for the Messiah would be "a light to lighten the Gentiles" (Luke 2:32). He shows that even Gentiles belong in the Messiah's circle.[73] Simeon's testimony openly teaches that Jesus will bring salvation to Gentiles and Jews alike.

Simeon understood something else—something much less glorious. In his message, we see little of the rejoicing of the angels. Here

---

[69] Brown, Mary, 57.

[70] Simeon is described as *eulabēs*, conscious about holy matters. Plummer, Commentary, 66.

[71] Plummer, Commentary, 67.

[72] Simeon knows his messianic scriptures well. His words echo Isaiah 52:10, "before all nations," and Isaiah 49:6, "light to the Gentiles, salvation unto the end of the earth." Plummer, Commentary, 68–69.

[73] Brown, BM, 443.

we glimpse a future suffering. "This child," he revealed, "is set for the fall and rising again of many of Israel; and for a sign which shall be spoken against" (Luke 2:34). History has proven the accuracy of Simeon's inspiration. The Lord did indeed divide Israel, causing most to fall and many to rise. Further, as Simeon's words show, Israel would not be able to ignore the Lord. Simeon was set "for a sign." The Greek, *semeion*, denotes a token impossible to ignore by which something else is made known.[74] In this case, what is made known is God's new covenant.

Simeon's words also reveal that the harsh reality that will divide Israel will not leave Mary unscathed. Indeed, Mary was told, "A sword shall pierce through thy own soul also" (Luke 2:35). The sword that would pass through Mary's heart was the discriminating sword, for "the thoughts of many hearts [would] be revealed" (Luke 2:35).[75] It would lay bare what people really were, exposing their deepest secrets and personal commitments, more especially of those who would oppose Him.[76]

The prophesied pain touched home when Mary's own children, for a time, rejected Jesus' messiahship.[77] It also touched home another time. The Joseph Smith Translation has Simeon say, "A spear shall pierce through him to the wounding of thine own soul" (JST Luke 2:35).[78] Thus, at home and at the cross, Mary carried in her soul the wounds of the sword and spear.

Softening the blow of the latter part of Simeon's blessing came the praise of the aged prophetess, Anna.[79] Her words are not recorded, but she shared her testimony when she "spake of him to all them that looked for redemption in Jerusalem" (Luke 2:38).

---

[74] Plummer, *Commentary*, 70.
[75] Fitzmyer, *Gospel*, 423.
[76] Compare Doctrine and Covenants 33:1.
[77] For example, see John 7:5, which states that his brothers did not "believe in him."
[78] In *The Holy Scriptures: Inspired Version*, Luke 2:35.
[79] Because of the ambiguity of the Greek, we have a difficult time in knowing just how old she was. According to one reading, she would have been over a hundred; according to another, eighty-four. For discussion, see Plummer, *Commentary*, 72.

Both Joseph and Mary "marveled at the things that were spoken of him" (Luke 2:33). Neither could grasp the full nature of the child with whom God had entrusted them. Nonetheless, they heard, pondered, believed, and acted.

The Visit of the Wise Men

The couple did not return to Nazareth, perhaps because rumor was still alive and active there or because they felt they wanted to raise Jesus in the city of David. Joseph seems to have found work in the area. Sections of the courtyard of Herod's temple were yet under construction, so employment was available for a skilled mason, carpenter, and stone cutter.[80] He was also able to find a house in the village for his family (see Matthew 2:11). The record suggests that the couple settled down with their new child. The months passed quietly.[81]

What kind of notoriety they may have had neither Matthew nor Mark say, but at the very least, the streets were not haunted by rumor. The record suggests that the infant and His family actually made very little stir, at least initially, for word never got back to the twisted, jealous, and ever-paranoid Herod, at least not from Bethlehem.[82] Eventually, however, it did arrive and was met with fear.

Herod's knowledge of the Child came from the visit of a foreign delegation who asked where they could find the future king of the Jews.[83] Matthew refers to them as "wise men from the east" and gives

---

[80] Brown, Mary, 59.

[81] One way of reading Matthew 2:16 suggests that the couple was there for as much as two years. Herod's death decree took in all who were two and under. According to S. Kent Brown, even though Herod was capable of much, he knew his limits and, therefore, would not have pushed much beyond this (Brown, Mary, 60). Because John was six months older than Jesus, Herod, not being able to distinguish among rumors, may have reached just beyond the dating of John's birth to sweep the infants into his death net. In that case, the couple was in Bethlehem for about eighteen months before being forced to flee.

[82] For a recent reevaluation of Herod, see Richard Neitzel Holzapfel, "King Herod," in *Masada and the World of the New Testament*, ed. John F. Hall and John W. Welch (Provo: BYU Studies, 1997), 35–73.

[83] Luke seems to know nothing of the magi. Admittedly, this is an argument from

no other information about them (Matthew 2:1).[84] Their title, however, was associated with Zoroastrian priests but also referred to men adept at lore, magic, interpretation of dreams, astrology, and astronomy. During the time of the Lord, the reputation of magi was mixed. Some were considered top scientists, whereas others were seen as charlatans and magicians.[85] Matthew shows them as wholly admirable. They seem to represent the best of the pagan priests who were sincere in seeking out the Lord. This description fits Matthew's thesis. He would be sensitive to anything that would show that Jesus was the universal Savior, and having righteous Gentiles recognize His star and come seeking Him fits his thesis perfectly.[86]

An issue arises about where pagan priests would get their knowledge of the Jewish Messiah. It certainly seems plausible that they got it from Jewish sources. Babylon had a strong population of Jews, some even serving in the government. Apparently, certain wise men developed an interest in Jewish matters. The Babylonian Jews were not without their messianic expectations, and some of those interested in prophecy would have expected some kind of celestial harbinger to mark the coming of their Lord. Bolstered by the prophetic oracle of Balaam (Numbers 24:17) that a star would come out of Jacob, some took the text literally and awaited the sign.[87] The magi may have responded accordingly. Thinking the king would be born in the Jewish capital, the believing magi approached Herod. Their

---

silence, but given Luke's sensitivity toward Gentiles, it is difficult to believe he would not have mentioned them. Plummer, *Commentary*, 73.

[84] The idea that they were kings may have come from Isaiah 49:7 and Psalm 72:10. Not until the eighth century do we find the names Caspar, Belthasar, and Melchior.

[85] See Philo, *On the Special Laws*, 3.18, 100–10, where he speaks of both kinds. W. K. L. Clarke, *Divine Humanity* (London: SPCK, 1936), 41–51, notes that the term is pejorative elsewhere in the scriptures and that *Didache* 2.2 warns the Christians away from such practices. C. S. Mann, "Epiphany—Wise Men or Charlatans?" in *Theology* 61 (1958): 495–500, argues that they were Jewish wise men who dabbled in astrology but gave up the tools of their trade—that is, incense and myrrh; Greek magical papyri show these were used as part of the incantation ritual.

[86] Brown, *BM*, 166–68.

[87] Albright, *Matthew*, 15. Matthew, however, does not cite a proof text for the star, possibly because he saw none.

question filled the king with consternation.[88] His agitation exposes the chasm that existed among the diverse groups of Jews at the time; like the Sadducees, Herod did not accept the prophetic books as authoritative (see JST Matthew 2:4).[89] The gathering of the political leaders (King Herod and his court) and the religious leaders (the chief priest and scribes) at the birth of Jesus to decide what would be His fate only foreshadowed the gathering of a similar group at the end of His ministry—the political leaders (Pilate and his court) and the religious leaders (chief priests and scribes).[90]

Herod's own wise men were able to answer the magis' inquiry. They knew the scriptures well and could tell him, based on Micah 5:2, that the Messiah would come out of Bethlehem.[91] Herod attempted to use the wise men as his informants, telling them to bring news of the of the Babe's whereabouts so he, too, might worship Him. In his dark heart, however, was anything but a desire to worship.

As the wise men traveled, to their delight, the star once again appeared and, more, acted as a guide to the very home of Jesus. Those exposed to Roman culture would not have found the story strange because their culture believed that stars announced the coming of great persons and could act as a guide to them.[92]

Just what this star was has led to much conjecture.[93] A comet, a conjunction between Jupiter and Saturn, a supernova—none of

---

[88] The Greek *tarassō* suggests strong mental agitation and consternation.

[89] Albright, *Matthew*, 12.

[90] Hagner, *Matthew*, 28.

[91] Matthew renders Micah 5:2 differently from both the Septuagint and the Hebrew Masoretic text. Both state that Bethlehem was "too small to be numbered among the thousands of Judah." The smallness of the site is designed to contrast, and therefore enhance, the greatness of the ruler who will come from there. Brown, *BM*, 184.

[92] For example, a star led Aeneas to the spot of the founding of Rome. Virgil, *Aeneid* 2.695–97.

[93] Some scholars have suggested that the wise men initially saw the beginning of the conjunction of Venus and Jupiter in the spring of 7 B.C. and left for Jerusalem. When they arrived, they experienced the very rare conjunction of Jupiter and Saturn (once every 794 years) in the Sign of the Fishes. Jupiter was the star of the universe, Saturn the star of Palestine, and the constellation of the Fishes represented the last days. For a discussion of possibilities, see Albright, *Matthew*, 13, and Brown, *BM*, 170–73.

these really work. A new star was, however, a sign in the western continent (see Helaman 14:5; 3 Nephi 1:21), suggesting its reality. Even so, a natural explanation may not be the answer. Matthew 2:9 gives the star a miraculous quality, having it lead the wise men to the home in Bethlehem. Whatever the magi first saw in the east, it motivated them to make a significant and fairly dangerous journey. Matthew's point is that divine guidance rewarded their faith.[94]

We can imagine the wonder of the young couple as these easterners knocked on their door and asked to see the royal king. Used to the demands of hospitality, Mary and Joseph would have welcomed and fed them. How long they stayed the record does not say. It does say that they left treasures: gold, incense, and myrrh. From as early as the second century, some, under the influence of Psalm 72:10, 11, 15 and Isaiah 60:6, have assigned symbolic meaning to the gifts.[95] In reality, they were presents worthy of royalty and a great blessing to the young family who would soon have to leave all and flee far from Judea.

The wise men did not fulfill Herod's request; warned by a dream, they left quietly, the last of the divinely appointed witnesses of the Lord's coming. Their testimony added to that of the peasant rural shepherds and the city-dwelling prophet and prophetess. "The testimonies concerning the Messiah's birth are from two extremes, the lowly shepherds in the Judean field, and the learned magi from the far east. We cannot think this is the result of mere chance, but that in it may be discerned the purpose and wisdom of God."[96] Each class of society had its representatives and its spokespersons.

Slaughter of the Babes

With the departure of the wise men, the attention the young family received may have quieted down, but it was too late. Herod had already heard enough to feel threatened. Probably feeling frustrated at the snub of the wise men and frightened at their news, he moved to

---

[94] Hagner, *Matthew*, 30.
[95] For a discussion on these, see Albright, *Matthew*, 13.
[96] Talmage, *JTC*, 109.

destroy the posed threat. He knew where to vent his wrath: Bethlehem. But to make sure, he included the wider area of Ephrathah near Bethlehem.[97]

The two villages probably had little more than five hundred souls living in them at the time. That means an estimate of fewer than forty babes would have been killed.[98] Because these were mere peasant children, their horror went unnoticed in any record that has survived.[99] That Josephus and others simply did not record the slaughter tells us more about the cruelty of the age than it does the lack of historical reality.[100] Matthew, however, saw great significance in the deed. Once again prophecy was fulfilled—here, unfortunately, with Rachael "weeping for her children" (Jeremiah 31:15).

The Flight into Egypt

Herod's insanely driven move did not accomplish its objective. In an inspired dream, an angel warned Joseph to move, and Joseph did not hesitate. Awakening his sleeping wife, he gave her the horrible news. They packed what they could and escaped into the night. Perhaps the very portable gold, incense, and myrrh made it possible to travel into Egypt and set up house until Joseph could find employment.[101] How long they stayed the record does not say. Herod's death

---

[97] The territory of Rachel's people was in Benjamin at Zalzah, about eleven miles north of Jerusalem. However, not long after the tribe settled there, the clan of Ephrathah moved close to Bethlehem (Micah 5:2). Brown, BM, 205–6.

[98] Even with Herod's expanded time frame and geographical area, probably fewer than 40 innocents were killed. The early Church greatly exaggerated the number: Byzantine tradition put the number at 14,000, Syrian at 64,000, and a few, influenced by the book of Revelation, 144,000. See Hagner, *Matthew*, 37.

[99] See Albright, *Matthew*, 19; Brown, BM, 204–5.

[100] Mounce, *Matthew*, 18.

[101] The anti-Christian Celsus (who opposed such Christian apologists as Origen during the early third century) preserved the tradition that Jesus worked in Egypt and there learned the magic arts, thus corroborating, if unintentionally, the essence of the biblical account. See Origen, *Contra Celsum* 1.28, 38. "Said R. Eliezer to them, 'But didn't Ben Stada [Jesus] bring witchcraft from Egypt by writing the formulas on his skin?'" Jacob Neusner, trans., *Babylonian Talmud* (Atlanta: Scholars Press, 1993), 48; Danby, *The Mishnah*, Shabbat 12.5.3.

must have come shortly after they left. Still, Herod was not the only enemy. There were others, apparently equally dangerous, from whom the couple needed to hide. So the Lord had them wait in seclusion until "they [were] dead which sought the young child's life" (Matthew 2:20).

This little window does give us a glimpse of the fear and even hostility that the news of the Lord's coming caused among powerful people. "The bitter opposition that would plague the ministry of Mary's Son almost thirty years later had already raised its head. But because Mary and Joseph spent those intervening years first in Egypt and then in Nazareth, far from Bethlehem and Jerusalem and centers of power, the opposition which had begun to flare in the early months of Jesus' life died down, giving Mary an opportunity to raise the Son out of the gaze of powerful and hateful eyes."[102]

The Return to Nazareth

Meanwhile, the family did its best in Egypt. An inspired dream informed Joseph that his family could safely go home (Matthew 2:20). Joseph needed no inspiration to tell him not to settle in Bethlehem. Herod's malevolent son, Archelaus, reigned over the area, making it one to avoid.[103]

Once again, Matthew assures his readers that all these events were foreseen. He cites Hosea 11:1, "called my son out of Egypt," to show providence at work and to tie the lives of Moses and Jesus together. Matthew does not overemphasize the Moses-Christ connection, but it does play in the background. Moses was Israel's physical savior, whereas Jesus would be its spiritual one.[104] Before the Lord could begin His saving work, however, He needed to grow up.

---

[102] Brown, *Mary*, 61–62.

[103] Archelaus was technically an ethnarch, not a king. He actually ruled over Judea, Samaria, and Idumea. His reign was short-lived. Because of his dictatorial and brutal ways, massacring three thousand Jews at one point, the Jews persuaded Rome to remove him. See Josephus, *War*, 2.6.2; *AJ*, 17. 13. 2.

[104] Hagner, *Matthew*, 34. Hosea 11:1 actually refers to the Exodus, but Matthew saw in it dual fulfillment and used it to explain the move to and from Egypt, ending in Nazareth. Matthew's quotation does not follow the LXX but suggests he had access to a Greek source that followed the Hebrew. See Brown, *BM*, 220.

Nazareth, despite its disadvantages, was the right place. So, in spite of rumor, the two were drawn back to family in Nazareth. During the time they were away, some of Mary and Joseph's other children would have been born, perhaps as many as three or four. Because Jewish tradition taught that the Lord blessed righteous women with children, Mary's growing family would have taken away much of her earlier reproach. That would mean they returned home as a respectful family, bringing to their parents grandchildren. So it was that Jesus grew up in the secluded and unmessianic village of Nazareth.[105]

Matthew shows his readers that the couple's return to Nazareth was foreseen. Everything happened "that it might be fulfilled which was spoken by the prophets, He shall be called a Nazarene" (Matthew 2:23). A problem is associated with Matthew's statement—unlike that of any other. In this case, no such prophecy is found in the Bible or any ancient source. Also, Matthew's introduction is different. He uses the plural, "prophets," suggesting that he was not looking at one but at several sources.[106] He could be saying, "What is found in the prophets generally is that he shall be called a Nazarene."[107] Thus, Matthew was able to account for Galilee as the place of the Lord's ministry (Matthew 4:12–16), and he was also able to justify unmessianic Nazareth as the Lord's hometown.

There the boy began to grow up. "Our knowledge of Jewish life in

---

[105] Nathaniel's words in John 1:46 suggest just how difficult it was to believe that the Messiah could come from the hamlet.

[106] Perhaps he is deriving a prophecy from several sources. Note how he does this in 26:54, 56 where no actual prophecy exists but where the general thought can be found in the Old Testament.

[107] Hagner, *Matthew*, 40–41. Matthew could be playing off *Nazaraios*, for it is quite defensively a derivation from Nazareth. However, if this is correct, it does not preclude echoes of other meanings. It could come from *Nazir*, one consecrated to God by a vow and usually transliterated as Nazirite (rendered *Naziraios* in the Septuagint as a transliteration of the Hebrew equivalent). It could be from *Neser*, the word for *branch*, which also ties to Immanuel in Isaiah 7:14 and fits with Matthew's overall plan. Finally, it could come out of the root *nasar*, carrying the sense "to watch, observe, and keep." "Nazarenus" probably comes from Jeremiah 31:6–7, where the watchman will call out to the hill country of Ephraim that the Lord has saved His people, the remnant of Israel. For a discussion, see Brown, *Birth*, 212–13 and Hagner, *Matthew*, 40–41.

that age justifies the inference that the boy was well taught in the law and the scriptures, for such was the rule. He garnered knowledge by study, and gained wisdom by prayer, thought, and effort. Beyond question He was trained to labor, for idleness was abhorred then as it is now; and every Jewish boy, whether carpenter's son, peasant's child, or rabbi's heir, was required to learn and follow a practical and productive vocation. Jesus was all that a boy should be, for His development was unretarded by the dragging weight of sin; He loved and obeyed the truth and therefore was free."[108] His parents continued their pattern of devotion, setting an example for the young man. Each year they went to Jerusalem for Passover. The large time commitment and financial sacrifice of the trip testify of their reverence for the law.

The Jerusalem Visit

Many Jewish men went to Jerusalem on Passover, Pentecost, and Tabernacles,[109] but the Dispersion kept most away. Still, all who could went up at least once a year. The law said nothing about women having to go; however, certain religious leaders had their opinions. For instance, Hillel and his followers prescribed the journey.[110]

The major Jewish holiday was the dual feast of Passover and Unleavened Bread, a week-long celebration commemorating the angel of death's sparing the firstborn of the children of Israel while taking those of the Egyptians.[111] Each year a lamb was roasted as directed by the law and a meal prepared. At sundown, families sat down to celebrate and eat.

When the Savior was twelve, Mary and Joseph took Him with

---

[108] Talmage, JTC, 112.
[109] As commanded in Exodus 23:14–17; 34:23; Deuteronomy 16:16.
[110] Plummer, Commentary, 74. Two Jewish scholars, Hillel and Shammai, both dying some years before the Lord's ministry began, drew many disciples. Hillel was known to be more humanitarian and liberal than his colleague, Shammai, who tended to take a very strict view of the law and its implementation. See Robert Goldenberg, "Hillel," ABD, 3:201–2.
[111] Exodus 5:1, 10:9, and 23:15–16 describe the two feasts.

them. According to the Mishnah, when a Jewish male was thirteen, the Jewish community welcomed him into the circles of adulthood.[112] From that time on, he was under the obligation to abide by the statutes of the law. That included attending the three pilgrim feasts dictated by the law of Moses if he was able.

Because Jesus was just twelve, He came to Jerusalem under no such obligation. Rather, the episode suggests the pious nature of His parents, for it was the custom among the most devout to take a younger son with them on the long and arduous journey.[113] Joseph and Mary may well have been preparing Jesus for His initiation ceremonies the coming year. By being at Jerusalem, He saw the rite take place and had a feel for what would be expected of Him.[114]

To avoid going through Samaria, an area inhabited by people antagonistic toward Jews, especially those traveling to the rival religious capital of Jerusalem, the Jews from Galilee usually traveled down to Jerusalem through the Jordan River Valley before ascending toward the Holy City. At times, however, when there were enough of them, they journeyed fairly safely across Samaria along the Patriarch's Way.[115]

Joseph's little band traveled in a company of relatives, friends, and other pilgrims. On the trip, women and children often started first to give them more time. The men usually followed. Older children could go with either group. All met together in the evening for dinner and bedtime.

The celebration of Passover and the Feast of Unleavened Bread lasted a full week. During that time, pilgrims enjoyed the Passover meal, temple services, and a general holiday atmosphere. After enjoying the festivities, Joseph and Mary started home. Neither realized that Jesus was not with them. Both may have thought He was

---

[112] Danby, *The Mishnah*, Niddah 5:6.

[113] Danby, *The Mishnah*, Hagiga 1:1. For a discussion, see Fitzmyer, *Gospel*, 440.

[114] Nyval Geldenhuys, *Commentary on the Gospel of Luke* (Grand Rapids: Eerdmans, 1988), 126.

[115] See David F. Graf, Benjamin Isaac, and Israel Roll, "Roads and Highways (Roman)," in Freedman, *ABD*, 5:782–87.

with the other—that is, until they met at dinnertime.[116] Mary may have had some of her other children in her care, which took her mind off her responsible and obedient eldest Son.[117] One other fact should be kept in mind: Jesus would have been viewed as nearly grown up in that society. The couple immediately turned back to find their Son, and "after three days they found him" (Luke 2:46). Very likely they did not search for three days but rather traveled out one day, back one day, and searched for part of a day.[118]

He may not have left because the attraction of the divine held Him. From what we can tell, this was His first experience with one of the great feasts. Here He may have sensed that the sacrificial rituals were a type of His own sacrifice, the prayers and psalms of joy were praises to Him, and the magnificent temple through whose courtyards He walked and under whose porticoes He sat was His. The Jewish leadership might have been corrupt and the high priest's office bought and sold for favor, but within the walls of that temple, the remnant of God's priesthood still blessed, and the sweet whispers of His Father's Spirit remained. Even the departure of the Lord's parents could not force the boy, now nearly a man, away from the wonder of His temple, His law, and its teachers.[119]

He may have known, even this early, that He Himself was destined to be a teacher. The law was to be His to interpret, explain, and fulfill. Thus, He seems to have been drawn to the discussions of the scribes and doctors of the law. Already, He had seen young men going through what would later be called the *Bar Mitzvah*. He seemed eager not only to query the doctors but also to share His own insights. And so He stayed behind in His and His Father's house.

Jesus was in the porticoes when Mary and Joseph found Him, as they were yet together. He was contentedly sitting with the doctors, "both hearing them, and asking them questions" (Luke 2:46). The

---

[116] Plummer, *Commentary*, 175.

[117] On the possibilities, see Geldenhuys, *Commentary*, 126; William Barclay, *The New Daily Study Bible* (Edinburgh: Saint Andrews Press, 2001), 35–36.

[118] Fitzmyer, *Gospel*, 442.

[119] Plummer, *Commentary*, 75.

discussions would most likely have revolved around the Torah and its place in contemporary Jewish life, a subject in which the Lord would have deep interest.

Luke shows us the Lord sitting, as a learner, taking full advantage of the moment. Later writers and embroiderers have made much of this event. One apocryphal story tells how Jesus overwhelmed various rabbis and scribes with His profound knowledge of the law.[120] The accounts, though overblown, may have preserved kernels of the truth.

The Joseph Smith Translation provides another view of the gathering—the doctors "were hearing him, and asking him questions" (JST Luke 2:46). Something extraordinary was going on, "as the demeanor of the learned doctors showed, for never before had such a student been found, inasmuch as 'all that heard him were astonished at his understanding and answers.' The incident furnishes evidence of a well-spent boyhood and proof of unusual attainments."[121]

Luke states that Jesus' parents were quite startled when they found Him.[122] Why this is so, the text does not say, but Mary's question suggests it was Jesus' unusual behavior that caused them such anxiety. "Son, why hast thou thus dealt with us?" she asked. "Behold, thy father and I have sought thee sorrowing" (Luke 2:48). Her rebuke suggests that a responsible child would not have acted in such a way.[123]

His answer suggests surprise on the Lord's part. They had brought Him to Jerusalem; how could they not know He would then be in his Father's house "and about [His] Father's business?" (Luke 2:49).[124]

---

[120] Evans, *Luke*, 46. A good example is *The Infancy Gospel of Thomas* 19:2. See Schneemelcher, *New Testament Apocrypha* 1:414–69 for an extensive collection of infancy tales.

[121] Talmage, *JTC*, 114.

[122] The Greek is very strong, *exeplagēsan*, meaning, "to be struck outside of one's self."

[123] Fitzmyer, *Gospel*, 433.

[124] The Greek in this passage is obscure. Jesus could be saying, "Did you not know that I had to be about my Father's business," as the KJV has it, or "Did you not know I would be in my Father's house?" as other translations have it. The setting of the Lord's question suggests the latter may be the correct nuance. See Plummer, *Commentary*, 77.

He seems perplexed that His earthly parents could not fathom that His duty to His divine Father transcended His duty to them. His statement reveals that He understood perfectly who His Father was and what His duties were. Luke emphasizes, however, that His parents "understood not the saying which he spake unto them" (Luke 2:50). They had not yet come to full understanding of the wonder of this Child they were raising. The story would continue to unfold, bit by bit, experience by experience.[125]

The story allows Jesus to speak for the first time in the New Testament, and as He does, He shows His awareness of who He is—the obedient Son of His Father. His witness adds a dimension to that of all the previous witnesses.[126] Also, the story highlights the independent nature of the Lord, which He would manifest throughout His ministry. He was self-reliant and had a strong personality, with but one objective best expressed in His words "Not my will, but thine, be done" (Luke 22:42). Whatever His feelings, He yielded to the wishes of Mary and Joseph and, we suspect, of His Father and went back with them to Nazareth where He "was subject unto them" (Luke 2:51). The way Luke phrased this statement implies that Jesus continued in His obedience to them.[127] His duty to His Father did not yet supersede His duty as a respectful and obedient Son of His earthly parents.[128]

The Lord's Young Adulthood

So, in spite of the pull of the temple and doctors of the law, Jesus returned to His unglamorous and hard life at Nazareth. We must keep in mind that at this point, He was probably the same age as Mary when the angel came to her and she entered into full adulthood. Further, at the temple, His status had clearly changed. He had become teacher and revealer, not just student.[129]

---

[125] Fitzmyer, *Gospel*, 443–45.
[126] Fitzmyer, *Gospel*, 436.
[127] He uses the imperfect verb *ēn* followed by the present participle.
[128] Fitzmyer, *Gospel*, 445.
[129] Brown, *Mary*, 65.

Even so, He had agreed to condescend, to be like His brethren. That did not mean the learned, the rich, the scholarly, or the noble. It meant the humble, the hard working, the poor. The scriptures had already told his lot: "He shall grow up before him [that is, God] as a tender plant, and as a root out of a dry ground: he hath no form nor comeliness; and when we shall see him, there is no beauty that we shall desire him" (Isaiah 53:2). He would eat "butter and honey" (Isaiah 7:15). Isaiah's words suggest that the environment in which Jesus grew up was "important in forming the person who subsequently chose to take upon Himself our sins."[130] He was a carpenter's son (Matthew 13:55) and a carpenter (Mark 6:3). He was one in a fairly large family where his brothers, James, Joses, Juda, and Simon, along with His sisters, toiled for the family's care (see Mark 6:3).

The absence of information about Jesus between birth and ministry was neither an accident nor an oversight. The Joseph Smith Translation adds nothing, even though it adds much about Melchizedek and Moses. Jesus' eternal Father wanted Him to grow up naturally, without the pressures that would come from other environments and situations. After His birth, Jesus virtually disappears from the biblical stage until His ministry begins. "I believe," writes Brigham Young University professor James Kearl, "that this *disappearance* of Jesus into childhood was not by chance but by heavenly design. There is something so important that occurs during these formative years that our Father in Heaven wanted His Son to experience it. In other words, it was important for Jesus to be not only the Son of God but also the child of Mary and Joseph" and to live in a family.[131]

The silence gives us the feeling that Jesus "had a *protected* childhood. Indeed, it remains protected in precisely the sense that we know virtually nothing about it and are clearly not supposed to."[132] Also, Jesus had an *extended* young adulthood. If ever there was anyone

---

[130] J. R. Kearl, "Christmas and Childhood," in *The Religious Educator* 2, no. 2 (2001): 112.
[131] Kearl, "Christmas," 114.
[132] Kearl, "Christmas," 114.

"who could have matured quickly and assumed His divinely appointed role, and mission, it is Jesus Christ, the literal Son of God." Yet, with great patience, His heavenly and earthly fathers allowed Jesus to mature slowly.[133] In a word, they allowed Him to have a life, His life, and so a reverent curtain hangs over it to this day.

Yet God has seen fit to give us some generalities. According to the Joseph Smith Translation, "Jesus grew up with his brethren, and waxed strong, and waited upon the Lord for the time of his ministry to come. And he served under his father, and he spake not as other men, neither could he be taught; for he needed not that any man should teach him" (JST Matthew 3:24–25).

Luke 2:52 properly reflects the emphasis the Gospel authors place on the importance of the young adulthood of Jesus when Luke says that "Jesus increased in wisdom and stature, and in favour with God and man." The Gospel of Luke passes over the period with brevity, moving on to more important matters—namely, the public ministry and Atonement.

These verses suggest that the Lord's childhood was less than normal. Still, even though He was the Son of God and possessed remarkable abilities, condescension demanded that He suppress them for a time so He could grow and be shaped like the rest of His Father's children.

We know, too, through John's testimony, that "he received not of the fulness at the first, but continued from grace to grace, until he received a fulness" (Doctrine and Covenants 93:13).

Apparently, it was necessary for the Lord to grow through this process. To do so, He first received grace, or divine assistance, from the Father. This favor He extended to His brethren. As He did so, He received even more grace. This process continued to the point that He eventually received a fullness of the glory of the Father. The implication of this process is interesting. In a very real way, Christ, Himself, was saved by grace.

Through Paul, we learn that "we have not an High Priest which

---

[133] Kearl, "Christmas," 114.

cannot be touched with the feeling of our infirmities; but was in all points tempted [that is, tried] like as we are, yet without sin" (Hebrews 4:15). His condescension demanded that he "[take] not on him the nature of angels; but he took on him the seed of Abraham" (Hebrews 2:16). Indeed, "in all things it behoved him to be made like unto his brethren, that he might be a merciful and faithful high priest in things pertaining to God. . . . For in that he himself hath suffered being tempted [that is, tried], he is able to succour them that are tempted" (Hebrews 2:17–18). Indeed, "though he were a Son, yet learned he obedience by the things which he suffered" (Hebrews 5:8).

Conclusion

Both Luke and Matthew teach us that the Lord's nature combined "the powers of Godhood with the capacity and possibilities of mortality."[134] The Child Jesus was to inherit the physical, mental, and spiritual traits, tendencies, and powers that characterized His parents: one immortal and glorified—God—the other mortal and human—Mary.[135]

These two Gospel writers, along with Nephi, testify that because of and through the wonder of a miraculous conception, Jesus was the Son of God. Indeed, a virgin, *the Virgin*, did conceive and yet retained her virginity. Only the power of God could do that. Thus, Jesus could only be God's Son.

The theme that runs through the Son of God's conception, birth, childhood, and young adulthood is condescension. He was God, yet He became clay; He lived poor, He worked hard, and He felt the full weight of mortality. Neither His divine nor His mortal parents spoiled or coddled Him. Neither did His environment. Just because He was the Son of God did not mean He received any earthly favors.

On the other hand, He was God. The record suggests, albeit tacitly, that there were times while He was growing up when the Father

---

[134] Talmage, *JTC*, 81.
[135] Talmage, *JTC*, 81.

permitted Him to use His divine power to bless His family.[136] These moments must have brought delight, but they could also have brought their own special challenge. Though He was God, He was not above His Eternal Father whose will He was determined to do. That may have meant that there were moments, even before Gethsemane, when Jesus' aching whisper could be heard, "Not my will but thine be done."

Sometime around His thirtieth birthday, the hour of His ministry drew nigh. As it did, He laid aside His private life, giving Himself fully to the service of God and His fellowmen. The powers of condescension, so strongly binding him in His youth and young adulthood, lessened. Though never fully free of its restraints, where faith was sufficient, He could reveal who He really was—the Son of God.

---

[136] Mary's interaction with the Lord at the marriage at Cana before His ministry began suggests she knew at least in part of His powers.

VI.
JESUS IN THE WILDERNESS: BAPTISM, FASTING, AND TEMPTATIONS

RICHARD NEITZEL HOLZAPFEL

The Spirit like a dove [descended] upon him.
MARK 1:10

Mark's Gospel opens abruptly, yet forcefully, "The beginning of the gospel of Jesus Christ, the Son of God" (Mark 1:1).[1] The first Greek word, *archē* ("beginning"), reminds us of Genesis 1:1 (LXX) and John 1:1.[2] However, Mark is not alluding to the creation or the beginning of the "Word" (John 1:1); rather, he is referring to the beginning of the "good news" (King James Version "gospel" from the old English word *godspel*, meaning "good story" or "good news") about Jesus Christ.[3] Even though, as we already know,

---

[1] No original text, identified as an *autograph*, has survived from antiquity. Therefore, we have access only to copies of copies, and we cannot always be sure that the current Greek manuscript reflects the original text as it was actually penned by the author. In this case, some ancient manuscripts lack "the Son of God." However, it seems highly likely that the phrase is original since the book's express purpose is to proclaim the good news about Jesus Christ, who is the Son of God (Mark 1:1); see discussion below.

[2] LXX, the Greek translation of the Old Testament completed in the second century B.C., is known as the Septuagint and is often identified by Roman numerals because of the tradition that it was translated in seventy days by seventy-two elders.

[3] *Jesus* is the English equivalent of the Greek form for the Old Testament name *Joshua*, whose Hebrew meaning is "*the Lord [Jehovah] saves.*"

Mark's Gospel moves toward a seemingly tragic end with Jesus' rejection, suffering, sorrow, and death in Jerusalem, we also know that it is not at all bad news but is rather "good news" because of the glorious events on the first day of the week (see Mark 16:6).[4]

What follows this opening volley is the retelling of a well-known and oft-repeated story about Jesus' wilderness experiences: His baptism, fasting, and temptations (see Acts 10:37; also 1:5).[5]

Mark continues his story by recording what happened immediately following Jesus' wilderness experiences when He began to proclaim the "good news" of the kingdom of God.[6] Jesus' words are recalled with a powerful sense of urgency: "The time is fulfilled, and the kingdom of God is at hand: repent ye, and believe the gospel" (Mark 1:15; see also Luke 3:9, where "the axe is [already] laid unto the root of the trees").[7] Mark is clear that Jesus not only proclaimed the "good news," an exact translation of the Greek, but also facilitated its effects through His own ministry, culminating in His suffering, death, and resurrection, as noted above.

When we read the four Gospels carefully, highlighting the similarities and differences among them as they discuss Jesus' wilderness

---

[4] For a full discussion of the important events at the end of Jesus' ministry, see Richard Neitzel Holzapfel and Thomas A. Wayment, eds., *From the Last Supper through the Resurrection: The Savior's Final Hours* (Salt Lake City: Deseret Book, 2003).

[5] The wilderness of Judea is an area stretching some twenty miles from the Jerusalem-Bethlehem plateau down to the Jordan River and the Dead Sea—a region usually identified as untamed by human activity but not necessarily uninhabitable. The higher elevations were used for herding, and the lower areas, nearer the Dead Sea, were generally considered barren. But the settlement at Qumran—the main settlement for those who collected the Dead Sea Scrolls—demonstrates some habitation. John the Baptist may have grown to adulthood in the wilderness (see Luke 1:80). Some modern translations of the New Testament provide an alternative English phrase, "desert region," for wilderness (see NIV Mark 1:4).

[6] Mark's first fifteen verses demonstrate complete unity framed by the announcement of the "good news" (Mark 1:1) and Jesus' arrival in Galilee to preach the "good news" (Mark 1:15). Between these two occurrences of the word *gospel* lie the events that form the basic underlying thesis of the whole Gospel narrative—Jesus is God's Beloved Son; He is empowered by His Father, and He goes forth by the Spirit.

[7] The term "good news" occurs seven times in Mark, four times in Matthew, none in Luke, twice in Acts, fifty-nine times in Paul's writings, and twice elsewhere in the New Testament.

experience and what immediately follows, we readily recognize that the Spirit is one of the themes that weave their way through these stories.

First, the Spirit falls upon Jesus when John baptizes Him in the wilderness (Mark 1:10; Matthew 3:16; Luke 3:21–22; John 1:32).[8] Second, the Spirit drives Jesus into the wilderness, where He fasts forty days and is tempted by the devil (Mark 1:13; Matthew 4:1–11; Luke 4:1–13). Third, Jesus returns to Galilee in the "power of the Spirit" (Luke 4:14).[9] Fourth, when He appears in Nazareth, following the wilderness experience, Jesus declares, "The Spirit of the Lord is upon me, because he hath anointed me to preach the gospel" (Luke 4:18).

The transition from John the Baptist's ministry centered at the Jordan River in the wilderness now gives way to Jesus' own ministry centered in the towns and villages in Galilee.[10] The public ministry, now begun in earnest, demonstrates, through Mark's quick, successive vignettes, that Jesus teaches with power and authority (Mark 1:21–22; Luke 4:31–32), casts out the unclean spirits (Mark 1:23–28; Luke 4:33–37), and heals all manner of diseases (Mark 1:33–34), demonstrating "how God anointed Jesus of Nazareth with the Holy Ghost and with power: who went about doing good . . . for God was with him" (Acts 10:38).

---

[8] Mark portrays the revelation as one received by Jesus alone, and Matthew portrays the revelation as being directed to the crowd (see Matthew 3:17). The JST provides another view, emphasizing John the Baptist's role as witness (see JST Matthew 3:45), adding, "This is my beloved Son, in whom I am well pleased. Hear ye him" (JST Matthew 3:46). Additionally, JST Mark, "Thou art my beloved Son, in whom I am well pleased. And John bare record of it" (JST Mark 1:9).

[9] We generally think of successive events: Jesus makes a journey to the wilderness where He is baptized, fasts for forty days (suffers temptation at the end), and then returns to Galilee. More time is likely involved than this commonly imagined scenario suggests. How long was Jesus in the wilderness *before* He was baptized? How long did He *remain* with John following His baptism? What was the length of time before He *returned* to Galilee following the temptations? The Gospel of John suggests that some activity took place in Judea *before* His return to Galilee (see John 3:22–24).

[10] The principal river in the Holy Land, the Jordan, begins in the north in the snows of Mount Hermon and ends in the south at the Dead Sea.

A New Beginning

Mark's account of the events immediately preceding the public ministry of Jesus is well known for its pithiness. With very few words (Mark 1:2–8), Mark demonstrates how suddenly and radically John the Baptist alters the social, political, and religious landscape of first-century Judaism when he announces that the coming of the "one mightier" than any prophet has at long last arrived (Mark 1:7).[11]

John the Baptist, like many of the Old Testament prophets before him, startles his compatriots by preaching a message that was meant to convict, convince, and challenge the people of Israel to change (repent)[12] and prepare themselves for another—who stands among them, though unknown to the Jews at the moment.[13] Jesus will,

---

[11] Born to righteous and devout parents of priestly descent in a small village in Judea, John the Baptist played a singular role at the beginning of Jesus' ministry. Each Gospel provides insights to John's ministry as a prophet, preacher, baptizer, and witness in the Judean wilderness east of Jerusalem, culminating with the baptism of Jesus at the River Jordan. Nevertheless, each Gospel author emphasized aspects of John's life, providing a context for each author's particular witness of Jesus. Luke alone, however, provides details of Jesus' birth and childhood (see Luke 1 and 3). Eventually, Herod Antipas arrested, imprisoned, and executed John. The JST provides additional mention of him during the Mount of Transfiguration experience (see JST Mark 9:3). For Jesus, John the Baptist symbolized the final transition from the Old Testament (covenant) and the beginning of the New Testament (covenant). The time of the law and the prophets had passed, and the time of the Messiah had arrived. John the Baptist, the last legal administrator of the Mosaic covenant, had one foot in each dispensation. Nevertheless, Jesus declared, "He was a burning and a shining light: and ye were willing for a season to rejoice in his light" (John 5:35). See also Jesus' other statements about John (Matthew 11:11, 18–19; 21:32; Luke 7:28, 33–34; John 5:35–36).

[12] Repent (Greek *metanoeō*), literally "to change one's mind," in the context of the preaching of John the Baptist and Jesus of Nazareth, is actually a call for a radical transformation. Repentance is not just an intellectual change of mind but is a behaviorally centered change from the heart, in which the individual, because of faith, forsakes sin and returns to God. As a result, John's message is not simply to inform but also to convert the reader to this radical transformation that brings gracious forgiveness that God continually offers men and women through the "one mightier than" prophet, Jesus Christ, who offers the "baptism of fire and the Holy Ghost" that can prevent a person from backsliding following the baptism of water.

[13] A common name during this period and especially popular among the priesthood, *John* means "The Lord is gracious," demonstrating that the call of repentance and reform was a gracious act by a merciful God.

nevertheless, soon be dramatically revealed to them: "There cometh one mightier than I after me, the latchet of whose shoes I am not worthy to stoop down and unloose" (Mark 1:7).

The time period is one of transition for the Jews, who have been without a prophet for hundreds of years.[14] Without warning, but not unanticipated, God intervenes dramatically and decisively in their history again—with far-reaching consequences when, as prophesied in the Old Testament, His messenger suddenly appears: "Behold, I send my messenger before thy face, which shall prepare thy way before thee" (Mark 1:2; compare LXX Exodus 23:20; Malachi 3:1).[15]

As noted earlier, John the Baptist enters the stage of human history at a decisive moment, ending a nearly five-hundred-year silence since the close of the Old Testament period and baptizing and preaching the "baptism of repentance for the remission of sins" (Mark 1:4).[16] John's baptisms were not like the repeatable, ritualistic washings performed at Qumran, which was located very close to

---

[14] For a fuller discussion of this important transitional period, see S. Kent Brown and Richard Neitzel Holzapfel, *Between the Testaments: From Malachi to Matthew* (Salt Lake City: Deseret Book, 2002).

[15] The KJV introduces the prophetic passages with the phrase, "As it is written in the prophets," and then quotes separate, but related, passages from LXX Exodus 23:20, Malachi 3:1, and, finally, Isaiah 40:3 (see Mark 1:2–3; Luke, however, quotes two additional verses). The earliest manuscripts read, "It is written in Isaiah the prophet." When later Christian scribes noticed the problem that the text included material beyond Isaiah, they changed the original to read, "As it is written in the prophets." For a full discussion of similar efforts by Christian scribes, see Bart D. Ehrman, *The Orthodox Corruption of Scripture: The Effect of Early Christological Controversies on the Text of the New Testament* (New York: Oxford University Press, 1993).

[16] Much has been made about John the Baptist's association with the Jewish group located at Qumran. And although we see similarities, such as locale (both were located near the Dead Sea), message (repentance and judgment), full-body immersions in water, and even an interest in the same passages of scripture referring to preparing the way in the wilderness (Isaiah 40:3), differences clearly are evident. First, John reached out to all people and did not plan to create a separate ascetic commune of holy men waiting for the end of time—like those at Qumran. Second, John's baptism, as noted above, was a one-time baptism administered by John himself. Third, and most significant, John identified Jesus as the one whose coming had been anticipated. Those at Qumran did not accept Jesus as the promised Messiah and were eventually killed by Roman soldiers during their sweep south toward Masada during the Jewish War in A.D. 68.

where John baptized. Nor was John the Baptist's invitation analogous to the baptism of a proselyte (if, in fact, baptisms as a sign of conversion to the Jewish religion were being performed at this time), which was apparently self-administered and represented the inclusion of one ethnic group (Gentiles) into another (Jews).[17] John was called the "baptizer," suggesting that people were required to receive baptism at his hand.[18]

John rekindled for the Jews in his generation vivid recollections of Old Testament prophets, particularly Elijah and Jeremiah.[19] John dressed like Elijah (Mark 1:6; compare 2 Kings 1:8); John preached like Jeremiah (Mark 1:4; cf. Jeremiah 18:11); and John acted like Elijah and Jeremiah by claiming a singular authority above political and religious rulers of his day (Mark 1:4, 6:16–29; compare 2 Chronicles 21:12 and Jeremiah 21–22).[20] In this particular case, John the Baptist offered forgiveness for sin independent of the temple and the priests in Jerusalem, even though he was himself a priest.[21]

This challenge to authority did not go unnoticed by the most dedicated and righteous lay priests of the various temple courses or among the Sadducees, who jealously controlled the temple itself. They recognized that John the Baptist manifested a special spirit of authority not witnessed among them in some time (John 1:19–25). For some, John represented a challenge to the status quo; for others who were more spiritually in tune, he represented an awakening from a deep and long spiritual sleep.[22]

---

[17] Luke emphasizes the fact that the Jews must make a fresh start because they had, through sin, forfeited their status as the "children of Abraham" (JST Luke 3:13).

[18] The New Testament provides two forms of John's title: the Baptist (*ho baptistēs*) as a formal title and the baptizer (*ho baptizōn*) as a nickname (see Mark 1:4).

[19] John the Baptist's role as forerunner elicits the identification to Elijah (Mark 6:15; 9:11–12; Matthew 11:14; 17:10–13).

[20] Scholars have some evidence that the above passages were associated with Elijah in early Judaism. Certainly, Jews of the period thought Jesus, the successor of John the Baptist, may have been Elijah or Jeremiah (see Matthew 16:14).

[21] Even Josephus was impressed with the prophetic mantle that fell upon John; see Josephus, *AJ*, 18.116–19.

[22] John the Baptist directly challenged Herod Antipas as the prophet Nathan did to David (Luke 3:19–20; 2 Samuel 12:1–12) and was eventually arrested, imprisoned, and

A significant number of Jewish leaders, many of whom were anxiously waiting for a new prophet to arise and who also anticipated the coming of the Messiah, made the long descent from Jerusalem down to the Rift Valley to the banks of the Jordan River (the closet point to Jerusalem is about twenty miles) to not only hear the "voice of one crying in the wilderness" but also to be baptized, "confessing their sins" (Mark 1:3, 5).[23] The Joseph Smith Translation emphasizes this point (see JST Matthew 1:33; JST Mark 1:4; JST Luke 3:12).

Jesus' Baptism

The transition from John to Jesus is outlined in the first chapter of Mark (Mark 1:2–8 deals with John the Baptist, and Mark 1:9–15 deals with Jesus of Nazareth).[24] In Matthew, Luke, and John, we have a similar transition (see Matthew 3:1–12 and 3:13–4:17; Luke 3:1–20 and 3:21–4:15; John 1:6–28 and 1:29–51).

Although Matthew, Mark, and Luke reveal little about John the Baptist's initial reason for going to the wilderness other than to preach and baptize, John informs us that, at some point, John the Baptist received instructions about what he was to do: "He that sent me to baptize with water, the same said unto me, Upon whom thou

---

executed by Herod Antipas, probably in A.D. 28 or 29.

[23] The Gospels do not provide an exact location for John the Baptist's ministry. However, the text indicates that Jesus was baptized at Bethabara, but in some manuscripts, Bethany, on the east side of the Jordan River, is identified as the site of Jesus' baptism (see John 1:28; 1 Nephi 10:9). Bethabara appears on the Medeba Map, a mosaic map in the floor of one of the sixth-century churches in the town by the same name, located about nineteen miles south of Amman, Jordan, on the King's Highway. It is a natural fording place east of Jericho. *Bethabara*, or *Beth-avara*, a Hebrew term, means "place of crossing." See D. Kelly Ogden, *Where Jesus Walked: The Land and Culture of New Testament Times* (Salt Lake City: Deseret Book, 1991), 37. The Gospel of John also indicates that John baptized at "Aenon near Salim" (see John 3:23). The location has been identified at the middle reaches of the Jordan River, where trade routes converge at a natural ford not far from the modern site of Tell Shalem, south of Beth Shan (ancient Scythopolis).

[24] Mark provides a pattern that draws our attention: the "Son of God," the first proclaimed (Mark 1:1), arrives in the wilderness last. The "voice crying in the wilderness," the second announced (Mark 1:2), arrives at Jordan last, creating a literary structure of ABBA—a perfect chiasm.

shalt see the Spirit descending, and remaining on him, the same is he which baptizeth with the Holy Ghost. And I saw, and bare record that this is the Son of God" (John 1:33–34). The setting for Jesus' baptism is straightforward. John the Baptist is in the wilderness, and Jesus must go to the wilderness to find John.[25] The focus, therefore, is on the messenger who prepares the way, on the one mighty, and on their meeting in the wilderness.

The Gospels emphasize that John not only baptized but also announced that the one following after him was mightier then he. This point is contrasted by the different baptisms each offered—one with water and the other with the Spirit (see Joel 2:28–29).[26] Jesus, according to Luke, fulfilled this distinction on the day of Pentecost (see Acts 1:5; cf. Acts 2).

Further, John the Baptist suggests that he and Jesus also differ in social status: one is not even worthy to perform a menial task fit for a slave (servant)—stooping down to untie the master's sandal strap (the Greek text of Matthew states, "I am not worthy to carry [away] his sandals") and wash His feet.[27] These words should not be read as an exaggeration, because they reflect John's sincere feeling of his abject unworthiness to baptize Jesus.

Mark's description of the baptism of Jesus is short and to the point: "And it came to pass in those days, that Jesus came from Nazareth of Galilee, and was baptized of John in Jordan. And straightway coming up out of the water, he saw the heavens opened, and the Spirit like a dove descending upon him: And there came a

---

[25] In early spring, the flood season was at its high point (see Joshua 3:15), and the shallow Jordan was now deep and cold, a time when people could have easily been baptized.

[26] The JST provides an interesting insight here: "I indeed have baptized you with water: but he shall not only baptize you with water, but with fire, and the Holy Ghost" (JST Mark 1:6), suggesting that Jesus did, in fact, perform baptisms Himself (John 3:23–26; JST John 4:1–4).

[27] JST Matthew states, "I indeed baptize you with water upon your repentance: and when he of whom I bear record cometh, who is mightier than I, whose shoes I am not worthy to bear (or whose place I am not able to fill), as I said, I indeed baptize you before he cometh, that when he cometh he shall baptize you with the Holy Ghost, and fire."

voice from heaven, saying, Thou art my beloved Son, in whom I am well pleased" (Mark 1:9–11).[28]

At the beginning, Mark provides a chronological context: "And it came to pass in those days," referring to John the Baptist's preaching in the wilderness, beginning about A.D. 27 (see below). Ironically, it is not all those who "went out unto" John from Judea (Mark 1:5) but the One coming from Nazareth who ultimately fulfills John's long-anticipated mission. Without any additional details, Mark reports that John baptized Jesus (Mark 1:9).[29] Mark adds, in language reminiscent of other apocalyptic writings, that the heavens open and God speaks (Mark 1:10–11). On this particular occasion, He speaks directly to Jesus: "Thou art my beloved Son, in whom I am well pleased" (Mark 1:11).[30]

In verse 10, we encounter Mark's first use of the word "immediately," one of his favorites. The Greek term, *euthus*, is often translated as "straightway," "anon," and "straitly" in the KJV.[31] In most cases,

---

[28] The straightforward account, storytelling at its best, provides the answers to several important and necessary questions: Who? "Jesus"; Where? "from Nazareth of Galilee"; What? "was baptized"; By whom? "John"; Where? "in the Jordan." The account then provides an interpretive element (Mark 1:10–11).

[29] Mark is the only Gospel to say explicitly that John baptized Jesus: "And it came to pass in those days, that Jesus came from Nazareth of Galilee, and *was baptized of John* in Jordan" (Mark 1:9; emphasis added). Matthew alludes to it, using the passive voice (see Matthew 3:16). Luke, however, is problematic because the baptismal passage (see Luke 3:20–21) follows John the Baptist's arrest (see Luke 3:18–20). Luke certainly knew that John baptized Jesus—so why the chronological rearrangement? It may have been an attempt to deal with some specific controversy at the time. Mostly likely, the issue at the time was competition among the followers of John the Baptist who did not accept Jesus of Nazareth and the Christian missionary efforts (see Acts 19:1–7). In this way, Luke may have simply wanted to counter attempts to exaggerate the importance of John the Baptist. Certainly, John the Baptist's disciples (including Andrew, Peter, and John), who later followed Jesus, realized that He, unlike John, performed remarkable miracles, including raising the dead. Neither the synoptic Gospels nor the Gospel of John informs the reader that John the Baptist did likewise; in fact, the Fourth Gospel categorically disallows it (see John 10:41).

[30] 2 Baruch 22:1 (James H. Charlesworth, ed., *The Old Testament Pseudepigrapha*, 2 vols. [Garden City: Doubleday, 1983], 1:629); Testament of Levi 2:6, 5:1, 18:6 (Charlesworth, 1:788, 789, and 795); Testament of Judah, 24:2 (Charlesworth, 1:801); Revelation 4:1; 11:19; 19:11.

[31] The Greek word appears some forty-seven times in Mark (see, for example, Mark

the reader should not take the word at face value—that is, literally. More often than not, "immediately" functions rhetorically—indicating that events are proceeding at a remarkable speed. For nearly thirty years, Jesus lived an apparently quiet and slow-paced life in an obscure and out-of-the-way village, away from the gaze of crowds and the interest of political and religious leaders of His day (see Luke 3:23).[32] Now, at the start of Jesus' ministry, Mark provides the reader with a striking word picture—Jesus expands His activity at an ever-increasing momentum until His final hours in Jerusalem, there to finish His work.

In Mark 1:11, we find allusions to Genesis 22:2 (identifying Jesus with Abraham's son Isaac; see discussion below); Psalm 2:7 (with the Davidic king); and Isaiah 42:1 (with the suffering servant)—reminding the reader of the special relationship that Jesus has with the Father.[33] Mark began his Gospel by declaring Jesus to be the "Son of God"; here, the Father proclaims Jesus as His "beloved Son." The Greek term translated here as "beloved" can also mean "unique" or "only." Jesus, as the unique or only Son, receives from the Father a full endowment of the Spirit, tethering the common theme of Spirit in the early stories of Jesus' ministry.

Although Mark had no reason to anticipate future discussion among second- and third-century Christians, much has been written about the meaning of the declaration "Thou art my beloved Son, in whom I am well pleased" (Mark 1:11).[34] For later Christians, Jesus

---

1:18, 20, 21, 28, 30, 42–43).

[32] JST Matthew provides this insight about this period: "And it came to pass that Jesus grew up with his brethren, and waxed strong, and waited upon the Lord for the time of his ministry to come. . . . And after many years, the hour of his ministry drew nigh" (JST Matthew 2:24, 26).

[33] The Book of Mormon provides a direct correlation to and interpretation of the passage: "Behold, they believed in Christ and worshipped the Father in his name, and also we worship the Father in his name. And for this intent we keep the law of Moses, it pointing our souls to him; and for this cause it is sanctified unto us for righteousness, even as it was accounted unto Abraham in the wilderness to be obedient unto the commands of God in offering up his son Isaac, which is a similitude of God and his Only Begotten Son" (Jacob 4:5).

[34] See Thomas A. Wayment's discussion on intentional scribal alterations of the

was the Son of God, but when He *became* the son of God was an important, relevant, and highly charged doctrinal issue, at least among a segment of the Christian movement. For some, He was always the Son of God (see John 1:1–2); for others, He was the Son of God from the moment of conception (see Luke 2:11); for another group, He was adopted as God's Son at baptism (see Acts 10:37–38); and for still another group, He became God's Son at the resurrection (see Acts 2:36).

Though each had a scriptural text to justify his position, the Gospel writers themselves all agree—but simply did not anticipate the later Adoptionist controversy of the second and third centuries. In opposition to Luke, the Adoptionists denied that Jesus had been born of a virgin (see the discussion below).

A more interesting question at this point may be, "When did God anoint Jesus?" Clearly, the Gospel authors believed that God actually did something to or for Jesus at the baptism. The nature of what He did is debated. Was Jesus anointed, elected, affirmed, identified, or declared at this time?

That Jesus Himself saw the event as significant can be seen in the discussion between Jesus and His detractors following the cleansing of the temple: "As he was walking in the temple, there come to him the chief priests, and the scribes, and the elders, and say unto him, By what authority doest thou these things? And who gave thee this authority to do these things?" (Mark 11:27–28).

Jesus responds, "I will also ask of you one question, and answer me, and I will tell you by what authority I do these things. The baptism of John, was it from heaven, or of men? answer me" (Mark 11:29–30). Thus, Jesus probably saw the event at Jordan as essential and possibly even as a defining moment upon which He based authority for His ministry.

We might ask, "Why did Jesus begin His ministry at this point, when others, who had come to Jordan, did not embark on a mission themselves?" Most likely, Jesus told His disciples of the experience in

---

New Testament text in "The Story of the New Testament," in this volume.

the wilderness and gave them an explanation of why He began His ministry—a ministry bound up in Jesus' wilderness experience that was highlighted by baptism, fasting, and temptations.

However, more than the physical acts of baptism and fasting for forty days gave Jesus a sense of mission at this time. The experiences following the baptism—God's voice and declaration, the devil's challenges, and Jesus' successful resistance to the temptations—are what provided Jesus the authority and power to begin His ministry.[35]

For Mark, then, Jesus came from Nazareth to find John. Now, after Jesus had been obedient to the will of God by heeding John's call for Israel to be baptized, the Father confirmed His blessing—the Spirit—upon His Son. Jesus is then ready to be tempted to see if, in fact, He is indeed worthy of that blessing—all of this in preparation for Him to begin His ministry in earnest.

The experience at Jordan reminds the modern reader of two other occasions when the voice of God is heard in the Gospels: on the Mount of Transfiguration (see Mark 9:7; Matthew 17:5; Luke 9:35; see also 2 Peter 1:16–17) and in the temple during Jesus' final week (see John 12:28).[36] The baptism also foreshadows Jesus' own death and resurrection.[37] Matthew and Luke, both of whom used Mark as the basis for their telling of the baptism, provide a window into the efforts of writers in the first-century Church to tell this story, as we see when we carefully examine the similarities and differences among the separate accounts.

---

[35] See Ben Witherington III, *New Testament History* (Grand Rapids: Baker, 2001), 118.

[36] Mark not only supports the main purpose of the book that Jesus Christ is the Son of God, as outlined in the prologue (Mark 1:1), by preserving the Father's witness, both at the baptism and on the Mount of Transfiguration, that Jesus is indeed His Son, but also supports it when Jesus is proclaimed "Son of God" by demons, who possessed special insight (Mark 3:11; 5:7); by Jesus Himself (Mark 12:6; 14:62); and, finally, at the end of the story, when the Roman soldier confirms what has already been announced (see Mark 15:39).

[37] This point would not have been missed by the original audience who gathered to hear the text read, as they knew that baptism was a symbol of death (going down into the water) and resurrection (coming up out of the water) (Romans 6:3–4).

Matthew records, "Then cometh Jesus from Galilee to Jordan unto John, to be baptized of him. But John forbad him, saying, I have need to be baptized of thee, and comest thou to me? And Jesus answering said unto him, Suffer it to be so now: for thus it becometh us to fulfill all righteousness. Then he suffered him. And Jesus, when he was baptized, went up straightway out of the water: and, lo, the heavens were opened unto him, and he saw the Spirit of God descending like a dove, and lighting upon him: and lo a voice from heaven, saying, This is my beloved Son, in whom I am well pleased" (Matthew 3:13–17).[38]

The Gospel of Mark: A Primary Source for the Evangelists

A question, a valid one to be sure, may naturally be raised at this point: Why did Matthew, a member of the Twelve (Mark 2:14; Matthew 9:9), use Mark, who was not one of Jesus' disciples, as a source for the Gospel of Matthew?

Mark's Gospel has often and repeatedly been identified as "Peter's memoirs."[39] Peter begins the story of Jesus with the reference to John the Baptist baptizing Jesus (see Acts 10:37–43) and seems to confirm that Mark provides us Peter's view in this case.[40] It does not seem unnatural for Matthew to rely upon Peter for the basic story line for three reasons. First, Peter was acquainted with Jesus earlier than Matthew. Second, Peter was a member of the inner circle of disciples (along with James and John). Finally, and maybe more to the point, Peter was most likely a disciple of John the Baptist.

Matthew, unlike Mark, identifies the Baptist's urgent message, "Repent ye: for the kingdom of heaven is at hand" (Matthew 3:2).

---

[38] JST Matthew clarifies what happened on this occasion: "Suffer me to be baptized of thee, for thus it becometh us to fulfil all righteousness. Then he suffered him, and John went down into the water and baptized him" (JST Matthew 3:43).

[39] See S. Kent Brown, "The Testimony of Mark," in *Studies in Scriptures, Vol. 5: The Gospels*, ed. Kent P. Jackson and Robert L. Millet (Salt Lake City: Deseret Book, 1986), 61–64.

[40] See Martin Hengel, *Studies in the Gospel of Mark* (Philadelphia: Fortress Press, 1985), 2–14.

Matthew also broadens the audience beyond Mark's account to include not only Jerusalem and Judea but also the Jordan Valley, "all the region round about Jordan" (Matthew 3:5). And Matthew provides additional material beyond Mark's regarding John the Baptist's confrontation with a group of Pharisees and Sadducees who came to him (Matthew 3:7–10).[41]

Matthew wants us to see that the early conflict between John the Baptist and the Pharisees and Sadducees was transferred to Jesus. From the standpoint of the Pharisees and Sadducees, it would have been only natural to see a continuity between John the Baptist's ministry and Jesus' ministry—to see Jesus of Nazareth as John the Baptist's successor (see Matthew 23:13–33).

The Focus of Matthew and Luke

Only Matthew provides the following information: "But John forbad him, saying, I have need to be baptized of thee, and comest thou to me? And Jesus answering said unto him, Suffer it to be so now: for thus it becometh us to fulfill all righteousness. Then he suffered him" (Matthew 3:14–15). We could naturally wonder about such an insertion when Mark and Luke did not feel it necessary to provide this particular information.

Explaining why Jesus, the sinless Son of God, needed to be baptized may have presented some challenges to the early Christians. Matthew, therefore, provides a context to explain and understand why Jesus was baptized: "Suffer [permit] it to be so now: for thus it becometh us [is fitting for us] to fulfill all righteousness," wording that is not found in Mark's account (Matthew 3:15).

Jesus, a son of the law—born "under the law" (Galatians 4:4)—was required to obey the law. At this point, John the Baptist was a legal representative of the law; therefore, even though He did

---

[41] John chastises these religious leaders because they should have known and understood the message; having failed to emphasize the call for renewal among the Jews, John was sent by God to call Israel to repentance in preparation for the coming of the Messiah.

not need baptism, Jesus was required to seek it at the hands of the legal administrator (see 2 Nephi 31:5–13).[42]

If, as is generally accepted, Matthew wrote to a Jewish audience, then we should not think it odd that the story of Jesus in the wilderness, both the baptism in Jordan and the subsequent forty-day wilderness and temptation period, must have had rich resonances with those familiar with the Hebrew scriptures, especially in their Greek translation (LXX), on several levels. The nuances are numerous, and although we cannot now reconstruct adequately what the original readers/hearers may have thought when they read/heard this passage, we can legitimately justify some reasons to believe that it was understood as fulfilling allusions made earlier in their scriptures.

First, they may have recalled the story of the Israelites' flight into the wilderness for forty years and their eventual entrance into the promised land through the Jordan River (see Exodus 19; Numbers 33).[43] By reenacting the Exodus—crossing from the eastern desert over the Jordan into the promised land—Jesus initiates a new beginning for Israel.

For Matthew's Jewish audience, the story of the baptism in Jordan, the accompanying revelation, and the descent of the Spirit may have also reminded them of the words found in Isaiah, "When thou passest through the waters, I will be with thee" (Isaiah 43:2).

Another possible context for Matthew's Jewish audience was Isaiah's prayer (see Isaiah 63:7–64:12). The Septuagint version shares a cluster of words, phrases, and ideas found in Matthew's account of the baptism:

---

[42] The author of Hebrews notes, "Though he were a Son, yet learned he obedience by the things which he suffered; and being made perfect, he became the author of eternal salvation unto all them that obey him" (Hebrews 5:8–9).

[43] Glenn A. Koch rightly argues that "not only are the biblical narratives 'archetypes' for use of the New Testament authors, but also the oral traditions/legends which sought to embellish those narratives" in "Jesus' Baptism and Temptations Accounts in Mark's Gospel," in Robert A. Kraft and Benjamin G. Wright, eds., *A Multiform Heritage: Studies on Early Judaism and Christianity in Honor of Robert A. Kraft* (Atlanta: Scholars Press, 1999), 42.

1. "brought them up out of the sea" (LXX Isaiah 63:11).
2. "he who put his holy spirit in their midst" (LXX Isaiah 63:11).
3. "A spirit from the Lord descended" (LXX Isaiah 63:14).
4. "you are our father" (LXX Isaiah 63:16).
5. "rend the heavens" (LXX Isaiah 64:1).
6. Isaiah's prayer ends with a plea: "Can you remain silent?" (LXX Isaiah 64:12).

For Matthew, the baptism of Jesus (with all the elements noted above) may have proved that God was no longer silent and that Isaiah's prayer is answered fully and finally in the voice from heaven, "This is my beloved Son, in whom I am well pleased" (Matthew 3:17).

Finally, the most poignant context of this story, for a Jewish audience, may have been the rich interrelationship among several narratives found in the Hebrew scriptures: first, Abraham's offering of his "beloved son" (Genesis 22:1–13), known as the *aqedah* ("binding"); second, the story of Joseph, Jacob's "favorite son," who was sold into Egypt for twenty pieces of silver at the instigation of Judah (*Judas* in Greek), who eventually saved his family from death (Genesis 37:3–28); third, the sacrifice required to redeem the "firstborn son" in ancient Israel (Exodus 34:19–20); and, finally, the Passover sacrifice of a "lamb" (Exodus 12:1–28).[44]

The most obvious parallel was with the "binding of Isaac." Jesus' death must have been seen as being prefigured in Isaac, as noted earlier. The familiarity of the Greek words used in both Matthew and Genesis (LXX) accounts would have been not only noticeable but also striking. The Hebrew term *yahîd* ("favored one") is consistently translated in the Septuagint as *agapētos* ("beloved") for each of the three times used (Genesis 22:2, 12, 16), the very word appearing in the Gospel accounts (see Matthew 3:17, for example). Matthew's audience would have just heard about Jesus' miraculous conception (Matthew 1:18-25), reminding them further of the connection with

---

[44] See Jon D. Levenson, *The Death and Resurrection of the Beloved Son: The Transformation of Child Sacrifice in Judaism and Christianity* (New Haven: Yale University Press, 1993).

Isaac's near-sacrifice (see Genesis 18:9–14). We should not feel the necessity of deciding among the various scenarios provided above, as they are intrinsically related.

Luke, like Matthew, provides a detailed context to Jesus' baptism, including chronological signposts—a six-fold synchronization formula: "In the fifteenth year of the reign of [Roman Emperor] Tiberius Caesar [A.D. 27], Pontius Pilate being governor of Judea [Roman governors, including Pilate's tenure of A.D. 26–36, ruled Judea after A.D. 6], and Herod [Antipas, Herod the Great's son] being tetrarch of Galilee [from A.D. 4 through 39], and his brother [Herod] Philip tetrarch of Ituraea and of the region of Trachonitis [from A.D. 4 through 33–34], and Lysanias [an unknown figure] the tetrarch of Abilene [a tetrarchy named after its chief town, Abila, about eighteen miles northwest of Damascus], Annas [the former high priest from A.D. 6 through 14 and head of the powerful priestly family] and Caiaphas [Annas's son-in-law and current high priest] being the high priests [from A.D. 18 through 36], the word of God came unto John the son of Zacharias in the wilderness" (Luke 3:1–2).[45]

Luke adds one more historical detail as he concludes the wilderness story: "And Jesus himself began to be about thirty years of age" (Luke 3:23).[46] Like other ancient people, the generation living in first-century Jewish Palestine was decimated by disease, accidents, and a high death rate during childbirth. Though Jesus may be considered a young man at thirty, according to modern Western standards, He was not considered young by His contemporaries. Obviously, many, if not most of His audience, would have been younger and, most likely, facing death within a decade or so.

Besides the chronological clues Luke provides, he also supplies the fullest account of John the Baptist's ministry (Luke 3:1–19) and,

---

[45] Annas was followed by his son Eleazar, his son-in-law Caiaphas, and then four more sons. Although no longer recognized by Roman authority, Annas continued, through his family, to wield tremendous power and influence (see John 18:12–14).

[46] Luke also provides details about John the Baptist's preaching before Jesus appears (see Luke 3:1–14; see also JST Luke 3:5 for additional information regarding what expectations existed regarding the mission of the Messiah).

as a result, offers us subtle and intriguing additions to the story of Jesus' baptism and temptations.[47]

Luke continues his story following his lengthy but informative narration of John the Baptist's ministry: "When all the people were baptized, it came to pass, that Jesus also being baptized, and praying, the heaven was opened, and the Holy Ghost descended in a bodily shape like a dove upon him, and a voice came from heaven, which said, Thou art my beloved Son; in thee I am well pleased" (Luke 3:21–22).[48]

Luke, the only Gospel writer to do so, indicates that Jesus was praying when the heavens opened (see Luke 3:21). Depicting Jesus in a praying mode is a common theme in Luke (see 5:16; 9:18). Still, addressing Jesus Himself, the voice from heaven states, "Thou art my beloved Son; in thee I am well pleased" (Luke 3:22).

An early manuscript, known as Codex Bezae (D 05), reads, "You are my son, today I have begotten you," reminding us of Psalm 2, a royal coronation hymn composed for the enthronement ceremonies of Davidic kings: "I will declare the decree: Thou art my Son; this day have I begotten thee" (Psalm 2:7).[49] This passage was understood in Adoptionist terms—that is, the new king was adopted as God's son on the occasion, and the Davidic king was God's son. Using this line of reasoning, some early Christians also supposed that Jesus had been adopted on the day of His baptism.

This means that the KJV, based on a later textual tradition, may, in fact, reflect scribal attempts to alter the words of the original text to make the passage conform to second- or even third-century

---

[47] Luke also provides details regarding John the Baptist's birth and childhood (see Luke 1:5–23, 39–44, 57–80); see also S. Kent Brown, "Zacharias and Elisabeth, Joseph and Mary," in this volume.

[48] JST Luke states, "Now when all the people were baptized, it came to pass, that Jesus also came unto John; and being baptized of him, and praying, the heaven was opened" (JST Luke 3:28).

[49] Codex Bezae Catabrigiensis (D 05), containing a Greek text on the left side and an Old Latin version on the right side, is an important manuscript written shortly before A.D. 400, but it reflects a form much older than the manuscript itself from the second century.

teachings by scribes who viewed themselves as more orthodox than their Adoptionist Christian brethren. The scribes' efforts to harmonize the text to the parallel in Mark was most likely an attempt to prevent the passages' misuse by other Christians who, at the time, argued that Jesus was adopted as God's Son, as noted in the discussion above.

We can identify other examples of such "orthodox corruptions of the text." For example, a scribe apparently changed an earlier text in the Gospel of Luke, seeking to avoid a similar confusion. Luke, as the text is recorded in the KJV but following later textual witnesses, clarifies that it was "Joseph and his mother" (Luke 2:43) who sought the young child Jesus rather than simply "his parents" who sought Him, as in the earliest Greek manuscripts.

The reading "his parents" was interpreted by Adoptionist Christians to mean that Joseph was the father of Jesus but that God adopted Jesus at the baptism.[50] What seems to be clear is that Luke, like other Gospel authors, was not always consistent with usage and never anticipated the doctrinal debates of the second and third centuries.

Another unique aspect of Luke's narrative is the statement that "the Holy Ghost descended in a bodily shape like a dove upon him" (Luke 3:22).[51] To John the Baptist, the event was a sign: "And John bare record, saying, I saw the Spirit descending from heaven like a

---

[50] The Nestle-Aland 27th edition restores the text as "egnosan oi goneis" (Luke 2:43), a reading from, as noted above, Bezae Catabrigiensis, but also from other important witnesses, including Codex Sinaiticus, Codex Vaticanus, and Codex Washingtonianus. The altered reading is supported by Codex Alexandrinus, Codex Ephraemi Syri Rescriptus, and several later Byzantine texts. For a fuller discussion, see Ehrman, *The Orthodox Corruption of Scripture*, 47–118.

[51] Joseph Smith stated, "The sign of the dove was instituted before the creation of the world, a witness for the Holy Ghost, and the devil cannot come in the sign of a dove. The Holy Ghost is a personage, and is in the form of a personage. It does not confine itself to the *form* of the dove, but in *sign* of the dove. The Holy Ghost cannot be transformed into a dove; but the sign of a dove was given to John to signify the truth of the deed, as the dove is an emblem or token of truth and innocence" (Joseph Smith, *TPJS*, 276, italics in original; see also 1 Nephi 11:27; 2 Nephi 31:8; Doctrine and Covenants 93:15.

dove, and it abode upon him. And I knew him not: but he that sent me to baptize with water, the same said unto me, Upon whom thou shalt see the Spirit descending, and remaining on him, the same is he which baptizeth with the Holy Ghost. And I saw, and bare record that this is the Son of God" (John 1:32–34).

The Gospel of John does not include a historical narrative of the baptism of Jesus itself but instead provides a retrospective. John seems to be cognizant that the story is already in circulation. He states, "The next day John seeth Jesus coming unto him, and saith, Behold the Lamb of God, which taketh away the sin of the world. This is he of whom I said, After me cometh a man which is preferred before me: for he was before me. And I knew him not: but that he should be made manifest to Israel, therefore am I come baptizing with water. And John bare record, saying, I saw the Spirit descending from heaven like a dove, and it abode upon him. And I knew him not: but he that sent me to baptize with water, the same said unto me, Upon whom thou shalt see the Spirit descending, and remaining on him, the same is he which baptizeth with the Holy Ghost" (John 1:29–33).

Unlike the synoptic Gospels, John may have provided us the only firsthand account of the story (Matthew, Mark, and Luke were not disciples of John the Baptist and, therefore, were not at Jordan during this period). Still, we may wonder why seemingly important details are often missing from John's account. Like many other stories, John apparently kept the details of intimate and personal events, such as Jesus' birth, His wilderness temptations, the Mount of Transfiguration, and even the institution of the sacrament, private.[52]

Of note, John informs us that even though the Baptist appears first on the scene, preaching and baptizing in the wilderness, Jesus, in reality, already existed before him: "This is he of whom I said, After me cometh a man which is preferred before me: for he was before me"

---

[52] On the other hand, John may have known that these stories are widely known and are in circulation at the time and therefore decided to provide those things he felt are necessary to advance his purpose: "These things are written, that you may believe Jesus is the Christ, and that believing you might have life through his name" (John 20: 31), instead of retelling these particular stories.

(John 1:30; see 1:15)—that is, "Before I was born, he already was." Because John has already told us that Jesus was, in the beginning, the firstborn, this statement makes perfect sense (see John 1:1; 8:56–57).

In this reflection on an earlier event, John provides his poignant and powerful designation for Jesus, "the Lamb of God" (John 1:29), used only here and in 1:36 in the Gospel of John. John uses "lamb" twenty-nine times as a way to identify Jesus in the book of Revelation (see Revelation 5:6, for example; compare John 21:15). Clearly, John did not invent this title but received it from his master, John the Baptist. It is likely an allusion to Isaiah 53:7–12, especially verse 7.[53]

Here, like Matthew, we find just beneath the surface an allusion to the Passover lamb, the ancient Israelite sacrificial rite where a sheep substitutes for the firstborn son destined for sacrifice, and the near-sacrifice of Isaac. For John, Jesus represents all three (Paul will also identify Christ with the Passover offering and also with Isaac, the beloved son *par excellence* of the Hebrew Bible; see Galatians 3:13–16). In an inextricable web of relationships, Jesus not only becomes but also supersedes each: "the *son* takes the place of the *sheep* who took the place of the *son*."[54]

John also provides the reason for John the Baptist's ministry in the wilderness: "I knew him not: but that he should be made manifest to Israel, therefore am I come baptizing with water" (John 1:31).

The Gospels' telling of Jesus' baptism at the hands of John the Baptist provides the reader with a concrete historical setting for the beginning of Jesus' ministry. Additionally, it provided the original audience an opportunity to understand how Jesus' ministry was a continuation of John the Baptist's ministry and also to understand how the one who was younger (Jesus) was actually ranked ahead of the other (John the Baptist), contrary to the custom of the day that gave status and respect to the older person.

---

[53] Paul utilizes the same identification in 1 Corinthians 5:7, where Jesus is associated with the Passover lamb (see Exodus 12:3–10).

[54] Levenson, *The Death and Resurrection of the Beloved Son*, 208.

Jesus' Temptations

Only the synoptic Gospels provide an account of Jesus being driven into the wilderness by the greatest known force—the Spirit—where the devil tempts Him.[55] However, the author of Hebrews may have also recalled the event (see Hebrews 2:17–18; 4:15–16; 5:2), and John may have alluded to it (John 6:15, 26–34; 7:1–4).

Certainly, this is one of the most dramatic stories in the New Testament, and it forms, for Matthew, Mark, and Luke, the last preparatory incidents introducing Jesus' public ministry and is directly linked to the story of the baptism.[56] For the synoptic authors, the sudden appearance of the "voice of one crying in the wilderness" (Mark 1:3) was certainly not an ordinary announcement but a bold challenge to the kingdoms of this world and to the prince of the power of the air himself (Revelation 1:5; Ephesians 2:2). We should not think that the challenge would go unanswered; in fact, the counter challenge begins almost immediately in the wilderness where Jesus is tempted.

Mark, our earliest source, does not provide details of the temptations themselves (see Mark 1:12–13). Matthew and Luke, on the other hand, record three specific temptations (see Matthew 4:3–9 and Luke 4:3–11).[57] Again, Mark's account is brief and to the point:

---

[55] Jesus was quite alone during this forty-day period, suggesting that Jesus Himself told the disciples about the experiences at some point, highlighting the importance of the events themselves.

[56] The temptations took place in three distinct places: first, in the wilderness region of the lower Jordan Valley; second, on a high mountain, traditionally identified as one of the abrupt cliffs near Jericho—Jebel Quruntul (Mount of Temptation); and third, on a high point of the temple, now generally identified as the "place of trumpeting" at the southwest corner of the temple area from which the priests sounded the trumpet to call the city's attention to important events; see Richard Neitzel Holzapfel and David Rolph Seely, *My Father's House: Temple Worship and Symbolism in the New Testament* (Salt Lake City: Bookcraft, 1994), 92–94.

[57] That Jesus performed miracles in behalf of others is demonstrated over and over again throughout the Gospels. Nowhere does He perform one in His own behalf. The temptations may explain the reason Jesus did not use His divine power for self-interest because doing so would have been a subtle, but significant, departure from a mission wholly dedicated to others—one that the devil tried to subvert by tempting Jesus to take

"Immediately the Spirit driveth him into the wilderness. And he was there in the wilderness forty days, tempted of Satan; and was with the wild beasts; and the angels ministered unto him" (Mark 1:13).

Mark's description is surprisingly strong: "the Spirit driveth him into the wilderness," whereas Matthew and Luke use the gentler verb "led" (Matthew 4:1; Luke 4:1). JST Matthew states, "Then was Jesus led up of the Spirit into the wilderness to be with God. And when he had fasted forty days and forty nights and had communed with God, he was afterwards an hungered, and was left to be tempted of the devil" (JST Matthew 4:1–2).[58]

Much has been made of the nuance of *tempting* versus *testing*. The Greek (*peirazō*), "to tempt," does have the idea of "to test" in secular Greek. Its basic meaning is to try something so the person doing the trying can discover what it is made of, what its character is like, or what the results are of testing it (2 Corinthians 13:5). God also tries people (1 Corinthians 10:13), and Satan can be called the tempter, *o peirazon* (Matthew 4:3; 1 Thessalonians 3:5). The term is used in Matthew 4:1 in a passive infinitive construction with the devil as the agent.[59]

However, such a distinction is problematic and diverts the reader from the essential aspect of the story. The Book of Mormon uses the English word *temptation* in relation to Jesus' mortal ministry: "He shall go forth, suffering pains and afflictions and temptations of every kind, and this that the word might be fulfilled which saith he will take upon him the pains and the sicknesses of his people" (Alma 7:11).

We cannot know with any certainty what Aramaic words Jesus

---

care of His needs by using His power to satisfy His hunger for food, acceptance, and power.

[58] The JST consistently, in all three accounts, indicates that the Spirit did not lead Jesus into the wilderness to be tempted (see JST Matthew 4:1; JST Mark 1:10; JST Luke 4:1). Several manuscript witnesses demonstrate early Christian scribes' efforts to reflect this understanding. See Thomas A. Wayment's discussion of intentional scribal alterations to the New Testament text in "The Story of the New Testament," in this volume.

[59] Arndt and Gingrich, GEL, "peirazō," 792.

used to retell the story to His disciples.[60] We have only the Greek translation of the words, preserved in the synoptic accounts. But Joseph Smith's choice of a specific English word seems to indicate that we should understand Jesus' experience in the wilderness as a temptation—without emphasizing the nuance of testing in its place.[61] We will return to this point again.

Mark provides a unique insight, not found in Matthew or Luke, that Jesus "was with the wild beasts" (Mark 1:13) during the forty-day period in the wilderness. Two different and distinct approaches have been taken by interpreters when they discuss this passage. First, the beasts represent the physical dangers of the wilderness, and the devil represents the spiritual dangers of the wilderness. The second interpretative trajectory suggests that Mark's allusion to the "beginning," that is, to Genesis 1:1, at the start of his account should make us think of the Garden of Eden and Jesus' role as the second Adam, restoring harmony to God's creation as it was in the garden.

The latter seems unlikely. In the first century, the wilderness was the abode of an abundance of wild animals, including carnivores such as lions, bears, cheetahs, jackals, leopards, and wolves. Mark's mention of wild animals, therefore, most likely highlights the danger of the experience that will end only when the devil leaves Jesus.[62]

Matthew and Luke add material to Mark's story, including, as noted above, the actual temptations themselves. We might naturally ask, "Were the temptations spiritual or temporal or a combination of both?" or "Did only three temptations occur, or are the three representative of the devil's frontal assault on Jesus following a fasting

---

[60] One context for retelling the story may well have been at the end of the ministry when Jesus informs Peter of a confrontation with the devil, who wanted to "sift [Him] as wheat" (Luke 22:31).

[61] The primary meaning, as noted in the 1828 Noah Webster's American dictionary, was "The act of tempting; enticement to evil by arguments, by flattery, or by the offer of some real or apparent good"; *Noah Webster's First Edition of an American Dictionary of the English Language*, reprint (San Francisco: Foundation for American Christian Education, 1987), s.v., "Temptation."

[62] The story recalls Daniel's test among the lions and the Lord's protection when He sent an angel (see Daniel 6:16–23).

period that would have been a period of hunger, thirst, and fatigue?" and, finally, "Do the temptations represent an internal conflict, or are they to be understood as coming from an external source?"

The temptations are as follows:

"If thou be the Son of God, command that these stones be made bread" (Matthew 4:3; Luke 4:3).[63]

"If thou be the Son of God, cast thyself down: for it is written, He shall give his angels charge concerning thee: and in their hands they shall bear thee up, lest at any time thou dash thy foot against a stone" (Matthew 4:6; Luke 4:9–11).

"And sheweth him all the kingdoms of the world, and the glory of them; and saith unto him, All these things will I give thee, if thou wilt fall down and worship me" (Matthew 4:8–9; Luke 4:5–7).

Although Matthew and Luke do not follow the same chronological order in presenting the temptations, they are the same (Matthew's second and third are Luke's third and second respectively).[64] On a superficial level, Matthew's temptations, probably the original order, take place at progressively higher altitudes, beginning with Jesus' being led up out of the Jordan to the "wilderness" and ending on an "exceeding high mountain" (Matthew 4:1, 8).

Several issues seem to be involved in the temptation narratives. First, Matthew and Luke inform us that the devil urged Jesus to choose an easier road to fulfill His divinely appointed call of service—a ministry bound up in healing, teaching, suffering, and death. Of course, the implication is that if Jesus had done so, the ultimate result would have been something dramatically different and, from our point of view, terribly different than what God had intended.

---

[63] Most likely to be understood as, "Since you are the Son of God," as the devil does not doubt who Jesus is but attempts to tempt Him to use His divine powers for self-preservation.

[64] Some commentators see the story as a theme of temptations initiated at various times during the entire six weeks and not at one specific moment. Although Matthew suggests that the temptations came at the end of the forty-day fast (Matthew 4:1), Mark and Luke give the impression that fasting and temptations interlaced the entire experience. (See also JST Mark 1:11, which provides the same interpretation. However, JST Luke 4:2 agrees with Matthew's lead that the temptations followed the fasting.)

Second, Jesus' loyalty to God is being tested by the values central to such loyalty as expressed in the *Shema*: "Hear, O Israel: The Lord our God is one Lord: and thou shalt love the Lord thy God with all thine heart, and with all thy soul, and with all thy might" (Deuteronomy 6:4–5).[65]

Finally, the passage demonstrates that the external threats constituted a real, not imaginary, opposition to Jesus' efforts to fulfill His mission as the Son of God. The story prepares the reader, and Jesus Himself, for the antagonism, malice, rejection, and betrayal that will confront Him throughout the entire public ministry. Surely He would be tempted to use His powers, as the unique and beloved Son of God, to overcome His enemies, just as He was in this instance. In this, Jesus remained loyal to God and His mission to us (see John 3:16–17).

Matthew writes:

> Then was Jesus led up of the Spirit into the wilderness to be tempted of the devil. And when he had fasted forty days and forty nights, he was afterward an hungered. And when the tempter came to him, he said, If thou be the Son of God, command that these stones [singular in Mark and Luke] be made bread. But he answered and said, It is written, Man shall not live by bread alone, but by every word that proceedeth out of the mouth of God [see Deuteronomy 8:3]. Then the devil taketh him up into the holy city, and setteth him on a pinnacle of the temple, and saith unto him, If thou be the Son of God, cast thyself down: for it is written, He shall give his angels charge concerning thee: and in their hands they shall bear thee up, lest at any time thou dash thy foot against a stone [Psalm 91:11–12]. Jesus said unto him, It is written again, Thou shalt not tempt the Lord thy God [LXX Deuteronomy 6:16]. Again, the devil taketh him up into an exceeding high mountain, and sheweth him all the kingdoms of the world, and the glory of them; and saith unto him, All these things will

---

[65] *Shema*, the first Hebrew word of the Jewish daily prayer or proclamation found in Deuteronomy 6:4. This prayer eventually became the basic theological confession of Judaism and a vital part of liturgy.

I give thee, if thou wilt fall down and worship me. Then saith Jesus unto him, Get thee hence [the same abjuration is used to Peter in Matthew 16:23], Satan: for it is written, Thou shalt worship the Lord thy God, and him only shalt thou serve [LXX Deuteronomy 6:13]. Then the devil leaveth him, and, behold, angels came and ministered unto him. (Matthew 4:1–11)

Matthew, keeping the Spirit theme to the forefront, tells his readers that Jesus is "led up of the Spirit" into the wilderness, and then Matthew introduces us to Jesus' arch enemy, the devil (Greek *periazon*), also identified appropriately as "the tempter" and additionally by the more familiar Jewish designation, "Satan" (Matthew 4:1, 3, 10). Again, the Joseph Smith Translation emphasizes the "Spirit" in the narrative when it highlights Jesus' movements as being facilitated by the Spirit itself and not by Satan, as the current Greek text suggests (see JST Matthew 4:5, 8; compare JST Luke 4:5, 9).

Matthew's Jewish audience would not have failed to see parallels between Jesus' fast for forty days and the forty-day fasts of Moses (Exodus 34:28; Deuteronomy 9:9, 18) and Elijah (1 Kings 19:8). Additionally, the forty-year wilderness experience of the ancient Israelites who were tested before entering the promised land may have come to mind for the Jewish audience.

In fact, most commentators see Deuteronomy 8 as the background to the temptations of Jesus (see Deuteronomy 8:1–5). Moses commanded the children of Israel, "Thou shalt remember all the way which the Lord thy God led thee these forty years in the wilderness, to humble thee, and to prove thee, to know what was in thine heart, whether thou wouldest keep the commandments, or no" (Deuteronomy 8:2). Jesus also quotes from this section in His first retort to the devil during the temptations (see Matthew 4:4; compare Deuteronomy 8:3).

Deuteronomy 6 provides another context of understanding. Here, Moses reminds the children of Israel about their tempting God in the wilderness: "Ye shall not tempt the Lord your God, as ye tempted him in Massah" (Deuteronomy 6:16).⁶⁶ Following forty days of fasting, Jesus was "afterward an hungred"—that is, *famished* (Matthew 4:2). At this point, according to some accounts, the devil approached Jesus to tempt Him—in Jesus' most vulnerable moment. Jesus was, by all accounts, hungry, alone, and exhausted at the end of forty days of fasting.

Jesus resists the enticing proposals offered by the devil. They are not only rebuffed but also categorically rejected. In each case, Jesus withstands the temptation and challenges the tempter by quoting scripture, demonstrating His rightful role as the sole interpreter of God's word and will in human affairs.⁶⁷ Even when the devil attempts to do the same, Jesus responds, "It is written again" (Matthew 4:7)—that is, "Scripture also says"—revealing Jesus' command of the scriptures even against those who would use scripture inappropriately. At the end of the temptation period, Matthew notes, "then the devil leaveth him, and, behold, angels came and ministered unto him" (Matthew 4:11).⁶⁸ Of passing interest, besides the phrase "Get thee hence, Satan," the only words of Jesus preserved in the account are His introduction and then quotation of scripture.⁶⁹

Luke's account, like Matthew's, provides more details than Mark's but omits the presence of wild beasts:

> And Jesus being full of the Holy Ghost returned from Jordan, and was led by the Spirit into the wilderness, Being forty days tempted of the devil. And in those days he did eat nothing: and when they were

---

⁶⁶ Matthew and Luke provide three specific temptations along with Jesus' responses, all of which are drawn from Deuteronomy.

⁶⁷ In each response, the context of the passage cited is fundamental to understanding what Matthew has in mind; see, for example, Jesus' first response, a quotation from Deuteronomy. Here the context is about the Lord's efforts to humble ancient Israel in the wilderness where He let them hunger but eventually fed them manna (Deuteronomy 8:3).

⁶⁸ Curiously, the JST deletes the reference to angels coming to administer to Jesus (JST Matthew 4:11).

⁶⁹ Most modern English versions omit a similar phrase found in Luke (see Luke 4:8) because early textual witnesses lack this statement, suggesting that a later scribe added it to Luke in an attempt to harmonize the accounts.

ended, he afterward hungered. And the devil said unto him, If thou be the Son of God, command this stone [unlike Matthew's plural "stones"] that it be made bread. And Jesus answered him, saying, It is written, That man shall not live by bread alone, but by every word of God. And the devil, taking him up into an high mountain, shewed unto him all the kingdoms of the world in a moment of time. And the devil said unto him, All this power will I give thee, and the glory of them: for that is delivered unto me; and to whomsoever I will I give it. If thou therefore wilt worship me, all shall be thine. And Jesus answered and said unto him, Get thee behind me, Satan: for it is written, Thou shalt worship the Lord thy God, and him only shalt thou serve. And he brought him to Jerusalem, and set him on a pinnacle of the temple, and said unto him, If thou be the Son of God, cast thyself down from hence: for it is written, He shall give his angels charge over thee, to keep thee: and in their hands they shall bear thee up, lest at any time thou dash thy foot against a stone. And Jesus answering said unto him, It is said, Thou shalt not tempt the Lord thy God. And when the devil had ended all the temptation, he departed from him for a season (Luke 4:1–13).

Luke, highlighting the theme of the Spirit, indicates that Jesus was "full of the Holy Ghost" following the baptism at Jordan and then was "led by the Spirit" into the Judean desert (Luke 4:1). Luke then turns to the temptations themselves. Except for a different chronological order, the temptations closely parallel Matthew's account (Matthew 4:1–11).[70] Most interestingly, Luke emphasizes that the devil departed "for a season" (Luke 4:13), or, more literally, "bided his time" or waited "until an opportune time, suggesting another battle in the future (Luke 22:3, 28, 31).

Unquestionably, the synoptic authors, the author of Hebrews, and Alma in the Book of Mormon believed that Jesus was not only tested

---

[70] Luke, in keeping with his temple theme, chose to end the temptations with Jesus' casting out of Satan from His Father's house; see Holzapfel and Seely, *My Father's House*, 92–94.

but also tempted. Having passed the period of temptation, Jesus begins His public ministry. The wilderness experience was, after all, another decisive moment in Jesus' ministry—a ministry where Jesus was to bind the devil (Matthew 12:28), release the devil's captives (Luke 4:18), and ultimately destroy the devil (Hebrews 2:14).

Communication and Communion in the Wilderness

The wilderness was certainly a place associated with negative references in the Jewish world. First, the wilderness was a terrible place (Numbers 20:5; Proverbs 21:19), a place of hunger, thirst, and deprivation (Psalm 107:4–5; Job 30:3), a place unsettled (Jeremiah 2:6; Job 38:26), a windswept place (Isaiah 21:1; Hosea 13:15; Job 1:19), a place haunted by beasts and demons (Deuteronomy 8:25; Isaiah 13:21; 34:14), a place where frightful noises were heard (Deuteronomy 32:10), and the domain of Cain (Genesis 4:12–16).

However, the wilderness was also a place of spiritual renewal for two of Israel's great prophets, Moses and Elijah (see Exodus 3:1–4:7; 1 Kings 19). Later, following His own wilderness experiences of baptism, fasting, and temptations, Jesus sought solitude in the wilderness again (Luke 5:16; John 11:54). There He communed and communicated with His Father.

The Gospels are virtually silent on the nature of Jesus' communion with God during this first wilderness period, except that the texts preserve a single sentence from at least one conversation—with His Father (Mark 1:11) and the notice that God sent angels to His Son to minister to Him in the wilderness following the temptations (see Mark 1:13).

The silence in the passage is deafening and, as a result, captures our attention and imagination. We can always find spaces between lines and letters—gaps that open wide for interpretation. We can reasonably believe that this long period of more than six weeks (at least forty days and forty nights) in the wilderness was not only filled with the events that were preserved by the pens of scribes through nearly two thousand years of textual history (the events of just two days) but also witnessed periods when Jesus communed and communicated with His Father.

In the sacred past, the Lord provided for the children of Israel, sometimes in dramatic ways, during their wilderness wanderings (Exodus 13:21–22; Numbers 10:33; Deuteronomy 8:3–5). In one account, the Lord sent His angel: "Behold, I send an Angel before thee, to keep thee in the way, and to bring thee into the place which I have prepared" (Exodus 23:20; compare 32:34). At times, their devotion to the Lord was exemplary: "I remember the devotion of your youth, how as a bride you loved me and followed me through the desert, through a land not sown" (NIV Jeremiah 2:2; Hosea 2:15).

Now, in the sacred present, —Jesus demonstrates His complete fidelity to the Father in the wilderness of Judea as they communed and communicated together—all in preparation for a ministry that was about to burst forth among His countrymen.

Conclusion

As Mark begins, John the Baptist, the people, and finally Jesus Himself gravitate toward the wilderness centripetally. Eventually, Jerusalem, the cities and towns of Judea, and, in fact, "all the region round about Jordan" are emptied of their inhabitants, and the river is flooded with them (Matthew 3:5–6). Following Jesus' baptism, fasting, and temptations, His ministry spread out from the wilderness centrifugally because His mission was not fulfilled in the wilderness, during His public ministry proper, or at the conclusion of His suffering, death, and resurrection; but His mission carried on beyond death—the end was really only the beginning.

Nevertheless, Jesus' baptism, fasting, and temptations were pivotal moments in His life and for His ministry. The importance of the events in the wilderness was highlighted when the disciples met, following Jesus' death and resurrection, to choose a replacement for Judas, who had fallen.

Peter informed the group assembled in the large upper room in Jerusalem that Judas' replacement among the apostles must be a witness of Jesus' resurrection and ascension—an obvious qualification in light of the calling.

At the other end of the chronological divide was what the synoptic authors claimed was a pivotal moment in Jesus' ministry—the baptism: "Wherefore of these men which have companied with us all the time that the Lord Jesus went in and out among us, *beginning from the baptism of John*, unto the same day that he was taken up from us, must one be ordained to be a witness with us of his resurrection" (Acts 1:21–22; emphasis added).

As noted earlier, the Spirit theme threads throughout the Gospels. First, the Spirit falls upon Jesus when John baptizes Him in the wilderness (Mark 1:9–10; Matthew 3:16; Luke 3:21–22; John 1:32). Second, the Spirit drives Jesus into the wilderness, where He fasts for forty days and is tempted by the devil (Mark 1:13; Matthew 4:1–11; and Luke 4:1–13). Third, Jesus returns to Galilee in the "power of the Spirit" (Luke 4:14). Fourth, Jesus declares that "The Spirit of the Lord is upon me, because he hath anointed me to preach the gospel" when He appears in Nazareth following the wilderness experience (Luke 4:18).

The events of the baptism, fasting, and temptations in the wilderness not only belong to the earliest strata of New Testament material about Jesus and set the tone for the whole public ministry of Jesus but also, in a fundamental and important way, emphasize "how God anointed Jesus of Nazareth with the Holy Ghost and with power: who went about doing good . . . for God was with him" (Acts 10:38).

PART 3

THE MINISTRY COMMENCES

VII.
JESUS' EARLY MINISTRY IN JUDEA AND JERUSALEM

THOMAS A. WAYMENT

He must increase, but I must decrease. He that cometh from above is above all: he that is of the earth is earthly, and speaketh of the earth: he that cometh from heaven is above all.

JOHN 3:30–31

Reconstructing the ministry of Jesus of Nazareth is no simple matter; it is a challenge that is compounded by the variety of accounts about Jesus' life. Anyone who has opened the New Testament has noticed differences among the Gospel accounts. Three of the Gospels, Matthew, Mark, and Luke, place Jesus' ministry in the framework of a one- to two-year ministry, and John includes information suggesting a two- to three-year ministry. Rather than use the familiar and often-tired scholarly arguments of why the dating of Matthew, Mark, and Luke are to be preferred against John's or vice versa for this period of Jesus' life, this chapter will look at the subject of Jesus' early Judean ministry, with particular emphasis on Jesus' relationship with John the Baptist.

Most Latter-day Saint reconstructions of the life of Jesus have contextualized it using the framework of a three-year ministry.[1]

---

[1] Latter-day Saint authors have unanimously adopted the framework of a three-year public ministry. See, for example, Robert J. Matthews, *Behold the Messiah* (Salt Lake City:

Surprisingly, many scholars today opt for a public ministry longer than the one-year ministry presented in the synoptic Gospels, even though they favor the historical reliability of those Gospels against the Gospel of John's three-year ministry.[2] The heart of the issue lies in Jesus' attendance at the Passover festival held every spring beginning on 15 Nisan and ending 21 Nisan.[3] The synoptic Gospels refer to only one Passover celebration, the one where Jesus was apprehended and tried as a criminal (Matthew 26:2; Mark 14:1; Luke 22:1).[4] John, on the other hand, makes reference to three separate Passover meals celebrated by Jesus (John 2:13; 6:4; 11:55).[5] The reference in John 5:1 to an unnamed feast could also be a Passover celebration and therefore would indicate that Jesus' public ministry included four Passover celebrations.[6] Another Passover may be implied by the synoptic Gospels when Jesus and His disciples are in Galilee plucking

---

Bookcraft, 1994), 59; McConkie, MM, 1:469; McConkie, DNTC, 3:188; Hugh B. Brown, *The Abundant Life* (Salt Lake City: Bookcraft, 1965), 314; John A. Tvedtnes, *The Church of the Old Testament* (Salt Lake City: Deseret Book, 1980), 1.

[2] See Marianne Meye Thompson, "The Historical Jesus and the Johannine Christ," in *Exploring the Gospel of John in Honor of D. Moody Smith*, ed. R. Alan Culpepper and C. Cliften Black (Louisville: Westminster/John Knox Press, 1996), 21–42; Francis J. Maloney, "The Fourth Gospel and the Jesus of History," *New Testament Studies* 46 (1999): 42–58.

[3] Nisan corresponds to March–April in the modern calendar. It was the first month of the Jewish calendar, and it began with the first new moon after the vernal equinox. Therefore, the Passover fell on the first full moon after the vernal equinox. See Grace Amadon, "Ancient Jewish Calendation," *Journal of Biblical Literature* 61 (1942): 229.

[4] The Gospel of Luke contains an added reference to the Passover in Luke 2:41.

[5] Other references to Passover in John are 2:23; 12:1; 13:1; 18:28, 39; 19:14.

[6] The footnote for John 5:1a refers to the "Koine Greek manuscripts of the Gospel (Byzantine)" to clarify which festival is being referred to in John. The note as it reads needs clarification. All Greek manuscripts of the New Testament are written in Koine Greek, as opposed to Attic or Classical Greek. The manuscripts of the New Testament are often separated into three or four classifications or families, of which the Byzantine family is historically the latest. For the passage in question, several ancient manuscripts contain the reading, "the festival," which indicates that this was the Passover. The manuscripts that include the reading span several centuries and text families and include the important New Testament codices Sinaiticus (fourth century), Ephraemi Syri Rescriptus (fifth century), and Athous Lavrensis (eighth/ninth century). The reading, "a festival" is found in p^{66} (circa A.D. 200). The earliness of the reading from p^{66} likely indicates that the unnamed feast was not originally referred to as a Passover feast.

grain, a springtime event. This event has traditionally been placed between the Passovers identified in John 2:13 and 6:4 and indicates, therefore, a fourth springtime in Jesus' ministry.[7]

The logical conclusion is that Jesus' ministry spanned a portion of a year in the synoptic account, whereas John's account mandates that Jesus' ministry lasted at least two years and probably three.[8] Combined with a third piece of evidence from the Gospel of John (John 5:1), the unspecified feast could indicate that the ministry lasted at least three years. The sheer number of events that took place during Jesus' public ministry speaks for a duration longer than the one-year period depicted in the synoptics. The issue is an important one, and further research will reveal that the Gospel authors were largely unaware of the beginnings of Jesus' public ministry, a possible result of their sources and, in some instances, the date of their conversions.

The Beginning of John the Baptist's Ministry

No Gospel account or other record purports to provide a personal eyewitness account of Jesus' baptism by John the Baptist or of Jesus' initial interactions with John.[9] The Gospel of Luke records that John and Jesus were related and that their mothers knew one another personally, but any contact between the two women was limited in the record to the period of the pregnancy (Luke 1:39–56). For whatever reasons, John and Jesus evidently did not remain in close contact with one another during their youth. A vague remembrance of their separate childhood and adolescent experiences is recorded in a passing reference in the Gospel of John where the Baptist says, "I

---

[7] Harold W. Hoehner, "History and Chronology of the New Testament," in Harold W. Hoehner, *Foundations for Biblical Interpretation: A Complete Library of Tools and Resources* (Nashville: Broadman & Holman, 1994), 477.

[8] Mark 6:39 refers to "green grass," an observation that inadvertently points to a public ministry longer than one year.

[9] The title "the Baptist" is the final form of an original epithet, "the baptizer" (*ho baptizōn*), a present active participle that carries with it the idea of repeated action. After his death around A.D. 26–29, the name appears to have shifted to a nominal form, "the Baptist." See Paul W. Hollenbach, "John the Baptist," in Freedman, *ABD*, 3:887.

knew him not" (John 1:31, 33).[10] Apparently, the two had grown up independently of each other, Jesus in the small village of Nazareth and John in the hill country of Judea, but they were brought together under the spirit and power of Elias rather than through family contacts.[11]

From the sources available to us, we cannot be certain how long John the Baptist had preached before his baptism of Jesus. Luke is the only author to provide any direct information on the issue when he says, "Jesus himself began to be about thirty years of age," a statement made in connection with Jesus' baptism (Luke 3:23). The statement, however, can confirm only Jesus' age when He was baptized, thus providing a relative age for John the Baptist, but it does not clarify when John began preaching. However, the Gospel of Luke links the beginning of John's ministry with the fifteenth year of the reign of Tiberius, which would indicate a date of A.D. 26 or early 27 (Luke 3:1–3).[12] Matthew's and Luke's inclusion of John's invective against the Pharisees, "O generation of vipers" (Matthew 3:7; Luke 3:7), leaves the impression that it cannot have been immediately before the beginning of the public ministry because by the time Jesus came to be baptized, John had already developed a well-defined set of

---

[10] The authenticity of this statement is unassailable. The historical context in which the Gospel of John was written makes such a statement by John a valuable piece of evidence for those who accepted John but denied Jesus. Pseudo-Clement, *Recognitions*, 1.54–60, reports that followers of John but not Jesus were a persistent problem into the second century.

[11] Zacharias and Elisabeth lived in the "hill country of Juda," a region that includes the area traditionally settled by Judah, son of Jacob (Numbers 13:26–30). Luke's phraseology suggests that Mary traveled from the hills of lower Galilee south to Judea (Luke 1:39). Luke mentions no city by name, and therefore the hometown of Zacharias and Elizabeth can remain only a conjecture. However, two sites are traditionally identified as possible locations: En Kerem, located on the western edge of modern Jerusalem, and the Palestinian village of Yatta (Jutta in KJV), located directly five miles south of Hebron (an ancient Jewish town—one of the Levitical cities in Joshua; see 15:15, 21:16).

[12] We derive the date of A.D. 27 by counting fifteen years forward from the date when the Roman Senate in A.D. 12 granted Tiberius tribunican powers for the second time and extended his imperium empire wide. See Barbara Levick, *Tiberius the Politician* (London: Thames and Hudson, 1976), 63.

enemies and had refined his prophetic harangue to include the Jewish aristocracy more narrowly. The Gospel of John, on the other hand, weaves the beginning of Jesus' ministry into the fabric of John's final days; therefore, the two could have overlapped for some time (John 3:22–24).

The Public Ministry of John the Baptist

John's family was part of a rural priestly family, his father of the course of Abia and his mother a descendant of Aaron (Luke 1:5).[13] Toward the beginning of his prophetic career, John chose an ascetic lifestyle and took on the appearance of a desert prophet. Matthew records that John wore "camel's hair, and a leathern girdle about his loins; and his meat was locusts and wild honey" (Matthew 3:4). Other Old Testament prophets had worn clothes similar to John's—namely Elijah, who wore "a girdle of leather about his loins" (2 Kings 1:8).[14] The parallel with Elijah may have been pointed out intentionally by the author of the Gospel of Matthew, as many people were already questioning whether John was Elijah.[15] This atypical clothing style has a strong parallel to the poor, landless class of Judean peasants.[16] From Matthew, we also learn that John spoke against Herod Antipas on the occasion of Herod's marriage to Herodias, his brother Philip's wife.

Josephus records that Herod Antipas had been married to the daughter of Aretas, the king of Arabia (located southeast of Herod's

---

[13] For a discussion of the course of Abia, see S. Kent Brown, "Zacharias and Elisabeth, Joseph and Mary," in this volume.

[14] Zechariah 13:4 relates that false prophets can be detected because they wear smooth clothing—and not the typical clothing of a prophet. Compare W. D. Davies and Dale C. Allison Jr., *Matthew*, International Critical Commentary, 3 vols. (Edinburgh: T & T Clark, 1988), 1:295.

[15] John 1:21 reads, "Are thou Elias? And he saith I am not." *Elias* in this passage is confused with *Elijah* in the passage, possibly as a result of the Greek text, which does not distinguish between the two names.

[16] For a similar assessment, see Robert J. Matthews, "A Voice in the Wilderness," in *Studies in Scripture, Vol. 5: The Gospels*, ed. Kent P. Jackson and Robert L. Millet (Salt Lake City: Deseret Book, 1986), 172–73.

tetrarchy). While in Rome, however, Antipas became infatuated with his brother Herod Philip's wife and secretly proposed that she leave her husband and marry him upon their joint return from Rome. Herodias, Philip's wife, made one request of her soon-to-be husband—Antipas had to divorce Aretas's daughter as a favor to Herodias.[17] The story, although scandalous, appears in a similar form in the New Testament with the addition that John challenged the legality of such a marriage. Invoking the legal precedent established in Leviticus 20:21, John publicly denounced the new liaison between uncle and sister-in-law. The relationship was particularly scandalous because Herodias was also Herod's niece through his half brother Aristobulus (Leviticus 18:13–16; 20:21).

The importance of the story lies in John's scathing rebuke of one of the most powerful men of Judea-Galilee. Very few families wielded more power than the Herodian clan, and John's tirade would certainly not go unnoticed. According to the synoptics and Josephus, John was imprisoned and executed for his condemnation of Herod Antipas and, more particularly, of Herod's marriage to Herodias (Matthew 14:1–13; Mark 6:17–19; Luke 3:19–20; Josephus, AJ, 18.5.2). John's criticisms of the powerful and corrupt Herodian clan must have been popular with the Jewish peasant population but highly unpopular with the aristocracy and the large non-Jewish population living in the region. Matthew's Gospel preserves a trace of the resulting division associated with John's teaching when it states, "John came unto you in the way of righteousness, and ye believed him not: but the publicans and the harlots believed him" (Matthew 21:32).

Our primary interest at this stage, however, is the point at which Jesus began to make contact with John and his followers. According to all Gospel accounts, Jesus came to John seeking baptism (Matthew 3:13).[18] According to the Gospel of John, it was John the Baptist who

---

[17] Josephus, AJ, 18.5.1.
[18] The Gospel of Mark is silent on the issue of John's location when he baptized Jesus, whereas Luke contains the ambiguous statement, "all the country about Jordan"

singled out Jesus from among those gathered at Jordan instead of Jesus making Himself known. John had been prepared to baptize the one mightier than he when that person was identified by a specific heavenly sign (John 1:33). Jewish leaders in Jerusalem and Herod Antipas's court in Galilee became alarmed with John's growing power and influence as the number of followers multiplied.[19] Jesus' initial interaction with John appears to have taken place as John was gaining greater public attention but prior to John's heated denunciation of Antipas.

The New Testament mentions two specific geographical locations for John's ministry: Bethabara, also identified as Bethany in the earliest manuscripts (see John 1:19–28), and Aenon near Salim (John 3:23).[20] Aenon is generally identified as being located in the Decapolis region—the political area on the east and west sides of the Jordan south of the Sea of Galilee. Bethabara is generally identified with Perea, just north of the Dead Sea, a region under Herod Antipas's control. It was most likely here that Herod Antipas was in a position to attempt to silence the prophet's criticism.

Jesus' Baptism by John

Jesus, by all accounts, traveled alone to see John and was preparing Himself for His public ministry. As He came into contact with the Baptist, Jesus made important contacts with men of faith who would later become His leading disciples. Andrew, Peter's brother, and an unnamed disciple, likely John the Beloved, were with John the Baptist before Jesus' baptism (John 1:37–40). Whether they saw the actual baptism of Jesus remains unclear. What we do know is that John the Baptist prophesied of Jesus and His future ministry during the same period when Jesus was baptized (John 1:29–34). Jesus

---

(Luke 3:3), although Luke 3:2 seems to imply this was the area around Jordan in Judea. The evidence from John 1:19 is inconclusive on the issue of locale.

[19] See Josephus, *AJ*, 18.5.2.

[20] The reading "Bethany" is found in papyri 66 (p^{66}; circa 200) and 75 (p^{75}; third century). The reading "Bethany" is found in a wide variety of later manuscripts.

appears to have left John's company shortly after His baptism to prepare Himself for the public ministry.

All three synoptic Gospels record that Jesus went into the wilderness alone during His forty-day fast (Matthew 4:1–11; Mark 1:12–13; Luke 4:1–13). The synoptic authors nearly always used the word *wilderness* to refer to the Judean wilderness, and this instance should not be considered an exception.[21] The Gospel authors' lack of precision in placing the event is insubstantial, as all three accounts are more focused on Jesus' primary concern to be alone. Leaving the designation "Judean" out of the phrase "Judean wilderness" may have been their way of heightening the idea of Jesus' solitary sojourn. Toward the end of His quiet separation in the wilderness, He was tempted by Satan to forego His mission and avoid the trials and pain that would certainly attend the public ministry (Matthew 4:3–10; Luke 4:3–12).

The next stage in Jesus' public ministry is difficult to reconstruct.[22] Jesus' youth was spent in and around Nazareth, but something in His late twenties or early thirties drew Him toward Judea. The Gospels all connect His early visit to Judea with the fiery and inspirational teaching of John the Baptist, combined with a foreboding sense that the public ministry was about to begin. The early connections between John and Jesus remain sufficiently obscure; however, all four Gospel accounts agree that His associations with John before John's arrest by Herod Antipas and John's imprisonment at Machaerus led Jesus to depart Judea or Nazareth and move to Galilee.[23]

This moment in time is of utmost importance if we are to understand Jesus' early ministry. The synoptic Gospels teach that after the

---

[21] The exceptions are Matthew 15:33, Mark 8:4, and Luke 15:4.

[22] For a useful discussion of possible reconstructions of Jesus' early ministry, see Peter Richardson, "What Has Cana to Do with Capernaum," *New Testament Studies* 48 (2001): 320–24.

[23] See Mathew 4:12; Mark 1:14; Luke 4:14; John 4:1–3. Only Luke confuses the issue by recording that Jesus returned to Galilee directly from His experiences in Judea. Josephus places John's imprisonment at Machaerus, the hilltop fortress north of the Dead Sea built by Herod Antipas's father, Herod the Great (*AJ*, 18.5.2).

arrest of John the Baptist, Jesus embarked on a one-year ministry that culminated in the Passover of the following year. The Gospel of John, however, teaches that Jesus' baptism preceded the miracle at Cana and was a prelude to an early Judean ministry, during which time the Baptist was still alive. The context of the early Judean ministry is difficult to reconcile with the synoptic accounts.

In reading Matthew's account closely, we will see a strong sense that the author is trying to understand Jesus' motives for moving away from His family in Nazareth and relocating to Capernaum. Consistent with the author's outlook elsewhere, Matthew sees it as Jesus' intentional effort to fulfill Old Testament prophecy.[24] Matthew may have been more interested in understanding the doctrinal implications of Jesus' move to Capernaum than in establishing its precise historical setting. According to the Gospel of Matthew, Jesus began His public ministry at the same moment John the Baptist was arrested, immediately calling disciples and teaching them the higher law of the Sermon on the Mount (Matthew 4:12–13, 18–22). Luke's description focuses on Jesus' return to His hometown of Nazareth in Galilee, for he says, "Jesus returned in the power of the Spirit into Galilee . . . and he came to Nazareth" (Luke 4:14–16). The intent of the Gospel of Luke appears to be on the reasons that Jesus moved to Capernaum rather than on the reasons He left Judea.[25]

The Gospel of John, however, outlines this early period of Jesus' ministry more completely. Rather than leave immediately for Galilee from Judea after hearing the news of John's arrest, Jesus was in Galilee by choice shortly after His baptism and was not under any suspicion in relation to John's arrest. In Cana, Jesus performed the miracle of changing water into wine in the presence of a few newly called disciples and then returned to Judea, where John was still active.

---

[24] In this instance, Matthew invokes the testimony of Isaiah to explain Jesus' motives in moving to Capernaum (Matthew 9:1–2). This way of understanding Jesus' ministry is evident throughout the Gospel of Matthew. For example, see Matthew 12:17 21.

[25] The Gospel of Mark is silent on this important juncture in Jesus' life. See Mark 1:15–16.

Before His departure to the wedding at Cana, Jesus had called four disciples. Three of them, Peter, Andrew, and Philip, were from Bethsaida, an area now identified with a site on the east side of the Jordan at the north end of the Sea of Galilee (John 1:35–44). At this time, Jesus also called the unnamed disciple, who should likely be identified with John the Beloved (John 1:37, 40).

Some scholars maintain that a call of Galilean disciples indicates that John the Baptist was also working in Galilee at this time, but such a thesis is unnecessary because Jesus probably met His future Galilean disciples when they came to listen to John teach in Perea.[26] Interestingly, in the Gospel of John's account of the call of the disciples, no mention is made of fishing nets, Peter's occupation, the Sea of Galilee, or any of the other descriptive markers that would indicate the call came after Jesus had returned to Galilee. Instead, John places the call of these early disciples in Perea and then relates that "the day following Jesus would go forth into Galilee" (John 1:43). This evidence, in support of the synoptic Gospels, reveals that Jesus traveled from Nazareth to Jordan, most likely in Perea, to be baptized by John and that during those early days of association with John's followers, He identified several future disciples from among those who had also come to hear John preach.

The Early Judean Ministry

For whatever reasons, now unknown to us, Jesus went into Galilee sometime following His baptism and fast in the wilderness. Nothing in the Gospel accounts suggests a break in the story between the baptism by John and the forty-day fast (Matthew 3:16–4:11; Mark 1:10–13; Luke 3:21–22; 4:1–13). Shortly after His stay in Cana, Jesus embarked on a brief period in His ministry that is known as the early

---

[26] John 1:19, 23 makes little sense if the baptism of Jesus took place in Galilee because on the day following His baptism, He called Peter, Andrew, the unnamed disciple, and Philip. The time reference provided in John 1:35 does not allow enough time for Jesus to be in Perea for the baptism and then travel to the Sea of Galilee to call disciples.

Judean ministry.[27] We cannot be certain which disciples accompanied Him on His journey from Cana to Jerusalem, but several key features of the story indicate that at least some of the disciples were present on this visit. The presence of disciples is implied in John 2:12–22 in connection with Jesus' cleansing of the temple. The author of the Gospel of John interjects, at the end of this story, the conclusion that "when . . . he was risen from the dead, his *disciples remembered* that he had said this unto them" (John 2:22; emphasis added). Also, John mentions in 3:22 that the disciples of Jesus were baptizing in Judea during this same visit. The final piece of evidence comes when Jesus returns from Judea to Galilee through Samaria, where His disciples were sent into the city to buy food (John 4:8).

The ramifications of this early Judean ministry for understanding the life of Jesus Christ are numerous. The Gospel of John places this early Judean ministry in John 2:13–4:42. They embarked on this ministry to participate in the Passover feast held every year in early spring (John 2:13). What is surprising about this early mission is that it immediately took on a negative tone with the Jewish leadership. Almost nothing of this early mission in Judea was positive, perhaps giving a few of the disciples an early glimpse into the pain and anguish that would come later.

Upon arriving in Jerusalem, Jesus went into the temple and cleansed its courts of those who changed money or sold oxen, sheep, and doves (John 2:14–16). What is remarkable about this early visit to the temple is not whether it is the first of two similar actions against the temple but rather how Jesus made such a provocative statement against the temple, thereby providing a clear context for what He had come to do.[28] A public action of this sort would not go

---

[27] For a Latter-day Saint discussion of this time period of Jesus' ministry, see Kay Edwards, "The Early Judean Ministry," in *Studies in Scripture, Vol. 5: The Gospels*, ed. Kent P. Jackson and Robert L. Millet (Salt Lake City: Deseret Book, 1986), 188–200. See also Paula Fredricksen, *Jesus of Nazareth, King of the Jews: A Jewish Life and the Emergence of Christianity* (New York: Alfred Knopf, 1999), 197–214.

[28] See Richard Draper, "Jesus' Prophecies of His Death and Resurrection," in Richard Neitzel Holzapfel and Thomas A. Wayment, eds., *From the Last Supper through the*

unnoticed by Jewish authorities and Roman officials, especially given its close proximity to the Antonia Fortress.[29] Because John in his Gospel wanted to tell the entire life of Jesus in terms of His atoning sacrifice, John likely saw the temple cleansing as a piece of the larger puzzle, an event that prefigured the final outcome of Jesus' life. Behind this early scene, however, is a brooding conflict between Jesus and the Jewish leadership in Jerusalem.

The immediate move to the story of Nicodemus continues the theme, as Nicodemus is afraid to visit Jesus by day but rather visits by night, claiming that "we know that thou art a teacher come from God: for no man can do these miracles that thou doest, except God be with him" (John 3:2).[30] The context of this statement has been called into question by modern interpreters who find no substance to support Nicodemus's claim that Jesus had performed miracles in Judea and also that a group of Jewish leaders had come to believe in them.[31] The Gospel of John does not mention any miracle, nor does it indicate that Jesus had taken time to teach in Jerusalem during this period. However, the themes of Jewish antagonism and resentment toward Jesus are consistent throughout the early Judean ministry.

Resurrection: The Savior's Final Hours (Salt Lake City: Deseret Book, 2003), 7–10.

[29] Jesus' actions against the temple are said to have taken place in the "*heiron*," the outer court of the temple or the court of the Gentiles, parts of which were clearly visible from the Antonia Fortress. When Jesus was questioned regarding His actions, He employed the noun "*naos*," referring definitively to the temple proper and not one of its outer courts. A perceived threat against the temple proper would have a much greater impact on Jews than on Romans, who would perceive either as an act of zealot rebellion. See Arndt and Gingrich, *GEL*, "naos," 665–66, and "heiron," 470.

[30] The "now" of John 3:1 appears to be the author's attempt to connect the visit of Nicodemus in close proximity with the cleansing of the temple. The visit of Nicodemus was clearly meant to be understood as a constituent element of the early Judean ministry. See Raymond E. Brown, *The Gospel According to John*, 2 vols. (Garden City, New York: Doubleday, 1966), 1:129. Haenchen is right to call into question the rabbinic parallels of rabbis studying into the night and therefore making Nicodemus's visit a friendly one. The context of the story simply will not allow this interpretation. See Ernst Haenchen, *John 1* (Philadelphia: Fortress Press, 1984), 199.

[31] The phrase "archōn tōn ioudaiōn" implies that Nicodemus was a leading member of the Sanhedrin. See Gerhard Delling, "archōn," in Kittel and Friedrich, *TDNT*, 1:488–89.

During His early ministry in Judea, Jesus was confronted for His actions against the temple (John 2:18); He was visited by a timid Nicodemus who may have been afraid of retribution (John 3:2); He faced questions from the disciples of John and certain Jews (John 3:25); and He left Judea after the Pharisees learned that He was baptizing more disciples than John (John 4:1–3). Nothing in the Gospels leads us to believe that the early Judean ministry was positive; therefore, Nicodemus's statements, when taken in context, fit into the overall impression of Jesus that He already had significant opposition among the Jewish leadership in Jerusalem during His early days in Judea.

The authors of all four Gospels imply that John had taught prior to Jesus' baptism, a point that is undisputed by scholars. By logical implication, therefore, if John came under scrutiny by Jewish leaders and authorities, would Jesus not also come under suspicion as one closely associated with John and his followers? Matthew and Luke see the arrest of John as the connecting element, but they do not relate any actions of Jesus that would call Him into suspicion when John was arrested. The Gospel of John, having access to better information about the early life of Jesus, makes the connection between Jesus and John explicit.

The contours of the early Judean ministry, when seen through the eyes of those opposed to Jesus, reveal a concerted effort by the Jerusalem Jewish leadership to assess the growing "problem" that Jesus and His disciples represented. By all accounts, John the Baptist was both a public and a private nuisance for Herod Antipas and his supporters. John's baptism attracted numerous followers and garnered the attention of the crowds, including both Pharisees and Sadducees (Matthew 3:7–10; Luke 3:7–9; John 1:19). Their quest to see John implies that they were willing to overcome doctrinal and practical differences. For reasons left unclear, John rebuked the Pharisees and Sadducees. Shortly after their denunciation by John, Jesus came to be baptized. By all Gospel accounts, John realized in Jesus the culmination of John's earthly ministry. He taught that Jesus was the Lamb of God and provided other prophetic insights into Jesus' mission (John 1:36).

Jesus then went to Galilee, particularly to Cana, and gathered disciples who would travel with Him to Judea. Upon returning to Judea, Jesus fell under the same suspicion that John was under. If the synoptics are correct in placing John's denunciation of Herod Antipas at this time, then the climate would have been more unwelcoming to Jesus and His new disciples, some of whom were earlier followers of the Baptist. Jesus was doing exactly what John had done—teaching the gospel with power and authority, gathering those who were willing to listen, and calling them to discipleship. From the eyes of the Jewish leaders, John's testimony of Jesus identified Him as the logical successor and a potential messianic candidate, a conclusion supported by the fact that He was picking up where John left off.

In this context, Jesus' actions in Judea may have been a consequence of John's already-established relationship with the Jewish leadership rather than Jesus' prior actions in Judea. In fact, Nicodemus's visit to Jesus, taken positively by the author of the Gospel, appears to be an attempt to gain a clearer picture of the ministry of Jesus. Originally, Nicodemus may have had no intentions of seeking out Jesus as a disciple— but rather seized the opportunity for making a surreptitious attempt to ascertain the threat posed by Jesus. Commentators have long been troubled by Nicodemus's facile questioning of Jesus, which at times is so painfully literal that Jesus rebukes him for his blatant ignorance (John 3:3–13).[32] Nicodemus had come unprepared to question Jesus, a fact made apparent by his simplistic, on-the-spot questions and answers. Obviously, the author of the Gospel of John told the story of Nicodemus as a way to retell the powerful teachings of Jesus, but the motives of Nicodemus have

---

[32] See Jeffrey R. Holland, "Lift up Your Eyes," *Ensign* (July 1993): 9, who said, "Nicodemus' response is confused. Conditioned by the Pharisaic literalism, he was either unwilling or unable to grasp the Savior's meaning and chose to give the reference to 'birth' its most immediate meaning." See also Neal E. Lambert and Richard H. Cracroft, "The Powerful Voices of the Gospels," *New Era* (January 1973): 42.

always been a question in the story.[33] Given Nicodemus's visit to Jesus in the night and his open concern to appease Jesus, we can plausibly see this visit as a subtle inquiry into who the Jewish leadership thought may have been the emerging leader among the Baptist movement.

After Nicodemus's departure into the night, the Gospel of John turns its attention to Jesus and His disciples, who were baptizing in the region of Judea. Contemporary with Jesus, John was also baptizing—but possibly at some distance in Aenon near Salim. The juxtaposition of these two figures leaves the indelible impression that Jesus is now the most important and renowned associate of John. John, in fact, may have moved out of the environs of Judea while Jesus entered them with authority and was openly doing the work of John. In John's Gospel, the Baptist's final statements in mortality were an open and powerful testimony of Jesus' coming mission (John 3:27–36).

The logical sequence is that Jesus returned to Judea to take over after John's departure. On that journey, known as the early Judean ministry, Jesus associated himself closely with the actions and teachings of the Baptist. Jewish authorities, concerned that John was too powerful, sent an emissary to question the person they believed was John the Baptist's successor. The report of their messenger is now lost, but the author of the Gospel of John understood it to be a powerful teaching moment, unfortunately giving Nicodemus nothing of substance to report. As John moved to Aenon near Salim, Jesus moved into Judea with His disciples and began preaching the word with power, unconcerned with any ramifications of His actions. The words of John the Baptist were literally fulfilled in those days when he said, "He must increase, but I must decrease" (John 3:30). John's ministry was waning as Jesus' was increasing dramatically.

The conclusion of the Judean ministry can be found in John 4:1–3, which reads, "When therefore the Lord knew how the Pharisees

---

[33] Keith J. Wilson, "The Message of Nicodemus," *The Religious Educator* 1 (2000): 57–70.

had heard that Jesus made and baptized more disciples than John, (though Jesus himself baptized not, but his disciples,) he left Judea, and departed again into Galilee." This theme can be found throughout the early Judean ministry. Jesus was the clear successor to John the Baptist, both in the eyes of John's followers and now in the eyes of the Pharisees. As the Gospel authors retold these events, they all focused on John the Baptist's decisive testimony of Jesus Christ. We should not be surprised that Jesus focused the early part of His ministry among those same followers and sought to harvest the field that had already been prepared. We know that some of the first disciples were followers of John, and Judea was a logical place for further missionary efforts among followers of the Baptist.

The motivation for Jesus' removal to Galilee at this stage of the ministry has also been called into question because Herod Antipas's rule extended into Galilee also; therefore, a flight into Galilee would not offer any protection from Herod Antipas or his minions.[34] The reasons for Jesus' removal to Galilee, however, may not be as unclear as previously thought. We know that many, if not all, of the early Apostles came from Galilee and that some success resulted from the gospel's being preached among their relatives. Peter, Nathaniel, and likely many others came to believe in Jesus as a result of a family member. Galilee offered a practical solution to the difficulties in Judea, and Jesus could continue to teach the gospel among the relatives and close friends of those who had already believed in John's teachings in Perea. The Galileans among John's followers were considerable, and, interestingly, the Gospels do not mention any Judean followers of John specifically. Instead, all of the known followers of John were Galileans.

Historically, John may have had many Judean followers whose names have now been forgotten, but the Gospels clearly make the point that Galileans were also found in that initial group. From Mark's and John's perspective, and to a lesser extent Matthew's and Luke's, Jesus' ministry grew out of His experiences with John the

---

[34] See Cecilia Peek, "Early Galilean Ministry and Miracles," in this volume.

Baptist. John came in the spirit and power of Elias to prepare the way for the Messiah. The logical corollary is that Jesus would take advantage of that preparation, teach the gospel to those who were ready first, and then move into those areas where the people had not been prepared to receive Him. John may have played a much greater role in preparing for the ministry of Jesus than the historical sources relate.

Summary

The importance of the early Judean ministry has most often been overlooked or underestimated. A closer look at the time period reveals many interesting details of the life of the Savior and of how the public ministry began. The beginning of Jesus' ministry coincides exactly with the period in which John the Baptist's ministry was ending. John was meeting with increasing hostility and friction from government and Jewish leaders. Jesus' appearance on the scene was not random; He appears to have purposely associated Himself with John the Baptist. Their preaching styles in the early days are very similar. As John came under suspicion from Herod Antipas, Jesus and John made it obvious that Jesus would succeed John in power and authority.

Jesus moved quickly and focused His attention in those regions where John had previously taught. That missionary work produced several converts who would later be called to serve among His twelve disciples. Upon hearing of John's arrest, according to the synoptic Gospels, Jesus moved to Galilee. Unfortunately, none of the authors of those accounts was converted to the gospel at that time; therefore, their respective accounts are not precise about His motivations for leaving Judea for Galilee. The Gospel of John, however, provides enough detail to give us a glimpse into the particulars of that period. Jesus, as an associate of John the Baptist, also came under suspicion, and the Jewish leadership had become aware of at least some of His activities. As the connections between Jesus and John became more profound and obvious, Jesus moved to Galilee and left Judea behind permanently. The later Gospel records reveal a great degree of tension between Jesus and the Jerusalem hierarchy—something that was likely spawned during the early ministry there. The reasons Jesus then retired to Galilee are not fully clear, but one likely possibility is that He moved there to continue work among the followers of John the Baptist.

Jesus' moves in those early days of the ministry appear calculated and controlled—not motivated by fear or forced in any way. He was in charge and was clearly moving in a direction that would result in the conversion of leading authorities for the future church. The public ministry had begun in earnest, and Jesus was faced with the daunting task of organizing the twelve disciples and teaching them so they could lead the Church following His death. Certainly He had a clear sense that this would come swiftly, and therefore His movement among followers of John is a silent testimony to the effectiveness and enduring message that John instilled in his followers. In Jesus' own eulogy of John, He said, "Among them that are born of women there hath not arisen a greater than John the Baptist" (Matthew 11:11; Luke 7:28). The Baptist had prepared the way for the early Judean ministry of Jesus in several important and fundamental ways beyond simply being the agent who baptized the Lamb of God.

VIII.
GALILEE AND THE CALL OF THE TWELVE APOSTLES

ERIC D. HUNTSMAN

And it came to pass in those days, that he went out into a mountain to pray, and continued all night in prayer to God. And when it was day, he called unto him his disciples: and of them he chose twelve, whom also he named apostles.

LUKE 6:12–13

Midway into the first Galilean ministry, Luke, in an account modeled partially on Mark and Matthew, notes that Jesus Christ separated twelve from the body of His disciples and gave them a special and significant appointment. The function, if not the actual title, of Apostle already existed,[1] special witnesses of Christ having been called in every age and Christ Himself having been an "apostle" of the One who appointed Him (Hebrews 3:1). Nevertheless, the Twelve in the meridian of time had a specific status as those who were with the Lord in His earthly ministry and were special witnesses of His resurrection. The importance of their role was a subject of prophecy long before their own ministries, and the Book of Mormon prophet Nephi knew of their specific and important title:

---

[1] Joseph Fielding Smith, *Doctrines of Salvation*, ed. Bruce R. McConkie, 3 vols. (Salt Lake City: Deseret Book, 1999), 3:151.

"*apostles* of the Lamb, for thus were the twelve called by the angel of the Lord" (1 Nephi 11:34; emphasis added).

Although Matthew combines the selection and naming of the Apostles with their actual receiving of authority in connection with their first mission, overall, the Gospel accounts suggest a cumulative process as they were first called as disciples and then chosen as members of the Twelve. At the time of their selection, Luke 6:13 stresses that Jesus specifically named them "apostles," suggesting the importance of the Greek term used in our texts and its presumed Hebrew or Aramaic antecedent. Literally, *apostolos* means "one sent forth," but the Greek term went through several stages of development before it acquired the general sense of a delegate, envoy, or messenger known from the New Testament.[2] Even within the New Testament, the usage varies from author to author, suggesting that the Greek translation used for Jesus' original designation of His special witnesses was not stagnant and that the writers saw it as more applicable to the Twelve after the resurrection than before.

Indeed, at the time of their selection, the original Twelve were still young in their discipleship, and their calling in Galilee was important as part of the preparation necessary for them to fulfill their later mission. The sequence provided by Luke 6:12–13 traces this development: Jesus prayerfully selected twelve special witnesses from those who had already become His disciples, and these He gave a specific title illustrative of their intended mission. The Gospel accounts document how these Twelve received explicit priesthood authority, were "sent out" on their first mission, obtained growing witnesses of the Savior's divinity and power, and finally received the further keys necessary for them to enjoy the fullness of the priesthood and to carry out their commission after Christ's resurrection and ascension. It was at this point that the Apostles were able to function fully in their calling, fulfilling the important apostolic qualifications cited by Luke and Paul and being sent out to all the world.[3]

---

[2] Arndt and Gingrich, GEL, "apostolos," 99. See the detailed discussion below.
[3] According to Luke in Acts, the qualifications for Apostles were that they be special

The Background of the Twelve: "He Called unto Him His Disciples"

Although the Twelve are frequently referred to as disciples, the synoptic Gospels agree that Jesus called the first Twelve Apostles from among a larger body of His followers, who were already called "disciples."[4] The Greek word for disciple, *mathētēs*, literally means "learner" and was a common term in Koine Greek for a pupil, apprentice, or adherent.[5] In the Gospels, the idea of learning (*manthanō*, from which *mathētēs* is derived) is connected closely to following (*akoloutheō*), and in this respect, the initiative always belongs to Jesus: He calls, and the true disciple follows.[6] According to Meier, "In this strict sense, discipleship meant following Jesus literally, physically. It therefore involved leaving home, family, and work, and exposing oneself to possible hardships and opposition from others, including one's own family."[7] Some scholars, such as Meier, distinguish, perhaps a little too finely, between "devoted adherents" who stayed home and supported the ministry—such as Mary, Martha, or Zachaeus—and true disciples. But the earliest followers of Jesus appear to have grown in their discipleship, learning from Jesus and accompanying Him to important events and only later abandoning their earlier lives completely. Then, like the early Restoration Apostles who were called from the number of those prepared by the experiences of Zion's Camp,[8] the men who were called as the Twelve

---

witnesses of the resurrection who were "men which have companied with us all the time that the Lord Jesus went in and out among us, beginning from the baptism of John, unto that same day that he was taken up from us" (Acts 1:21–22).

[4] See, for instance, Heber F. Peacock, "Discipleship in the Gospel of Mark," *Review and Expositor* 75 (1978): 555–56; J. Andrew Overman, "Disciple," in Bruce M. Metzger and Michael D. Coogan, eds., *The Oxford Companion to the Bible* (Oxford: Oxford University Press, 1993), 168.

[5] Arndt and Gingrich, *GEL*, "mathētēs," 486.

[6] Hans Weder, "Disciple, Discipleship," trans. Dennis Martin, in Freedman, *ABD*, 2:207–8.

[7] John P. Meier, "The Circle of the Twelve: Did It Exist during Jesus' Public Ministry?" *Journal of Biblical Literature* 116 (1997): 636–37.

[8] Lawrence R. Flake, *Prophets and Apostles of the Last Dispensation* (Provo, Utah: Brigham Young University, Religious Studies Center, 2001), 317; Ivan J. Barrett, *Joseph Smith*

were prepared during their early period of discipleship, following the Savior through the early Judean and Galilean phases of His ministry, learning from both His words and deeds, and suffering with Him from the growing opposition against Him.

The region around the Sea of Galilee was the home of at least eleven of the Twelve, and geographic, kinship, and occupational ties bound some of the earliest known disciples to each other and, perhaps in some cases, to Jesus Himself. The story of the earliest calls to discipleship, however, began in Bethabara, across the Jordan River.[9] John 1:35–51 begins the account of the earliest disciples, Andrew and another follower of John the Baptist, presumably the later Apostle John.[10] After hearing the Baptist's testimony, "Behold

---

and the Restoration (Provo, Utah: BYU Press, 1973), 294–97.

[9] The evidence of the manuscripts is divided over whether the place where John was baptizing was Bethany or Bethabara (see Raymond E. Brown, *The Gospel According to John I–XII: A New Translation with Introduction and Commentary* [New York: Doubleday, 1966], 44–45). Origen, *Commentary on the Gospel of John*, 6.40, preferred Bethabara because he could not find a Bethany across the Jordan. Verse 9 of 1 Nephi 10 identifies the site with Bethabara.

[10] This "other" disciple is most often identified with the Beloved Disciple elsewhere mentioned in the Gospel, and this character is explicitly connected with the author in John 21:20–24. The ancient assumption that John the Apostle was the author of the Gospel was widely supported (e.g., Irenaeus *Against Heresies*, 3.1.1; the Latin anti-Marcionite Prologue to John; *Muratorian Canon*, 9–34; Clement of Alexandria as quoted by Eusebius, *Church History*, 6.14.7). Although it has become popular in some scholarly circles to contest John's authorship (see Brown, *The Gospel According to John I–XII*, lxxxviii–cii; R. Alan Culpepper, *John: The Son of Zebedee, the Life of a Legend* [Minneapolis: Fortress Press, 2000], 72–85), several scholars strongly support or at least admit the possibility of John's authorship (see Leon Morris, *The Gospel According to John*, The New International Commentary on the New Testament, rev. [Grand Rapids: William B. Eerdmans, 1995], 4–25; Francis J. Moloney, *The Gospel of John*, Sacra Pagina 4, ed. Daniel J. Harrington [Collegeville, Minnesota: Liturgical Press, 1998], 6–9; Stephen S. Smalley, *John: Evangelist and Interpreter* [Exeter, England: Paternoster Press, 1978], 75–90).

Latter-day revelation confirms the identification of the Apostle John as the author of the Johannine corpus, at least for the Gospel and the Book of Revelation and implicitly for 1 John (see 1 Nephi 14:18–27; Ether 4:16; Doctrine and Covenants 7; 77:1–15; 88:141), and this position is almost universally accepted in LDS scholarship. See C. Wilfred Griggs, "The Testimony of John," in *Studies in Scripture, Vol. 5: The Gospels*, ed. Kent P. Jackson and Robert L. Millet (Salt Lake City: Deseret Book, 1986), 109–10; Jonn D. Claybaugh, "What the Latter-day Scriptures Teach about John the Beloved," in

the Lamb of God!" (John 1:36), these two left their former master and began to follow after Jesus. Their actual discipleship, however, did not begin until Jesus saw them following and asked what they were seeking. Their question "Where dwellest thou?" signaled their willingness to give up their own homes and occupations to follow Him. Jesus' response, "Come and see," then represented His formal invitation for them to follow Him as full disciples (John 1:38-39).

The role of John the Baptist in preparing disciples for Jesus was a significant part of his call.[11] Although John the Baptist was the first witness of Christ in the public phase of His ministry, the infancy narratives found in Matthew 1–2 and Luke 1–2 show that others had preceded him in recognizing who Jesus really was, and many of their testimonies would have been known to him because of family connections. His mother, Elisabeth, and Jesus' mother, Mary, were relatives, close in personal relationship if not necessarily in kinship.[12] Rather than being a new revelation to John, the sign of the Spirit descending upon Jesus at His baptism may have been both a confirmatory sign and a signal that the public ministry was beginning.

Such kinship connections and previous preparation may have played a role in the readiness that the earliest disciples displayed in following Jesus. Andrew, after joining Jesus, went the next day and found his brother Simon, testified that Jesus was the Messiah, and brought him to Jesus (John 1:40–42). Jesus had not yet returned to

---

Daniel K Judd, Craig J. Oster, and Richard D. Draper, eds., *The Testimony of John the Beloved*, 27th Annual Sidney B. Sperry Symposium (Salt Lake City: Deseret Book, 1998), 16–20; and John F. Hall, *New Testament Witnesses of Christ: Peter, John, James, and Paul* (American Fork, Utah: Covenant Communications, 2002), 107–10.

[11] See. H. Dean Garrett, "The Calling and Mission of the Twelve (Matthew 10)," in *Studies in Scripture, Vol. 5: The Gospels*, ed. Kent P. Jackson and Robert L. Millet (Salt Lake City: Deseret Book, 1986) 227–28.

[12] The KJV translation of *sungenis* as "cousin" in Luke 1:36 is misleading because it actually means "kinswoman" or "female relative" without denoting the degree of connection (see Arndt and Gingrich, *GEL*, "suggenis," 772). Nevertheless, as S. Kent Brown, *Mary and Elisabeth* (American Fork, Utah: Covenant Communications, 2002), 31–32, 39, notes, they were clearly familiar to each other, perhaps because of family property near each other and the habit later seen of Mary's family regularly visiting Jerusalem for feasts.

Galilee, so He was apparently still in the vicinity of Bethabara, raising the possibility that Peter, too, may have been a disciple of John the Baptist or at least had come to hear him preach.[13] The text does not explicitly indicate that John introduced his brother James to Jesus at this point; however, when Jesus seemingly called Peter and Andrew a second time when He later found them fishing on the Sea of Galilee (Matthew 4:18–22, Mark 1:16–20; Luke 5:1–11), James and John were called together immediately thereafter.[14] Their father Zebedee was a business partner of Peter and Andrew in the Galilean fishing industry, and this working relationship together with the apparent similarity of the names of John and Jonah, the father of Peter and Andrew, might be a sign that the two families were related.[15] Additionally, harmonizations of the lists of the women at the cross suggests that the mother of James and John was Salome and that she may have been the sister of Mary, the mother of Jesus.[16] Although this connection seems to be supported by some early Christian evidence,

---

[13] Raymond E. Brown, "The Twelve and the Apostolate," in *The New Jerome Biblical Commentary*, 1378 (§138). For the possibility that Peter, and indeed other of the early disciples, was first taught and prepared by John the Baptist, see Robert J. Matthews, *Behold the Messiah* (Orem, Utah: Granite Publishing, 1994, repr. 2003), 109.

[14] Note, however, that in Codex Sinaiticus (fourth century) and some later manuscripts that "he first (*prōton*) findeth his [own] brother in John 1:41 appears as "he was the first (*prōtos*) to find his brother," with a masculine singular nominative adjective *prōtos* rather than an adverb, leading some to propose that Andrew was "the first" to find his brother, suggesting that John then went and found his brother, James. See Brown, *Gospel According to John I–XII*, 75–76; Morris, *The Gospel According to John*, 139–40; and Garrett, "The Calling and Mission of the Twelve," 228.

[15] Luke 5:10; see JoAnn Ford Watson, "Zebedee," in Freedman, *ABD*, 6:1055. Although Matthew 16:17 describes Peter as "Simon Bar-Jonah," that is "son of Jonah," the best manuscripts of John 1:42 and 21:15–17 read "Simon, son of John." For the possible confusion of the Hebrew names Jonah and Yohan, see Brown, *Gospel According to John I–XII*, 76, and Raymond F. Collins, "John (8)," in Freedman, *ABD*, 3:886–87; Hall, *New Testament Witnesses of Christ*, 53–55. Certain names often were kept within the family, being given in alternate generations or to nephews or other collaterals. Hall, *New Testament Witnesses of Christ*, 112, writes, "While tenuous, the hypothesis that Peter and Andrew were first cousins to John and James, sons of their uncle Zebedee, is not entirely implausible."

[16] Matthew 27:55–56; Mark 15:40; John 19:25.

the assumption cannot be accepted as conclusive.[17] Nevertheless, these four disciples may already have known Jesus and may even have been aware of the divine promises that had been made regarding His future mission. This fact, together with the earlier call of Andrew, John, Peter, and perhaps James in John 1:35–42, explains the readiness of the brothers to leave everything at the "second call." As with John the Baptist, rather than unexpected revelations, the signs and calls that were issued at the beginning of the Galilean ministry may have been simply the signals that the long-awaited work of the Savior had begun.

After these initial calls, Jesus went into Galilee proper (John 1:43), where the account in John of Jesus' early disciples continues with the calls of Philip and Nathaniel. Here again earlier connections appear to have been important. Philip, for instance, was from Bethsaida, a town on the northeastern shore of the Sea of Galilee in the tetrarchy of Herod Philip, which John 1:44 identifies as the hometown of Andrew and Peter. The two brothers apparently moved from Bethsaida to Capernaum—a village on the northwestern shore of the Sea of Galilee in the tetrarchy of Herod Antipas—because this would allow their fishing business the tax benefits of operating in Antipas's territory, as repeatedly crossing the frontier between the two tetrarchies would have allowed each tetrarch to tax them.[18]

Why Philip seems to have relocated into Antipas's tetrarchy is unclear, although the possibility that he, too, had business dealings

---

[17] See, in particular, *Protoevangelium of James*, 19–20. Culpepper (*John*, 8–9, 23 notes 6–7), reviews the evidence cautiously. It receives a more confident assessment from Brown, *The Gospel According to John I–XII*, 904–7; Morris, *The Gospel According to John*, 716–17; Richard J. Bauckham, "All in the Family: Identifying Jesus' Relatives," *Bible Review* 16.2 (April 2000): 23, and Hall, *New Testament Witnesses of Christ*, 110–13.

[18] Jerome Murphy-O'Connor, "Fishers of Fish, Fishers of Men: What We Know of the First Disciples from Their Profession, *Bible Review* 15.3 (June 1999): 27. Murphy-O'Connor notes that although there were thirteen ancient harbors around the Sea of Galilee, the only town that salted and processed fish for export was Taricheae (Magdala in Hebrew), which meant "the fish factory" in Greek. Taricheae was in the tetrarchy of Galilee, so based in Bethsaida, Peter and his associates would have needed to pay a customs fee to bring them into Antipas's territory.

with Andrew and Peter is intriguing. The fishing industry was an important business in the ancient world, especially within Jewish circles because observant Jews needed to know they were buying fish from reliable suppliers who were following the proper kosher rules in the selection, drying, and salting of the fish. This fact combined with the information that Zebedee, Peter, and Andrew had hired men and multiple boats suggests that they were reasonably prosperous, in contradiction to the usual image of these early disciples as poor fishermen. Additionally, Simon (the Hellenized form of *Shimon*), Andrew, and Philip are all Greek names, indicating that these early disciples were part of a mixed cultural area, where they knew at least "marketplace Greek."[19]

Next, Philip found Nathaniel, apparently someone whom he already knew, to share the exciting news that he had found the Savior prophesied by Moses and the prophets (John 1:45). Here again Jesus extended the actual call to discipleship—in this instance in a dramatic fashion by indicating that He had known Nathaniel, "an Israelite in whom there was no guile," by revelatory means before He even met him in person (John 1:47–48).[20] Nathaniel was from Cana in Galilee (John 21:2), but other than the probable relationship that may have already existed between Philip and Nathaniel, we do not know of any other connections between Nathaniel and the other early disciples or Jesus. Neither do we know anything of his profession, although he appears to have been a student of the Jewish scriptures, appearing in a familiar rabbinic pose seated beneath a fig

---

[19] Muphy-O'Connor, "Fishers of Fish," 24–27. See also JoAnn Ford Watson, "Philip (6)," in Freedman, *ABD*, 5:311. Philip, in particular, appears to have been conversant in Greek, since the Greeks who wanted to meet Jesus in John 12:20–22 approached him first.

[20] Brown, *The Gospel According to John I–XII*, 83, 86–88; Raymond F. Collins, "Nathaniel (3)," in Freedman, *ABD*, 4:1030–31; Garrett, "The Calling and Mission of the Twelve," 228–29. What exactly was meant by "in whom there is no guile" is enigmatic. Does it reflect positively on Nathaniel, showing his willingness to accept and follow Jesus, or is it somewhat ironic given Nathaniel's earlier, disparaging characterization of Nazareth as being the kind of town from which one would not expect anything good to come? (John 1:46).

tree in prayer, meditation, or study.[21] The important lesson learned from the calling of Nathaniel is the fact that Jesus knew, and knows, the heart and desires of those whom He calls.

According to John's account, the early disciples of Jesus began to accompany Him to social and religious functions, the first being the wedding held at Cana, the hometown of Nathaniel (John 2:1–11; 21:2). John keeps the identities of the bride and groom at this wedding anonymous, thus focusing the attention on Jesus and what He does.[22] When He and Mary were invited, the disciples were as well, either because they too knew the participants or because they were recognized as part of Jesus' intimate circle, almost with the status of family.

John describes the miracle of turning water into wine as the first of the "signs" performed by Jesus, with symbolism significant enough that it "manifested forth his glory; and his disciples believed on him" (John 2:11).[23] After the miracle, the first disciples accompanied Jesus

---

[21] Collins, "Nathaniel (3)," 4:1030.

[22] Much has been written concerning the possible identity of the bridegroom at this wedding. An early third-century Latin preface to John identifies John the son of Zebedee as the groom, explaining the role of Mary if John's mother, Salome, was her sister (see Brown, *The Gospel According to John I–XII*, 97). In harmony with his preference for anonymity, John would not be expected to name himself (indeed, he never even mentions the name of Jesus' mother). Although rarely suggested, Nathaniel, as a native of Cana, could have been the bridegroom, occasioning the invitation of his new master and friends (although this does not explain the prominence of Mary in the account, unless here too some family relationship existed).

Bruce R. McConkie, MM, 1:448–49, suggested that "some member of the Holy Family," presumably another son of Mary, was being married. See also Talmage, *JTC*, 135–36, and McConkie, *DNTC*, 1:135–36. Earlier, nineteenth-century LDS proposals often focused on the role of Jesus at the wedding. See Orson Hyde, "The Marriage Relations," in Young, *JD*, 82, although this does not fit well the circumstances described in the text.

[23] "Signs" or "miraculous signs" is a better translation for the Greek *semeia*. Rather than downplaying the reality and power of Christ's miracles, this translation emphasizes that what is truly important is what they symbolize or teach about Jesus or what He can do instead of focusing on the act itself. For the symbolism, see Brown, *The Gospel According to John I–XII*, 103–11; Morris, *The Gospel According to John*, 163–64. LDS discussions of the miracle or sign of water-into-wine tend to focus on Jesus' power over the elements (see Talmage, *JTC*, 136–38; McConkie, MM, 1:453–54; Fred E. Woods, "The Water Imagery in John's Gospel: Power, Purification, and Pedagogy," in Bruce A.

to Jerusalem for the Feast of the Passover, giving occasion to the early Judean ministry.[24] In Jerusalem, they would have seen Jesus cleanse the temple (John 2:13–25), learned of Jesus' discourse with Nicodemus on the new birth (John 3:1–12), and heard about His discourse on the water of life with the Samaritan woman at the well (John 4:4–42) before completing the circle by returning to Cana, where they witnessed the healing of the nobleman's son (John 4:43–54).

Although the early disciples spent time with Jesus at such events and began to learn from His words and deeds, the accounts in the synoptic Gospels suggest they did not yet completely leave their earlier lives to follow Jesus.[25] Gospel harmonies frequently have Jesus return to Nazareth after the early Judean ministry (Luke 4:16–30), and when He is rejected in His hometown, He seems to be alone. Apparently, His disciples returned to their homes and vocations after the pilgrimage to Jerusalem because when Jesus came to Capernaum after His rejection at Nazareth, He found Peter, Andrew, and the sons of Zebedee fishing. This, then, was the occasion of the "second call," at which point the disciples began to accompany Jesus full time (Matthew 4:13–22; Mark 1:16–20; Luke 5:1–11). In the subsequent days and weeks, they witnessed, among other things, their Master teach with power, cast out an unclean spirit, heal Peter's mother-in-law, cleanse a leper, and give strength to a man afflicted by palsy.[26]

Throughout the course of the Galilean ministry, Jesus' following increased. Using language associated with discipleship, Matthew 4:25 reports that multitudes from Galilee, the Decapolis, Judea, and

---

VanOrden and Brent L. Top, eds., *The Lord of the Gospels*, The 1990 Sperry Symposium on the New Testament [Salt Lake City: Deseret Book, 1991], 192–93). Much remains to be discussed regarding the importance of the Johannine themes of blood/water and mortality/divinity or eternal life. Suggesting the transition from the premortal and divine Word to earthly Jesus, this miracle could be a symbol of the Incarnation, explaining its use as the first of the "signs" of who Christ really was and how it "manifested . . . his glory" to His disciples.

[24] See Thomas A. Wayment, "Jesus' Early Ministry in Judea and Jerusalem," in this volume.

[25] Garrett, "The Calling and Mission of the Twelve," 229.

[26] See Cecilia M. Peek, "Early Galilean Ministry and Miracles," in this volume.

Perea "followed him," using a tense of the word *akoloutheō* that commonly indicates discipleship. The vast majority of these disciples remain nameless in the Gospel texts, but the texts do feature a few individuals.

The body of full-time disciples grew with the call of a certain tax collector from his customs booth. He is named Matthew in Matthew 9:9, and the name Levi in Mark 2:14 and Luke 5:27 may be a tribal designation rather than a name, hence "Matthew the Levite."[27] Because there were more Levites in this period than could be afforded regular employment in the temple, this theory proposes that well-educated Levites like Matthew may have been forced to find occupations elsewhere where their skills would be useful. As a Herodian tax collector for Antipas (not, as often presumed, one of the publicans like the Zacchaeus of Luke 19:1–10 who was employed by the Roman administration of Judea), Matthew collected tolls in Capernaum on goods crossing between Antipas's territories and those of his brother, Herod Philip. Consequently, Matthew was the very type of official whom Peter and Andrew had moved from Bethsaida to avoid.

Later, after the formal call of the Twelve from among the larger body of disciples, others are mentioned as travelers with Jesus. These include Mary Magdalene, probably from the important fish-processing center of Magdala; Joanna, the wife of an important Herodian official; and an otherwise unknown woman named Susanna. All of these were women of moderate to considerable means, Luke 8:2–3 noting that they helped support Jesus and the traveling disciples out of their personal resources.[28] Another female follower from Galilee who traveled with Jesus as far as Jerusalem was

---

[27] R. T. France, *Matthew: Evangelist and Teacher* (Grand Rapids: Academic Books, 1989), 66–70. The issue is, however, complex. See Dennis C. Duling, "Matthew (Disciple)," in Freedman, *ABD*, 4:618–22.

[28] *Diōkonoun*, translated as "ministered unto" in the KJV, can mean simply "served" in a domestic sense, but the combination with *ek tōn huperarchontōn autais*, meaning "private means or resources" (translated as "substance"), suggests that these women both had more-than-average means and were free to manage and dispose of their property.

Salome, perhaps the mother of James and John. If so, this relationship explains her presence on the road to Jerusalem when she interceded, apparently without much understanding, on behalf of her sons' position (Matthew 20:20–28). Another woman present at the final Jerusalem events was Mary the wife of Clopas (John 19:25). Clopas was traditionally identified as the brother of Joseph the carpenter,[29] which makes his wife the (step) paternal aunt of Jesus and adds to the number of early disciples who may have had longstanding connections with the Savior[30] Intriguing but less certain is that this Clopas can be identified with either Alphaeus, whose son James would be called to the Twelve,[31] or "Cleopas," one of the two disciples on the road to Emmaus following Jesus' resurrection (Luke 24:18).[32] Matthew is also identified as "the son of Alphaeus" at Mark 2:14, revealing a possible connection between these two disciples and future Apostles.[33]

John's account records that Jesus went to Jerusalem for another "feast" (John 5:1), presumably one of the three annual pilgrimage festivals.[34] Although the disciples are not specifically mentioned here

---

[29] Hegesippus, as quoted in Eusebius, *Church History* 3.32.6; 4.22.4. See Bauckham, "All in the Family: Identifying Jesus' Relatives," 23–24.

[30] For an interesting comparison of these connections to the ties of kinship among the leadership in the early and modern restored Church, see McConkie, MM, 2:113–14n2.

[31] James is identified as the son of Alphaeus at Matthew 10:3 but as the son of Mary, the wife of Clopas at Mark 15:40. Defenders of this position note that although the similarities are not apparent in English, Alphaeus and Clopas are variant Greek forms for the same Aramaic name of Ḥalphai. See F. F. Bruce, *The Acts of the Apostles: Greek Text with Introduction and Commentary*, 3d rev. ed. (Grand Rapids: William B. Eerdmans, 1990), 105–6, and Morris, *The Gospel According to John*, 717n63.

[32] I. Howard Marshall, *The Gospel of Luke*, The New International Greek Testament Commentary (Grand Rapids: William B. Eerdmans, 1978), 894; Morris, *The Gospel According to John*, 717n63.

[33] See R. T. France, *The Gospel of Mark*, ed. I. Howard Marshall and Donald A. Hagner (Grand Rapids: William B. Eerdmans, 2002), 133–34, although he notes the oddity that Matthew and James are not listed together in the apostolic lists, as are both Peter and Andrew as well as James and John.

[34] The three pilgrimage festivals were Pesach (Passover), Shavuot (Pentecost or Weeks), and Sukkot (Tabernacles). The text lacks an article before "feast," making it unlikely that the celebration referred to here was Passover. Brown, *The Gospel According*

as they were at the earlier Passover, if they accompanied Jesus, they would have witnessed the healing of the lame man at the Pool of Bethesda and the subsequent controversy that ensued because the miracle was performed on the Sabbath (John 5:1–18). Jesus' discourse on the Divine Son (John 5:17–47) follows this healing, and the synoptics record further controversy over the Sabbath, the restoration of a man's withered hand, and then the healing of many (Matthew 12:1–21; Mark 2:23–3:12; Luke 6:1–11). Prepared by the teachings and miracles of Jesus, some of His followers were now ready for a special call.

Selecting the Apostles: "Of Them He Chose Twelve"

Before Jesus called twelve from the body of His disciples, Luke 6:12 records that He retired to a mountain where He spent the night in prayer, emphasizing the care He took and the inspiration He sought in this selection.[35] The number twelve was significant, representing the twelve tribes of Israel and symbolizing that in Jesus, a new Israel was being established. All three synoptic Gospels and Acts contain lists of the twelve men Jesus chose. These lists are essentially the same, and each arranges the Twelve into groups of four. They occasionally differ in their order and disagree only in regard to the figures of Thaddeus and Judas "of James," who was probably the son rather than the brother of an otherwise unspecified James.[36]

Matthew 10:2–4	Mark 3:16–19	Luke 6:14–16	Acts 1:13
Simon Peter	Simon Peter	Simon Peter	Peter
Andrew, his brother	James, son of Zebedee	Andrew, his brother	James
James, son of Zebedee	John, brother of James	James	John
		John	Andrew
			Philip

---

to John I–XII, 206, proposes Pentecost, suggesting a rather short stay in Galilee after Jesus' return from Passover. For other proposals, see Morris, *The Gospel According to John*, 265n6.

[35] McConkie, MM, 2:104.

[36] *Ioudas Iakōbou* is most naturally rendered "son of James," as in the NAV, NIV, NRSV, and NJB, rather than "brother of James," as in the KJV.

John, his brother	Andrew	Philip	Thomas
Philip	Philip	Bartholomew	Bartholomew
Bartholomew	Bartholomew	Matthew	Matthew
Thomas	Matthew	Thomas	James, son of
Matthew	Thomas	James, son of	Alphaeus
James, son of	James, son of	Alphaeus	Simon the Zealot
Alphaeus	Alphaeus	Simon the Zealot	Judas "of James"
(Lebbaeus)	Thaddeus	Judas "of James"	
Thaddeus	Simon "the	Judas Iscariot	
Simon "the	Cananean"		
Cananean"	Judas Iscariot		
Judas Iscariot			

The first group of four consists of two pairs of brothers, with Matthew and Luke keeping Peter and Andrew together but with Mark and Acts putting Andrew last, in recognition of the special role that Peter, James, and John served within the Twelve.

These four, plus Philip, were among the earliest disciples called to follow Jesus. Bartholomew is not mentioned elsewhere; his name, however, is a patronymic (*bar Talmai*, meaning "son of Tolmai"). Since the ninth century, his lack of a given name has allowed commentators to identify this "Bartholomew" with Nathaniel, suggesting that he was Nathaniel the son of Tolmai.[37] Nowhere in the texts is this identification explicit, however.

Another figure, Thomas, emerges as an active character in the account of John (John 11:16; 14:5; 20:27–28), although no other details are preserved in the synoptics. Thaddeus, whose name appears as Lebbaeus in some manuscripts of Matthew 10:3,[38] is usually associated with Jude, the son of James, as these are the only two names where the four lists diverge substantively. Consequently, Mark's and Matthew's use of the name *Thaddeus* may have been intended to differentiate him more completely from Judas Iscariot.[39]

---

[37] Brown, "The Twelve and the Apostolate," 1378 (§140). This has been the position taken by most LDS authorities. See Talmage, *JTC*, 222; McConkie, *MM*, 2:109.

[38] William F. Albright and Christopher S. Mann, *Matthew* (New York: Doubleday, 1971), 116; JoAnn Ford Watson, "Thaddeus," in Freedman, *ABD*, 6:435.

[39] Marshall, *The Gospel of Luke*, 240. The possibility cannot be ruled out that the

The epithet *Kananaios*, rendered "Canaanite" in the KJV and "Cananaean" in the NRSV, was not an ethnic identifier but a Greek transliteration of the Aramaic *qanā'nā* meaning "enthusiast." Luke rightly rendered this disciple as "the one called a zealot." Although the term *zēlōtēs* later applied to a political nationalist party, the New Testament regularly uses it in a religious rather than in a political sense.[40] As a result, although Simon has been seen as a reformed revolutionary, he may have been simply an ardent and religious enthusiast.

All of the Twelve so far were from the Galilean region, either from Galilee proper or perhaps the territories of Herod Philip to the north and east of the Sea of Galilee. Judas Iscariot, the final member of the Twelve, is often viewed as the sole member of the group from Judea. This identification arises from one interpretation of the meaning of his epithet *Iscariot*, often understood to be from the Hebrew *'iš qĕriyyôt* meaning "a man of Kerioth," a Judean town. Alternate interpretations have been attempted, however, and these allow Judas, too, to be from Galilee. *Iscariot* could come from *sikarios*, a Greek transliteration of the Latin *sicarius*. This term uniformly means "assassin" or "revolutionary," suggesting that perhaps Jesus' followers did have a (partially) reformed revolutionary in their midst, even if it was not Simon the Zealot. Another possibility is that it comes from the root *šāqar*, "false one," indicating retrospectively that he was a false disciple.[41] Complicating the issue, however, is John 6:71, where the Greek actually reads, "he spoke of Judas *son of Simon Iscariot*," suggesting that both Judas and his father bore the title "Iscariot." Although Judas and his father, Simon, may both have had revolutionary tendencies or

---

composition of the Twelve could have changed. Meier, "The Circle of the Twelve," 648, notes, "Jesus' ministry lasted for two years and some months . . . [and] we should not be astonished that, sometime during two years of the ministry, at least one member left the group. Any number of reasons might be suggested for the departure: voluntary leave taking, dismissal by Jesus, illness, or even death. Whatever the cause, it may well be that one member of the Twelve departed and was replaced by another disciple."

[40] France, *the Gospel of Mark*, 162.

[41] Brown, "The Twelve and the Apostolate," 1379 (§145); William Klassen, "Judas Iscariot," in Freedman, *ABD*, 3:1091–92; France, *the Gospel of Mark*, 163.

may have been in some way false, the most natural interpretation is that they were both from the Judean town of Kerioth.[42]

These, then, were the twelve men who, as trusted and intimate companions, took on an almost familial role, a point that Mark 3:13–35 illustrates. After recounting Jesus' calling of the Twelve (Mark 3:13–19), Mark includes instances of rejection and opposition—that of "his own people from home" (Mark 3:19–21 NAV)[43] and the scribes who have come from Jerusalem (Mark 3:22).[44] At the end of this passage, the crowd tells Jesus that His mother and brother are outside waiting for Him, to which He responds, "Who is my mother, or my brethren? And he looked round about on them which sat about him, and said, Behold my mother and my brethren! For whosoever shall do the will of God, the same is my brother, and my sister, and mother" (Mark 3:32–35). Because of their willingness to do the will of God, the Twelve took the place of, or a place equal to, Jesus' family.

The Meaning of the Title: "Whom Also He Named Apostles"

The testimony of Luke emphasizes that Jesus specifically called the Twelve "apostles" (Luke 6:13), indicating a divine origin and importance to the title He gave them and encouraging a further examination of the meaning and use of the term. New Testament usage, however, requires the consideration of two different issues. The first is how a Greek term with a secular origin came to have an

---

[42] Brown, *The Gospel According to John I–XII*, 1:298.

[43] In this scene, Jesus' activities in Capernaum have so alarmed *hoi par autou* (literally "those from or at his side") that they come, presumably from Nazareth, to take hold of Him to preserve His own reputation and that of His family. While the KJV renders *hoi par autou* as "his friends," the NIV and NRSV render it "his family" and the NJB "his relations." Although Jesus' brothers are known to have not been fully converted until later in his ministry or even until after His resurrection, the presence of His mother in Mark 3:31 has made these uncomfortable readings for some. In view of this sensitivity, perhaps the "his own people" of the NAV is the most prudent course. See the discussion by France, *The Gospel of Mark*, 165–67.

[44] France, *The Gospel of Mark*, 156–57.

almost exclusively religious meaning. The second concerns how the different New Testament writers used the word. "Apostle" appears with surprising infrequency in the Gospel accounts, although Luke uses it more often in Acts, perhaps indicating that the term best described the function of the Apostles after the Resurrection. The term is even more frequent in the writings of Paul, but at times he uses it differently than Luke.

Standard discussions of the title *apostolos* note that it derives from the verb *apostellō*, meaning "to send forth." This converges smoothly with the function of the Twelve whom Jesus sent forth to preach and bear their witness of who He was. This was not, however, the sense of *apostolos* in classical Greek before the New Testament. Originally an adjectival form employed only later as a noun, *apostolos* was most commonly used in classical literature in connection with seafaring, particularly regarding the dispatch of a fleet or expedition.[45]

Related to this was the idea of an embassy sent out with a message, although this usage retained its naval connection because most ambassadors in the Greek world traveled by sea.[46] This is the sense in which Josephus used the term when he recorded the embassy sent by the Jews to Augustus to complain about Archelaus; this use of the term, rare in Jewish writings in Greek, may have arisen because the embassy would necessarily have traveled by sea.[47] In other Greek documents roughly contemporary with or shortly after the New Testament, the use often varied widely, as indicated by references in papyrus records where *apostolos* can mean anything from an export license to cargo dispatched by an order or bill.[48] Extant classical

---

[45] For example, Lysias, 19, "On the Estate of Aristophanes," 21; Demosthenes, *Orationes* 3.5, 18.80. See Karl H. Rengstorf, "apostoloi," in Kittel and Friedrich, *TDNT*, 1:407–8, and Walter Schmithals, *The Office of Apostle in the Early Church*, trans. John E. Steely (Nashville: Abingdon Press, 1969), 96–98.

[46] Herodotus, *Historiae*, 1.21, 5.38; Plato *Epistulae*, 346a. See Hans D. Betz, "Apostle," in Freedman, *ABD*, 1:309.

[47] Josephus, *AJ*, 17.11.1 (§300), which is Josephus's only secure use of the term. Poorly attested is the variant *apostlos* for *apodasmon* in *AJ*, 1.6.4 (§146). On embassies traveling by sea, see Rengstorf, in Kittel and Friedrich, *TDNT*, 1:413.

[48] Henry G. Liddell and Robert Scott, *A Greek-English Lexicon*, 9th ed., rev. by Henry

Greek literature does not attest the use of the term for religious figures—the only possible parallel for New Testament usage being the Cynic and Stoic sages who were seen as being "sent from Zeus" to proclaim the truth.[49] In this case, however, the philosopher was a *kēryx* ("herald") or an *angellos* ("messenger"), not an *apostolos*, although a connection appears in the regular use of these nouns with a passive form of the verb.[50]

Another important fact is that *apostolos* was probably not the actual word Jesus used when He "named" (Luke 6:13) His twelve special followers. Because Jesus presumably spoke Aramaic in His ministry, the Greek term *apostolos* may have been adopted some time afterward as either a translation or an explanation of an original Hebrew or Aramaic term. This original word and not the Greek translation may account for the familiar meaning of "one sent out as an authorized representative or agent" familiar to students of the New Testament.[51] Although Old Testament Hebrew does not preserve a noun for "a sent one," *šālûach*, a passive participle meaning "having been sent," is used in 1 Kings 14:6 to describe the prophet Ahijah's being sent to the wife of Jeroboam.[52] A similar passive

---

S. Jones (Oxford: Clarendon Press, 1996), s.v. "apostolos," 220, for *Der Gnomon des Idios Logos, Berliner griechische Urkunden V* (Berlin: 1895), 162, and *The Oxyrhynchus Papyri III*, ed. B. P. Grenfell and A. S. Hunt (London, 1903), 522.1. See Rengstorf, in Kittel and Friedrich, *TDNT*, 1:408 for additional examples, including P.Oxy. 9.1197 for shipments of corn and BGU 5.64 for a passport; also, F. Agnew, "On the Origin of the Term Apostolos," *Catholic Biblical Quarterly* 38 (1976): 51–53, for P. Lond (Greek Papyri in the British Museum; London, 1910), 4.1339, 4.1343, and 4.1393, which give examples of Egyptian papyri with meanings more closely approaching the sense of *agent*.

[49] Rengstorf, in Kittel and Friedrich, *TDNT*, 1:409–13; Betz, in Freedman, *ABD*, 1:309.

[50] For example, Epictetus *Diatribari*, 3.22.23: "angelos apo tou Dios apestaltai," or "a messenger sent from Zeus."

[51] S. Kent Brown, "Apostle," *Encyclopedia of Mormonism*, ed. Daniel H. Ludlow (New York: Macmillan, 1992), 1:60.

[52] Francis Brown, Samuel R. Driver, and Charles A. Briggs, *A Hebrew English Lexicon of the Old Testament* (Oxford: Clarendon Press, 1907, repr. 1953), s.v. šālûah 1018; Ludwig Koehler, Walter Baumgartner, and Johann J. Stamm, *The Hebrew and Aramaic Lexicon of the Old Testament*, trans. M. E. J. Richardson, 5 vols. (New York: Brill, 1994–2000), 4:1511–16. See also Jeremiah 49:14; Ezekiel 23:40; 2 Chronicles 36:15. Significantly, in at least one Septuagint manuscript tradition, Ahijah is described as an

participle, the Aramaic šĕlîaḥ, appears in Daniel 5:24 and Ezra 7:14.[53] Outside of the Old Testament, the participle šĕlîaḥ regularly began to serve as a substantive and comes to represent a later Jewish institution—that of a legally commissioned agent, fully empowered to represent the person who sent him. The rabbis said that "a man's šĕlîaḥ, is as himself."[54] Additionally, by the second century A.D., rabbinic literature employed true nouns šālûaḥ in Mishnaic Hebrew and šĕlûḥä in Aramaic that meant "messenger, agent, or deputy."[55] Although it is by no means clear that this meaning was fully established for šĕlîaḥ at the time of Christ or even in the early Christian period, Jesus probably employed some such word connoting the sense of sending or commissioning a representative when He named the Twelve "his apostles."[56]

---

apostolos. Although rendered actively in 3 Kingdoms 12:6 (LXX) ("I send grievous tidings to you"), Rengstorf, "apostolos," in Kittel and Friedrich, *TDNT*, 1:413, notes that the Codex Alexandrinus renders it "I am a grievous messenger sent to you."

[53] Brown, *Hebrew and English Lexicon*, s.v. šĕlîaḥ, 1115; Koehler, *Hebrew and Aramaic Lexicon of the Old Testament*, 5:1994–95. In both these passages, however, the Septuagint Greek rendering uses *apestaltō*, an aorist passive indicative form of the verb *apostellō*, rather than the noun *apostolos*.

[54] *Mishna Berakhot*, 5:5. See Rengstorf, "apostolos," in Kittel and Friedrich, *TDNT*, 1:413–20; Schmithals, *The Office of Apostle in the Early Church*, 98–105; Otto Betz, "Apostle," *The Oxford Companion to the Bible*, 41.

[55] Marcus Jastrow, *A Dictionary of the Targumim, the Talmud Babli and Yerushalmi, and the Midrashic Literature*, 2d ed. (New York: 1903; repr. Judaica Press, 1971), s.v. šālûaḥ, 1579; Michael Sokoloff, *A Dictionary of Jewish Palestinian Aramaic of the Byzantine Period*, 2d ed. (Baltimore: Johns Hopkins Press, 2002), s.v. šĕlûḥa [šālûaḥ], 553.

[56] Schmithals, *The Office of Apostle in the Early Church*, 105–10, however, strongly disputes the seeming connection. Compare with Hans Freiherr Von Campenhausen, *Ecclesiastical Authority and Spiritual Power in the Church of the First Three Centuries*, trans. J. A. Baker (Stanford: Stanford University Press, 1969), 22, who confidently writes, "The very word 'apostle' is nothing other than a literal translation of a Jewish legal term, namely *shaliach*, which denotes a person of a plenipotentiary representative, whose task it is to conduct business independently and responsibly for the one who has assigned him these powers for a particular service." For an overview of the scholarly debate, see Brown, "The Twelve and the Apostolate," 1380–81 (§150–52).

Rengstorf, "apostolos," in Kittel and Friedrich, *TDNT*, 1:429, arrived at the compromise position that although we do know what term Jesus actually used, He would have used a word such as šĕlîaḥ; see also J. A. Kirk, "Apostleship since Rengstorf," *New Testament Studies* 21 (1974–75): 259.

Although *apostolos* did later come to be the standard Greek translation of *šĕlîaḥ*,[57] Jesus clearly did not establish the apostleship, a priesthood office, by basing it solely upon some existing Jewish model. However, the sense of a fully empowered agent whom the Lord sent as His representative does seem to have influenced how the writers of the New Testament rendered this idea in Greek. Thus, because *šĕlîaḥ* (or some similar expression) was associated with the idea of sending (*apostellō*), in the earliest Christian writings *apostolos* lost its original naval connotations and went beyond the idea of an embassy to take on the definitive sense of a personal agent empowered to represent and act for the one who sent him. Once it became the dominant understanding of the Greek term, this sense of *apostolos* then expanded outside of Christian circles.

The frequency and occurrences of *apostolos* in the New Testament, however, suggests that its use and meaning were originally somewhat fluid. The Gospels, other than Luke, use this term surprisingly rarely and usually in the plural (*apostoloi* and related forms). The only secure use in Mark, presumably the oldest Gospel, is in Mark 6:30 when the Twelve return from their first mission.[58] Matthew also uses the term only once, at the beginning of his list of the Apostles (Matthew 10:2). John also has a single occurrence of the word

---

[57] Eusebius, *Commentary on Isaiah* 18:1–2 refers to Jewish *apostoloi* being sent out from Jerusalem to the Diaspora, and Rengstorf, *TDNT* 1:414 interprets Jerome, *Commentary on Galatians* 1:1 as demonstrating that *apostolos* is the translation of *šĕlîaḥ* (via the Latin *Slias*). More important, *šlîḥā* is the regular translation of *apostolos* into Syriac found in the Peshitta (*LexSyr* 780b).

[58] Some manuscripts suggest that Mark, presumably the oldest Gospel, uses it at Jesus' selection of the Twelve in Mark 3:14: "And he ordained twelve [*whom he named apostles*], that they should be with him, and that he might send them forth to preach." For the possibility that "whom he named apostles" in these manuscripts is a gloss taken from Luke, see Frederick C. Grant, *The Gospel According to St. Mark, Exegesis*, The Interpreter's Bible 7 (Nashville: Abingdon Press, 1979), 685–86, and France, *The Gospel of Mark*, 157. Bruce M. Metzger, *A Textual Commentary on the Greek New Testament* (Stuttgart: United Bible Societies, 1971), 80, notes the strong external evidence for this variant and includes the phrase in brackets in the Greek text "to reflect the balance of probabilities." If the phrase "whom he named apostles" stood in the original, it would provide early textual evidence supporting Luke's witness that Jesus gave the Twelve a specific title (see Marshall, *The Gospel of Luke*, 238).

apostolos at John 13:16, and there it is used in such a nontechnical sense that it is not even evident in the KJV translation: "The servant is not greater than his lord; neither *he that is sent* [*apostolos*] greater than he that sent him" (emphasis added).[59] By contrast, there are thirty-one references in the writings of Luke, six in his Gospel and twenty-five later in Acts.[60] Because Luke seems to have written after Mark and Matthew, an initial hypothesis could be that using *apostolos* as the Greek rendering of the Twelve's title caught on slowly and that Luke had a major role in establishing its usage.

Nevertheless, this does not take into account the use of the word in the epistles, most of which were probably written before any of the Gospels. In the general epistles, the writings of Peter use *apostolos* three times, and Jude uses it once.[61] Paul, however, uses the term thirty-five times, in both the singular and the plural.[62] Hebrews 3:1 provides an additional single reference that refers to Christ as an Apostle.

Because the writings of Paul appear to be the earliest in the New Testament, some secular scholars have proposed that the term was a postresurrectional title read anachronistically into the mortal ministry or that the term originated in Greek Christianity after the beginning of the gentile mission and hence did not necessarily have a direct connection with Jesus or the original Twelve.[63] In this view, even though the Gospels were written after Paul, their authors did not regularly include the term *apostle*, preferring, particularly in the

---

[59] John's failure to use the term *apostolos* in a technical sense is difficult to explain. On the one hand, because John does not seem to be aware of the synoptic Gospels, this usage, or lack thereof, might serve as a sign of early composition, at least before Luke. On the other hand, if the later date that is traditionally proposed is accepted, then John has purposefully avoided the term to focus instead on his theme of discipleship.

[60] Luke 6:13; 9:10; 11:49; 17:5; 22:14; 24:10; Acts 1:2, 26; 2:37, 42, 43; 4:33, 35, 36; 5:2, 12, 18, 29, 40; 6:6; 8:1,14,18; 9:27; 11:1; 14:14; 15:2, 4, 6, 23; 16:4.

[61] 1 Peter 1:1; 2 Peter 1:1; 3:2; Jude 1:17.

[62] Romans 1:1; 11:13; 16:7; 1 Corinthians 1:1; 4:9; 9:1, 2, 5; 12:28, 29; 15:7, 9 (x2); 2 Corinthians 1:1; 8:23; 11:5,13 (x2); 12:11, 12; Galatians 1:1, 17, 19; Ephesians 1:1; 2:20; 3:5; 4:11; Philippians 2:25; Colossians 1:1; 1 Thessalonians 2:6 (v. 7 in Greek manuscripts); 1 Timothy 1:1; 2:7; 2 Timothy 1:1, 11; Titus 1:1.

[63] Brown, "The Twelve and the Apostolate," 1381 (§153).

case of Mark and Matthew, the designation "the twelve," usually as a number alone and sometimes with the word for disciple.[64]

This position, of course, does not satisfactorily deal with the evidence of Luke, who applies *apostoloi* almost exclusively to the original Twelve, noting that when Judas was replaced, his replacement had to come from the body of disciples who had not only been witnesses of the resurrection but who had also been with Christ from the beginning of His ministry (Acts 1:21–22). Luke's usage in both his Gospel and in Acts is consistent, the only possible exception being his reference to Paul and Barnabas as *apostoloi* in Acts 14:4 and 14, as Paul at least had not been with Jesus in His mortal ministry and, in this instance, Paul and Barnabas were "sent out" by local Church officials.[65] Because Mark and Matthew antedate Luke, the rarity of the term in these Gospels must be explained. Perhaps a satisfactory translation for the Hebrew or Aramaic term used by Jesus had not yet been settled upon; perhaps they were always seen as a group, making "the twelve" a more natural designation; or perhaps, as today, the frequent use of the title was avoided out of respect for the priesthood office.[66] On the other hand, if the term *apostolos* had already become

---

[64] Mark uses "the twelve" ten times (Mark 3:14; 4:10; 6:7; 9:35; 10:32; 11:11; 14:10, 17, 20, 43) and Matthew five or six times (Matthew 10:1, 5; 26:14, 20, 47; "disciples" with "the twelve" in Matthew 20:17 does not appear in all the Greek manuscripts). The expression "the twelve disciples" appears in Matthew 11:1 and possibly in 20:17.

[65] This instance might reflect their earlier role as emissaries or representatives of the Church in Antioch, which set them apart for that particular mission (see Bruce, *Acts of the Apostles*, 318–19, and Ben Witherington, *New Testament History: A Narrative Account* [Grand Rapids: Baker Academic, 2001], 235–36). Richard L. Anderson, *Understanding Paul* (Salt Lake City: Deseret Book, 1983), 35, argues strongly for full apostolic ordination and membership among the Twelve. Indeed, from a Latter-day Saint perspective, they easily could have filled subsequent vacancies that occurred among the Twelve, although ordination to the priesthood office of Apostle does not always include automatically being set apart to the Twelve. See Joseph Fielding Smith, *Doctrines of Salvation*, comp. Bruce R. McConkie, 3 vols. (Salt Lake City: Bookcraft, 1956), 3:153; Hall, *New Testament Witnesses of Christ*, 236–38.

[66] See Talmage, *JTC*, 214. "So great is the sanctity of this special calling that the title 'Apostle' should not be used lightly as the common or ordinary form of address applied to living men called to this office. The quorum or council of the Twelve Apostles as existent in the Church today may be better spoken of as the 'Quorum of the Twelve,' the 'Council of the Twelve,' or simply as the 'Twelve,' than use of the more sacred term."

the more common form in Greek Pauline circles before the Gospels were written, this could explain why Luke, who had been closely associated with Paul and his mission, used it more often in his Gospel and then increasingly in Acts.

In the Pauline corpus, however, the use of the term is fluid. For instance, Paul uses *apostolos* in a simple, nontechnical sense at least twice. In Philippians 2:25, he applies it to Epaphroditus, who was serving as the commissioned representative of the Church at Philippi but did not function specifically in a priesthood office, leading the KJV, NIV, and NRSV to translate it as "messenger" here rather than "apostle." Likewise, after commending Titus in 2 Corinthians 8:23, Paul mentions other brethren, whom he calls "the messengers of the churches (*apostoloi ekklēsiōn*)." In Romans 16:7, Paul also refers to Andronicus and Junia(s) as Apostles, but here they may simply be missionaries.[67] In 2 Corinthians 11:5 and 12:11, on the other hand, he refers to his opponents who preach a different Jesus or different gospel derogatorily as "these 'super' apostles (*huperlian apostolōn*)," which does not come across as clearly in the "very chiefest apostles" of the KJV. That he does not see them as genuine Apostles is clear when in 2 Corinthians 11:13 he denounces them directly as *pseudapostoloi* or "false apostles."

By contrast, all of Paul's other uses were concerned with legitimate and special authority, and that may have affected Luke's later practice. Nineteen times Paul refers to himself as an Apostle to legitimize his position, notably in the opening formulae of ten of his letters and when his own authority was questioned. Paul's expression "an apostle *of Jesus Christ*" emphasizes that this is a specific and divine commission rather than *apostolos* used in a general sense. Whereas the original Apostles were thought of as a group and hence were commonly referred to as "the twelve" rather than as "apostles" in the

---

[67] *Iounian* can be either the feminine singular accusative of Junia or the masculine singular accusative of Junias (perhaps short for Junianus). Ancient commentators frequently saw these two as a husband and wife pair (see J. A. Fitzmeyer, *Romans* [New York: Doubleday, 1992], 737–40), in which case we would presume that they were "ambassadors" or missionaries "sent out" in a general sense.

synoptic Gospels, after Paul himself received an apostolic commission and authority, he regularly began to use what had become the accepted Greek rendering of whatever term Jesus had used when He "named" His first twelve Apostles.[68]

Nevertheless, an often-overlooked explanation lies in the fact that although called, ordained, and even "sent out" for short missions during Jesus' mortal ministry, the Apostles did not fully serve in their calling until after the Passion, Resurrection, and Ascension. They were chosen and ordained, to be sure, but while their Lord was with them, their main role was to be His twelve companions, to learn from Him, and to follow Him. Indeed, although Luke employs the term *apostoloi* in his Gospel more often than Mark and Matthew, he uses "the twelve" just as often.[69] After using "apostles" twice in Acts, 1:2 and 26, in much the same way as he did in his Gospel, after Pentecost, Luke's use of the term suddenly increases in frequency, appearing twenty-three more times, whereas the designation "the twelve" appears only once more.[70] In Acts, the Twelve truly were "sent out," and this is the type of mission filled by Paul and Peter in their letters.

Thus, what had also been used in general terms for any messenger or agent became the exclusive appellation for those who had been individually commissioned by Jesus Christ, either in His ministry or after His resurrection; they then fulfilled that commission by taking their apostolic witness to the world. Although additional Apostles

---

[68] Whether Paul ever referred explicitly to Peter and the Twelve as apostles depends upon the reading of 1 Corinthians 15:7 (Anthony C. Thistelton, *The First Epistle to the Corinthians*, NIGTC [Grand Rapids: Eerdmans, 2000] 1203–8). Verses 5–8 of chapter 15 comprise a list of all those who had seen the Risen Lord: starting with Cephas and the Twelve, the resurrected Lord was seen next by more than five hundred disciples, then by James the brother of the Lord, "then of all the apostles" (v. 7), and finally by Paul himself. Read inclusively the reference to "all the apostles" could refer to Peter and the Twelve earlier in the list (although this reading would also include the more than five hundred as well), but elsewhere where Paul speaks of apostles in the plural, he does explicitly seem to be referring to the Twelve alone (1 Corinthians 4:9; 9:5; 12:28–29; 15:9; 2 Corinthians 11:13; Galatians 1:17; 1:19; 2:20; 3:5; 4:1; 2 Thessalonians 2:6).

[69] Luke 8:1; 9:1;["his twelve disciples"] 9:12; 18:31; 22:3, 47.

[70] Acts 2:37, 42; 4:33, 35, 36; 5:2, 12, 18, 29, 40; 6:6; 8:1, 14, 18; 9:27; 11:1; 14:14; 15:2, 4, 6, 23; 16:4.

such as Paul and Barnabas may have been appointed to occupy vacancies among the original Twelve,[71] as has sometimes been the case in this dispensation, some special witnesses may have been ordained Apostles but may not have been members of the Twelve, raising the possibility of a body of ordained witnesses that was at times slightly larger than the innermost circle of twelve.[72] As a result, in the New Testament texts, a picture emerges of a set of concentric circles around the figure of the Savior. In the broadest circle were all the disciples, those who accepted Jesus as Lord and endeavored to follow Him. Within this group were those who were sent out on specific missions, such as the Seventy whom Jesus "sent out" (*apesteilen*) later in the Galilean ministry (Luke 10:1). Such missionaries and later the agents of individual churches, such as Epaphroditus (Philippians 2:25), may have been called *apostoloi* in a general sense.[73] Then, within this circle were those who had a special, divine witness of the Savior, in particular those who had received a special commission

---

[71] "We have no record that states that in the days of the apostles of old that any one was ever ordained to be an apostle and not to be a member of the Council of the Twelve" (Joseph Fielding Smith, *Doctrines of Salvation*, 3:153).

[72] The 2004 *Deseret Morning News Church Almanac* (Salt Lake City: Deseret News, 2004), 71, lists eleven officially recognized Apostles who were not members of the Council of the Twelve at the time of their ordinations. Included in this list are Joseph Smith and assistant presidents of the Church Oliver Cowdery and Hyrum Smith. Three others—Brigham Young Jr. (1864), Joseph F. Smith (1866), and Sylvester Q. Cannon (1938)—were eventually set apart as members of the Quorum of the Twelve, but four of those listed—John W. Young (1864), Daniel H. Wells (1857?), Joseph A. Young (1864), and Alvin R. Dyer (1967)—never were. The case of Amasa M. Lyman is particularly involved. He became a member of the Twelve during the period of Orson Pratt's disaffection (1842), was released from the Twelve upon Pratt's reinstatement in 1843, returned to the Twelve in 1844, and was eventually dropped from the Quorum in 1867.

For the possibility that there were more New Testament Apostles than simply the original Twelve, see Meier, "The Circle of the Twelve," 637–38.

[73] Compare Joseph Fielding Smith, *Doctrines of Salvation*, 144, "The term apostle is recognized in the Church in the sense in which it is defined in the dictionary. Men have been called apostles who have been sent forth with the gospel message even when they have not been ordained to that particular office. The seventies of the Church are at times referred to as the seventy apostles, because they are the missionaries of the Church and are sent out with the message of salvation and as witnesses for Christ into all the world, although they do not hold the office of apostle in the restricted sense."

and a specific priesthood ordination, for whom the term *apostolos* has special significance. Ultimately, of course, the term became most closely associated with the Twelve and their successors.[74]

Given Authority, Commissioned, and Further Taught

Mark 3:14 makes the purpose of the Twelve's apostolic appointment clear: "He ordained twelve, *that they should be with him*, and *that he might send them forth* (*apostellē*) to preach" (emphasis added). Although their ultimate purpose was to go forth and preach the gospel, this clause is secondary to the first purpose clause, "that they should be with him," supporting the idea that they were not fully "sent out" until after his ascension. Although *epoiēsen* is rendered "ordained" in the KJV, the word literally means "make" and usually has the sense of "make ready, prepare, or appoint."[75] Although Jesus called and named the Twelve "apostles" in Mark 3:13–14 and Luke 6:13, He did not formally give them "power and authority" until He commissioned them and "sent them" on their first mission (Mark 6:7 and Luke 9:1–2).[76] This break is not as apparent in Matthew's account because he seems to have reordered some events to highlight the Sermon on the Mount, thus delaying the account of the calling of the Twelve until they were empowered and sent on their first mission (Matthew 10:1–42).[77] Whether the Twelve were called, trained, and

---

[74] Although we have difficulties identifying when Paul was ordained an Apostle and became a member of the Twelve (see Anderson, *Paul*, 35–36, and Matthews, *Behold the Messiah*, 330–31), his own career may illustrate these different types of "apostolic" calls. The mission recounted in Acts 14 seems to be a "sending out" by local Church officials, but Paul's vision of Christ made him an Apostle in the sense of a special witness. Whereas Latter-day Saints have no doubt that he was subsequently ordained an Apostle, the New Testament does not specifically mention when, or whether, he ever took a place in what we would term "the Quorum of the Twelve."

[75] Arndt and Gingrich, "poieō," *GEL*, 680–81.

[76] Rengstorf, "apostolos," 428–29; Matthews, *Behold the Messiah*, 112–13.

[77] Matthew's structure divides the body of his Gospel (between the infancy narrative at the beginning and the passion and resurrection narratives at the end) into five alternating blocks of narrative and discourse. The first narrative block, Proclamation of the Kingdom (3:1–7:29), precedes the first and important discourse, the Sermon on the Mount (5:1–7:29), which is followed by the second narrative block, the Galilean

then later "ordained" in the conventional sense of receiving priesthood authority or whether they were actually ordained at their call and then further set apart or otherwise commissioned for their first mission is not in itself important.[78] What is significant is that after they were chosen, Jesus knew they needed to "be with him" to develop their apostolic testimonies. A vital part of this was the instruction received in the Sermon on the Mount (Matthew 5:1–7:29), some of which was apparently repeated on another occasion in the so-called Sermon on the Plain (Luke 6:17–49).[79] Portions of the sermon were directly prefaced with "these are the words which Jesus taught his disciples that they should say unto the people" (JST Matthew 7:1), and their coming apostolic commission was foreshadowed later in the sermon when Jesus directed them, "Go ye into the world, saying unto all, Repent, for the kingdom of heaven has come nigh unto you" (JST Matthew 7:9).

Events after the Sermon on the Mount are beyond the stated scope of this volume, but a few subsequent incidents have bearing upon the call of the Twelve, their preparation for their apostolic mission, and their reception of full authority. This preparatory period included such important teachings as parables of the sower, the seed, the wheat and the tares, and the mustard seed (Matthew 13:1–43; Mark 4:1–34; and Luke 8:4), each giving the Twelve insights into their missionary work. They further witnessed miraculous demonstrations of God's power, which they, as Apostles, would exercise themselves. Among these miracles were the healing of the servant of a "centurion" (Matthew 8:5–13; Luke 7:1–10),[80] the raising of the

---

Ministry (8:1–10:42). Many of the events of the Galilean ministry, however, including the calling of the Twelve, appear to actually have preceded the Sermon on the Mount.

[78] Note, however, JST Luke 8:1, "the twelve who were ordained of him."

[79] See John H. Hall and John W. Welch, *Charting the New Testament* (Provo, Utah: Foundation for Ancient Research and Mormon Studies, 2002), charts 9–3 and 9–4, and Matthews, *Behold the Messiah*, 115–25, as well as Frank F. Judd, "The Setting of the Sermon on the Mount"; Andrew C. Skinner, "A Reading of the Sermon on the Mount: A Restoration Perspective"; and Thomas A. Wayment, "The Sermon on the Plain," in this volume.

[80] Because this event occurred in Antipas's Galilee, where there were no official

widow's son at Nain (Luke 7:11–17), the calming of the sea (Matthew 8:18–27; Mark 4:35–41; Luke 8:22–25), the casting out of the legion of devils (Matthew 8:28–9:1; Mark 5:1–21; Luke 8:26–40), the healing of the woman with the issue of blood (Matthew 9:20–22; Mark 5:25–34; Luke 8:43–48), and the healing of the dumb and blind (Matthew 9:27–34).

Additionally, Jesus singled out Peter, James, and John to witness the special miracle of the raising of Jairus's daughter (Matthew 9:18–19, 23–26; Mark 5:22–24, 35–43; Luke 8:41–42, 49–56). As a result, when Jesus gave the Twelve their commission and sent them on their first mission, He was able to direct them, "As ye go, preach, saying, The kingdom of heaven is at hand. Heal the sick, cleanse the lepers, raise the dead, cast out devils: freely ye have received, freely give" (Matthew 10:7–8).

When Jesus "sent out" the Apostles on their first mission, He specifically restricted them to Israel, restraining them from preaching to Gentiles or Samaritans (Matthew 10:5). As successful as this first, limited mission was (Mark 6:30; Luke 9:10), further preparation was necessary for them as Jesus' companions before they were ready to witness the culminating acts of the Savior's mission and truly go forth to all the world. Pivotal among these was the feeding of the five thousand (Matthew 14:14–21; Mark 6:34–44; Luke 9:11–17; John 6:3–14), which, in addition to being a stunning sign of Jesus' divine power, preceded Jesus' walking on the Sea of Galilee and the delivery of His discourse on the bread of life.

When the disciples saw Jesus walking toward them on the water and became frightened, in all three accounts Jesus calmed them by proclaiming, "It is I" (Matthew 14:27; Mark 6:50; John 6:20). Rendered *ego eimi* in Greek, this statement echoes the sacred tetragrammaton YHWH of the Hebrew scriptures, implicitly identifying

---

forces before A.D. 44, the "centurion" would probably have been either a Herodian officer trained and functioning along Roman lines or perhaps a Roman military attaché working with Antipas's forces. See Marshall, *The Gospel of Luke*, 279.

Jesus with the Jehovah of the Old Testament.[81] This may have been what inspired Peter to join Jesus on the water, and his partial success can be seen as a tentative attempt to do as his Master was doing.

The bread of life discourse that followed (John 6:35–58) was a turning point in the Galilean ministry, for Jesus' direct teachings about His identity as the "bread come down from heaven" and His "hard sayings" about His followers needing to eat His flesh and drink His blood led many former disciples to no longer follow Him (John 6:66).[82] Significantly, at this point of decision, the Twelve remained faithful, strengthened by their growing apostolic testimonies that Jesus was the Christ: "Then said Jesus unto the twelve, Will ye also go away? Then Simon Peter answered him, Lord, to whom shall we go? thou hast the words of eternal life. And we believe and are sure that thou art that Christ, the Son of the living God" (John 6:67–69). More healings, a second miraculous feeding, this time of four thousand, and additional teachings followed. Then, at Bethsaida, the original home of Peter, Andrew, and Philip, came the healing of a blind man (Mark 8:22–26). Though this was not an unprecedented miracle, the timing had symbolism beyond the act: the Apostles, Peter foremost among them, began to see Jesus for who He really was.

Peter's Declaration, the Transfiguration, and Priesthood Keys

At Caesarea Philippi, Jesus asked His disciples, "Whom do men say that I am?" (Mark 8:27; compare with Matthew 16:13 and Luke 9:18). Although others thought that Jesus was John the Baptist, Elijah, or some other prophet, Peter stood forth and boldly declared, "Thou art the Christ, the Son of the living God" (Matthew 16:16; JST Mark 8:31; JST Luke 9:20).

Whereas the disciples had earlier "believed" and even "been sure" (John 6:69) after the bread of life discourse, Peter's apostolic witness

---

[81] Brown, *The Gospel According to John I–XII*, 533–38, although he and France, *The Gospel of Mark*, 273n71, have some reservations in this instance.

[82] Talmage, *JTC*, 316–19; McConkie, *MM*, 2:365–87.

was now a firm testimony given through revelation by the Father. Accordingly, James E. Talmage has written, "The confession by which the apostles avowed their acceptance of Jesus as the Christ, the Son of the living God, was evidence of their actual possession of the spirit of the Holy Apostleship, by which they were made particular witnesses of their Lord."[83]

This declaration by Peter then led Jesus to make the important proclamation, "Thou art Peter (*Petros*) and upon this rock (*petra*) I will build my church" (Matthew 16:18). *Petros*, the name Jesus gave Peter at his initial call, means an isolated rock or stone, whereas *petra*, a feminine noun, means bedrock, the type of rock of which a tomb was hewn, or the foundation of an impregnable position or rocky fortress.[84]

Thus, although Peter's subsequent apostolic career revealed that he was indeed a rock, the rock upon which the Church would be built was the rock from which Peter as an Apostle was hewn. Joseph Smith taught, "Jesus in His teachings says, 'Upon this rock I will build my Church, and the gates of hell shall not prevail against it.' What rock? Revelation!"[85] Helaman 5:12 helps clarify what particular revelation the prophet may have meant: "Remember that it is upon the rock of our Redeemer, who is Christ, the Son of God, that ye must build your foundation."[86] In the context of Peter's preceding declaration, then, Jesus' statement may be interpreted to mean that the Church would be built upon the apostolic testimony of Christ that comes through revelation (cf. Ephesians 2:20).

Christ's next promise to Peter, "I will give unto thee the keys of the kingdom of heaven: and whatsoever thou shalt bind on earth shall be bound in heaven: and whatsoever thou shalt loose on earth shall be loosed in heaven" (Matthew 16:19), indicates the final step in Peter's apostolic preparation. This declaration and Jesus' promise

---

[83] Talmage, *JTC*, 336–37.
[84] See "petra," and "Petros," in Arndt and Gingrich, *GEL*, 654–55.
[85] Joseph Smith, *TPJS*, 274.
[86] See Matthews, *Behold the Messiah*, 250–51, for other scriptural examples of the image of Christ as "the rock."

of the keys of the kingdom precede the first of several "passion predictions" wherein Jesus began to prophesy of His suffering, death, and resurrection, specific parts of His messianic mission of which His Apostles would be witnesses.[87]

After this first prediction, all three synoptic Gospels recount a sacred event, the Transfiguration (Matthew 17:1–13; Mark 9:2–13; Luke 9:28–37), at which Peter, James, and John received a further witness and, according to latter-day revelation, the promised keys of the kingdom. Although the Transfiguration cannot be fully treated here, it was critical in the development of the apostleship. Jesus' taking His three closest disciples onto a mountaintop to have a visionary experience had important parallels with Exodus 24, where Moses took three companions onto Mount Sinai to meet with God.[88]

The appearance of Moses and Elijah (KJV "Elias") had much symbolism, given their roles as representatives of the law and the prophets and their eschatological associations, but their most important function is one not mentioned in the Gospel texts. Modern revelation and parallels with the 1836 experience of Joseph Smith and Oliver Cowdery in the Kirtland Temple (Doctrine and Covenants 110) confirm that here Jesus' leading Apostles received important authority that enabled them to lead the Church after His departure.[89] Joseph Smith taught, "The Savior, Moses, and Elias, gave the keys to Peter, James, and John, on the mount, when they were transfigured before him."[90] Additionally, these keys were received in connection with their endowment and the audible voice of God proclaiming Christ as His Beloved Son, what Peter later

---

[87] Matthew 16:21–23; 17:22–23; 20:17–19; Mark 8:31–9:1, 30–37; 10:3–5; Luke 9:19–27, 43–45; 18:31–34; John 12:20–36.

[88] Bruce Chilton, "Transfiguration," in Freedman, *ABD*, 6.640–41; Marshall, *The Gospel of Luke*, 383; France, *The Gospel of Mark*, 348.

[89] Matthews, *Behold the Messiah*, 253–54.

[90] Smith, *TPJS*, 158; Joseph Fielding Smith, *Doctrines of Salvation*, 2:109–12. See Robert J. Matthews, "Tradition, Testimony, Transfiguration, and Keys," in Kent P. Jackson and Robert L. Millet, eds., *Studies in Scripture, Vol. 5: The Gospels* (Salt Lake City: Deseret Book, 1986), 305–8.

associated with "a more sure word of prophecy" (2 Peter 1:19),[91] whereby they received the greatest of witnesses.

The Twelve Empowered and Prepared for the Road to Jerusalem

Peter, James, and John were charged not to share all their experiences on the Mount of Transfiguration until after Jesus' resurrection (Matthew 17:9; Mark 9:9; Luke 9:36). Nevertheless, shortly thereafter Jesus affirmed that they had received the vital keys necessary to exercise the sealing power and enjoy the fullness of the priesthood in His Sermon on the Church (Matthew 18:1–35): "Whatsoever ye shall bind on earth shall be bound in heaven: and whatsoever ye shall loose on earth shall be loosed in heaven" (Matthew 18:18).[92] Thus empowered and prepared, the Twelve were ready to leave Galilee and accompany their Master to Jerusalem to become final witnesses of His mission and then take up the leadership of the Church.

An important parallel emerges from the experience of the latter-day Quorum of the Twelve Apostles at the end of Joseph Smith's ministry before the Prophet went to Carthage. The first quorum in this dispensation had gone through a similar pattern of early discipleship, followed by being called, growing in understanding, gaining a deeper witness, being sent on missions, and finally receiving the necessary keys to direct the Church. According to Joseph Fielding Smith, "A short time before his martyrdom, the Prophet bestowed upon the Twelve apostles—who constitute the second quorum in the

---

[91] Joseph Fielding Smith, *Doctrines of Salvation*, 2:165; McConkie, *DNTC*, 1:400. On 1 Peter 1:19, see Doctrine and Covenants 131:5, "The more sure word of prophecy means a man's knowing that he is sealed up unto eternal life, by revelation and the spirit of prophecy, through the power of the Holy Priesthood."

[92] Although Jesus could have been speaking specifically to Peter, James, and John or suggesting that through them all the Twelve would receive these keys, McConkie, *DNTC*, 3:424, writes, "Now we find our Lord announcing that all of the Twelve possessed these same sealing powers and keys; either the remaining nine apostles had received them sometime between the Transfiguration and the occasion of this sermon or they received them at this time. After his resurrection, we shall find Jesus again specifying that all of the Twelve held these keys. (John 20:21–23)."

Church—all the keys and all the ordinances and priesthood necessary for them to hold in order to carry on this great and glorious work of universal salvation."[93] The Prophet's preparation of the latter-day Twelve before Carthage mirrored the Savior's own acts as He approached Calvary.

After sacred instruction and ordinances at the time of the Last Supper, Jesus prayed the following to the Father during His great Intercessory Prayer: "As thou hast sent me *into the world*, even so have I also sent them into the world" (John 17:18; emphasis added). This prayerful intent at the time of the Last Supper became a formal commission during His resurrection appearance to ten of the Twelve:

> Then the same day at evening, being the first day of the week, when the doors were shut where the disciples were assembled for fear of the Jews, came Jesus and stood in the midst, and saith unto them, Peace be unto you. And when he had so said, he shewed unto them his hands and his side. Then were the disciples glad, when they saw the Lord. Then said Jesus to them again, Peace be unto you: *as my*

---

[93] Joseph Fielding Smith, *Doctrines of Salvation*, 3:154. Note the following:

From Parley P. Pratt: "Before I went east on the 4th of April last, we were in council with Brother Joseph almost every day for weeks, says Brother Joseph in one of those councils there is something going to happen; I dont [don't] know what it is, but the Lord bids me to hasten and give you your endowment, before the temple is finished. He conducted us through every ordinance of the holy priesthood, and when he had gone through with all the ordinances he rejoiced very much, and says, now if they kill me you have got all the keys, and all the ordinances and you can confer them upon others, and the hosts of Satan will not be able to tear down the kingdom, as fast as you will be able to build it up; and now says he on your shoulders will the responsibility of leading this people rest, for the Lord is going to let me rest a while. Now why did he say to the Twelve on YOUR shoulders will this responsibility rest" (*Times and Seasons* 5.17 [September 15, 1844], 651).

From Wilford Woodruff: ". . . has the Prophet Joseph found Elder Rigdon in his councils when he organized the quorum of the Twelve, a few months before his death, to prepare them for the endowment? And when they received their endowment, and actually received the keys of the kingdom of God, and oracles of God, keys of revelation, and the pattern of heavenly things; and thus addressing the Twelve, exclaimed, 'upon your shoulders the kingdom rests, and you must round up your shoulders, and bear it; for I have had to do it until now. But now the responsibility rests upon you. It mattereth not what becomes of me'" (*Times and Seasons* 5.20 [November 2, 1844], 698).

Father hath sent me, even so send I you. And when he had said this, he breathed on them, and saith unto them, Receive ye the Holy Ghost: Whose soever sins ye remit, they are remitted unto them; and whose soever sins ye retain, they are retained. (John 20:19–23; emphasis added)

In this episode, all the cardinal features of the apostolic call are put into place. First, His chosen disciples became witnesses of His divinity, particularly of the reality of His resurrection. Second, He formally sent them forth as He had prayed in the upper room, not just to Israel or on a limited mission but to the whole world.[94] Third, endowed with a special measure of the Holy Ghost, they were prepared to go forth with full priesthood keys to act in the place of Christ Himself. The idea later encapsulated in the rabbinic maxim "A man's *šēliaḥ* is as himself" had, in John's view, first applied to Jesus, whom the Father had sent into the world. The narrative of Acts affirms that following the Resurrection, the Forty-Day ministry, and Pentecost, they began to function fully in their unique and complete role as Apostles of the Lord Jesus Christ, thus fulfilling what Joseph Fielding Smith defined as "the true calling of the apostles of Jesus Christ," which "is to hold the fullness of the priesthood and to proclaim the gospel in all the World."[95]

---

[94] As we would expect in light of Johannine usage, the Greek here does not use forms of *apostellō* for the sending forth of both Jesus and the disciples: "Peace be unto you: as my Father hath sent me (*apestalken me*), even so send I you (*pempō humas*)." Nevertheless, when we look at the parallels with the Intercessory Prayer in John 17:18, the intent is clear, leading F. F. Bruce, *The Gospel of John* (Grand Rapids: William B. Eerdmans, 1983), 391, to write: "Now comes the actual sending. The technical term 'apostle' is avoided by John, but by the use of the cognate verb *apostellō* [for himself] he indicates that the disciples now become effectively apostles in the sense of 'sent ones.' The Son's mission in the world is entrusted to them, since he is returning to the Father."

[95] Joseph Fielding Smith, *Doctrines of Salvation*, 3:144.

IX.
JESUS TEACHES AT JACOB'S WELL

GAYE STRATHEARN

Whosoever drinketh of the water that I shall give him shall never thirst; but the water that I shall give him shall be in him a well of water springing up into everlasting life.

JOHN 4:14

Early in Jesus' ministry, John records that Jesus "must needs go through Samaria" (John 4:4) on His way from Judea to Galilee. The need that John refers to was not geographical. Since He was probably already in the Jordan Valley (John 3:31–4:3), Jesus could "have easily have gone north through the valley and then up into Galilee through the Bethshan gap, avoiding Samaria."[1] But He had work to do in Samaria, so He traveled instead to "Sychar, near to the parcel of ground that Jacob gave to his son Joseph" and near to Jacob's Well (John 4:5–6).[2] At this well, after his disciples had left to

---

[1] Raymond E. Brown, *The Gospel According to John I–XII: A New Translation with Introduction and Commentary* (New York: Doubleday, 1966), 169. According to Josephus, it "was the custom of the Galileans" to pass through Samaria when they were going to Jerusalem until the time of the Judean procurator, Cumanus (A.D. 48–52; see also Luke 9:51). At that time, some Samaritans from the village of Ginea ambushed a group of Galileans traveling to Jerusalem (*AJ*, 20.6.1).

[2] "Scholars have not agreed about the location of Sychar," although there is a general consensus that Jacob's Well has been correctly identified as the tourist site located

buy food, Jesus met with the Samaritan woman and helped her and a group of villagers recognize Him as the Messiah (John 4:8). The interest in this event is fourfold. First, when Jesus gave His commission to the Twelve, He specifically instructed them not to engage in missionary work among the Samaritans (Matthew 10:5). Yet, in this instance, He seems to have gone out of His way to travel through Samaritan territory and to seek out this Samaritan woman. Second, this incident plays a major role in the structure of John's Gospel. The event is a prime example of how Jesus, as one who comes from above (John 3:31), helps His earthly disciples gain an eternal perspective of who Jesus is and what He came to earth to accomplish.[3] Third, the account of Jesus' interaction with the Samaritan woman shows a good knowledge of Samaritan beliefs and practices. Fourth, the account of Jesus teaching the Samaritan woman and the other members of her city is the most prominent evidence to suggest that John's Gospel was directed, at least in part, to a Samaritan audience.[4]

---

on the eastern edge of modern Nablus and now housed in a structure built by the Greek Orthodox Church (John J. Rousseau and Rami Arav, *Jesus and His World: An Archaeological and Cultural Dictionary* [Minneapolis: Fortress Press, 1995], 131, 267). One possible site for Sychar is the village of 'Askar. It is situated at the foot of Mount Ebal, about one mile north of Jacob's well. "This was based on Epiphanius who named two different cities, Sychar and Shechem (*Versio Antiqua*, 253)" (Rousseau and Arav, *Jesus and His World*, 267). Brown, however, says that this identification "is probably wrong on several counts: (a) the site is a medieval settlement; (b) the dubious similarity of name is useless since the Arabic name 'Askar does not reflect an ancient designation of the site but simply that the place has served as a military campsite; (c) 'Askar has a good well of its own, a fact which makes the woman's journey to Jacob's well inexplicable" (Brown, *The Gospel According to John I–XII*, 169). Jerome is the first to equate it with the ancient Israelite city of Shechem (*Letter 58, To Eustochium* 13). Shechem (also known as Tell Balatah) is only about 250 feet from Jacob's well (Brown, *The Gospel According to John I–XII*, 169). John Hyrcanus destroyed it at the end of the second century B.C., and no archaeological evidence shows that the city was ever rebuilt. However, a village was built near its site (Josephus, *AJ*, 13.9.1; Lawrence E. Toombs, "Shechem [Place]," in Freedman, *ABD*, 5:1185; Rousseau and Arav, *Jesus and His World*, 268).

[3] Craig R. Koester, *Symbolism in the Fourth Gospel: Meaning, Mystery, Community*, 2d ed. (Minneapolis: Fortress Press, 2003), 4–8, 47–50.

[4] Edwin D. Freed, "Did John Write His Gospel Partly to Win Samaritan Converts?" *Novum Testamentum* 12 (1970): 231–56; George Wesley Buchanan, "The Samaritan

Before we can fully appreciate Jesus' interaction with the Samaritans in John 4, we must first be clear about who the Samaritans were in the New Testament. Why did animosity exist between the Samaritans and the Jews? What differentiated the Samaritans' sect from that of Judaism? When did the Samaritans become a distinct sect in their own right? All these questions are pivotal for our understanding of the intricacies of Jesus' interaction with them as well as our understanding of His discussion with His disciples at Jacob's Well.

Recent research into the origins of Samaritanism has shown that the issue is much more complex than simply identifying them as the "descendants of (1) foreign colonists placed [in northern Israel] by kings of Assyria and Babylonia (2 Kings 17:24; Ezra 4:2, 10); [and] (2) Israelites who escaped at the time of the captivity."[5] In the discussion that follows, we will see that, although they enjoyed a definite continuity with the preexilic house of Israel,[6] the Samaritans did not emerge as a sect that was *distinct* from their southern relatives in Judea until the Hasmonean period (167–63 B.C.). This was a time of intense struggle, as Judeans and Samaritans alike suffered under the political and religious oppression of the Seleucids. However, when the Jewish Hasmonean family (also known as the Maccabees) rose up in rebellion against the Seleucids, the Samaritans chose not to participate. This choice added fuel to a fire of distrust and animosity that had been smoldering for generations but now ignited into a blaze of secession.[7]

Origin of the Gospel of John," in *Religions in Antiquity: Essays in Memory of Erwin Ramsdell Goodenough* (Leiden: E. J. Brill, 1968), 149–75; Koester, *Symbolism in the Fourth Gospel*, 20–21. Note Bruce Hall's cautions against uncritically accepting the influence of Samaritanism on the Gospel: "Some Thoughts about Samaritanism and the Johannine Community," in *New Samaritan Studies of the Société d'Études Samaritaines: Essays in Honour of G. D. Sixdenier*, ed. Alan D. Crown and Lucy Davey (Sydney: Mandelbaum Publishing, University of Sydney, 1990), 207–15.

[5] BD, "Samaritans," 768.

[6] Alan D. Crown, "Another Look at Samaritan Origins," in *New Samaritan Studies*, 133–55.

[7] The antipathy we find between Samaritans and Jews in the New Testament is just one manifestation of deeply entrenched tensions between Israelite tribes in the north and those in the south. These tensions date back to premonarchial times and may even

The Origin of the Samaritans and Their Religion

Two aspects, in particular, complicate the issue of Samaritan origins. First, ancient texts do not always make a distinction between the Samarians and the Samaritans.[8] Yet Samaritan scholarship has concluded that this distinction is critical because of the inaccuracy of identifying all Samarians as Samaritans.[9] Samarians were people who lived in the geographical and political realm of Samaria. In contrast, Samaritans were "a well defined and self-conscious religious sect employing a version of the Pentateuch called the Samaritan Pentateuch as its sacred text and honoring Mount Gerizim as the proper place of worship."[10] Any discussion of Samaritan origins, therefore, must be grounded in the development of these two characteristics. More than any other issues, the combination of these two elements

---

reflect the inherent differences between the agricultural pursuits of the northern tribes vis-à-vis the herding pursuits of the south. King David recognized these tensions and established his capital city of Jerusalem in a politically neutral zone (Yohanan Aharoni, *The Land of the Bible: A Historical Geography*, rev. and enl. ed., trans. A. F. Rainey [Philadelphia: Westminster Press, 1979], 29–30). But any ameliorating effects of that decision were soon negated by the political decisions made by both Solomon and Rehoboam (1 Kings 12:1–16).

[8] Josephus uses both of these terms but is inconsistent in his usage. See Rita Egger, "Josephus," in *A Companion to Samaritan Studies*, ed. Alan D. Crown, Reinhard Pummer, and Abraham Tal (Tübingen: J. C. B. Mohr [Paul Siebeck], 1993), 139. See also Rita Egger, "Josephus Flavius and the Samaritans: Aspects of the Origin of the Samaritans and of Their Early History," in *Proceedings of the First International Congress of the Société d'Études Samaritaines*, ed. Abraham Tal and Moshe Florentin (Tel Aviv: Chaim Rosenberg School for Jewish Studies, Tel-Aviv University, 1991), 109–14.

[9] According to Josephus, some "Samarians" had a distinctly Hellenistic outlook (*AJ*, 12.5.5). These Samarians wanted to "distance themselves from the religious traditions of the past and sought to assert their distinct identity by calling themselves Sidonians" (Robert T. Anderson and Terry Giles, *The Keepers: An Introduction to the History and Culture of the Samaritans* [Peabody, Massachusetts: Hendrickson Publishers, 2002], 28). This group probably named the Mount Gerizim temple Jupiter Hellenius (Josephus, *AJ*, 12.5.5; compare 2 Maccabees 6:1–6).

[10] Anderson and Giles, *The Keepers*, 9. Later Samaritans, probably under the influence of Islam, developed a five-point creed: "We say: My faith is in thee, YHWH; and in Moses son of Amram, thy servant; and in the Holy Law; and in Mount Gerizim Bethel; and in the Day of Vengeance and Recompense" (James A. Montgomery, *The Samaritans: The Earliest Jewish Sect* [Philadelphia: Winston, 1907; repr. New York: KTAV, 1968], 207.

separated, and continues to separate, Samaritanism from Judaism. The second of these characteristics, worship at Mount Gerizim, is at the heart of the Samaritan woman's confusion about Jesus' identity in John 4:19–20 and is also the reason that the Samaritans rejected Jesus in Luke 9:51–56.

The second issue that complicates our search for the origins of the Samaritans is that Samaritan and Jewish accounts are fundamentally different, and both versions are heavily laced with polemic. Jewish accounts of Samaritan origins are grounded primarily in two Old Testament passages, 2 Kings 17 and Ezra 4. Verse 7 in 2 Kings 17 describes how the northern tribes of Israel were deported because they "sinned against the Lord their God." They "built them high places in all their cities, . . . they set them up images and groves in every high hill, . . . they burnt incense in all the high places, as did the heathen whom the Lord carried away before them; . . . they served idols, . . . they rejected [the Lord's] statutes, and his covenant . . . and they left all the commandments of the Lord their God, and made them molten images, even two calves, and made a grove, and worshipped all the host of heaven, and served Baal." In addition, "they caused their sons and their daughters to pass through the fire, and used divination and enchantments, and sold themselves to do evil in the sight of the Lord, to provoke him to anger " (vv. 9–17).

Verse 23 then says "the Lord removed Israel out of his sight, as he had said by all his servants the prophets. So was Israel carried away out of their own land to Assyria." In Sargon's annals, we learn that he "besieged and conquered Samaria [and] led away as booty 27,290 inhabitants of it,"[11] but we should not assume that this figure represents the entire population or even the majority of the population.[12]

---

[11] J. B. Pritchard, ed., *Ancient Near Eastern Texts Relating to the Old Testament*, 3d ed. (Princeton: Princeton University Press, 1969), 284–85. Sargon is here taking credit for the work of his predecessor, Shalmaneser V, who was the one who laid siege to Samaria (J. A. Thompson, *The Bible and Archaeology*, 3d ed. [Grand Rapids: William B. Eerdmans, 1982], 142). Sargon probably was involved in the deportation because this took place over a number of years (A. Kirk Grayson, "Sargon," in Freedman, *ABD*, 5:984).

[12] Robert T. Anderson, "Samaritans," in Freedman, *ABD*, 5:941; Menachem Mor,

A common practice of the Assyrians after they deported a conquered people was to repopulate the area with other conquered peoples. Thus, 2 Kings 17:24 states that "the king of Assyria brought men from Babylon, and from Cuthah, and from Ava, and from Hamath, and from Sepharvaim, and placed them in the cities of Samaria instead of the children of Israel: and they possessed Samaria, and dwelt in the cities thereof."[13]

The new settlers soon found themselves plagued with an infestation of lions that they could not repel. Therefore, they petitioned the Assyrian king to return one of the deported priests so he could teach them how to properly worship the god of the land. Verse 29 is important. It reads, "Every nation made gods of their own, and put them in the houses of the high places which the Samaritans had made, every nation in their cities wherein they dwelt." This is the only place in the King James Version of the Old Testament where we find the term *Samaritans* (*haššōmĕrōnîm*); it refers specifically to the Assyrian colonists who worshiped their own gods and learned to worship the God of Israel as well. "So they feared the Lord, and made unto themselves of the lowest of them priests of the high places, which sacrificed for them in the houses of the high places. They feared the Lord, and served their own gods, after the manner of the nations whom they carried away from thence" (2 Kings 17:32–33). The Jewish historian Josephus specifically identifies this incident as the origin of the Samaritans (*AJ*, 9.14.3).

The important question, though, is whether *haššōmĕrōnîm* here should be translated as *Samarians* or *Samaritans*. The major difficulty with identifying them as the Samaritans of the New Testament is that

---

"The Persian, Hellenistic and Hasmonaean Period," in *The Samaritans*, ed. Alan D. Crown (Tübingen: J. C. B. Mohr [Paul Siebeck], 1989), 1. One scholar estimates that the population of Samaria at the time of the deportation was around 560,000 souls (C. S. Chang, "A New Examination of Samaritan Origins and Identity in the Light of Recent Scholarship" [Ph.D. dissertation, Sydney, 1990], as cited in Crown, "Another Look at Samaritan Origins," 137).

[13] In Jewish sources, the Samaritans are often labeled the Cutheans (*kutim*) to emphasize that they were foreign imports (for example, Josephus, *AJ*, 9.14.3). See also Lawrence Schiffman, "Cutheans," in *A Companion to Samaritan Studies*, 63–64.

very little evidence is available of any pagan religious practices in the Samaritan religion.[14] According to our definitions, and in contrast to Josephus, we can more accurately refer to this group as Samarians.[15] Thus, the New Revised Standard Version translates *haššōměrōnîm* as "the people of Samaria."

Ezra 4 describes the rebuilding of the Jerusalem temple after the Babylonian captivity. A group described as the "adversaries of Judah and Benjamin" offered its services to rebuild the temple because, as they said, "We seek your God, as ye do; and we do sacrifice unto him since the days of Esar-haddon king of Assur, which brought us up hither" (vv. 1–2). This latter statement certainly links the adversaries with the Assyrian colonists of 2 Kings 17. However, we must be cautious in interpreting these passages. Some evidence indicates that during the time between the exiles of the northern and southern kingdoms, remnants from the north continued to contribute to the temple, entered the temple, and even participated in its sacrifices.

During the reign of Josiah, people "from Manasseh and Ephraim, and of all the remnant of Israel" made contributions to the temple treasury (2 Chronicles 34:9). In addition, Jeremiah recorded that eighty men from Shechem, Shiloh, and Samaria ritually prepared themselves and brought sacrifices to the Jerusalem temple (Jeremiah 41:5). Therefore, we have to ask ourselves whether these northerners were the product of intermarriages and were still allowed to participate in the Jerusalem temple or whether some of the northerners possibly remained isolated from the Assyrian colonists and continued in the traditions of their fathers. Unfortunately, the texts in the Old Testament are not more specific than indicated.

---

[14] R. J. Coggins, *Samaritans and Jews: Origins of Samaritanism Reconsidered* (Oxford: Basil Blackwell, 1975), 18. See also James D. Purvis, *The Samaritan Pentateuch and the Origin of the Samaritan Sect* (Cambridge, Massachusetts: Harvard University Press, 1968), 95. The one clear exception to this statement is the Samaritan aversion for an anthropomorphic god. The Aramaic Targum has reworked any passages that suggest God has a body (Abraham Tal, "Samaritan Literature," in *The Samaritans*, 444–45). This point, however, is not indicative of the adoption of Assyrian religion but of Greek philosophy.

[15] For a further discussion on the identity of *haššōměrōnîm*, see also John Bowman, "The History of the Samaritans," *Abr-Nahrain* 18 (1978): 101–2.

In contrast, however, when the northerners offered their services to rebuild the temple in Ezra 4, "Zerubbabel, and Jeshua, and the rest of the chief of the fathers of Israel, said unto them, Ye have nothing to do with us to build an house unto our God; but we ourselves together will build unto the Lord God of Israel" (Ezra 4:3). The "people of the land," whom I understand to be the Samarians, saw this rejection as an affront to them. They reacted by unsuccessfully trying to prevent the rebuilding of the Jerusalem temple (Ezra 4:4–6; 5). This incident clearly placed a wedge in the relations between the north and the south, the repercussions of which carried into New Testament times. This incident may have led the Samarians to build their own holy place on Mount Gerizim.[16] Even so, we can interestingly note that Josephus indicates they continued to have access to the Jerusalem temple into the Roman period (AJ, 18.2.2).[17]

The Samaritan version of their origins is quite different from the Jewish one. Unfortunately, much of what we know from the Samaritans about their origin and religion comes from sources that were written after the first century A.D. but probably incorporate earlier traditions.[18] The Samaritans consider themselves to be the "true descendants of the ten tribes of Israel" who are the "guardians of the Law" (šamerim).[19] According to Samaritan records, Jews split with them when the ambitious Eli moved the ark of the covenant from Shechem to Shiloh because he did not want to serve under Uzzi, a

---

[16] Yitzhak Magen has found the remnants of a stone structure, dating from the Persian period, that represents a holy place ("Mount Gerizim—A Temple City," Kadmoniyot 33, no. 2 [2000]: 96–98 [Hebrew]).

[17] Gospel of Thomas 60 may also be evidence that Samaritans were allowed to offer sacrifice in the Jerusalem temple.

[18] The principal sources are the following: Abu 'l-Fath, Kitab Al-Tarikh, trans., Paul Stenhouse (Sydney: Mandelbaum Trust, University of Sydney, 1985); The Samaritan Chronicle Tolidah, The Samaritan Book of Joshua, and Chronicle Adler. Extracts from the last three can be found in John Bowman, Samaritan Documents Relating to the History, Religion and Life, Pittsburgh Original Texts and Translation Series 2 (Pittsburgh: Pickwick Press, 1977).

[19] This is in contrast to the term šŏměrōnîm, "which name they believe to have pejorative implications" (Menachem Mor, "Šamerim," in A Companion to Samaritan Studies, 210–11).

young high priest who was a descendant of Phineas.[20] Eli's actions initiated the transition from *Rhwth*, the age of Divine Favor, to the *Fanūta*, the age of Divine Wrath. The Samaritans believe that the *Fanūta* will continue until the coming of the Taheb, an eschatological prophet who will restore the *Rhwth*. The concept of a taheb is grounded in the prophecy that God would raise up a "Prophet . . . like unto [Moses]" (Deuteronomy 18:18). Secondary developments variously describe him as being part of the eschatological scene, coming from the east, possessing the staff of Aaron and the Manna, bringing the holy tabernacle, and revealing truth.[21] This Taheb is what the Samaritan woman is probably referring to when she says, "I know that Messias cometh, . . . [and] when he is come, he will tell us all things" (John 4:25).

As noted earlier, the two elements of Samaritan theology that characterize it as a distinct religious entity are its use of the Samaritan Pentateuch as its sacred text and its insistence that Mount Gerizim is the proper place of worship. Both of these elements are important factors in helping us determine the origins of the Samaritan sect.

The Samaritans, like the Sadduccees, rejected the prophetic and historical books of the Hebrew Bible, although they do have a version of the book of Joshua. Their Pentateuch consists of the five books of Moses but includes certain textual changes that emphasize the importance of Mount Gerizim, rather than Jerusalem, as the central place of worship (see Josephus, *AJ*, 13.3.4).[22] These changes can be dated fairly accurately to the Hasmonean period,[23] which means that

---

[20] Abu'l-Fath, *Kitab Al-Tarikh*, 47–48; Richard White, "Eli," in *A Companion to Samaritan Studies*, 85.

[21] Ferdinand Dexinger, "Rhwth," in *A Companion to Samaritan Studies*, 202–4.

[22] The Samaritan Pentateuch is based on an early proto-Samaritan text "similar to several texts that have been found at Qumran" (Emanuel Tov, "Proto-Samaritan Texts and the Samaritan Pentateuch," in *The Samaritans*, 397–407). "The proto-Samaritan can be understood as a Palestinian text type descended from an Old Palestinian textual tradition" (Purvis, *The Samaritan Pentateuch*, 80).

[23] Purvis comes to this conclusion based on the Samaritan Pentateuch's script (the way the letters are formed), orthography (the way words are spelled), and textual tradition (how the text has evolved over time) (*The Samaritan Pentateuch*, 87; for a full

during this period, we see an effort by some Samarians to distinguish themselves and their worship from the Jews and their canon of scripture. During this time, we see the first concrete evidence that they began to use their scriptures as an ideological weapon against their Jewish opponents.[24]

The second element that distinguishes Samaritanism from Judaism revolves around their worship on Mount Gerizim. Even in the Hebrew Bible, Mount Gerizim was a sacred site. Here the tribes of Simeon, Levi, Judah, Issachar, Joseph, and Benjamin congregated and declared the Lord's blessings after they entered the promised land (Deuteronomy 11:29; 27:11–12; Joshua 8:33). In the Samaritan Pentateuch, Mount Gerizim, rather than Mount Ebal, is the place where Israel was to build an altar to the Lord (contrast the Jewish version of Deuteronomy 27:4–8). In fact, it also places this reworking of Deuteronomy 27 as the final commandment in their list of Moses' Ten Commandments.[25] Samaritans attach to Mount Gerizim the same type of sacredness that the Jews identify with Jerusalem: they believe that Mount Gerizim was the site of the Garden of Eden, the place where Abraham brought Isaac to offer as a sacrifice, and the place where Noah landed after the flood.[26]

For a number of years, archaeological excavations failed to find

---

discussion, see pp. 16–87).

[24] Judith E. Sanderson, *An Exodus Scroll from Qumran: 4QpaleoExod^m and the Samaritan Tradition* (Atlanta: Scholars Press, 1986), 317–20.

[25] The tenth commandment in the Samaritan Pentateuch reads as follows: "And when the Lord your God brings you into the land of the Canaanites which you are entering to take possession of it, you shall set up these stones and plaster them with plaster, and you shall write upon them all the words of the Law. And when you have passed over the Jordan, you shall set up these stones, concerning which I command you this day, on Mount Gerizim. And there you shall build an altar to the Lord your God, an altar of stones; you shall lift up no iron tool upon them. You shall build an altar to the Lord your God of unhewn stones; you shall offer burnt offerings, and shall eat there; and you shall rejoice before the Lord your God. That mountain is beyond the Jordan, west of the road, toward the going down of the sun, in the land of the Canaanites who live in the Arabah, over against Gilgal, beside the oak of Moreh in front of Shechem" (Bowman, *Samaritan Documents*, 23–24).

[26] Robert T. Anderson, "Gerizim, Mt," in *A Companion to Samaritan Studies*, 100.

the Samaritan temple on Mount Gerizim.[27] Recent excavations, however, may have changed that. Yitzhak Magen has identified the temple precinct and the temple itself dating to the Hellenistic period. Among the archaeological finds are areas of "sheep bones, some of them charred, [which] may have been the remains of the paschal or other sacrifices offered by the Samaritans on Mount Gerizim,"[28] a fragmentary inscription mentioning both a priest (*cohen*) and priests (*cohenim*),[29] and another inscription where "the Samaritans call their temple the 'House of YHWH' [Yahweh or Jehovah]."[30] The most significant, however, are the remnants of the foundation wall of the Hellenistic period temple. This temple seems to be an extension of the earlier Persian period holy place.[31]

According to Josephus, the Samaritan priesthood descended from Manasseh, a brother of the Jewish high priest, who married the daughter of Sanballat, the governor of Samaria (cf. Nehemiah 13:28–31).[32] The building of a temple on Mount Gerizim undoubtedly

---

[27] Their excavations were limited by the presence of a Byzantine period Christian church on the site.

[28] Yitzhak Magen, "Gerizim, Mount," in *The New Encyclopedia of Archaeological Excavations in the Holy Land*, ed. Ephraim Stern, 4 vols. (New York: Simon & Schuster, 1993), 2:487.

[29] Yitzhak Magen, "Mount Gerizim and the Samaritans," in *Early Christianity in Context: Monuments and Documents*, ed. F. Manns and E. Alliata, Studium Biblicum Franciscanum 38 (Jerusalem: Franciscan Printing Press, 1993), 98, 106. See also "Replica of the Temple Found in Samaria," *Biblical Archaeological Review* 21, no. 5 (September/October 1995): 24, 85, and Yitzhak Magen, "Mount Gerizim—A Temple City," 74–118.

[30] Ephraim Stern and Yitzhak Magen, "Archaeological Evidence for the First Stage of the Samaritan Temple on Mount Gerizim," *Israel Exploration Journal* 52 (2002): 56.

[31] Magen, "Mount Gerizim—A Temple City," 96–98.

[32] According to Josephus, the elders of Jerusalem demanded that Manasseh divorce his wife or lose his right to officiate in the temple. His father-in-law, Sanballat, countered the Jewish threats by promising to build a temple "like that at Jerusalem" wherein Manasseh could officiate. Josephus reports that there were "many priests and Levites" who were in a similar situation to that of Manasseh and followed him (*AJ*, 11.8.2–4). However, Nehemiah records a very similar experience occurring during the Persian period (Nehemiah 13:23–28). Josephus may have conflated two governors named Sanballat (Crown, "Another Look at Samaritan Origins," 146–48). Archaeological evidence confirms that more than one governor of Samaria was named Sanballat (Frank M. Cross Jr., "The Discovery of the Samaria Papyri," *The Biblical Archaeologist* 26 [1963]:

created a significant wedge in the relationship between Samarians and Jews, but it does not appear to have caused an immediate, irreparable schism.[33] We know that other Jewish temples existed in Egypt, in Leontopolis, and in Elephantine that were apparently tolerated by the Jerusalem authorities.[34] Nevertheless, for the Jewish authorities, "a temple in the north of Palestine was more of a direct threat."[35]

The first concrete evidence for a Samaritan religious self-awareness that was independent of Judaism arose during the Hasmonean period. This was a time of tremendous political and religious turmoil for both Samaria and Judea. Under the political control of the Seleucid, Antiochus Epiphanes IV, both regions experienced intense religious oppression (2 Maccabees 6:2). Significantly, however, when the Hasmoneans rose up in rebellion against the Seleucids, the Samaritans did not join with them in the fight for religious freedom. Even though they would have clearly benefited by removing the Seleucids from power over them, they apparently did not believe they would experience any more religious freedom under the Hasmoneans than they experienced under the Seleucids.[36] Therefore, they saw themselves as a religion that was distinct from Judaism. This assessment was later confirmed when John Hyrcanus (134–104 B.C.), one of the Hasmonean leaders, treated the Samaritans as Gentiles. In a military campaign in which he attacked "the unprotected cities of Syria,"[37] he also attacked Samaria, Shechem, and the temple on

---

110–21). This initial temple may not have been much more than an altar that was developed into a full temple during the Hellenistic period.

[33] Ferdinand Dexinger, "Limits of Tolerance in Judaism: The Samaritan Example," in *Jewish and Christian Self-Definition*, vol. 2 of *Aspects of Judaism in the Graeco-Roman Period*, ed. E. P. Sanders et al. (Philadelphia: Fortress Press, 1980), 100–2.

[34] Coggins, *Samaritans and Jews*, 112. In circa 400 B.C., Jews at Elephantine considered the Samarians to be Jewish. They wrote to leaders in both Jerusalem and Samaria asking for help to rebuild their temple (Crown, "Another Look at Samaritan Origins," 149; Anderson and Giles, *The Keepers*, 24).

[35] Purvis, *The Samaritan Pentateuch*, 11–12.

[36] Anderson and Giles, *The Keepers*, 29. See also Mor, "The Persian, Hellenistic and Hasmonean Period," 16–17.

[37] Anderson and Giles, *The Keepers*, 29. Significantly, John Hyrcanus treated the

Mount Gerizim (Josephus, *AJ*, 13.9.1).[38] The temple on Mount Gerizim was never rebuilt.

One scholar has suggested that Hyrcanus's actions against Mount Gerizim, in particular, may have been motivated by the fact that the Samaritans could trace the lineage of their high priest, through Manasseh, to the legitimate Zadokite line. This lineage was in contrast to the Hasmoneans, who belonged to the priestly Jehoiarib family but who usurped the high priestly duties by political appointment from the Seleucid ruler Alexander Balas in 152 B.C. (1 Maccabees 10:18–20; Josephus, *AJ*, 13.2.2).[39] Therefore, the issue became more than simply a question of where the temple should be located; it also became an issue of who had a legitimate claim to the high priestly office. Not coincidentally, during the Hasmonean period, the Samaritans, as we have seen, began to create their own set of scriptures, separate from those used by the Jews.

By the time Jesus conversed with the Samaritans at Jacob's Well, these events were firmly entrenched in the religious psyche of both the Samaritans and the Jews. By understanding these events, we are now in a better position to appreciate how the Master Teacher was able to invite Samaritans to raise their sights above their political and religious antipathies for the Jews and recognize in Jesus "the Christ, the Saviour of the world" (John 4:42).

Jesus and the Samaritans at Jacob's Well

Immediately prior to John's account of Jesus' journey into Samaria, John recorded a conversation between John the Baptist and his disciples that has a bearing upon our subject. John's disciples were concerned that Jesus was having greater success than John. As John reassured his disciples that such a situation was necessary, he made a

---

Idumeans with greater respect than the Samaritans. He afforded them a special status if they would circumcise themselves (Josephus, *AJ*, 13.9.1), but the Samaritans, who were already circumcised, did not receive the same considerations.

[38] Magen, "Gerizim, Mount," 487.
[39] Mor, "The Persian, Hellenistic and Hasmonean Period," 17–18.

statement that becomes a theme in John's Gospel: "He that cometh from above is above all: he that is of the earth is earthly, and speaketh of the earth: he that cometh from heaven is above all" (John 3:31). Jesus himself made a similar comment while conversing with the Pharisees: "Ye are from beneath; I am from above: ye are of this world; I am not of this world" (John 8:23).

The experience at Jacob's Well contains two examples in John's Gospel where Jesus, who comes from above, engages people whose outlook is limited by an earthly perspective.[40] One is His experience with the Samaritan woman, and the other is His conversation with His own disciples. On both occasions, Jesus used the opportunity to teach those with whom He spoke; but in his conversation with the Samaritan woman, we see Him guiding her to raise her sights and recognize and embrace His eternal identity rather than questioning and dismissing Him because of the limitations of her religious and political assumptions.

"How is it that thou, being a Jew, askest drink of me?"

As soon as Jesus asked the Samaritan woman for a drink, she recognized Him as a Jew. Her response acknowledged the deep-seated antipathy between the two groups. "How is it that thou, being a Jew, askest drink of me, which am a woman of Samaria? For the Jews do not have friendly relations [*sunchrōntai*] with the Samaritans" (John 4:9; author's translation).[41] Initially, all the woman saw was an enemy. In contrast to her limited vision, Jesus crossed the boundaries between Jews and Samaritans. He saw in the woman something much more than a Samaritan. So He helped her elevate her sights. To do so, He used the very earthly, daily task of drawing water.

Water is a precious commodity in the Holy Land. When Jehovah delivered the Israelites from Egypt, He warned them that "the land,

---

[40] Others include Nicodemus (John 3), the multitude seeking another miraculous feeding (John 6), the Pharisees (John 8), the disciples (John 11), and Peter (John 13).

[41] Arndt and Gingrich, *GEL*, 775. *Sunchrōntai* cannot simply mean "to have dealings with" because at this point in time, Jesus' disciples were dealing with Samaritans in the city as they bought food from them (John 4:8).

whither thou goest in to possess it, is not as the land of Egypt, . . . but the land, whither ye go to possess it, is a land of hills and valleys, and drinketh water of the rain of heaven. . . . And . . . if ye shall hearken diligently unto my commandments . . . , I will give you the rain of your land in . . . due season, the first rain and the latter rain" (Deuteronomy 11:10–14). Water, therefore, was a gift from God, conditional upon obedience to His commandments. In both Judea and Samaria, the people relied on wells and cisterns to collect water during the rainy seasons to ensure their survival during the hot, dry summers. Jacob's Well is "located at the entrance to the ravine which separates Mount Ebal from Mount Gerizim."[42] It "is a large deep shaft, about 7 1/2 feet in diameter and 100 feet deep," situated in an area that "would have been a natural stopping place on a journey from Judea to Galilee through Samaria."[43]

When the Samaritan woman came to the well, her mind was focused on the grind of her daily chore. The chore was one she clearly wished she could forgo (John 4:15). But the Master Teacher used that chore to teach the woman about the things of eternity. While she was fixated on the physical water and the difficulty of obtaining it without a bucket (*antlēma*), He reminded her of the living water that would be "a spring (*pēgē*) of water bubbling up (*hallomai*) into eternal life" (John 4:14; author's translation).[44] Later, Jesus specifically declared, "If any man thirst, let him come unto me, and drink" (John 7:37). This was the "gift of God" that Jesus was offering not just to the Jews but also to a Samaritan woman (John 4:10). It was a greater gift than the well Jacob dug that had supplied water for millennia, because the water Jesus offered would last for eternity.[45] It was a gift

---

[42] Zdravko Stefanovic, "Jacob's Well," in Freedman, *ABD*, 3:608.

[43] According to John, the well is both a spring (*pēgē*; John 4:6) and a reservoir for rainwater (*phrear* = cistern; John 4:11–12). This remarkably accurate description of the well is still valid today (Rousseau and Arav, *Jesus and His World*, 131).

[44] Elder McConkie teaches, "Where there are prophets of God, there will be found rivers of living water, wells filled with eternal truths, springs bubbling forth their life-giving draughts that save from spiritual death" (*DNTC*, 1:151–52).

[45] No specific mention of Jacob's well is made in the Old Testament. All we are told is that Jacob bought a parcel of land near Shechem and erected an altar there (Genesis

that came freely (*dōrean*; cf. Matthew 10:8) from God without the laborious effort required for drawing water from a well that was a hundred feet deep! But to receive the gift, the Samaritan woman had to come to recognize who Jesus was—to recognize that He was much more than a Jew and that He was not an enemy of her people.

"I perceive that thou art a prophet"

Only after Jesus had gained the woman's attention with the hope of living water did He move to help her raise her sights. To do so, He had to accomplish two things. First, He had to bring her to a point where she felt a sense of sin and therefore a need for help. Second, He had to establish His authority as God's representative on earth.[46] He accomplished both in a masterful teaching moment. By instructing her to call her husband, He simultaneously raised a mirror of spiritual introspection and opened the door for her to see Jesus from a higher spiritual perspective. He revealed to her that even though they had just met, He knew who she was: more than the fact that she was a Samaritan, she was a woman who had had five husbands but was now living with a man who was not her husband (John 4:16–18).

This revelation clearly affected the woman. Later, she told the men in her village that Jesus "told me all things that ever I did" (John 4:29). In light of the details recorded in John, this statement appears to be a hyperbole, but it illustrates how profound the revelation of her life was to the woman. She now saw this man at the well in a different light. She knew that Jesus was much more than a Jew: "Lord [*kurios*], I perceive that you are a prophet" (John 4:19; author's translation). This was a significant realization for her. The Samaritans did not accept the prophetic books of the Old Testament; but, as we have noted earlier, they did anticipate the coming of a prophet like unto Moses, an expectation that was based on Deuteronomy 18:15–18.

33:18–20). However, the woman clearly knew of a tradition that dated back to the time of Jacob.

[46] Wayne Jackson, "Jesus and the Samaritan Woman," n.p. Online: christiancourier.com/feature/november2000.htm (accessed August 30, 2004).

This prophecy indicates that the Lord would put His words "in [the prophet's] mouth; and he shall speak . . . all that I shall command him. And it shall come to pass, that whosoever will not hearken unto my words which he shall speak in my name, I will require it of him" (Deuteronomy 18:18–19). Then, the Deuteronomist declares that if the prophet is not sent from God, his prophecies will not come true, and therefore the people should not be afraid of him (Deuteronomy 18:20–22). Because Jesus' revelations were true, the woman was obligated to acknowledge Jesus as a prophet and recognize that what He said came from God.

With this realization, however, the woman was clearly faced with an internal quandary. On the one hand, she recognized Jesus as a prophet; on the other, she was torn by the reality that "our fathers worshipped in this mountain; and ye say, that in Jerusalem is the place where men ought to worship" (John 4:20). Two items are important about this statement. First is her comment that "our fathers worshipped in this mountain." "This mountain" is a clear reference to Mount Gerizim that provided the topographical background for their conversation.[47] As we have noted, the centrality of Mount Gerizim was canonized in the Samaritan Pentateuch. Worship on "this mountain" was and continues to be *the* theological difference that separates the Samaritans and the Jews. Second, the past tense of the verb (*aorist*), showing that her ancestors worshiped on Mount Gerizim, reflects the historical reality that their temple had been destroyed by John Hyrcanus more than a hundred years before. Although the Samaritans never rebuilt their temple, through the intervening centuries they have always recognized the sanctity of Mount Gerizim and have continued to offer sacrifices on it.

"I know that Messias cometh"

Jesus' response to the question of where to worship was again calculated to move the Samaritan woman's perspective to an even

---

[47] Robert J. Bull, "An Archaeological Footnote to 'Our Fathers Worshipped on this Mountain', John 4:20," *New Testament Studies* 23 (1977): 460–62.

higher level: "Woman, believe me, the hour cometh, when ye shall neither in this mountain, nor yet at Jerusalem, worship the Father" (John 4:21). The physical temple on Mount Gerizim had been destroyed. The physical temple in Jerusalem would also be destroyed in the near future. The purpose of temples has always been to provide a way for individuals to ritually leave behind the things of the world and enter the presence of God. The Samaritan woman was so consumed by the Jewish-Samaritan debate over the correct location for the temple that she had not realized that Jesus was the ultimate way to enter the presence of the Father. He was the Word who enabled humans to come to know the Father while they were still in mortality (John 1:1, 14; 14:6–14). As Elder Jeffrey R. Holland has taught, "It is the grand truth that in all that Jesus came to say and do, including and especially in His atoning suffering and sacrifice, He was showing us who and what God our Eternal Father is like, how completely devoted He is to His children in every age and nation. In word and deed Jesus was trying to reveal and make personal to us the true nature of His Father, our Father in Heaven."[48]

At this point, the Samaritan woman did not know what she worshiped (John 4:22). As a Samaritan, she had rejected the continuous revelation of God through the Old Testament prophets; she apparently did not appreciate the true purpose of the temple; and she did not understand the implications of her declaration that Jesus was a prophet. Salvation was "of the Jews" (John 4:22) because the prophet standing before her was the source of salvation and because He, as she had quickly recognized at the beginning of their interaction, was a Jew.

So Jesus taught her the elements of "true worship." True worship is not always a function of location, nor is it a function of having a physical building in which to worship (cf. Alma 32:4–12). Rather, Jesus taught that what is most important is that true worshipers "worship [the Father] in spirit and in truth"; in fact, that process is an absolute requirement (John 4:24). Thus, Elder Bruce R. McConkie

---

[48] Jeffrey R. Holland, "The Grandeur of God," *Ensign* (November 2003): 70.

taught that "our purpose is to worship the true and living God and to do it by the power of the Spirit and in the way he has ordained. The approved worship of the true God leads to salvation; devotions rendered to false gods and which are not founded on eternal truth carry no such assurance."[49] According to the Joseph Smith Translation, Jesus then taught that God would send His Spirit to those who "worship . . . in truth (JST John 4:26).

Again, the woman was confused. The only thing the Samaritans anticipated from their worship was the coming of a Taheb: "I know that Messias cometh, which is called Christ: when he is come, he will tell us all things" (John 4:25). Although she uses the term *messiah*, we need to remember that the Samaritan hope was very different from its Jewish counterpart. The Samaritans certainly did not anticipate that the Messiah would be a Davidic king! Instead, their Taheb was a restorer who would reinstitute the age of divine favor. Having created the teaching moment, Jesus was then ready to reveal fully His identity to the Samaritan woman. *He* was the fulfillment of this Samaritan hope; *He* was the prophet "like unto [Moses]" (cf. 3 Nephi 20:23). But, in making that identification, he went further. He applied the divine title to Himself. Literally, He says, "I Am (*egō eimi*), the one who speaks to you" (John 4:26; author's translation; cf. John 8:58; Exodus 3:11–14).[50]

Jesus was indeed the prophet like unto Moses, but He was also God who directed Moses. In both of these roles, He had indeed come to tell her "all things" (John 4:25). No doubt the Samaritan woman understood exactly what Jesus was saying. John tells us that she "then left her waterpot" (John 4:28). She had come to the well with her waterpot in search of water, and she left with water, but not the kind she could carry in a pot. She had found the living water that Jesus had promised her.

Like Lehi in his vision of the tree of life, as soon as she realized what she had received, she yearned to share it with others. She

---

[49] Bruce R. McConkie, "How to Worship," *Ensign* (December 1971): 129.
[50] Brown, *The Gospel According to John I–XII*, 172–73, 533–38.

returned to Sychar and invited the villagers to "come, see a man, which told me all things that ever I did: is not this the Christ?" (John 4:29). The inclusion of the Greek particle *mēti* at the beginning of the question indicates that she did not expect a positive answer. This usage is probably why she invited them to come and see for themselves rather than rely on her witness.

"This is indeed the Christ, the Saviour of the world"

Just as the Samaritan woman was leaving the well, Jesus' disciples returned with the food they had bought. With the Samaritan woman before them, Jesus used the opportunity to give His earthbound disciples a glimpse into His mission and into what God had prepared for the Samaritans. "My meat is to do the will of him that sent me, and to finish his work" (John 4:34). That work included sowing seeds among the Samaritans, which the disciples would reap after Jesus had left them. The disciples' reaction when they saw the Savior conversing with the Samaritan woman suggests that they were not immune from some of the antipathy for the Samaritans that was common among the Jews (John 4:27). Jesus encouraged them, "Lift up your eyes, and look on the fields." Perhaps He was inviting them to elevate the perception of the land of Samaria. Instead of seeing it as a place to be avoided, they should recognize it as fields that were "white already to harvest" (John 4:35; cf. Doctrine and Covenants 4).

With the Samaritan woman, Jesus had sown a seed that was about to bear fruit, but the disciples would also participate in a later harvest. Using the prophetic past tense, Jesus said, "I sent you to reap that whereon ye bestowed no labour: other men laboured, and ye are entered into their labours" (John 4:38). After Jesus' resurrection, He modified the apostolic commission He gave in Matthew 10:5 that they were not to go "into any city of the Samaritans." On the Mount of Olives, He would specifically command them that after they had received the Holy Ghost, they were to "be witnesses unto me both in Jerusalem, and in all Judea, and *in Samaria*, and unto the uttermost part of the earth" (Acts 1:8; emphasis added). Acts records a partial fulfillment of this prophecy in the work of Philip, Peter, and John in Samaria (Acts 8).[51] Jesus' journey into Samaria was not just to teach the Samaritan woman but also to teach His disciples and help both sides overcome their prejudices.[52]

As Jesus finished teaching His disciples, we learn that "many of the Samaritans of that city believed on him for the saying of the woman, which testified, He told me all that ever I did" (John 4:39). The Samaritans were so taken with His teachings that they implored Him to stay with them. He agreed, and the result was that "many more believed because of his own word" (John 4:41). They received a personal testimony that was independent of the Samaritan woman's and testified that they knew "this is indeed the Christ, the Saviour of the world" (John 4:42). They had learned that Jesus was not just a Jew, not just a prophet, and not just a messiah. He was the Savior of the Jews, of the Samaritans, and of the world.

Conclusion

A fourth-century Christian, Ephraem the Syrian, wonderfully summarized Jesus' interactions with the Samaritan woman: "Our Lord came to the fountain of water as a hunter. . . . He cast a bait for the dove so that through it he might capture the entire flock. . . . She first saw him as someone thirsting; and then as a Jew; then as a prophet, and after that as God. As someone thirsting, she persuaded him; as a Jew, she recoiled from him, as a learned one, she interrogated him, as a prophet she was reprimanded, and as the Messiah she worshipped him."[53] Although Jesus had some success among the

---

[51] With the exception of Acts 8, we have little specific knowledge of post-resurrection missionary work among the Samaritans. Two of the most famous Christians from Samaria were Simon Magus and Justin Martyr.

[52] Jesus' teachings and experiences were very pro-Samaritan. Besides John 4, see also the parable of the good Samaritan (Luke 10:25–37) and the cleansing of the ten lepers (Luke 17:11–19). In addition, note significantly that when the Pharisees attempted to slur Jesus, they called Him "a Samaritan, and hast a devil." In response, Jesus refuted the accusation of having a devil but ignored being labeled a Samaritan (John 8:48–52).

[53] Ephrem, *Commentary on Tatian's Diatessaron* 12.16, 18. English translation from Carmel McCarthy, *Saint Ephrem's Commentary on Tatian's Diatessaron: An English*

Samaritans this time, later He would receive a different reaction. On that occasion, the Samaritans did not have one of their own to introduce the Messiah to them. Perhaps that is one reason they could not accept that Jesus was committed to Jerusalem rather than Mount Gerizim (Luke 9:51–53).[54] Both of these incidents remind modern readers that nationality is not what determines or precludes salvation; rather, salvation comes from how individuals respond to the Savior's attempts to raise their sights from an earthly to a heavenly perspective and how they respond to His universal invitation, "Come, follow me."

Translation of Chester Beatty Syriac MS 709 with Introduction and Notes (Journal of Semitic Studies Supplement 2; Oxford: Oxford University Press, 1993), 198–99.

[54] George R. Beasley-Murray, *John* (Word Biblical Commentary 36; Waco, Texas: Word Books, 1987), 64.

X.

EARLY GALILEAN MINISTRY AND MIRACLES

CECILIA M. PEEK

Jesus came into Galilee, preaching the gospel of the kingdom of God, and saying, The time is fulfilled, and the kingdom of God is at hand: repent ye and believe the gospel.

MARK 1:14–15

This beginning of miracles did Jesus.

JOHN 2:11

Shortly after His baptism and forty-day stay in the wilderness, Jesus began His public ministry. Each of the synoptic Gospels closely associates the start of that ministry with Jesus' return from those forty days spent in the wilderness, where He successfully withstood the temptations of Satan and experienced the ministrations of angels (Matthew 4:1–11; Mark 1:12–13; Luke 4:1–14).[1] Fresh from His encounter with devilish and heavenly forces, Jesus is said to have entered His ministry "in the power of the Spirit" (Luke 4:14).

---

[1] Mark's account is by far the most abbreviated of the descriptions, comprising only two short verses. The Gospel of John omits any reference to this scene. For a full discussion of the event, see Richard Neitzel Holzapfel, "Jesus in the Wilderness: Baptism, Fasting, and Temptations," in this volume.

That Jesus' period of fasting lasted forty days conjures thoughts of the forty days Moses spent with the Lord as that prophet received and recorded the terms of God's law for Israel (Exodus 34:27–28; 24:18).[2] Moses' experience occurred at a critical juncture in his prophetic career—just before he introduced God's covenant to the children of Israel. Moses, empowered by God and purified by the divine encounter, mediated that covenant. A time of private fasting and prayer seems to be the necessary precursor to the public pronouncements made by Jesus as well.

The similarities between Jesus and Moses are surely not accidental. By establishing this connection between the two figures, the Gospels implicitly portray Jesus as at least the equal of Moses in His religious practice and preparation and proclaim Him as the one to mediate a new covenant for Israel.[3]

Jesus' forty-day wilderness experience further recalls the forty years the Israelites spent in the wilderness after they had left the bondage of Egypt and were being prepared to inherit the land of promise (Exodus 16:35; Numbers 14:33–35). At the end of those forty years, the people were finally given leave to enter the land intended for them and to create ancient Israel as a nation—in other words, to establish the earthly kingdom of God. When Jesus returned from His forty-day stay in the wilderness, He immediately began to announce the approach of the kingdom of God. Mark, for example, tells us that "Jesus came into Galilee, preaching the gospel of the kingdom of God, and saying, The time is fulfilled, and the kingdom of God is at hand" (Mark 1:14–15). Matthew calls it the "kingdom of heaven" (Matthew 4:17). Here the emphasis is not on any earthly

---

[2] The connections between Jesus and Moses are numerous and interesting, but they are beyond the scope of the present discussion. The interested reader may look to Dale C. Allison, *The New Moses* (Minneapolis: Fortress Press, 1993) and Frank F. Judd Jr., "Jesus as the New Moses in the Gospel of Matthew" (M.A. thesis, Brigham Young University, 1995).

[3] Hebrews 9:15 calls Jesus "the mediator of the new testament." The term rendered "testament" in the KJV—*diathēkē*—can be translated *covenant*. See Arndt and Gingrich, *GEL*, 228. Compare Genesis 6:18 (LXX).

realm but on a heavenly one, and in the synoptic accounts, Jesus' preparation in the wilderness anticipates the establishment of God's heavenly kingdom, with Jesus as the spiritual *locus* of this new kingdom.

The Gospels thus create a compelling context for the start of Jesus' public career, one that recalls the accomplishments of Israel's greatest age and of its greatest ancient prophet and prepares the reader for similarly epic achievements in Jesus' ministry. Where the individual Gospel narratives locate the start of that ministry and what words and deeds mark its beginning are matters of great significance, as they were chosen to introduce and frame the whole of Christ's ministry and mission.

The Location of the Early Ministry

That Jesus began His ministry in Galilee seems clear—it is where His first sermons were given and His first miracles performed in each of the Gospels. None of the accounts, with the exception of Matthew, offers any explicit rationale for Jesus' choice of location. Mark associates Jesus' move into Galilee with the fate of John the Baptist. Matthew makes a similar connection but also describes His presence in Galilee as a fulfillment of prophecy. Luke, for his part, seems to relate the start of Jesus' ministry in Galilee to the fact that His boyhood home of Nazareth was there. John, meanwhile, displays less concern for the geography of Christ's ministry than for the symbolic implications of its earliest deeds.

Mark's record describes Jesus' arrival in Galilee with these words: "After that John was put in prison, Jesus came into Galilee" (Mark 1:14). The phrase "after John was put in prison" (*meta de to paradothēnai ton Iōannēn*) would be better translated "after John was handed over" and provides, at the very least, a chronological indication: Jesus went to Galilee *after* John was arrested.[4] The statement allows for the possibility of a cause-and-effect relationship between John's arrest

---

[4] Or "delivered up." See Arndt and Gingrich, *GEL*, "paradidōmi," 761–63.

and Jesus' move into Galilee, although the statement by no means guarantees such a relationship. In other words, Mark may have viewed John's imprisonment as the reason for Jesus' move into Galilee, but he does not explicitly state that. The verb used to describe Jesus' departure is *ēlthen*, which merely indicates that Jesus "came into Galilee," without asserting anything about what motivated the Savior's move.

Matthew's words help clarify and elaborate on Mark: "When Jesus had heard (*akousas*) that John was cast into prison (*paredothē*), he departed (*anechōrēsen*) into Galilee" (Matthew 4:12).[5] Here the implications seem to be more than chronological and the verb describing Jesus' move less neutral than that found in Mark's Gospel. Jesus left for Galilee after He had *heard* of John's arrest.[6] Unlike Mark's description, in which there is no assertion that Jesus actually knew of John's fate, Matthew's participle (*akousas*) implies that Jesus left His current location for Galilee after and/or because He got word of John's imprisonment.

Matthew's term "departed" (*anechōrēsen*) takes the place of Mark's simple "came" and can mean "withdrew" or "took refuge."[7] The word is used earlier (Matthew 2:22) to describe Joseph's decision to go into Galilee rather than into Judaea after his return with Mary and Jesus from Egypt: "When he heard that Archelaus did reign in Judea in the room of his father Herod, he was afraid to go thither: notwithstanding, being warned of God in a dream, he turned aside [*anechōrēsen*] into the parts of Galilee."

Later (Matthew 12:14–15), Jesus "withdrew" (*anechōrēsen*) when He realized that the Pharisees were plotting "how they might destroy

---

[5] W. D. Davies and Dale C. Allison, *A Critical and Exegetical Commentary on the Gospel According to St. Matthew*, International Critical Commentary, 3 vols. (Edinburgh: T & T Clark, 1988), 1:375, where they call Matthew's version "redactional." The verb in Matthew 4:12 translated "was cast into prison" means "was handed over" or "delivered up."

[6] It may be that John's disciples informed Jesus of John's fate. See Paul Gächter, *Das Matthäus-Evangelium: Ein Kommentar* (Innsbruck: Tyrolia, 1963), 120.

[7] Arndt and Gingrich, *GEL*, "anachōreō," 75. Compare Davies and Allison, *The Gospel According to Matthew*, 1:376.

him." Finally, after recounting the violent death of John the Baptist, Matthew says, "When Jesus heard [*akousas*] of it, he withdrew [*anechōrēsen*] thence by ship into a desert place apart" (Matthew 14:13). In this latter instance, Jesus once more heard fearful tidings of John before His departure.

These examples suggest that Matthew may sometimes use the verb *anechōrēsen* when "fear for one's life provides the motivation for [the] scripturally attested move."[8] Are we then to understand from Matthew that Jesus' life was already in danger in the south and that He began His ministry in Galilee primarily to protect Himself? That the circumstance of John's arrest was a frightening matter may well be implied by the verb used to describe Jesus' departure, but the Gospel writer does not necessarily mean to imply that Jesus was driven into Galilee by fear. A more thorough consideration of Matthew's text is instructive.

To return to Matthew's account of Joseph the carpenter's departure into Galilee: Although Joseph was admittedly afraid to go to Judea, fear seems not to have been his only, or indeed his chief, concern. Immediately before announcing the move "into the parts of Galilee," Matthew tells the reader that Joseph was "warned of God in a dream" (Matthew 2:22). The author's decision to locate the dream just before the move to Galilee rhetorically suggests that it was the most immediate impetus for the move and that Joseph's primary concern here, as elsewhere, was obedience to God's will for himself and his family.[9] Further, Matthew asserts that Joseph had to settle in Galilee, specifically Nazareth, to fulfill a prophetic foretelling that Jesus would "be called a Nazarene" (Matthew 2:23). More important to Matthew than Joseph's fear about Judea was the will of God

---

[8] Davies and Allison, *The Gospel According to Matthew*, 1:376, where they say it is "historically plausible that Jesus . . . became cautious or even went into hiding after John was arrested."

[9] Joseph is regularly advised of God's will through revelatory dreams, and he regularly heeds the warnings in those dreams. See Matthew 1:20–25; 2:13–15, 19–21. Compare the dream given to the men from the east who had presented gifts to the young Jesus in Matthew 2:12.

expressed in a dream and in an earlier prophetic prediction that took Joseph to Galilee.

As for Jesus' departure into "a desert place apart" after the death of John the Baptist, some scholars assume that Jesus withdrew to escape from Herod.[10] This is not explicit in the text, however, and elsewhere in His ministry, Jesus is said to have sought the retreat of solitude at a turning point in His life. After His baptism, for example, Jesus went into the wilderness, proving Himself before the assault of Satan and the ministering of angels, prior to beginning His public ministry (Matthew 4:1–11; Mark 1:12–13; Luke 4:1–13). John the Baptist's death, marking the definitive end of that prophet's mission as a forerunner to Christ, may represent a similar transitional moment for Jesus, and His removal to "a desert place apart" may have been an occasion for the thoughtful recollection of John's career and preparation for the next phase of His own.[11] That is not to say that Jesus' move into Galilee after His temptation in the wilderness was in pursuit of a place for quiet contemplation—the start of His ministry was hardly quiet. We may, however, judge that Matthew may use the verb "withdraw"—elsewhere without explicitly suggesting that the removal was born of fear.

Notably, Jesus' move to Galilee did not constitute "a change in jurisdiction, for Herod Antipas, who laid hands on John, also had charge of Galilee."[12] If Jesus feared what Herod might do to Him, the new location (still within Herod's jurisdiction) held no promise of safety.

In answer to this reasoning, we might note, with Plummer, that the term used to describe John's arrest—*paredothē*—means "was delivered up," placing the focus on those who surrendered John to the authorities rather than on the officials who received him into

---

[10] See, for example, Raymond. E. Brown, *Introduction to the New Testament* (New York: Doubleday, 1997), 187.

[11] Interestingly, Jesus seeks a desert place, which induces us to recall the fact that John was a "voice of one crying in the wilderness" (Matthew 3:3; Mark 1:3; Luke 3:4; John 1:23).

[12] As Davies and Allison, *The Gospel According to Matthew*, 1:376, rightly note.

custody.[13] In this reading, it was not so much fear of Herod as fear of those who had handed John the Baptist over to Herod that motivated Jesus' relocation to Galilee.

We can, however, judge from Matthew's account of later episodes in Jesus' life that He made no effort to escape pain, arrest, punishment, and even death at the end of His mortal ministry (Matthew 26:36–27:50). Most tellingly, Matthew describes Jesus' willingness to submit to the fearful ordeal in the Garden of Gethsemane with the words, "O my Father, if it be possible, let this cup pass from me: nevertheless not as I will, but as thou wilt" (Matthew 26:39). When the soldiers arrived at the garden to arrest Jesus and the disciple drew his sword in defense, Jesus asked, "Thinkest thou that I cannot now pray to my Father, and he shall presently give me more than twelve legions of angels? But how then shall the scripture be fulfilled, that thus it must be?" (Matthew 26:53–54). In Matthew's view, Jesus clearly could have forestalled the suffering in the garden and the arrest had He wished, but instead He chose to fulfill the scriptures concerning His fate—His behavior was not governed by fear.[14]

If Jesus did not flee to Galilee in fear, we must still ask why Jesus chose that location and what Matthew sees as the relationship between John's fate and the start of Jesus' ministry. As noted above, Matthew is careful to characterize events in Jesus' life as fulfillment of Old Testament prophecies.[15] Immediately following his general statement about Jesus' departure into Galilee, the Gospel writer includes a more specific description: "Leaving Nazareth, he came and

---

[13] Alfred Plummer, *A Critical and Exegetical Commentary on the Gospel According to St. Luke*, International Critical Commentary (Edinburgh: Clark, 1981), 115.

[14] Significantly, here too Jesus' behavior is a fulfillment of prophecy.

[15] For examples of these so-called "formula citations," see Matthew 1:22–23; 2:15, 17–18, 23; 4:12–16; 21:4–5; 27:35. For a full discussion, see Robert H. Gundry, *The Use of the Old Testament in Matthew's Gospel*, Novum Testamentum Supplements 18 (Leiden: Brill, 1967); Krister Stendahl, *The School of St. Matthew and Its Use of the Old Testament*, 2d ed. (Philadelphia: Fortress, 1968), and Bruce M. Metzger, "The Formulas Introducing Scripture in the New Testament and the Mishnah," *Journal of Biblical Literature* 70 (1951): 297–307. For a summary discussion and additional bibliography, see Brown, *Introduction*, 207–8.

dwelt in Capernaum, which is upon the sea coast, in the borders of Zabulon and Nephthalim: that it might be fulfilled which was spoken by Esaias the prophet, saying, The land of Zabulon, and the land of Nephthalim, by the way of the sea, beyond Jordan, Galilee of the Gentiles; the people which sat in darkness saw great light; and to them which sat in the region and shadow of death, light is sprung up" (Matthew 4:13–14).[16] These verses provide the scriptural justification for Jesus' decision; the withdrawal from one location to another becomes not a casual geographical fact but rather the realization of a divine commission, one foretold by the ancient prophets.

On another level, the imprisonment of John the Baptist may be said to reveal the dangers of the ministry generally and foreshadow the dangers of Jesus' ministry specifically. Mention of the difficulties John must face underscores from the start of Christ's public life that "the proclamation of the kingdom will encounter major obstacles."[17] More particularly, Jesus personally will face dangerous obstacles throughout His remaining life and will, like John, eventually be arrested and cruelly put to death. The fate of John the Baptist anticipates that of the Savior (Matthew 4:12; 14:3–12; Mark 1:14; 6:17–29; Luke 3:19–20).[18] The precise verb Matthew uses for the arrest of John is elsewhere used to foretell and describe the arrest and passion of Jesus (Matthew 17:22–23; 20:18–19; 26:2, 14–16, 48) and underscores "the parallelism between the Messiah and his herald."[19] The removal of the forerunner not only looks ahead to the fate of the one foretold but likewise signals His arrival. John's forced retirement seems to be the "divine cue" for Jesus to begin His labor.[20]

---

[16] Recall that Joseph's earlier removal into Galilee also constituted a fulfillment of prophecy.

[17] Brown, *Introduction*, 128.

[18] See Davies and Allison, *Gospel of Matthew*, 1:375–76.

[19] Davies and Allison, *Gospel of Matthew*, 1:375, with note 49. See Bruce D. Chilton, "God in Strength: Jesus' Announcement of the Kingdom," in *Studien zum Neuen Testament und seiner Umwelt* (Freistadt: F. Plöchl, 1979), 65, 70–71. Compare Matthew 10:17–21, where the same term is used to characterize the prophesied persecution of Jesus' disciples.

[20] Ernst Lohmeyer, *Das Evangelium des Matthäus* (Göttingen: Vandenhoeck und

If, however, the threat of arrest was one Jesus could and would confront later in His life, why would He move to avoid a confrontation at the beginning of His public ministry? The answer seems to be primarily a matter of timing. At this early stage of His career, as He says elsewhere, His "hour [was] not yet come"[21] (John 2:4). Although He was not afraid to face a fate similar to that faced by John the Baptist, it was not yet the time, and He needed to avoid anything that could disrupt His mission before its completion. He had other work to do before His hour *was* come in the culminating work of His suffering in Gethsemane, His arrest, His trials, His death on the cross, and His resurrection.

Unlike Matthew, Luke makes no mention of John the Baptist's fate, as a chronological indicator or otherwise, when he describes the beginning of Jesus' ministry. He does rehearse the forty-day fast and the encounter with Satan, but he ends this section of his narrative thus: "Jesus returned in the power of the Spirit into Galilee: and there went out a fame of him through all the region round about" (Luke 4:14). Luke offers no explicit reason for Jesus' move to Galilee. He does, however, say He "returned" (*hupestrepsen*) to that place. The early geographical focus of Luke's account is Nazareth of Galilee, which was the native home of Jesus' youth; and, indeed, at the start of Jesus' ministry in Galilee, Luke locates Him first in Nazareth. Jesus' boyhood home seems a likely place to begin His ministry, but Luke represents that His efforts to preach in the synagogue there met with amazement, hostility, and rejection (Luke 4:14–30).[22]

Luke's location of the beginning of Jesus' ministry in Nazareth seems to serve several functions.[23] First, the story of Jesus' rejection at

---

Ruprecht, 1962), 63.

[21] John 2:4. Compare John 7:30; 8:20; 12:23, 27; 13:1; 17:1. See C. K. Barrett, *The Gospel According to St. John*, 2d ed. (Philadelphia: John Knox/Westminster Press, 1978), 191.

[22] The same story is told in Mark 6:1–6 and Matthew 13:54–58, although much later and in a more abbreviated form in those two Gospels.

[23] The *content*, as opposed to the *location*, of Jesus' first sermon as rehearsed in Luke's Gospel is of critical importance and will be discussed below.

Nazareth may be part of Luke's "theological geography" and may help explain Jesus' extended ministry in Capernaum, as one would have expected "Jesus of Nazareth" to be most active in His native home.[24]

The rejection as related in Luke involves, moreover, great danger to Jesus—the angry crowd from the synagogue drove Him from the city to the top of the hill, from which they were going to "cast him down headlong" (Luke 4:29). The account may, therefore, serve a purpose similar to that in part served by Matthew's and Mark's references to John the Baptist—namely, to highlight from the very start of the ministry the threats that would almost unrelentingly confront Jesus and the establishment of the kingdom of God.

Furthermore, Nazareth was a suitable context for the Isaiah passage Jesus quoted in His first recorded presentation in the synagogue (Isaiah 61:1–2). Therein the ancient prophet foretold the beginning of the Messiah's mission to the poor, and Jesus' presence in Nazareth may be said to mark that beginning, Nazareth being itself a city of no great reputation or wealth. As Nathanael asked, "Can there any good thing come out of Nazareth?" (John 1:46).

The reconstruction of the start of Jesus' ministry in the Gospel of John is unique. John gives no exact account of Jesus' baptism and makes no reference to the forty-day fast or wilderness confrontation with Satan. He does, however, flesh out John the Baptist's testimony of Jesus as "the Lamb of God, which taketh away the sin of the world" (John 1:29) and as "the Son of God" (John 1:34). John's Gospel then outlines the transfer of the first disciples from John the Baptist to Christ (John 1:35–42). John afterward locates Jesus in Galilee, where He "findeth Philip and saith unto him, Follow me," amazes Philip's friend Nathanael with His knowledge of that man's past activity, and promises "greater things than these" (John 1:43, 50). Once in Galilee, Jesus performs what John calls His first miraculous sign—*sēmeion*,[25] by transforming water into wine at the wedding in Cana of

---

[24] Brown, *Introduction*, 237.
[25] Arndt and Gingrich, *GEL*, "sēmeion," 920–21.

Galilee (John 2:1–11).[26] So John, like the synoptic Gospels, begins the work of Jesus' public ministry in Galilee, but he gives no explanation of why Jesus chose to go to there.

The Gospel of Mark's Account and Its Implications

In what was apparently intended to be read as the first day of Jesus' public ministry, Mark "familiarizes his reader with the type of things done in proclaiming the kingdom."[27] Particularly prominent are Jesus' public preaching, His first miracle, and the spread of His fame—things that prove typical of His entire mission. Mark's account, widely believed to have been the first of the Gospel narratives,[28] describes the start of Jesus' ministry thus: "After that John was put in prison, Jesus came into Galilee, preaching the gospel of the kingdom of God, and saying, The time is fulfilled, and the kingdom of God is at hand: repent ye, and believe the gospel" (Mark 1:14–15).

Jesus initiated His ministry with words that announced the new proximity of the kingdom of God and the response men and women should have to its approach (to Christ's approach). The verb rendered "is at hand" is *engizō*, "to come near" or "approach."[29] Jesus was saying that the kingdom of God had drawn near but, as Brown describes it, that kingdom had "not yet fully arrived."[30] Jesus called upon His listeners to "repent and believe (have faith) in the Gospel," implying that the complete arrival of God's kingdom depends upon people being in a state to receive it.[31] And men and women must *change* to achieve the receptive state. The term translated "repent" is *metanoeite*.[32] A careful look at the Greek verb is instructive. The verb

---

[26] This miracle and some of its implications will be considered in due course.
[27] As Brown, *Introduction*, 129, points out.
[28] On the question of Mark being the earliest of the synoptic Gospels, see Arthur J. Bellinzoni Jr., ed., *The Two-Source Hypothesis: A Critical Appraisal* (Macon, Georgia: Mercer University Press, 1985); Mark S. Goodacre, *The Synoptic Problem: A Way through the Maze* (London and New York: Sheffield, 2001).
[29] Arndt and Gingrich, *GEL*, "engizō," 270.
[30] Brown, *Introduction*, 128.
[31] See Brown, *Introduction*, 128.
[32] Arndt and Gingrich, *GEL*, "metanoeō," 640.

consists of the prefix, *meta*, and the main root, *noeō*. The prefix *meta* is commonly used to express the idea of change. *Noeō* comes from the same root as the Greek noun *noos*, which means "mind." The injunction to repent is, in effect, an injunction to change one's mind. This is not a trivial requirement. In fact, it suggests a profound transformation. In Classical Greek, the word *noos* may be variously translated "mind," "thought," "reason," "intellect," "purpose," "will," "heart," "design," or, we might say, "mind as the active principle of the universe."[33] In light of this, Jesus' commandment to repent, *metanoeite*, becomes a call for the transformation of the individual, the remaking of the self at the most profound level. Christ calls upon His listeners to become completely new creatures. Closely linked to that change, and in an interactive and inextricable relationship with it, is faith: We must believe the gospel as a sometimes precursor to, sometimes result of, the necessary transformation.

After this expression of the gospel message, Jesus called the first disciples to join Him—an essential addition to Christ's labor of preparing people to receive God's kingdom (Mark 1:16–20).[34] Mark then rehearses the Savior's visit to a synagogue of Capernaum, detailing the Jewish audience's reaction to the doctrine Jesus taught and the first miracle of His ministry:[35]

---

[33] H. G. Liddell, R. Scott, H. S. Jones, and R. McKenzie, *A Greek English Lexicon* (Oxford: Clarendon Press, 1968), "noos," 1180–81. This collection of terms closely (and interestingly) approximates the use of the term *intelligence* in Latter-day Saint scripture. See, for example, Abraham 3:21–22; Doctrine and Covenants 93:29–30.

[34] The calling of the first disciples will not be treated here. See Eric D. Huntsman, "Galilee and the Call of the Twelve Apostles," in this volume.

[35] Of the extensive bibliography interpreting Christ's miracles generally, we may profitably look to the following: Colin Brown, *Miracles and the Critical Mind* (Grand Rapids: William B. Eerdmans, 1984); Reginald H. Fuller, *Interpreting the Miracles* (Philadelphia: John Knox/Westminster Press, 1963); Anton Fridrichsen, *The Problem of Miracle in Primitive Christianity* (Minneapolis: Fortress Press, 1972); H. Hendrickx, *The Miracle Stories of the Synoptic Gospels* (London: Chapman, 1987); Howard C. Kee, *Miracle in the Early Christian World: A Study in Sociohistorical Method* (New Haven and London: Yale University Press, 1983), 161; Alan Richardson, *The Miracle-Stories of the Gospels* (London: SCM, 1941); Hendrick Van der Loos, *The Miracles of Jesus*, Novum Testamentum Supplements 9 (Leiden: Brill, 1965). For a useful collection of essays, see David Wenham and Craig L. Blomberg, eds., *The Miracles of Jesus* (Sheffield, England: JSOT Press, 1986).

And they went into Capernaum; and straightway on the sabbath day he entered into the synagogue, and taught. And they were astonished at his doctrine: for he taught them as one that had authority, and not as the scribes. And there was in the synagogue a man with an unclean spirit; and he cried out, saying, Let us alone; what have we to do with thee, thou Jesus of Nazareth? art thou come to destroy us? I know thee who thou art, the Holy One of God. And Jesus rebuked him, saying, Hold thy peace, and come out of him. And when the unclean spirit had torn him, and cried with a loud voice, he came out of him. And they were all amazed, insomuch that they questioned among themselves, saying, What thing is this? what new doctrine is this? for with authority commandeth he even the unclean spirits, and they do obey him. And immediately his fame spread abroad throughout all the region round about Galilee. (Mark 1:21–28)

Mark tells the reader nothing of the content of Jesus' speech in the synagogue, although he makes much of the audience's reaction to that speech: "They were astonished at his doctrine: for he taught them as one that had authority, and not as the scribes" (Mark 1:22). We might wonder why the author excludes any description of the words that inspired such a reaction. We might be intended to assume, since Mark introduces no unique doctrine in the intervening verses, that Christ simply continued preaching the gospel of the kingdom (Mark 1:14), announcing the approach of God's kingdom and calling people to repentance and to faith. This may well be the case, but it remains significant that any particular words Jesus used to inspire His listeners are not included. Perhaps Mark omits them to turn his readers' attention to the speaker Himself. The audience was "astonished" at Christ's "doctrine"—not just because of what He said but also because of how He said it and, by implication, because of who He is: "He taught them as one that had authority, and not as the scribes." The word rendered "authority" is *exousia*, which is better translated "power."[36] It is not only a matter of Jesus' style and status but also of

---

[36] Arndt and Gingrich, *GEL*, "exousia," 352–53.

His personal impact. In Mark, the emphasis in the scene is not on any particular words Jesus spoke—because Jesus Himself embodies the message of the kingdom and the power of that message.

In immediate counterpoint to the Savior's forceful teaching, a man in the synagogue possessed of a demon called out to Jesus, and the Savior performed the first known miracle of His ministry by cleansing the man of the possessing spirit (Mark 1:23–26). This was a crucial moment in Jesus' ministry.[37] Immediately pursuant to His proclamation of the gospel message, which included the announcement that God's kingdom was drawing near, He was confronted by a representative of the kingdom of the enemy and had to test and prove His superiority over that representative. From this exchange, Jesus emerges not just as a preacher but also as a miracle worker.[38] As the encounter with the demoniac shares certain features with pagan wonder stories, some have supposed that the account of this Gospel miracle (and others) has been "formulated... so as to assimilate Jesus to the typical miracle-working divine man... with which the Hellenistic world was familiar."[39] Because of the presumed similarities, Jesus is sometimes "dismiss[ed] as a typical exorcist or magician of his

---

[37] See Kee, *Miracle in the Early Christian World*, 160; Brown, *Introduction to the New Testament*, 129; Fuller, *Interpreting the Miracles*, 70.

[38] His inaugural miracle as recounted by Mark has received significant attention. See, for example, Fuller, *Interpreting the Miracles*, 35 with note, 48–49, 54, 70, 75, 76 with note, 84; Kee, *Miracle in the Early Christian World*, 161–63, 204–5; Van der Loos, *The Miracles of Jesus*, 127–29, 181, 206, 268, 363, 367–68, 372, 378–81, 436, 536, 552, 594; Brown, *Introduction*, 129; Compare Howard C. Kee, "The Terminology of Mark's Exorcism Stories," *New Testament Studies* 14 (1968): 232–46.

[39] Barry L. Blackburn, "Miracle Working Theioi Andres in Hellenism (and Hellenistic Judaism)," in *The Miracles of Jesus*, ed. D. Wenham and C. L. Blomberg (Sheffield, England: JSOT Press, 1986), 185. Compare L. Bieler, *Theios Aner*, 2 vols. (Vienna: Oskar Höfels, 1935–36), 2.25–36; Hans Windisch, *Paulus und Christus* (Leipzig: Hinrichs, 1934), 101–14. A contrasting view is represented in C. Holladay, *Theios Aner in Hellenistic Judaism* (Missoula, Montana: Scholars Press, 1977), 22–43. See also Edwin Yamauchi, "Magic or Miracle? Diseases, Demons, and Exorcisms," in *The Miracles of Jesus*, ed. D. Wenham and C. L. Blomberg (Sheffield, England: JSOT Press, 1986), 131–32; Van der Loos, *The Miracles of Jesus*, 127; 368–71, 380–81; Fuller, *Interpreting the Miracles*, 48.

time."[40] That critical differences do exist between the accounts of Jesus' miracles and those of pagan magicians and that Jesus is, in fact, quite unlike a "typical exorcist or magician" seem clear. Among several key distinctions described by scholars,[41] three points deserve particular notice.

First-century exorcists often made use of elaborate magical incantations and, sometimes, actions. The words of the incantations required precise recitation and exact fidelity to a specific "content, intonation, and rhythm"—if they were to have the desired effect.[42] In particular, knowing the true name of an entity would give a person power over it. As Van der Loos has remarked, "If the magician was able to speak the right name at the right moment, he became master of the situation, for neither gods nor demons could resist the name; if they were called they had to appear."[43] But Mark does not record any distinctive magical words or gestures and no use of the demon's name—Jesus speaks only a few, quite ordinary words and controls the demon by His "authoritative" word.[44] This, it should be noted, is in sharp contrast to the demon's proclamation of Jesus' name, which, among other things, seems to have been the unclean spirit's attempt to control Jesus.[45] He names Jesus in an effort at defense and resistance but discovers that no word, even an accurate one, used against the true Word is sufficient to overpower Him. We may recall the impact of Jesus' speech in the synagogue just preceding the encounter with the demon when He spoke with "power" (*exousia*). Quite unlike the special incantations recited by magicians or the name uttered by

---

[40] Brown, Introduction, 129n3.
[41] See references in note 39. See also John P. Meier, *Mentor, Message and Miracles*, vol. 2 of *A Marginal Jew: Rethinking the Historical Jesus*, 3 vols. (New York: Doubleday, 1994), 2:537–52. Cf. Paul J. Achtemeier, "Mark, Gospel Of," in Freedman, *ABD*, 4:555.
[42] Yamauchi, "Magic or Miracle," 132.
[43] Van der Loos, *The Miracles of Jesus*, 323. Compare Ludwig Blau, *Das altjüdische Zauberwesen* (Graz: Akademische Druck-und Verlagsamst, 1974), 123.
[44] Van der Loos, *The Miracles of Jesus*, 381. Cf. Yamauchi, "Magic or Miracle," 133.
[45] Van der Loos, *The Miracles of Jesus*, 379–80, where he notes, "By speaking this name [Jesus of Nazareth] the demoniac opposes power to power; his knowledge of the true name must adjure the power of his opponent."

magician or demon, *any* words the Savior speaks are words of power, for He is the Word and has power in Himself.

Furthermore, many magicians would identify themselves with a deity familiar to the victim of the demon to overawe and compel the possessed.[46] Jesus, by contrast, did not identify Himself to the possessed, nor did He say anything about His relationship to God. It was the demon who identified Jesus for the audience: "I know thee who thou art, the Holy One of God" (Mark 1:24). But Jesus silenced him. That the demon knew Jesus' true identity and that Jesus forbade him to speak are elements of the account that have received considerable attention, and various interpretations of the scene are possible.[47] As for Jesus' failure to identify Himself in the exchange with the possessed man, we might argue that the performance of the miracle by the simple act of command constitutes a declaration of who and what Jesus is. Unlike the magicians, the Savior had no need to name Himself—in His command itself and in the demoniac's obedience thereto, His divine power and identity were manifest.

Finally, a moral element exists, although not always an explicit one, in Jesus' exorcisms that distinguishes Him from other miracle workers. Even anciently, it was recognized that Jesus, unlike traditional pagan magicians, called His followers to lives of moral transformation,[48] and, as we shall see, such an invitation is implicit in this exorcism represented by Mark.

Many of the same themes and motifs found in the pagan tradition are likewise documented in Jewish literature, and parallels can

---

[46] Van der Loos, *The Miracles of Jesus*, 380.

[47] Those interested in this part of the exchange should look to William Wrede, *The Messianic Secret*, Issues in Religion and Theology 1, trans. J. C. G. Greig (London: Clarke, 1971); Christopher M. Tuckett, ed., *The Messianic Secret* (Philadelphia: Fortress, 1983); Haikki Räjsänen, *The "Messianic Secret" in Mark's Gospel* (Edinburgh: T & T Clark, 1990); Talmage, *JTC*, 181–83, 187n6.

[48] Blackburn, "Miracle Working," 185. For Origen's defense against Celsus, who accused Jesus of mere magic, see Henry Chadwick, *Origen Contra Celsum*, Society of Biblical Literature Dissertation Series 64 (Cambridge: Cambridge University, 1980); Eugene V. Gallagher, *Divine Man or Magician? Celsus and Origen on Jesus* (Chico, California: Scholars Press, 1982).

certainly be found between Jesus' miracles and Jewish miracle stories.[49] There is, in fact, greater similarity in the types of miracles performed by Jesus and those described in *Jewish* miracle narratives: raising the dead, nature miracles, miraculous feedings, exorcisms, and healings.[50] And the Jewish tradition may, as Fiebig argues, deserve priority when we make comparisons. But at least one important difference seems to exist between the performance of the miracle by Jesus and the performance by the average Jewish miracle worker. Old Testament prophets and rabbis tended to accomplish their miracles through intensive prayer, through their relation to God, and through the use of God's name.[51] Jesus, who also taught that fasting and prayer were necessary conditioning prior to performing a miracle, often healed the sick by invoking His own authority as the Son of God (Matthew 9:1–8; 17:14–21; Mark 9:29).

The performance of any miracle at this juncture would have proved in *deed* the power the Jewish audience had just witnessed in Jesus' *words*, and the inclusion of this miracle account in Mark no doubt in part serves this purpose. But that the first recorded instance of a miracle should be an exorcism is significant on many levels.

Cosmic forces seem to be at work in the encounter. Of the many types of miracles in Mark's Gospel, none represents the confrontation between the power of good and the power of evil as obviously and forcefully as an exorcism of an unclean spirit. Unlike the healing of a person suffering from fever, leprosy, or paralysis, an unclean spirit cannot seem neutral or innocent—it is closely associated with Satan. As scholars note, the demoniac spoke of himself in the plural, the

---

[49] Blackburn, "Miracle Working," 196–98, where he lists numerous of these themes and motifs. Paul Fiebig, *Jüdische Wundergeschichten des neuentestamentlichen Zeitalters unter besonderer Berücksichtigung ihres Verhältnisses zum Neuen Testament* (Tübingen: J. C. B. Mohr, 1911), 74, long ago pointed the way to the likenesses between Jewish miracle narratives and the miracles recounted in the New Testament.

[50] P. Fiebig, *Jüdische Wundergeschichten*, 74; Blackburn, "Miracle Working," 196–97; Van der Loos, *The Miracles of Jesus*, 133.

[51] Martin Dibelius, *Die Formgeschichte des Evangeliums* (Tübingen: J. C. B. Mohr 1933), 131–39. In this section, Dibelius discusses two types of miracle stories—those he calls theodicy legends and those he calls personal legends.

possessed man presumably spoke for the demon in him, and the demon spoke for the fraternity of evil spirits and their shared interest.[52]

This shared interest, or concern, is the threat posed to the demons by Jesus, not just in this encounter but in the greater battle between the kingdom of God represented by Christ and the kingdom of Satan embodied by the possessed man.[53] The demon itself clearly understood this, fearing its own downfall and that of its master: "Art thou come to destroy us?" Satan's subjects know Jesus for who He is—"I know thee who thou art, the Holy One of God"—and want nothing to do with Him.[54] The demon's fear was justified, for Jesus "rebuked him, saying, Hold thy peace, and come out of him," and the evil spirit had to comply: "And when the unclean spirit had torn him, and cried out with a loud voice, he came out of him" ((Mark 1:24–26).

The word rendered "rebuke" is a forceful term, translatable variously as "lay a penalty on," "censure," "punish," or "penalize."[55] Kee points out that the expression is "a technical apocalyptic term . . . which implies the commanding power of Jesus to control the agent of Satan."[56] Likewise, the phrase weakly translated "hold thy peace" really means "be muzzled" or "be shut up with a muzzle,"[57] suggesting Jesus' ability not only to silence the unclean spirit but also to bind it and impede its power to do injury. In this confrontation, it becomes clear that Satan's power was indeed threatened by the advent of the kingdom of God as preached by Jesus (Mark 1:14–15).[58] The successful exorcism of the demon foretells and foreshadows the eventual eschatological triumph of God's kingdom over Satan's kingdom through the victory of Christ.

---

[52] Van der Loos, *The Miracles of Jesus*, 380.
[53] Fuller, *Interpreting the Miracles*, 49, 70. Cf. Brown, *Introduction*, 129.
[54] Fuller, *Interpreting the Miracles*, 49, reads the account of the demoniac's perception of Jesus' true identity and the threat He represents as preaching "the coming and manifestation of the Messiah."
[55] Arndt and Gingrich, GEL, "epitimaō," 384.
[56] Kee, *Miracle in the Early Christian World*, 161.
[57] Arndt and Gingrich, GEL, "fimoō," 1060.
[58] See Kee, *Miracle in the Early Christian World*, 160.

Although the forces in play are cosmic in scope and nature, the battle was waged in and over one man. That the man is unnamed suggests he is to stand for every man, and the battle over the possession of this one man's body signifies the battle eternally waged between Christ and Satan over every individual soul. We must remember that Jesus began His ministry by proclaiming the kingdom and enjoining men to repent, to change themselves fundamentally.[59] By including as His first miracle an exorcism, in which He cleansed a man of an invading evil, Jesus, as Mark demonstrates, showed His ability to effect what He commands. He can cleanse and purify us from within and can, in fact, transform us from unclean to clean, from unholy to holy. Jesus' first miracle symbolizes His teaching, performs in deed what He proclaims in word, and uses only His word to bring it about—no magical paraphernalia and no secret incantations. He embodies the power, and any words He speaks can be words of power, issuing, as they do, from Him.

A further suggestion of the scene is that there is power in the words of the gospel Jesus brings, power for men and women, should they submit to those words and to the Savior Himself, to be purified and transformed into new men and women. That this is implied by the exchange becomes evident from the audience's reaction to Jesus' miracle: "What thing is this? what new doctrine is this? for with authority commandeth he even the unclean spirits, and they do obey him" (Mark 1:27). It is clear from their response that the observers recognized some connection between the power with which Jesus caused the miraculous healing of the possessed man and His doctrine: "What new doctrine is this?" The word of Christ uttered as command and doctrine is linked to His ability to purify and to transform.[60]

Mark's description of Jesus' actions in the synagogue becomes

---

[59] For the meaning and implications of the term translated "repent," see above.

[60] On the relationship of word and miracle, see the still useful, if rather dated, work by O. Perels, *Die Wunderüberlieferung der Synoptiker in ihrem Verhältnis zur Wortüberlieferung* (Stuttgart: Kohlhammer, 1934), throughout, especially chapters one and two. Cf. Van der Loos, *The Miracles of Jesus*, 280–86.

particularly meaningful when read in the context of the opening message of the ministry.⁶¹ Jesus begins by preaching that men must change (*metanoeite*), and His first miracle symbolizes and realizes this doctrine. As typified by the miraculous cleansing of the possessed man, Jesus demonstrates that He has the power to transform any sinful man into a new, purified entity.⁶² In his account of Jesus' earliest ministry, Mark, in fact, creates a paradigm for the gospel as a whole.

The Gospel of Matthew's Prophetic Framework

In Matthew, as in Mark, Jesus' forty-day stay in the wilderness provides the active backdrop for the beginning of the Savior's ministry, with the same Mosaic connections and implications discussed above. But the more immediate context for the debut of Jesus' teachings and deeds is a citation from Isaiah, one that highlights Matthew's particular theological interests. The author quotes the prophecy, in part, to explain Jesus' decision to go to Galilee and, more specifically, Capernaum.⁶³ In addition to providing scriptural justification for Jesus' geographical situation, however, the particular verses of Isaiah establish a prophetic framework for the initiation of His ministry: "Leaving Nazareth, he came and dwelt in Capernaum ... That it might be fulfilled which was spoken by Esaias the prophet, saying, The land of Zabulon and the land of Nephthalim, by the way of the sea, beyond Jordan, Galilee of the Gentiles; the people which sat in darkness saw great light; and to them which sat in the region

---

⁶¹ Kee, *Miracle in the Early Christian World*, 161. Kee actually refers specifically to the defeat of the demon in the synagogue in Capernaum as "paradigmatic for the Gospel as a whole." But I believe the exorcism of the demon must be viewed as part of a larger introductory framework, which includes the news that the kingdom of God "is at hand," the call to repentance, and the power of Jesus' initial teaching in the synagogue, and that that larger framework may be called "paradigmatic."

⁶² The term Mark most commonly uses for miracles is *dynamis*, meaning an "act of power." See Arndt and Gingrich, *GEL*, "dunamis," 262–63. Compare Brown, Introduction, 133n16.

⁶³ See discussion under "Location" above. 2 Kings 15:29. See S. L. Edgar, "Respect for Context in Quotations from the OT," *New Testament Studies* 9 (1962): 58.

and shadow of death, light is sprung up. From that time Jesus began to preach, and to say, Repent: for the kingdom of heaven is at hand" (Matthew 4:13–17).

Scholars have noted the suitability of Capernaum as the site for the introduction of Jesus' ministry, for Zebulon and Naphtali were, of the peoples attacked by the Assyrians, among the first tribes of Israel to be exiled, and "it would be appropriate for the kingdom to be restored where it was initially dissolved."[64] In context, Isaiah foretold the birth of a son of the house of David, who would reestablish and expand the kingdom: "of the increase of his government and peace there shall be no end, upon the throne of David" (Isaiah 9:7). Matthew clearly applies this prophecy to Jesus and sees Him as the Messiah and the bringer of the promised deliverance.[65] But the restoration of the kingdom as conceived by Matthew and described by Isaiah seems a primarily spiritual business, and the dawning of light upon those in darkness and shadow (Isaiah 9:2) is to be understood as a reinterpretation of the physical plight of the ancient Israelites in terms of their (from Matthew's perspective) contemporary condition of spiritual darkness.[66] The implications of the passage become explicitly spiritual when Matthew tells the reader that Jesus proclaims the approach of a *heavenly* kingdom (Matthew 4:17), not merely to restore but also, we may assume, to supersede the preexilic kingdom of Israel.

That the extent of the kingdom Jesus proclaims would exceed ancient Israel's physical and psychic boundaries is underscored by the use of the phrase "Galilee of the Gentiles" (Matthew 4:15). The word used here for "Gentiles" is *ethnōn*, which can also be translated

---

[64] Davies and Allison, *Gospel of Matthew*, 1:382. Compare A. S. Geyser, "Some Salient Passages on the Restoration of the Twelve Tribes of Israel," in *L'Apocalypse johannique et l'Apocalyptique dans le Nouveau Testament*, ed. J. Lambrecht (Leuven: Leuven University Press, 1980), 307.

[65] Cf. Davies and Allison, *Gospel of Matthew*, 1:380.

[66] For multiple examples of darkness as a symbol of sin and spiritual bankruptcy, see Davies and Allison, *Gospel of Matthew*, 1–385. For the Messiah as the bringer of light, see O. Michel, "Das Licht des Messias," in *Donum Gentilicium*, ed. E. Bammel, C. K. Barrett, and W. D. Davies (Oxford: Oxford University Press, 1978), 140–50.

"nations."[67] Davies and Allison have called Matthew's use of this phrase "the key to and the reason for the quotation of Isaiah's text,"[68] arguing that the Gospel writer has a theological interest in "linking the Messiah and the Gentiles" early in the account of the Savior's life "so that the end will be foreshadowed in the beginning: although Jesus must minister only to the lost sheep of the house of Israel, the kingdom will eventually embrace the Gentiles,"[69] or, we might say, all "nations." In this reading, Matthew's description of Jesus' presence in Galilee is a fulfillment not only of the specific geographical prophecy uttered by Isaiah but also of an implied (and elsewhere articulated) prophecy of the spread of the gospel and the promises of God beyond the Jewish nation.

The Gospel of Matthew's Summary and Message

Following the statement that Jesus departed into Galilee after John the Baptist's arrest and the characterization of this move as a fulfillment of prophecy, Matthew reviews Jesus' first teaching and miracles. Of the synoptic accounts, Matthew's contains the most summary description of Jesus' early ministry, omitting any report of the Jewish reaction to His message or of a specific miracle encounter at this stage of His career. Matthew's record of the first message proclaimed by Jesus is very like that given in Mark: "Repent: for the kingdom of heaven is at hand" (Matthew 4:17), and it lends itself to similar interpretation, with the added layers of meaning facilitated by the inclusion of the Isaiah prophecy.[70] As for the very general depiction of Jesus' ministry, it can likewise be understood and explicated in terms of its rhetorical context. Matthew's description

---

[67] Indeed, in the King James translation of Isaiah 9:1, one of the verses here cited by Matthew, the phrase is rendered "Galilee of the nations." Compare Arndt and Gingrich, GEL, "ethnos," 276.

[68] Davies and Allison, *The Gospel of Matthew*, 1:383.

[69] Davies and Allison, *The Gospel of Matthew*, 1:385; Brown, *Introduction*, 178, infers from Matthew's use of the phrase "Galilee of the Gentiles" that the Gospel is addressed to "a mixed congregation of many Gentiles."

[70] Specific to Matthew, see Matthew 21:43; 28:19. Compare Mark 16:15, Luke 24:47, Acts 1:8.

sets up a particular order of performance in Jesus' ministry and provides the realization of the universal reach of Jesus and His message as foreseen in the phrase "Galilee of the Gentiles."

Jesus, we are told, "went about all Galilee, teaching in their synagogues, and preaching the gospel of the kingdom, and healing all manner of sickness and all manner of . . . disease among the people" (Matthew 4:23). Though not providing a specific example at this juncture, Matthew, like Mark, links Jesus' power to heal to His doctrine: Jesus teaches and preaches and heals. The structure suggests that the teaching of the gospel is a precursor to the healing miracles.[71] That Matthew intended such a connection is borne out by further reading of his Gospel. The Sermon on the Mount, for example, anticipates and contextualizes the particular miracles detailed in chapters 8 and 9 of Matthew.[72] Furthermore, Jesus' disciples are commanded not only to preach the kingdom of heaven but also to heal every disease and infirmity,[73] signifying that the labor of preaching the gospel is closely tied to the healing of those in need. In this construction, Jesus' word precedes and, in the end, effects the healing associated with physical and spiritual infirmity.[74]

Additional implications of Matthew's synopsis become clear if we consider the rhetorical emphases of his text:

> *And* Jesus went about
> *all* Galilee, teaching in their synagogues,
> *and* preaching the gospel of the kingdom,
> *and* healing
> *all* manner of sickness
> and
> *all* manner of disease among the people.

---

[71] Perels, *Die Wunderüberlieferung der Synoptiker*, chapters one and two. Cf. Van der Loos, *The Miracles of Jesus*, 280–86; Yamauchi, "Magic or Miracle," 133.

[72] Davies and Allison, *The Gospel of Matthew*, 1:413.

[73] Cf. Matthew 4:17 and 10:6; 4:24 and 10:1. A parallelism is noted and discussed by Davies and Allison, *The Gospel of Matthew*, 1:412.

[74] See Dennis C. Duling, "The Therapeutic Son of David," *New Testament Studies* 24 (1978): 393–99.

THE MINISTRY COMMENCES

> *And* his fame went throughout
> *all* Syria:
> *and* they brought unto him
> *all* sick people that were taken with diverse diseases
> *and* torments,
> *and* those which were possessed with devils,
> *and* those which were lunatick,
> *and* those that had the palsy;
> *and* he healed them.
> And there followed him great multitudes of people from Galilee,
> *and* from Decapolis,
> *and* from Jerusalem,
> *and* from Judea,
> *and* from beyond Jordan (Matthew 4:23–25; emphasis added).

Two different adjectives are used in the Greek text to signify what is translated into King James's English as "all," but some form of one or the other of those two adjectives occurs five times in just two verses.[75] Further, the word *kai*, meaning "and," is used fourteen times in the Greek version of these three verses.[76] The repeated use of the terms for "all" and of the connective *kai* persuades readers that they are hearing a long and all-inclusive list of the places Jesus goes, of the activities He engages in, of the sicknesses He heals, and of the areas from which potential followers are drawn. The rhetoric of the passage underscores the universal reach of Jesus' message and blessing. He preaches throughout *all* Galilee, and His fame spread through *all* Syria,[77] suggesting that His word is intended for and is being heard by

---

[75] See Arndt and Gingrich, *GEL*, "holos," 704, and "pas," 782.

[76] This is an instance of what is known as *polysyndeton*: the "use of a conjunction between each clause." See R. A. Lanham, *A Handlist of Rhetorical Terms: A Guide for Students of English Literature*, 2d ed. (Berkeley and Los Angeles: University of California, 1991), 117.

[77] Brown, *Introduction*, 178, suggests that Matthew makes particular mention of Syria "perhaps because the Gospel was written there." For a full discussion of the possible site of this Gospel's composition, see Brown, *Introduction*, 212–16. For a bibliography of scholars treating the various possibilities, see Davies and Allison, *Gospel of Matthew*,

everyone. And although Matthew neglects to elaborate any specific healing story at this point of the story, his summary of the sicknesses cured covers a wide range of ills, signifying that Jesus' healing power can reach and overpower every evil.[78]

Matthew's Gospel confirms the universality not only of Jesus' reach but also of His attraction in the final verse of chapter 4: great multitudes came to Him "from Galilee, and from Decapolis, and from Jerusalem, and from Judea, and from beyond Jordan." Consideration of each of the locations named by Matthew is beyond the scope of this discussion.[79] The point to be made here is that Jesus draws and, we may assume, welcomes vast numbers of people to Him and that these potential followers come from a wide range of locations. Indeed, with the places listed, Matthew "manages to cover the compass—Galilee (NW), the Decapolis (NE), Judea (SW), Transjordan (SE)—as well as name the centre of the world, Jerusalem."[80] Matthew's list describes the geographical impact of Jesus' ministry: people from all points of the compass do come and, presumably, will come to Jesus for His word and His power. The whole of Matthew's summary announces and confirms the magnitude of Jesus' ministry: His ability to reach, attract, and transform men and women is limitless.

Rejection and Liberation in the Gospel of Luke

Luke follows Mark and Matthew in locating the start of Jesus' public ministry in Galilee. He further adheres to Mark's account by recording that Jesus' first miracle was healing the possessed man in the synagogue at Capernaum. Luke differs from the other synoptic Gospels, however, in that he precedes the visit to Capernaum with an

---

1:138–39.
[78] Davies and Allison, *Gospel of Matthew*, 1:416.
[79] Such has been undertaken elsewhere by others. See, notably, Emil Schürer, *The History of the Jewish People in the Age of Jesus Christ (175 B.C.–A.D. 135)*, rev. and ed. Geza Vermes et al., 3 vols. (Edinburgh: T & T Clark, 1973–87), 2:125–27; Davies and Allison, *Gospel of Matthew*, 1:420. On the Decapolis specifically, see G. A. Smith, *The Historical Geography of the Holy Land*, 30th ed. (London: Collins, 1966), 397–408.
[80] Davies and Allison, *Gospel of Matthew*, 1:420.

appearance in Nazareth, where Jesus gives the first articulated discourse of His adult ministry:

> And Jesus returned in the power of the Spirit into Galilee: and there went out a fame of him through all the region round about. And he taught in their synagogues, being glorified of all. And he came to Nazareth, where he had been brought up: and, as his custom was, he went into the synagogue on the sabbath day, and stood up for to read. And there was delivered unto him the book of the prophet Esaias. And when he had opened the book, he found the place where it was written, The Spirit of the Lord is upon me, because he hath anointed me to preach the gospel to the poor; he hath sent me to heal the brokenhearted, to preach deliverance to the captives, and recovering of sight to the blind, to set at liberty them that are bruised, to preach the acceptable year of the Lord. And he closed the book, and he gave it again to the minister, and sat down. And the eyes of all them that were in the synagogue were fastened on him. And he began to say unto them, This day is this scripture fulfilled in your ears. (Luke 4:14–21)[81]

That Luke places a story of rejection at the very outset of Jesus' ministry is telling. It has been noted already that this account, in part, sets the stage for the relentless obstacles Jesus would face throughout His life. But other considerations may also be at work. Plummer accounts for Luke's assignment of this story "to the opening of the ministry, as being typical of the issue of Christ's ministry."[82] Jesus was,

---

[81] Mark and Matthew likewise report a visit to Nazareth, although much later in their Gospel narratives (Mark 6:1–6; Matthew 13:53–58). It is unclear whether Luke is referring to the same appearance in Nazareth described later by the other synoptic authors. If so, he has apparently transposed it to the beginning of Jesus' ministry. Brown, *Introduction*, 237, treats it as an expanded version of the same incident related by Mark and Matthew. As previously mentioned, Brown believes that Luke relates the story of Jesus' rejection at Nazareth to account for the Savior's extensive presence and activity in Capernaum. Davies and Allison, *Gospel of Matthew*, 1.420.

[82] Plummer, *The Gospel According to Luke*, 118.

as Plummer reminds us,[83] eventually rejected by the Jews, and the localized rejection by His own native people at Nazareth foreshadows the final rejection by His people, Israel.

Moreover, Luke's is not just a tale of rejection but, as mentioned above, of life-threatening rejection: "[They] rose up, and thrust him out of the city, and led him unto the brow of the hill whereon their city was built, that they might cast him down headlong" (Luke 4:29). Although the Savior's opponents did not succeed at Nazareth, the violence of the scene prepares the reader not only for future difficulty and rejection but also for Jesus' "ultimate fate"—His death on the cross.[84]

As important to the event as the rejection itself is the content of Jesus' presentation in the synagogue that elicited such a furious response from His listeners. Here, as elsewhere in His ministry, Jesus cites the prophet Isaiah. The passage He quotes is a "composite text" abridged from Isaiah 61:1–2 and 58:6.[85] The language used in Luke's account is, with minor variations, very close to the language of the Septuagint for these verses.[86] The Isaiah passage cited is a so-called "Jubilee text" and seems to constitute, in fact, the clearest reference in the synoptic Gospels to any of the Hebrew Jubilee texts.[87] The Jubilee involves, as Ringe points out, three primary images: "The

---

[83] Plummer, *The Gospel According to Luke*, 118.

[84] Compare Brown, *Introduction*, 237.

[85] S. H. Ringe, *Jesus, Liberation, and the Biblical Jubilee* (Philadelphia: Fortress Press, 1985), 38.

[86] Compare Ringe, *Jesus, Liberation, and the Biblical Jubilee*, 38.

[87] Brown, *Introduction*, 237; Ringe, *Jesus, Liberation, and the Biblical Jubilee*, 36. For a full definition of the Jubilee and discussion of the Jubilee Tradition in Hebrew scripture, see Ringe, *Jesus, Liberation, and the Biblical Jubilee*, 16–32. Compare R. B. Sloan, *The Favorable Year of the Lord: A Study of Jubilary Year Theology in the Gospel of Luke* (Austin, Texas: Schola, 1977), who likewise recognizes and discusses the significance of the Jubilee to this passage in Luke. Ringe, *Jesus, Liberation, and the Biblical Jubilee*, 102, points us to other recent studies of Luke that discuss the citation from Isaiah but fail to underscore its character as a Jubilee text. From a fairly sizeable bibliography, we may see, for example, Robert C. Tannehill, "The Mission of Jesus According to Luke IV.16–30," in *Jesus in Nazareth*, ed. Erich Grässer et al. (New York and Berlin: Walter de Gruyter, 1972), 51–75; D. H. Hill, "The Rejection of Jesus at Nazareth [Luke 4:16–30]," *Novum Testamentum* 13 (1971): 161–80.

announcement of God's reign by one anointed by the Holy Spirit to be a messenger, the proclamation of good news to the poor, and the declaration of 'release' from captivity to various forms of imprisonment and enslavement."[88]

All these images figure in Jesus' quotation. He speaks of one who has been "anointed to preach the gospel to the poor"; He refers to one who is "to preach deliverance to the captives" and "to set at liberty them that are bruised"; He speaks of one who is "to preach the acceptable year of the Lord," this last alluding to the announcement of God's reign. Jesus clearly meant to apply the terms of the Jubilee text to Himself, for, after quoting the Isaiah passages, He proclaimed to His listeners' attentive silence, "This day is this scripture fulfilled in your ears" (Luke 4:18–21). We must ask why Jesus cited a Jubilee text and related it to Himself at the inauguration of His ministry and how the chosen text helped define that ministry.

Some of the particular language of the Isaiah citation deserves elaboration as it applies to Jesus and to Luke's representation of His ministry. First, Jesus significantly cited an Isaiah passage making use of the term "anointed" (*ekrisen*), the word at the root of the title *Christ, the anointed one*. Plummer has commented on the verb translated "he hath sent me" (*apestalken*), which in the perfect tense implies "he has sent me, and I am here."[89] The choice of this term for "sent" also implies a "special relation between sender and sent" and "adds the idea of a delegated authority making the person sent to be the envoy or representative of the sender."[90] Jesus, to whom the text applies, is, by implication, the authoritative representative of God, who has sent Him. Further, the word used for captives (*aixmalōtois*) traditionally means "prisoners of war."[91]

Although this term appropriately applies to captives in political

---

[88] Ringe, *Jesus, Liberation, and the Biblical Jubilee*, 36.
[89] Plummer, *The Gospel of Luke*, 121.
[90] Plummer, *The Gospel of Luke*, 121. Cf. Huntsman's discussion of the word *apostolos* in "Galilee and the Call of the Twelve Apostles," in this volume.
[91] Liddell et al., *Greek English* Lexicon, "*aixmalōtos*," 45. Compare Plummer, *The Gospel of Luke*, 121.

exile, it may also recall the eternal battle waged between God and Satan and confirms that Jesus, as God's representative, is empowered not only to preach but also to effect the liberation of those souls who have been taken prisoner by the forces of Satan and sin.[92] It is clear from these comments and considerations that the images of the Jubilee text quoted by Jesus, including the figures of return from exile and of liberation from enslavement, aptly describe and prefigure the redemptive work of Jesus' ministry.[93]

The listeners in the synagogue were, Luke tells us, "amazed" at Jesus' "words of grace" (Luke 4:22). The term translated "amazed" implies astonishment, not necessarily admiration.[94] As for the phrase "words of grace," it can reasonably mean the "message of God's promises and blessings recorded in Isaiah,"[95] but it may also refer to the redeeming grace of Jesus' life and atonement that is foreseen by the Jubilee text. That the audience failed to understand this secondary implication is clear from their question, "Is not this Joseph's son?" (Luke 4:22). For it is "not as Joseph's son but as God's son that Jesus speaks the gracious words."[96] Jesus anticipated their final response and rejection, saying, "Ye will surely say unto me this proverb, Physician, heal thyself: whatsoever we have heard done in Capernaum, do also here in this country. And he said, Verily I say unto you, No prophet is accepted in his own country" (Luke 4:24). In other words, they would request signs and miracles like those He would yet perform in Capernaum, but they would not believe.

The reaction of those in the synagogue changed from amazement to anger when Jesus evoked miracles performed by the ancient Israelite prophets Elijah and Elisha and reminded His listeners that

---

[92] Compare the discussion of Mark 1: 23–26 above.
[93] Compare Plummer, *The Gospel of Luke*, 121; Ringe, *Jesus, Liberation, and the Biblical Jubilee*, 40.
[94] Arndt and Gingrich, GEL, "thaumazō," 444–45. Compare Plummer, *The Gospel of Luke*, 124.
[95] Ringe, *Jesus, Liberation, and the Biblical Jubilee*, 40.
[96] Ringe, *Jesus, Liberation, and the Biblical Jubilee*, 40; cf. Tannehill, "The Mission of Jesus," 53. See Luke 2:48–49.

their wonders were done for non-Israelites (Luke 4:25–27).[97] When the people in the synagogue heard this, they were furious, and they drove Jesus out of the synagogue and to a hill from which they were about to cast Him down to His death. But Jesus escaped, and "passing through the midst of them went his way" (Luke 4:30).[98]

The miracle and meaning of Jesus' escape from the angry crowd are underscored by the context of the Isaiah passage He so recently quoted. His departure recalls the release imagery of the Jubilee text, as those who were intending to kill Him and who seemed to have Him in their power found that He was marvelously freed from their control—not by any outside agent or assistance but of Himself.[99] Jesus' escape identified Him as the liberator described and foretold by Isaiah.

Luke immediately follows the rejection at Nazareth with his account of those events Mark places first: Jesus' removal to Capernaum, His teaching there, and the healing of the demoniac in the Capernaum synagogue, using language very similar to what we find in Mark's Gospel (Luke 4:31–37). Luke's description of the encounter with the possessed man in the synagogue lends itself to an interpretation similar to that put forward in the discussion of the miracle as recounted by Mark. But Luke's version of events in Capernaum takes on added meaning when read in the context of Jesus' earlier appearance in the synagogue at Nazareth. There Jesus cited the Jubilee text, which traditionally brought "a gracious message to those in captivity, promising them release."[100] With this background, we can see that

---

[97] See 1 Kings 17; 2 Kings 5.

[98] For the traditional interpretation of the scene, see Joseph A. Fitzmyer, *The Gospel According to Luke I–IX* (Garden City, New York: Doubleday, 1981), 537; Tannehill, "The Mission of Jesus," 59–62; H. Anderson, "Broadening Horizons: The Rejection at Nazareth Pericope of Luke 4:16–30 in Light of Recent Critical Trends," *Interpretation* 18 (1964): 266–72. Contrast L. C. Crockett, "Luke 4:25–27 and Jewish Gentile Relations in Luke-Acts," *Journal of Biblical Literature* 88 (1969): 177–83. Cf. Ringe, *Jesus, Liberation, and the Biblical Jubilee*, 44.

[99] Plummer, *The Gospel of Luke*, 129, comments that "they had asked for a miracle, and this was the miracle granted to them."

[100] Plummer, *The Gospel of Luke*, 121.

the exorcism of the possessed became an ironic realization of the promise of liberty. When we contemplate the release of a prisoner, we typically imagine the freeing of someone from an external captor or prison. In the exorcism, Jesus drove out the demon that held the man captive from within. The one released from external boundaries was the demonic captor, whereas the one from whom the demon was expelled was the freed captive. This seems to suggest that the essential liberation is not from any earthly bondage but from those demons, real and figurative, that keep men and women in subjection to Satan. With the cleansing of the demoniac, Jesus proved that He can release and redeem each prisoner of sin.

The Gospel of John's Unique Contribution

John's Gospel begins quite differently from any of the synoptic accounts, and his description of the start of Jesus' ministry is likewise unique. John does locate Jesus in Galilee, although it is unclear from John's reconstruction whether Jesus' arrival in Galilee should be understood to mark the beginning of His *public* ministry, as His earliest recorded exchanges there are rather private matters. At this point in John's narrative, we see no indication of Jesus' preaching in the synagogue or appearing in any other public venue, in either Nazareth or Capernaum. In His first recorded act in Galilee, Jesus found Philip and said to him, "Follow me" (John 1:43). This Philip did, announcing to his associate Nathanael what Philip discovered: "We have found him, of whom Moses in the law, and the prophets, did write, Jesus of Nazareth, the son of Joseph" (John 1:45).

Nathanael went with Philip to see Jesus, and when Jesus proved to know and recognize him, having already seen him in vision when Nathanael was sitting under the fig tree, Nathanael declared, "Thou art the Son of God; thou art the King of Israel" (John 1:49). In response, Jesus promised Nathanael that he would see greater things than what he had witnessed thus far (John 1:50). Nathanael's recognition of and wonder at Jesus' true identity did not depend upon the delivery of a powerful sermon or the performance of a powerful miracle—he believed because Jesus knew him, and knew him by revelation, even before their encounter. Jesus' knowledge of Nathanael and Nathanael's faith in Jesus are very personal matters.

John next relates Jesus' attendance at a wedding:

> And the third day there was a marriage in Cana of Galilee; and the mother of Jesus was there: and both Jesus was called, and his disciples, to the marriage. And when they wanted wine, the mother of Jesus saith unto him, They have no wine. Jesus saith unto her, Woman, what have I do to with thee? mine hour is not yet come. His mother saith unto the servants, Whatsoever he saith unto you, do it. And there were set there six waterpots of stone, after the manner of the purifying of the Jews, containing two or three firkins apiece. Jesus saith unto them, Fill the waterpots with water. And they filled them up to the brim. And he saith unto them, Draw out now, and bear unto the governor of the feast. And they bare it. When the ruler of the feast had tasted the water that was made wine, and knew not whence it was: (but the servants which drew the water knew;) the governor of the feast called the bridegroom, and saith unto him, Every man at the beginning doth set forth good wine; and when men have well drunk, then that which is worse: but thou hast kept the good wine until now. This beginning of miracles did Jesus in Cana of Galilee, and manifested forth his glory; and his disciples believed on him. (John 2:1–11)

This is a profoundly important scene in John's Gospel—the moment he chooses to represent what he calls the "beginning of miracles" done by Jesus. Unlike the other evangelists, John does not use the designation *dunamis* (act of power) for *miracle*. Instead, he calls them *ergon* (work) or *sēmeion* (sign). In his description of this scene at the wedding, John uses the term *sēmeion*: "this beginning of *signs* did Jesus" (John 2:11; author's translation). The marvelous transformation of water into wine was thus not exclusively a manifestation of Jesus' power but also a manifestation of His identity.[101] The miracle

---

[101] As Brown, *Introduction*, 340n15, characterizes it, a sign is a miraculous deed "that

performed at the wedding in Cana is in John's report the inaugural sign of Jesus' ministry, the first act to reveal who and what Jesus is.

In Cana, then, Jesus found Himself at a wedding celebration where they had run out of wine. His mother, who apparently had some close connection to the wedding party, pointed out to Jesus that they had no wine. In answer to her observation and her implicit request for His assistance, Jesus said, "Woman, what have I to do with thee? mine hour is not yet come" (John 2:4). Both the tenor and content of the exchange between Jesus and His mother have been adequately discussed by others,[102] but, as Barrett rightly concludes, Mary could not regard her son's response as an outright refusal of her implied request.[103] This is clear from her reaction to His answer. She must have expected some sort of intervention by Jesus, as she advised the servants to do whatever He told them (John 2:5). Jesus, in turn, ordered the servants to fill six water pots, containing more than 120 gallons each, with water. The headwaiter sampled the liquid they newly contained and discovered wine therein—wine of such quality that he was amazed it had not been brought forward earlier in the celebration (John 2:6–10).

Readings and explanations of the wedding in Cana are numerous, including several book-length studies, and it is well beyond the scope of this discussion to consider all the possible interpretations of the scene.[104] Still, as a matter of such primary importance to John's

---

manifest[s] who Jesus is, his purpose, his glory, and/or his relation to the father." Cf. W. Nicol, *The Sēmeia in the Fourth Gospel*, Novum Testamentum Supplements 32 (Leiden: Brill, 1972).

[102] Barrett, *The Gospel According to John*, 191; Brown, *Interpretation*, 340; Paul Gächter, "Maria in Kana," *Zeitschrift für Katholische Theologie* 55 (1931): 351–402; E. J. Kilmartin, "The Mother of Jesus Was There," *Sciences Ecclésiastiques* 15 (1963): 213–26; M. Thirian, *Mary, Mother of All Christians* (New York: Herder & Herder, 1964), especially 117–19.

[103] Barrett, *The Gospel According to John*, 191.

[104] Of the vast bibliography, see, for example, Barrett, *The Gospel According to John*, 153–55; M. E. Boismard, *Du Baptême à Cana* (Paris: Cerf, 1956), 133–59; J. Breuss, *Das Kanawunder: Hermeneutische und Pastorale Überlegungen aufgrund einer Phänomenologischen Analyse von John 2,1–12* (Fribourg: Schweizerisches Katholisches Bibelwerk, 1976); Brown, *The Gospel According to John I–XII*, 97–110; J. P. Charlier, *Le Signe de Cana* (Bruxelles: Pensée Catholique, 1959); J. D. M. Derrett, "Water into Wine," *Biblische*

reconstruction of Jesus' life, we must consider, at least in part, what may be read into the miraculous act at the wedding and John's inclusion of it at this point in his narrative. What are we to make of this water transformed to wine? Of many reasonable and powerful readings of the scene,[105] it is Jesus' act of creation and transformation that is of particular interest in the context of this chapter. The setting is significant in this regard. Marriage is the legal and sacred precursor to the human act of procreation, when husband and wife bring into existence beings completely new in the world. Jesus' transformation of the water into wine is likewise a creative act, bringing into existence something previously unknown. It is thus the appropriate first sign (*sēmeion*) of the Word (*logos*), through whom, according to John, "all things were made" (John 1:3).[106]

Zeitschrift 7 (1963): 80–97; R. J. Dillon, "Wisdom Tradition and Sacramental Retrospect in the Cana Account (John 2:1–11)," *Catholic Biblical Quartely* 24 (1962): 268–96; E. Haible, "Das Gottesbild der Hochzeit von Kana," *Münchener Theologische Zeitschrift* 10 (1959): 189–99; E. Little, *Echoes of the Old Testament in the Wine of Cana in Galilee (John 2:1–11) and the Multiplication of the Loaves and Fish (John 6:1–15): Towards an Appreciation* (Paris: J. Gabalda, 1998); W. Lütgehetmann, *Die Hochzeit von Kana zu Ursprung und Deutung einer Wundererzählung im Rahmen Johanneischer Redaktionsgeschichte* (Regensburg: Friedrich Pustet, 1990); Rudolph Schackenburg, *Das Erste Wunder Jesu* (Freiburg: Herder, 1951).

[105] Brown, *Introduction*, 340, suggests that the wine "represents the revelation and wisdom that [Jesus] brings from God" and the fulfillment of Old Testament "prophecies of abundance of wine in the messianic days." The wine thus provided is evidence that the messianic days have arrived and that Jesus Himself is the Messiah. Barrett, *The Gospel According to John*, 189 and 192, expresses the view that the wine is "meant to show the suppression of Judaism in the glory of Jesus" because "it was Jewish purificatory water which stood in the water pots and was made the wine of the Gospel." In this view, the water in the pots represents the comparative "poverty" of water as a medium for "purification and for the satisfaction of thirst" compared to the rich blessing of the blood of Christ (the wine) for "cleansing . . . and for drink." Cf. Van der Loos, *The Miracles of Jesus*, 610; K. L. Schmidt, *Der Johanneische Charakter der Erzählung vom Hochzeitswunder in Kana* (Leipzig: Harnack-Ehrung, 1921), 40–41; F. F. Bruce, *Second Thoughts on the Dead Sea Scrolls* (Grand Rapids: William B. Eerdmans, 1956), 135. Latter-day Saint analyses of the scene have, for their part, paid particular attention to the miracle as an evidence of Jesus' power over the elements. See Bruce R. McConkie, MM, 1:453–54; Talmage, JTC, 146–49.

[106] Compare Barrett, *The Gospel According to John*, 193.

That the act symbolizes and recalls Jesus' eternal creative role is perhaps underscored by the fact that there are *six* water pots whose contents He changes. Origen saw in the six pots an allusion to the six days of creation, and in Cana, as in the beginning, the creative work was accomplished by the word of God.[107] We may recall the Old Testament language describing the creation: "God said, let there be light, and there was light" (Genesis 1:3). God's word alone was sufficient to create the physical universe, and in His mortal incarnation, Jesus' word alone was sufficient to create the richest wine from mere water.

The making of the wine at the wedding, however, was clearly not an act of creation *ex nihilo*. It was rather a re-creation, a remaking, of something better out of something that was already good. In Cana, Jesus showed His ability to transform the physical world, but the act implies His power also to transform the psychic world. Jesus can, by the power of His word, transform water into wine. As that wine becomes a symbol of His blood, He demonstrates that He can, by the atoning act in which that blood is spilt, transform sinful men into holy ones.

This act symbolizing Jesus' ability to transform a physical substance at its most basic level proclaims His ability to bring about profound spiritual transformation as well. The altered substance was, it must be remembered, hidden in vessels, and the change was not discovered until the headwaiter tested the inner content of those vessels.

This reasoning suggests that the transformation Jesus can effect in His faithful followers is not primarily a change of the outer but rather of the inner, man. As the water in the vessels was made wine, rich and red, it points to the inner man being made new by the blood of Christ, and this critical metamorphosis is bound up with obedience to Jesus' word, for John says that Jesus' mother instructed the servants thus: "Whatsoever he saith unto you, do it" (John 2:5). In response to Jesus' command, the transforming miracle was wrought.

---

[107] Origen, *De Principiis*, 4.2.5. Compare Van der Loos, *The Miracles of Jesus*, 610.

If this episode points to the creation of new, holy men from the substance of sinful ones by the power of Christ's atonement, then John aptly says that this first miracle "manifested forth his glory" (John 2:11), for God's work and glory are, as declared to Moses, "to bring to pass the immortality and eternal life of man" (Moses 1:39). The miracle in Cana thus signifies Jesus' power to accomplish the work of salvation—in the transformation of the water into wine— and the work of exaltation—in the transformation of the water into the *best* wine.

Conclusion

Each of the four evangelists frames his representation of Jesus' ministry with a beginning that anticipates and confirms what that individual evangelist considers central to the content and outcome of that ministry.

Mark represents the call to faith and repentance, an authoritative sermon, and an exorcism in which the Savior's message is realized in a miracle of transformation.

Matthew likewise includes the call to repentance but also lists all the types of miracles done and all the people and places reached by Jesus, highlighting the universal scope of His Gospel and advocating the extension of His blessings to all of God's children.

Luke foreshadows the sorrowful end of Jesus' mortal ministry, but with the implied promise that the Savior's death ultimately brings life and liberty. Luke relies upon the Jubilee text, Jesus' escape from the angry mob in Nazareth, and His healing of the possessed man in Capernaum to give life to the promise implied in Jesus' death.

John, like Mark, relates a miracle of transformation and seeks to announce in Jesus' earliest acts His ability to accomplish the changes He enjoins. Mark's narrative does so with the driving of an evil spirit out of the unnamed man in the synagogue at Capernaum. The first miracle of John's account looks to a result more profound and lasting. In Cana, Jesus does not drive out an invading evil, but he works a *substantive* transformation, for the Savior has the power not just to cleanse us but also to completely remake us. This supernal promise of re-creation that introduces Jesus' ministry is, in fact, the purpose and result of all His work in and beyond His mortal mission.

XI.
THE SETTING OF THE SERMON ON THE MOUNT

FRANK F. JUDD JR.

When Jesus had ended these sayings, the people were astonished at his doctrine: For he taught them as one having authority, and not as the scribes.

MATTHEW 7: 28–29

The Sermon on the Mount is a masterful discourse. Many consider it to be the greatest sermon ever given.[1] On one occasion, Elder Ezra Taft Benson suggested, "Each of us would do well to periodically review [the Savior's] teachings in the Sermon on the Mount so that we are totally familiar with His way."[2] This chapter will discuss certain aspects of the cultural and doctrinal setting of the Sermon on the Mount that will help us better understand the meaning and significance of the sermon.[3]

Brigham Young offered this important insight on scripture study:

---

[1] See Ezra Taft Benson, *Come unto Christ* (Salt Lake City: Deseret Book, 1983), 37; Anthony W. Ivins, in Conference Report, October 1920, 48; Bruce R. McConkie, "Upon This Rock," *Ensign* (May 1981): 75; Thomas S. Monson, "The Way Home," *Ensign* (May 1975): 15; Sterling W. Sill, *That Ye Might Have Life* (Salt Lake City: Deseret Book, 1974), 268, and Joseph Fielding Smith, in Conference Report, October 1941, 95.

[2] Benson, *Come unto Christ*, 37.

[3] For summaries of the history of interpretation of the Sermon on the Mount, see Hans Dieter Betz, *The Sermon on the Mount* (Minneapolis: Fortress Press, 1995), 1–50, and Ulrich Luz, *Matthew 1–7* (Minneapolis: Fortress Press, 1989), 218–23.

"Do you read the scriptures, my brethren and sisters, as though you were writing them a thousand, two thousand, or five thousand years ago? Do you read them as though you stood in the place of the men who wrote them? If you do not feel thus, it is your privilege to do so, that you may be as familiar with the spirit and meaning of the written word of God as you are with your daily walk and conversation."[4] If we are to read the Sermon on the Mount in this way, we will benefit from some basic background information. This orientation will help us to "read them as though [we] stood in the place of the men who wrote them," as Brigham Young encouraged us to do.

Social Context and Matthean Setting

Jesus of Nazareth was not the only Jewish man in Palestine during the first century to gather people around him to demonstrate the purposes of God. Josephus, a first-century Jewish historian, describes certain men who led groups of people onto a mountain or into the wilderness to show miraculous signs that God would soon deliver His people. These kinds of movements were often put down with military force.[5] Also, other men preached messages concerning the imminent judgment or deliverance of God. These types of preachers were likewise not favorably received by the ruling class.[6] Although the Savior also attracted large groups of followers, taught about the future judgments of God, and often encountered opposition, distinct differences are evident between Jesus of Nazareth and these other individuals. Whereas other movements were focused upon popular and physical deliverance from political enemies, the miracles and the message of Jesus were primarily concerned with personal and spiritual healing and our relationship with God through obedience.

According to the Gospel of Matthew, following the imprisonment

---

[4] Brigham Young, in *JD*, 7:333.
[5] For the references, see Richard A. Horsley and John S. Hanson, *Bandits, Prophets, and Messiahs: Popular Movements in the Time of Jesus* (Harrisburg, Pennsylvania: Trinity Press International, 1999), 161–72.
[6] For the references, see Horsley and Hanson, *Bandits, Prophets, and Messiahs*, 172–87.

of John the Baptist, the Savior went to Galilee for the early stages of His ministry.[7] While in Galilee, two sets of brothers—Peter and Andrew as well as James and John—became followers of Jesus, who continued to teach and perform miracles throughout the region of Galilee.[8] Stories about the Savior's wisdom and power spread rapidly: "His fame went throughout all Syria. . . . And there followed him great multitudes of people from Galilee, and from Decapolis, and from Jerusalem, and from Judea, and from beyond Jordan" (Matthew 4:24–25). Because He saw the crowds of people approaching Him, Jesus "went up into a mountain" and gave this wonderful sermon (Matthew 5:1).[9] Thus, the Savior gave the Sermon on the Mount on a mountain in Galilee early in His ministry.[10]

Audience and Purpose

Who was Jesus' audience for the Sermon on the Mount? The opening verse of the sermon gives the impression that Jesus privately addressed the sermon to His disciples and not to the general populace: "Seeing the multitudes, he went up into a mountain: and when he was set, his disciples came unto him" (Matthew 5:1). The Joseph

---

[7] See Matthew 4:12. According to Josephus, John the Baptist was imprisoned and eventually executed at a prison in Machaerus, on the east side of the Dead Sea. See Josephus, AJ, 18.5.2 (§§116–19).

[8] See Matthew 4:18–23.

[9] The area that has become traditionally associated with the place Jesus gave the Sermon on the Mount is located just off the north shore of the Sea of Galilee and is often called the Mount of Beatitudes. See Jerome Murphy-O'Connor, *The Holy Land*, 4th ed. (New York: Oxford University Press, 1998), 277–81, and Jack Finegan, *The Archaeology of the New Testament*, rev. ed. (Princeton: Princeton University Press, 1992), 92–94.

[10] The precise date of the beginning of Jesus' ministry is disputed and is very difficult to ascertain with certainty. The Gospel of Luke says that John the Baptist began baptizing in the fifteenth year of the reign of the Emperor Tiberius (see Luke 3:1). Because Tiberius became emperor following the death of Augustus in approximately A.D. 14, John the Baptist probably began his public ministry sometime between A.D. 28 and 30. Jesus seems to have started His own ministry shortly thereafter. See John P. Meier, *A Marginal Jew: Rethinking the Historical Jesus*, 3 vols. (New York: Doubleday, 1991, 1994, 2001), 1:372–86, and E. P. Sanders, *The Historical Figure of Jesus* (London: Penguin Press, 1993), 282–90.

Smith Translation supports this interpretation,[11] twice affirming that Jesus was addressing His disciples[12] and then concluding the sermon in the same way: "When Jesus had ended these sayings *with his disciples...*" (JST Matthew 7:36; emphasis added).[13]

But the final verse of the sermon also suggests that Jesus' audience included more than just disciples: "When Jesus had ended these sayings, *the people* were astonished at his doctrine" (Matthew 7:28; emphasis added). The Greek word translated as "multitudes" (Matthew 5:1) as well as "people" (Matthew 7:28) in the Gospel of Matthew is *ochlos*, and it consistently refers not to disciples of the Savior but to the various groups of curious onlookers who were present when Jesus preached or performed miracles during His ministry.[14] Thus, while Jesus was teaching His disciples, others were apparently present and heard this wonderful sermon. The Joseph Smith Translation supports this conclusion by explicitly contrasting the two groups: "When Jesus had ended these sayings with *his*

---

[11] John Welch considers the JST of the Sermon on the Mount to be a "third telling of the speech" (the second being the Sermon at the Temple in 3 Nephi 12–14). See John W. Welch, *Illuminating the Sermon at the Temple and the Sermon on the Mount* (Provo, Utah: Foundation for Ancient Research and Mormon Studies, 1999), 31. The approach of this chapter is, however, that the JST is simply additional information about the Sermon on the Mount in Matthew 5–7. Monte Nyman made this important observation: "The JST Sermon on the Mount may differ from the sermon recorded in 3 Nephi because either the sermons were actually slightly different or the Prophet enlarged or improved the JST text to ensure proper understanding. This was the Prophet's prerogative. The original words were understood by the Nephites but needed to be refined for our understanding today." See Monte S. Nyman, *The Most Correct Book* (Salt Lake City: Bookcraft, 1991), 25–26.

[12] See JST Matthew 6:1 and 7:6.

[13] David Yarn noted, "The unity of the Sermon on the Mount is further reinforced if we remember that the Lord was addressing his followers and not a throng of hecklers, unbelievers, and idly curious folk." See David H. Yarn Jr., "The Sermon on the Mount," *Ensign* (December 1972): 55.

[14] For the occurrences of *ochlos* in the Gospel of Matthew, see John R. Kohlenberger III, Edward W. Goodrick, and James A Swanson, *The Exhaustive Concordance to the Greek New Testament* (Grand Rapids: Zondervan, 1995), 4063–64. J. R. C. Cousland concluded that the term *ochlos* is used not for disciples of Jesus but "to refer to the Jewish people as distinguished from their leaders." See J. R. C. Cousland, *The Crowds in the Gospel of Matthew* (Leiden: Brill, 2002), 22 and throughout.

disciples, the people were astonished at his doctrine" (JST Matthew 7:36; emphasis added).[15]

The Joseph Smith Translation also indicates that in the Sermon on the Mount, Jesus instructed His disciples what they should then teach to the people. For example, at the beginning of the Beatitudes in the JST, the Savior blesses His disciples and also "they who shall believe on your words, when ye shall testify that ye have seen me and that I am" (JST Matthew 5:3).[16] Later in the sermon, the JST records that Jesus taught His disciples, "Go ye into the world, saying unto all, Repent, for the kingdom of heaven has come nigh unto you" (JST Matthew 7:9).[17] Using this evidence, some scholars have concluded that the Sermon on the Mount was addressed exclusively to the Twelve who were to testify of Christ and should therefore be considered "apostolic preparation."[18] But a closer look at the evidence reveals that the Sermon on the Mount was intended as preparation for all disciples and not exclusively for Apostles.

Distinct and important differences exist between disciples and Apostles. The word "disciple" is a translation of the Greek *mathētēs*, and it refers to a pupil or apprentice.[19] Hence, "the term 'disciple'

---

[15] Robert Cloward concluded: "The JST makes clear that the Sermon was directed to the disciples, and it was the people who were merely listening who compared his teaching with the scribes and were astonished at his doctrine." Robert A. Cloward, "The Sermon on the Mount in the JST and the Book of Mormon," in *Joseph Smith Translation: The Restoration of Plain and Precious Things* (Provo, Utah: BYU Religious Studies Center, 1985), 167.

[16] In this same JST passage, Jesus also says to His disciples, "Blessed are they who shall believe on your words, and come down into the depth of humility, and be baptized in my name" (JST Matthew 5:2).

[17] See also JST Matthew 7:1, 4, 7, 9.

[18] The term is from Robert L. Millet, "Joseph Smith and the New Testament," *Ensign* (December 1986): 33, and Joseph Fielding McConkie, Robert L. Millet, and Brent L. Top, *Doctrinal Commentary on the Book of Mormon*, 4 vols. (Salt Lake City: Bookcraft, 1987–92), 4:63. Daniel Ludlow also concludes that portions of the Sermon on the Mount were "intended *only* for apostles." See Daniel H. Ludlow, "How to Get the Most from Your Study of the New Testament," in *Selected Writings of Daniel H. Ludlow* (Salt Lake City: Deseret Book, 2000), 77; emphasis in original.

[19] The Greek verb *mathēteuō* means "to be a pupil." See Arndt and Gingrich, *GEL*, 609–10. See also Hans Weder, "Disciple, Discipleship," in Freedman, *ABD*, 2:207.

means one who is accepted by contract to be a student, much as one would become an apprentice in a trade."[20] On the other hand, the term "apostle" is a translation of the Greek *apostolos* and has reference to a delegate or messenger.[21] Thus, the word "apostle" means "someone who is 'sent' and who shares the authority of the one who sends, as his representative."[22]

These comments mean that disciples and Apostles are not necessarily the same. All Apostles are disciples, but not all disciples are Apostles. The Gospel of Luke makes this clear: "When it was day, he called unto him his disciples: and of them he chose twelve, whom *also* he named apostles" (Luke 6:13; emphasis added). The Gospel of Matthew, however, does not normally distinguish between a disciple and an Apostle, often referring to the Twelve Apostles as the twelve disciples,[23] but it does indeed recognize that not all disciples are

---

[20] S. Kent Brown, C. Wilfred Griggs, and Thomas W. Mackay, "Footnotes to the Gospels: The Sermon on the Mount," *Ensign* (January 1975): 30. M. Russell Ballard offered this explanation: "The word disciple comes from the Latin word *discipulus*, meaning 'pupil' and implying learning or knowledge. Many people think that to be a disciple means simply to follow, with an unfortunate connotation of following blindly. Becoming a true disciple is nothing of the sort. It requires us to learn and to know of Jesus Christ, to study the principles of truth for ourselves and to receive answers; in other words, to receive knowledge. Once we have knowledge of the simple principles of the Restoration, coupled with a deep and abiding faith in the truths we do not yet know, we become true disciples of Jesus Christ, and not simply followers." See M. Russell Ballard, "Steadfast in Christ," *Ensign* (December 1993): 51.

[21] The Greek verb *apostellō* means "to dispatch" or "to send." See Arndt and Gingrich, *GEL*, 122. See also Hans Dieter Betz, "Apostle," in Freedman, *ABD*, 1:309, and Robert J. Matthews, *Behold the Messiah* (Salt Lake City: Bookcraft, 1994), 103.

[22] Donald A. Hagner, *Matthew 1–13* (Dallas: Word Books, 1993), 265. In a revelation given to the Prophet Joseph Smith, the Lord stated, "The Twelve Apostles [are] special witnesses of the name of Christ in all the world—thus differing from other officers in the church in the duties of their calling. . . . The Twelve [are] being sent out, holding the keys, to open the door by the proclamation of the gospel of Jesus Christ" (Doctrine and Covenants 107:23, 35). Brigham Young taught, "The calling of an Apostle is to build up the Kingdom of God in all the world; it is the Apostle that holds the keys of this power, and nobody else. If an Apostle magnifies his calling, he is the word of the Lord to his people all the time." See Brigham Young, in *JD*, 6:282. On the responsibilities of an Apostle in general, see Edward J. Brandt, "And He Gave Some, Apostles," *Ensign* (July 1999): 14–19.

[23] See, for example, Matthew 10:1–2; 11:1; 20:17. See also Daniel H. Ludlow, A

Apostles: "When the even was come, there came a rich man of Arimathea, named Joseph, *who also himself was Jesus' disciple*" (Matthew 27:57; emphasis added).[24] Joseph of Arimathaea is called a disciple but is not included on the Matthean list of Apostles.[25] Consequently, when the Gospel of Matthew tells us that the Savior directed the Sermon on the Mount to His disciples, it does not necessarily mean that He was speaking only to his Apostles.[26] Concerning Matthew 5:1, David Hill stated, "The word 'disciples' ... may be more comprehensive in its meaning than the Twelve ... and may denote all those who wished to hear the teacher's instruction."[27]

Robert Cloward concludes that in the Sermon on the Mount, "disciples" refers to the Savior's "newly ordained Twelve Apostles and other faithful followers."[28] But this conclusion needs to be clarified. In the Gospel of Matthew narrative, by the time of the Sermon on the Mount, only four of the Twelve have explicitly become followers of the Savior: Simon Peter, Andrew, James, and

---

Companion to Your Study of the Book of Mormon (Salt Lake City: Deseret Book, 1976), 291, and M. Catherine Thomas, "The Sermon on the Mount: The Sacrifice of the Human Heart," in *Studies in Scripture, Vol. 5: The Gospels*, ed. Kent P. Jackson and Robert L. Millet (Salt Lake City: Deseret Book, 1986), 237.

[24] Note the observation of Robert Cloward: "In Matthew ... the word disciple is ambiguous. The Twelve are called disciples (see Matthew 10:1; 11:1), but the word may also refer to any group of followers such as the disciples of John the Baptist (see KJV Matthew 9:14; 11:2)." See Cloward, "The Sermon on the Mount in the JST and the Book of Mormon," 167.

[25] For the Matthean list of Apostles, see Matthew 10:2–4.

[26] Catherine Thomas concludes that "no teaching in the sermon need be seen as specific to the Twelve only." See Thomas, "The Sermon on the Mount: The Sacrifice of the Human Heart," 237.

[27] David Hill, *The Gospel of Matthew*, New Century Biblical Commentary (Grand Rapids: William B. Eerdmans, 1972), 109. For similar comments, see also W. D. Davies and Dale C. Allison Jr., *The Gospel According to Saint Matthew*, International Critical Commentary, 3 vols. (Edinburgh: T & T Clark, 1988–97), 1:425, and Herman N. Ridderbos, *Matthew* (Grand Rapids: Zondervan, 1987), 86.

[28] Cloward, "The Sermon on the Mount in the JST and the Book of Mormon," 167. Catherine Thomas also concludes that the Sermon on the Mount was directed toward "the newly ordained twelve" as well as toward "that larger group of disciples also present." See Thomas, "The Sermon on the Mount: The Sacrifice of the Human Heart," 237.

John.[29] Significantly, according to the Matthean narrative, Matthew himself had not become a follower of Jesus by the time of the Sermon on the Mount.[30] In the Gospel of Matthew, the Twelve are not even commissioned until chapter 10.[31] So although in the Sermon on the Mount the term "disciple" includes some *who would become* members of the Twelve as well as other faithful followers, it does not strictly refer to the Twelve Apostles. They are not commissioned until later, and at least one of them is not yet a follower of Jesus.

A comparison with the Sermon at the Temple in 3 Nephi 12–14 offers some insights.[32] The Sermon at the Temple is clearly addressed to more than just the Nephite Twelve.[33] "When Jesus had spoken

---

[29] See Matthew 4:18, 21.

[30] See Matthew 9:9.

[31] In the Gospel of Luke, the commission of the Twelve occurs before the Sermon on the Plain (see Luke 6:13–49). The scope of this chapter does not cover the debate over whether the Sermon on the Plain is Luke's version of the Sermon on the Mount or whether it is a different sermon on a different occasion in which the Savior repeated similar teachings to those in the Sermon on the Mount. Bruce R. McConkie prefers the former interpretation, and James E. Talmage and Robert J. Matthews prefer the latter interpretation. This chapter is concerned with the Sermon on the Mount, and according to the Gospel of Matthew narrative, the commission of the Twelve occurs after the sermon. For references to the above interpretations, see Robert J. Matthews, *Behold the Messiah* (Salt Lake City: Bookcraft, 1994), 110, 122; McConkie, *DNTC*, 1:214; McConkie, *MM*, 115, and Talmage, *JTC*, 246–47.

[32] For a side-by-side comparison of the Gospel of Matthew's Sermon on the Mount and the Book of Mormon's Sermon at the Temple, see Jeffrey R. Holland, *Christ and the New Covenant* (Salt Lake City: Deseret Book, 1997), 371–94, and Welch, *Illuminating the Sermon at the Temple and the Sermon on the Mount*, 255–76.

[33] Although the Nephite Twelve are consistently called disciples rather than Apostles, they functioned as Apostles to the Nephites. Concerning this point, Joseph Fielding Smith taught, "While in every instance the Nephite twelve are spoken of as disciples, the fact remains that they had been endowed with divine authority to be special witnesses for Christ among their own people. Therefore, they were virtually apostles to the Nephite race, although their jurisdiction was, as revealed to Nephi, eventually to be subject to the authority and jurisdiction of Peter and the twelve chosen in Palestine. According to the definition prevailing in the world an apostle is a witness for Christ, or one who evangelizes a certain nation or people. 'A zealous advocate of a doctrine or cause.' Therefore the Nephite twelve became apostles, as special witnesses, just as did Joseph Smith and Oliver Cowdery in the Dispensation of the Fulness of Times." See Joseph Fielding Smith, *Answers to Gospel Questions*, 5 vols. (Salt Lake City: Deseret Book, 1957–66), 1:122.

these words unto Nephi, and to those who had been called, (now the number of them who had been called, and received power and authority to baptize, was twelve) and behold, he stretched forth his hand *unto the multitude,* and cried unto them" (3 Nephi 12:1; emphasis added). The Nephite multitude apparently consisted of disciples, or pupils who were discussing and learning about the Savior.[34] "A great multitude gathered together, of the people of Nephi, round about the temple which was in the land Bountiful; and they were marveling and wondering one with another, and were showing one to another the great and marvelous change which had taken place. And they were also conversing about this Jesus Christ, of whom the sign had been given concerning his death" (3 Nephi 11:1–2). These Nephites were disciples indeed and not merely curious onlookers, for the resurrected Savior instructed them to teach the gospel to the rest of the people: "More blessed are they who shall believe in your words because that ye shall testify that ye have seen me, and that ye know that I am" (3 Nephi 12:2).[35] Therefore, it was not merely the Twelve who were commissioned to teach the people.[36]

The majority of the teachings of the Sermon at the Temple, therefore, were directed toward the disciples in general and not only to the

---

[34] They are referred to as "more righteous" than those who had been destroyed during the destruction at Christ's death (3 Nephi 9:13).

[35] 3 Nephi 12:1 seems to suggest that this Nephite multitude was not baptized yet: "Blessed are ye if ye shall believe in me and be baptized, after that ye have seen me and know that I am." We know, however, that Nephi had baptized many Nephites before the destruction (3 Nephi 7:26) and that the "more righteous" of them were spared and survived (3 Nephi 9:13). Joseph Fielding Smith explained, "Nephi was baptized *and so was everybody else* although they had been baptized before. The Church among the Nephites before the coming of Christ was not in its fulness and was under the law of Moses. The Savior restored the fulness and gave to them all the ordinances and blessings of the gospel. Therefore, it actually became a new organization, and through baptism they came into it." See Joseph Fielding Smith, *Answers to Gospel Questions,* 3:205; emphasis added. Thus, these Nephite disciples were already baptized, and the Savior is speaking of rebaptism under the new organization under the gospel of Jesus Christ.

[36] After the resurrected Savior left the Nephites on the first day of His visit, the Nephite disciples immediately spread the word throughout the night so that those who were not present at the Sermon at the Temple could arrive in time to see the Lord the next day. See 3 Nephi 19:1–3.

Nephite Twelve. This point becomes very apparent in the middle of the Sermon at the Temple when the Savior, in fact, changes His audience: "When Jesus had spoken these words he looked upon the twelve whom he had chosen, and said unto them . . ." (3 Nephi 13:25). Then, Jesus taught the Nephite Twelve to "take no thought for the morrow" (13:34) concerning "your life, what ye shall eat, or what ye shall drink; nor yet for your body, what ye shall put on" (13:25) because "heavenly Father knoweth that ye have need of all these things" (13:32). The Savior's admonition to the Nephite Twelve was "seek ye first the kingdom of God and his righteousness, and all these things shall be added unto you" (13:33). The text then informs us, "When Jesus had spoken these words he *turned again to the multitude*, and did open his mouth unto them" (14:1; emphasis added). In the Sermon at the Temple, the verses in 3 Nephi 13:25–34 are the only verses directed exclusively to the Twelve.[37]

In summary, the entirety of the Sermon on the Mount was directed toward the "disciples," with a "multitude" of others apparently within earshot, whereas the Sermon at the Temple was directed toward all disciples generally, with the exception of a few verses that were directed toward the Twelve specifically.[38] Thus, we would not be quite accurate in calling the Sermon on the Mount "apostolic preparation" as some have suggested. Though it contains important instructions for Apostles, it is more generally "missionary preparation" than primarily "apostolic preparation."[39]

---

[37] We should note that neither the Sermon on the Mount nor the JST contains this change of audience in the middle of the sermon. See Matthew 6:25–34. Consider the conclusion of Catherine Thomas: "No teaching in the sermon need be seen as specific to the Twelve only." See Thomas, "The Sermon on the Mount: The Sacrifice of the Human Heart," 237. Therefore, the Savior probably felt those particular teachings were appropriate for those who preach the gospel, whether Apostle or general disciple.

[38] See Cloward, "The Sermon on the Mount in the JST and the Book of Mormon," 168.

[39] The phrase "missionary preparation" is from Catherine Thomas, "The Sermon on the Mount: The Sacrifice of the Human Heart," 237. Robert Cloward also concluded that "Jesus was training missionaries in the Sermon on the Mount" and called it a "missionary training sermon." See Robert A. Cloward, "The Savior's Missionary Training Sermon in 3 Nephi," in Monte S. Nyman and Charles D. Tate Jr., eds., *Third*

Astonishment

The last verse of the sermon raises another issue: "When Jesus had ended these sayings with his disciples, *the people were astonished* at his doctrine" (JST Matthew 7:36; emphasis added). What was it that caused the people to be "astonished"?[40] The Greek verb *ekplēssō* carries the meaning of being "filled with amazement to the point of being overwhelmed."[41] The word is used numerous times in the Gospels to describe reactions to Jesus. Careful consideration of these instances helps us understand why various groups of people were astonished at Jesus, which in turn allows us to deduce why the people would have been astonished at Jesus at the conclusion of the Sermon on the Mount.

One of the few references to Jesus as an adolescent informs us that when Jesus interacted with the learned doctors at the temple, "all that heard him were astonished at his understanding and answers" (Luke 2:47). The Gospel of Luke tells us that the young Jesus was "hearing them [the doctors], and asking them questions" (Luke 2:46). It is noteworthy that the Joseph Smith Translation changes this to "they [the doctors] were hearing *him*, and asking *him* questions" (JST Luke 2:46; emphasis added). Thus, the JST emphasizes that it was not merely Jesus' questions but His answers—His teachings—that filled people with amazement.[42]

After the beginning of Jesus' ministry, we learn that when He visited His hometown of Nazareth, "he began to teach in the synagogue:

Nephi 9–30: This Is My Gospel (Provo: BYU Religious Studies Center, 1993), 128 and throughout.

[40] Elder Marvin J. Ashton observed, "Those who saw and heard Him were not only astonished, but frightened, bewildered, and amazed as well in His life and performances. They were inclined to talk among themselves about His unusual skills, conduct, and background." See Marvin J. Ashton, "Come and See," *New Era* (December 1989): 4.

[41] Arndt and Gingrich, GEL, 308.

[42] Concerning this, Robert J. Matthews observed: "This clarification is necessary in order to make the event newsworthy. There is nothing essentially divine for a twelve-year-old boy to listen to his elders. But to be able to teach them and astound them in the knowledge of the scriptures is an event worth reporting." See Robert J. Matthews, "A Greater Portrayal of the Master," *Ensign* (March 1983): 9.

and many hearing him were astonished" (Mark 6:2).[43] But what was it that astonished His audiences? The Gospel of Luke tells us that crowds in Capernaum "were astonished at his doctrine: for *his word was with power*" (Luke 4:32; emphasis added).[44] This type of power is aptly illustrated by an incident in the Gospel of John. When soldiers sought Jesus in the Garden of Gethsemane, Jesus responded, "I am he" (John 18:5). The text reports that "as soon then as he had said unto them, I am he, they went backward, and fell to the ground" (John 18:6).

Yet it was not merely the words that came out of the Savior's mouth that exhibited power and resulted in astonishment. The Gospel of Matthew records concerning Jesus' teaching about the resurrection of the dead that "when the multitude heard this, they were astonished at his doctrine" (Matthew 22:33). The Joseph Smith Translation redirects the reference concerning the source of the astonishment: "When the multitude heard *him*, they were astonished at his doctrine" (JST Matthew 22:32; emphasis added). This wording seems to emphasize that there was something about the Savior Himself, as well as His words, that caused the people to be astonished. After the Savior healed a deaf man with a speech impediment, those who were present at the time of the miracle "were beyond measure astonished, saying, He hath done all things well: he maketh both the deaf to hear, and the dumb to speak" (Mark 7:37). On another occasion, Jesus healed a man possessed with an evil spirit. Those who witnessed this miracle "were all amazed at the mighty power of God" (Luke 9:43).

These references indicate that it was the power of Jesus Himself, as well as of His teachings, that filled people with amazement.[45] Elder

---

[43] The JST clarifies this by adding "and many hearing him were astonished *at his words*" (JST Mark 6:2; emphasis added). For other references to people being generally astonished at the teachings of Jesus, see Matthew 13:54; 19:25; 22:33; Mark 10:26; 11:18.

[44] See also Mark 1:22. Note also that in JST Luke 4:32, "his word was with power" (Luke 4:33) becomes "his *words were* with power" (emphasis added).

[45] A connection seems apparent among witnessing powerful deeds, learning true

James E. Talmage observed, "Many of those who were so signally privileged and blessed as to personally hear the Master were astonished at His doctrine and deeply moved by the simple and convincing presentation.... Our Lord was qualified to teach as He did, not only by reason of the sufficing fact that He bore the Father's commission, but because He had done and was doing just what He required of others. The authority of Divine precept was united in Him with that of unimpeachable example. The burden of all scriptural direction relating to the attainment of a place in the Kingdom of God is: Do the works that are prescribed."[46]

Authoritative Teaching

But an additional reason for the astonishment of the crowds has to do with the authority to which the Savior appealed for His teaching. The law of Moses was "the divinely revealed law that governed the house of Israel from the time of Moses until the atonement of Jesus Christ."[47] The commandments of the law of Moses were written down and are contained in the Old Testament books of Exodus, Leviticus, Numbers, and Deuteronomy. At the time of the Savior, the law of Moses had been the law of the land for Jews in Palestine for more than a thousand years and was revered as the ultimate authority on the will of God concerning His people.[48]

The Gospel of Matthew specifically says that when Jesus concluded the Sermon on the Mount, "the people were astonished at his doctrine: *for he taught them as one having authority, and not as the scribes*"

---

doctrine, and exhibiting astonishment. In other words, deeds can teach and then astonish. When Paul showed forth the power of God by temporarily blinding the sorcerer Elymas, the proconsul Sergius Paulus "was amazed *at the teaching* of the Lord" (Acts 13:12; emphasis added). See also Mark 1:27.

[46] James E. Talmage, *The Vitality of Mormonism* (Boston: Gorham Press, 1919), 283.

[47] Kent P. Jackson, "Law of Moses," in Dennis L. Largey, ed., *Book of Mormon Reference Companion* (Salt Lake City: Deseret Book, 2003), 504.

[48] See the early Jewish references in Stephen E. Robinson, "The Law after Christ," *Ensign* (September 1983): 69–70. A similar reverence seems to have existed among some Nephites in the New World. The priests of Noah taught that salvation came by keeping the law of Moses (Mosiah 12:31–32).

(Matthew 7:28–29; emphasis added). Georg Strecker describes the difference between the teaching of the scribes and of Jesus as follows: "Different from the Jewish scribes, the Son of God does not formulate his instruction in connection with and as interpretations of inherited doctrinal opinions."[49] These "inherited doctrinal opinions" were a body of oral traditions (also called the oral law) that developed after the time of Moses and to which many Jews looked for answers about the written law of Moses and its application to daily living.[50] The New Testament sometimes refers to this oral law as the "tradition of the elders."[51]

An early Jewish document entitled *Pirke Aboth* (Sayings of the Fathers) reveals how some Jews explained the origin of the oral law: "Moses received the [oral] Torah[52] on Sinai, and handed it down to Joshua; Joshua to the elders; the elders to the prophets; and the prophets handed it down to the Men of the Great Assembly. They said three things: Be deliberate in judgment; raise up many disciples; and *make a fence round the Torah*" (*Pirke Aboth* 1.1; emphasis added).[53] To "make a fence round the Torah" means to create specific legislation that, when obeyed, would prevent a person from breaking the written law of Moses. Thus, at least in theory, the oral law was intended to prevent *breaking* commandments rather than to prevent *keeping* commandments.[54] For example, the written law of Moses

---

[49] Georg Strecker, *The Sermon on the Mount: An Exegetical Commentary* (Nashville: Abingdon Press, 1988), 173.

[50] Note the assessment of Francis Wright Beare: "Such authority as the scribes exercised rested upon their knowledge of the law of Moses, and especially on the traditional interpretations of its provisions given by their predecessors, which constituted the 'oral law.'" See Francis Wright Beare, *The Gospel According to Matthew* (San Francisco: Harper & Row, 1981), 200.

[51] See Matthew 15:2 and Mark 7:3, 5.

[52] The Hebrew word *torah* is normally translated as "law." Herbert Danby concludes that this particular instance of the term *torah* is a reference to the oral law rather than to the written law of Moses. See Herbert Danby, *The Mishnah* (Oxford: Oxford University Press, 1933), 446n2.

[53] The second use of the word *torah* has reference to the written law of Moses. The translation is from Joseph H. Hertz, *Sayings of the Fathers* (New York: Behrman House, 1945), 13–15.

[54] Of the instances where the oral law is mentioned in the New Testament, most are

states, "Remember the sabbath day, to keep it holy. Six days shalt thou labour, and do all thy work: But the seventh day is the sabbath of the Lord thy God: in it thou shalt not do any work" (Exodus 20:8–10). But what constitutes work? The written law of Moses prohibits work but does not always define it precisely. The oral law, however, specifically explains what constitutes work.[55] Though the written law does not allow a person to "go out of his place on the seventh day" (Exodus 16:29), Jewish oral tradition explains how far a person can walk on the Sabbath (that is, a "sabbath day's journey")[56] before he is considered to have gone "out of his place."[57] As Stephen E. Robinson has observed, these oral traditions "were attempts of later teachers to 'fine tune' the Law of Moses."[58]

When questions arose about scriptural interpretation and religious practices, Jewish teachers (that is, scribes) appealed to this body of oral tradition for answers and protested when the disciples of Jesus did not follow these guidelines.[59] For example, on one occasion, Jesus

---

negative. For example, in Mark 7:10–13, Jesus condemns the *corban* tradition that allowed individuals to dedicate their property or inheritance to God, thus depriving their elderly parents of needed temporal support. Jesus rightly viewed this application of the oral tradition as giving license to breaking the command to "honor thy father and thy mother" (Exodus 20:12). It must be remembered, however, that the underlying intent of these traditions, as expressed in *Pirke Aboth*, was nonetheless honorable, even if some of the traditions may have been misguided.

[55] Some of the oral traditions were later written down and compiled in a collection called the *Mishnah*. The *Mishnah* tractate *Shabbath* lists thirty-nine "main classes of work" (*Shabbath* 7.2). See Danby, *The Mishnah*, 106.

[56] Acts 1:12. In this light, note the warning of the Savior: "Pray ye that your flight be not in the winter, neither on the sabbath day" (Matthew 24:20).

[57] The tradition seems to be that a "sabbath day's journey" was two thousand cubits, or approximately a thousand yards, beyond the walls of the city. According to Exodus 16:29, the Lord informed each Israelite not to "go out of his place on the seventh day." This two-thousand-cubit limit seems to have been derived from Numbers 35:5, which states that this was the distance outside the city walls of Levitical cities to be considered the suburbs of the city. According to Acts 1:12, Jerusalem was a Sabbath's day journey from the Mount of Olives. On this matter, see Lawrence H. Schiffman, "Sabbath's Day Journey," in *Harper's Bible Dictionary*, ed. Paul J. Achtemeier, rev. ed. (New York: HarperCollins, 1996), 955.

[58] Robinson, "The Law after Christ," 69.

[59] See Brown, Griggs, and Mackay, "Footnotes to the Gospels: The Sermon on the Mount," 31.

and His disciples were walking through some wheat fields on the Sabbath and plucking handfuls of the grain.[60] Some Pharisees objected, saying, "Why do they on the Sabbath day that which is not lawful?" (Mark 2:24). The written law of Moses prohibits plowing and harvesting on the Sabbath: "Six days shalt thou work, but on the seventh day thou shalt rest: in earing time and in harvest thou shalt rest" (Exodus 34:21).[61] But what is considered plowing and harvesting? The Pharisees were appealing to an oral tradition that interpreted plucking grain with one's hands to be harvesting grain.[62] There are a number of examples of these kinds of traditional prohibitions. For instance, Philo, a first-century Jewish philosopher, taught concerning Sabbath observance, "It is not permitted to cut any shoot or branch, or even a leaf, or to pluck any fruit whatsoever" (Philo, *Life of Moses*, 2.22).[63] The New Testament contains other instances of conflicts between Jesus and Jewish teachers concerning the oral law's authority to interpret the prohibitions contained in the written law of Moses.[64]

The Savior cites another Jewish tradition: "Ye have heard that it hath been said, Thou shalt love thy neighbor, and hate thine enemy" (Matthew 5:43). The written law certainly taught, "Thou shalt love thy neighbor as thyself" (Leviticus 19:18). But the written law never

---

[60] See Mark 2:23. In the KJV, "corn" and "ears of corn" in this verse are translations of the Greek words *sporimos* and *stachus*. More accurate translations are "grain field" and "heads of grain." See Arndt and Gingrich, GEL, 939 and 941–42.

[61] The KJV phrase "earing time" is a translation of the Hebrew word ḥārîš, which means "plowing time." See Francis Brown, S. R. Driver, and Charles A. Briggs, *A Hebrew and English Lexicon of the Old Testament* (Oxford: Clarendon Press, 1951), 361.

[62] Note the comment of Bruce R. McConkie: "Their act violated, not the Mosaic law forbidding servile work on the Sabbath, but the rabbinical interpretations prevailing. . . . To rub ears of grain together in the hands was considered to be threshing, to blow away the chaff, winnowing." See McConkie, DNTC, 1:204.

[63] See also Jerusalem Talmud, *Shabbath*, 9c: "Plucking is reaping," and *Jubilees* 2.29: "They should not prepare on the Sabbath anything which will be eaten or drunk, which they have not prepared for themselves on the sixth day." For these and other references, see Davies and Allison, *The Gospel According to Saint Matthew*, 2:307. The Mishnah prohibits "plowing," "reaping," "threshing," and "winnowing" on the Sabbath (Mishnah, *Shabbath* 7.2). See Danby, *The Mishnah*, 106.

[64] See Mark 7:5; 2:18–20.

dictated hating one's enemy. This directive seems to have been part of the oral tradition of at least some Jews.[65] The Essenes, who likely prepared the Dead Sea Scrolls, taught their adherents, "Love all the sons of light . . . and hate all the sons of darkness" (1QS 1.10–11).[66] The Savior did not agree with this traditional perspective and taught instead the exact opposite: "But I say unto you, Love your enemies, bless them that curse you, do good to them that hate you, and pray for them which despitefully use you, and persecute you" (Matthew 5:44). D. A. Carson concluded, "The teachers of the law taught derivatively, that is, by referring to the authorities. But Jesus taught with his own authority."[67] Thus, real authority lay in the declarations of the Savior Himself rather than in the unreliable assertions of tradition.

Concerning the Sermon on the Mount, John Meier observes that the crowds "are astonished not at *what* he says but *how* he says it."[68] Jesus did not appeal to oral tradition for answers; rather, He spoke with unprecedented authority.[69] Whereas the scribes would have responded with, "Our tradition says . . . ," Jesus responded with "I say unto you . . . !" Robert A. Guelich explains, "Jesus never used the familiar prophetic formula of 'Thus saith the Lord,' did not simply stay with general proverbial platitudes as found in Wisdom teaching, made no reference to the tradition or the Law in a fashion of the scribes; rather, he taught *as one who had authority.*"[70]

One might be tempted to say that Jesus was replacing the oral

---

[65] On this issue, see Larry E. Dahl, "The Higher Law," *Ensign* (February 1991): 10.

[66] The translation is from Geza Vermes, *The Complete Dead Sea Scrolls in English* (New York: The Penguin Press, 1997), 99.

[67] D. A. Carson, *The Sermon on the Mount: An Evangelical Exposition of Matthew 5–7* (Grand Rapids: Baker, 1978), 135. See also Thomas, "The Sermon on the Mount: The Sacrifice of the Human Heart," 250.

[68] John P. Meier, *Matthew* (Wilmington: Michael Glazier, 1980), 76.

[69] As Herman Hendrickx noted, "He does not speak as one who merely explains or passes on the tradition." See Herman Hendrickx, *The Sermon on the Mount*, rev. ed. (London: Geoffrey Chapman, 1984), 176.

[70] Robert A. Guelich, *The Sermon on the Mount: A Foundation for Understanding* (Waco: Word Books, 1982), 418; emphasis in original. For similar comments, see also Robert H. Gundry, *Matthew: A Commentary on His Literary and Theological Art* (Grand Rapids: William B. Eerdmans, 1982), 137, and Ridderbos, *Matthew*, 157.

tradition of Jewish teachers with His own oral tradition. After all, both the declarations of oral tradition and of Jesus built a "fence" around the law of Moses in the sense that, if followed, they both prevented breaking the core commandments. But there is a key difference, for while the oral law contained the traditions of human wisdom, the declarations of Jesus were a revelation from God.[71] Thus, the Joseph Smith Translation appropriately clarifies the source of Jesus' authoritative teachings: "He taught them as one having authority *from God*, and not *as having authority from* the scribes" (JST Matthew 7:37; emphasis added).[72]

Fulfillment of the Law

Jesus' authoritative expressions concerning the *written* law also filled His audience with awe. Because the law of Moses was considered of utmost importance and sacredness, one of the most offensive elements of the new Christian movement, in the eyes of many Jews, was the scandal that Jesus would dare to "change the customs which Moses delivered us" (Acts 6:14).[73] What was the Savior's real attitude toward the law of Moses?

At the beginning of the Sermon on the Mount, Jesus declared, "Think not that I am come to destroy the law, or the prophets: I am not come to destroy, but to fulfil" (Matthew 5:17). In this respect, we must remember that the sacrifices of animals were not symbolic of the *birth* of Jesus but rather of His *death*.[74] This interpretation means that

---

[71] See Robert L. Millet, "Looking beyond the Mark: Why Many Did Not Accept the Messiah," *Ensign* (July 1987): 62, and Robert L. Millet, "Joseph Smith and the New Testament," *Ensign* (December 1986): 33.

[72] The irony of this statement is that Jesus, as Jehovah, was God. When the resurrected Christ visited the Nephites, He declared, "I am he that gave the law, and I am he who covenanted with my people Israel" (3 Nephi 15:5).

[73] See also Acts 6:11–14; 11:1–2; 15:1–2.

[74] This is something many Nephites misunderstood. After the sign of Christ's birth was given, some Nephites attempted "to prove by the scriptures that it was no more expedient to observe the law of Moses. Now in this thing they did err, having not understood the scriptures" (3 Nephi 1:24). Eventually, these Nephites "were convinced of the error which they were in, for it was made known unto them that the law was not fulfilled in every whit" (3 Nephi 1:25).

"fulfillment" of the law of Moses was not to happen during the mortal ministry of the Savior but after His crucifixion. Consequently, during His mortal ministry, Jesus supported full compliance with the written law of Moses. For example, after Jesus healed a man afflicted with leprosy, He instructed the man, "Go thy way, shew thyself to the priest, and offer for thy cleansing those things which Moses commanded, for a testimony unto them" (Mark 1:44). Jesus was referring to the requirements in Leviticus for those who had been cured of leprosy so they might be restored to a state of ritual cleanliness.[75] Consequently, the Savior taught in the Sermon on the Mount concerning the written law, "Till heaven and earth pass, one jot or one tittle shall in no wise pass from the law, till all be fulfilled. Whosoever therefore shall break one of these least commandments, and shall teach men so, he shall be called the least in the kingdom of heaven: but whosoever shall do and teach them, the same shall be called great in the kingdom of heaven" (Matthew 5:18–19).

But what did Jesus mean when He stated that the law of Moses would be "fulfilled"? To answer this question, we must realize that there was a difference between the "fulfillment" of the sacrificial portions of the law and the "fulfillment" of the ethical portions of the law. Ritual aspects of the law would be "fulfilled" in the sense that they would cease once the events toward which they pointed actually occurred. As Amulek taught, "It is expedient that there should be a great and last sacrifice, and then shall there be, or it is expedient there should be, a stop to the shedding of blood; then shall the law of Moses be fulfilled; yea, it shall be all fulfilled, every jot and tittle, and none shall have passed away. And behold, this is the whole meaning of the law, every whit pointing to that great and last sacrifice; and that great and last sacrifice will be the Son of God, yea, infinite and eternal" (Alma 34:13–14).[76]

---

[75] See Leviticus 13–14. On leprosy in general, see David P. Wright and Richard N. Jones, "Leprosy," in Freedman, *ABD*, 4:277–82.

[76] See also Alma 25:15: The Nephites "did keep the law of Moses; for it was expedient that they should keep the law of Moses as yet, for it was not all fulfilled . . . believing that they must keep those outward performances until the time that he should be

The moral teachings contained in the law, however, were fulfilled in a different manner. Certainly, prohibitions such as those against adultery and murder were not lifted after the Savior's crucifixion. Jesus did not teach, "You have heard that it was said, 'Thou shalt not *murder* or *commit adultery.*' But I say unto you, 'Thou shalt!'" These commandments in the law of Moses are not done away; adultery and murder are still prohibited. As Jesus said, "Think not that I have come to destroy the law" (Matthew 5:17). Rather than being destroyed, these ethical obligations were raised to a higher level. W. D. Davies concludes, "We cannot speak of the Law being annulled in the antitheses, but only of its being intensified in its demand, or reinterpreted in a higher key."[77]

The ethical demands of the law of Moses were intensified in a specific way. Whereas the Mosaic law was primarily concerned with outward actions like committing adultery or murder, the fulfilled law or new law of the gospel is concerned also with inward intents of the heart, such as lustful thoughts and anger toward others.[78] In the Joseph Smith Translation, Jesus summarized this new and more stringent understanding: "I give unto you a commandment that ye *suffer none of these things to enter into your heart*" (JST Matthew 5:31; emphasis added).[79] Thus, if a person does not think bad things, he or she will be much less likely to do bad things. President Gordon B. Hinckley has summarized this concept: "Unclean thoughts lead to

---

revealed unto them." After His resurrection, the Savior taught the Nephites: "In me is the law of Moses fulfilled. . . . And ye shall offer up unto me no more the shedding of blood; yea, your sacrifices and your burnt offerings shall be done away, for I will accept none of your sacrifices and your burnt offerings" (3 Nephi 9:17, 19).

[77] W. D. Davies, *The Sermon on the Mount* (Cambridge: Cambridge University Press, 1966), 29. Marion D. Hanks stated that the Savior "wanted those who were the salt of the earth, the light of the world, to rise to nobler heights than the old law had required." See Marion D. Hanks, "The Royal Law," *Ensign* (May 1992): 10.

[78] Note the assessment of Catherine Thomas: "Where the *outward act* of murder was earlier forbidden, now the *inner state* of anger, of contempt, of condemnation, of mocking one's brother was proscribed." See Thomas, "The Sermon on the Mount: The Sacrifice of the Human Heart," 243; emphasis added.

[79] See also 3 Nephi 12:29.

unclean acts."[80] A direct link exists among the thoughts of our heart, our actions, and our very essence as people. Elder Joseph B. Wirthlin has taught, "All evils to which so many become addicted begin in the mind and in the way one thinks. Experience teaches that when the will and imagination are in conflict, the imagination usually wins. What we imagine may defeat our reason and make us slaves to what we taste, see, hear, smell, and feel in the mind's eye. The body is indeed the servant of the mind."[81] In other words, "thoughts lead to acts, acts lead to habits, habits lead to character—and our character will determine our eternal destiny."[82] These insights highlight the importance of the Savior's command that we "suffer none of these things to enter into [our] heart." As the writer of Proverbs declared, "As he thinketh in his heart, so is he" (Proverbs 23:7).[83]

But how is this intensification of the commands in the law of Moses considered a "fulfillment"? Jesus clearly stated, "I am not come to destroy, but to fulfil" (Matthew 5:17). The Greek verb translated as "to fulfill" is *plēroō*, and it carries a number of similar meanings, including "to make full" and "to complete."[84] The divine teachings of the Savior in the Sermon on the Mount "make full" or "complete" the moral requirements within the law of Moses. Various scholars have described how this is so.[85] Stephen E. Robinson summarizes, "The demand of the Law of Moses has been expanded, has been *filled* to its *fullest* extent. Where there is no hatred or greed, there can be

---

[80] Gordon B. Hinckley, "Be Ye Clean," *Ensign* (May 1996): 48. See also Gordon B. Hinckley, "Stand True and Faithful," *Ensign* (May 1996): 92. David O. McKay taught, "Every action is preceded by a thought. If we want to control our actions, we must control our thinking." See David O. McKay, quoted in Thomas S. Monson, "That We May Touch Heaven," *Ensign* (November 1990): 47.

[81] Joseph B. Wirthlin, "Pondering Strengthens the Spiritual Life," *Ensign* (May 1982): 24.

[82] Ezra Taft Benson, "Think on Christ," *Ensign* (March 1989): 2.

[83] David O. McKay taught, "Tell me what you think about when you do not have to think, and I will tell you what you are." See David O. McKay, *Gospel Ideals*, 401.

[84] See Arndt and Gingrich, *GEL*, 827–29.

[85] For summaries of the interpretations of this concept, see Guelich, *The Sermon on the Mount*, 138–42, and Roland H. Worth, *The Sermon on the Mount: Its Old Testament Roots* (New York: Paulist Press, 1997), 20–30.

no murder; where there is no lust, there can be no adultery. With the coming of Christ, the ethical portion of the Law had not been abolished; it had been caught up by, included in, and expanded to a broader application—its intention, its potential as an ethical standard, had been *fulfilled*."[86] Thus, we might say that in the Sermon on the Mount, Jesus taught the most complete or full understanding of the intent of the moral obligations of the law of Moses.[87]

Conclusion

The Sermon on the Mount was addressed to all disciples of Jesus. The teachings of the Savior contained in this wonderful sermon are for the benefit of Apostles as well as new converts, all of whom should in turn teach them to others. Before the coming of Jesus Christ, the law of Moses was the will of God for His people. The prophet Mormon said that prior to the resurrected Savior's visit among the Nephites, they "did keep the law of Moses; for it was expedient that they should keep the law of Moses as yet, for it was not all fulfilled . . . believing that they must keep those outward performances until the time that [Jesus Christ] should be revealed unto them" (Alma 25:15). But as Abinadi taught the Nephites, "The time shall come when it shall no more be expedient to keep the law of Moses" (Mosiah 13:27). The lesson is that when God gives His people new commandments, new revelation takes precedence over past revelation.[88] Unfortunately, some who heard the new revelations of the

---

[86] Robinson, "The Law after Christ," 71; emphasis in original.

[87] See Davies, *The Sermon on the Mount*, 30, and Floyd V. Filson, *A Commentary on the Gospel According to St. Matthew*, Black's New Testament Commentary (London: A & C Black, 1960), 83. Note the conclusion of Marion D. Hanks: "[The Savior] fitted those teachings [of the law of Moses] into the higher and holier context of the law of love he had come to invoke among God's children." See Hanks, "The Royal Law," 10.

[88] John Taylor taught, "Adam's revelation did not instruct Noah to build his ark; nor did Noah's revelation tell Lot to forsake Sodom; nor did either of these speak of the departure of the children of Israel from Egypt. These all had revelations for themselves, and so had Isaiah, Jeremiah, Ezekiel, Jesus, Peter, Paul, John, and Joseph. And so must we, or we shall make a shipwreck." See John Taylor, *Millennial Star* (1 November 1847): 323. Note also the conclusion of Bruce R. McConkie: "There is, of course, no salvation in believing in a dead prophet and stopping there. A living prophet must be found, first,

Savior did not embrace them, preferring to hold on to traditions and revelations of the past.[89]

Because past revelations are written in scripture, another important lesson is that "the written Law and God's will [are] not always identical, and that the will of God expressed in revelation always [has] precedence over the written Law."[90] This is the lesson that Nephi learned. The written law of Moses clearly stated, "Thou shalt not kill" (Exodus 20:13), but the Spirit of the Lord instructed Nephi to kill Laban.[91] After initially hesitating, Nephi determined to "obey the voice of the Spirit" (1 Nephi 4:18). As disciples of Christ, we must also learn to be obedient to the current will of God, whatever it might be.[92]

Elder Dallin H. Oaks explained, "What makes us different from most other Christians in the way we read and use the Bible and other scriptures is our belief in continuing revelation. For us, the scriptures are not the ultimate source of knowledge, but what precedes the ultimate source. The ultimate knowledge comes by revelation . . . through those we sustain as prophets, seers, and revelators."[93] In the Sermon on the Mount, Christ gave His ancient disciples new revelation to interpret (in the case of the ethical portions of the law of Moses) and to supersede (in the case of the ritual portions of the law

---

to interpret God's word in terms of today." See McConkie, *DNTC*, 1:621.

[89] Bruce R. McConkie observed: "For nearly 1,500 years righteous Israelites had sought salvation through conformity to the laws and ordinances revealed by Moses and the prophets. Now those among whom Jesus ministered erroneously assumed that the preaching of the ancients and the powers of past prophets were sufficient to give them a hope of eternal life." See McConkie, *DNTC*, 1:506.

[90] Robinson, "The Law after Christ," 70.

[91] See 1 Nephi 4:10–18.

[92] Joseph Smith explained, "God said, 'Thou shalt not kill;' at another time He said, 'Thou shalt utterly destroy.' This is the principle on which the government of heaven is conducted—by revelation adapted to the circumstances in which the children of the kingdom are placed. Whatever God requires is right, no matter what it is, although we may not see the reason thereof till long after the events transpire." See Smith, *TPJS*, 256.

[93] Dallin H. Oaks, "Scripture Reading and Revelation," *Ensign* (January 1995): 7. Bruce R. McConkie taught, "There is no salvation in reading the Bible and stopping there. People must find a living oracle." See Bruce R. McConkie, in Conference Report, October 1949, 78.

of Moses) previous written scripture. In our day as well, Jesus Christ gives His modern disciples new revelation through His living prophets to explain and sometimes to replace previous directives.[94]

Applying the original counsel of Brigham Young, disciples of Christ should strive to read the Sermon on the Mount as though they were present when the Savior originally taught these words.[95] Even if they have read the Sermon on the Mount many times before, modern disciples can feel the power of the Savior and the authority of His teachings whenever they study this wonderful sermon. As latter-day disciples, we can feel the same astonishment that those first disciples experienced when we encounter this sermon and embrace the challenge to live a higher standard of righteousness. If we will do these things, we will realize that "if we will only hearken to those teachings, we may come back again into the presence of God, the Father, and His Son Jesus Christ."[96]

---

[94] In a revelation to the Prophet Joseph Smith, the Lord stated: "What I the Lord have spoken, I have spoken. . . . Whether by mine own voice or the voice of my servants, it is the same" (Doctrine and Covenants 1:38).

[95] Recall the statement by Brigham Young: "Do you read the scriptures, my brethren and sisters, as though you were writing them a thousand, two thousand, or five thousand years ago? Do you read them as though you stood in the place of the men who wrote them? If you do not feel thus, it is your privilege to do so, that you may be as familiar with the spirit and meaning of the written word of God as you are with your daily walk and conversation." See Young, in *JD*, 7:333.

[96] Joseph Fielding Smith, in Conference Report, October 1941, 95.

XII.
A READING OF THE SERMON ON THE MOUNT: A RESTORATION PERSPECTIVE

ANDREW C. SKINNER

Think not that I am come to destroy the law, or the prophets: I am not come to destroy, but to fulfil.

MATTHEW 5:17

Human expression cannot fully capture the meaning and significance of the Sermon on the Mount. One of the greatest and most profound of all of our Lord's discourses, the Sermon on the Mount was and is many things, reflecting truth as a multifaceted diamond reflects light.

The Sermon signaled the inauguration of a new dispensation of the gospel. It provides a window into the Savior's personality and character. It summarizes the essence of Christ-like behavior. It describes the characteristics and makeup of those who will inhabit the celestial kingdom. It compares the old law with the new. It teaches *all* people how to live and how to pray, yet it was addressed to a specific group of individuals and constitutes one of the most significant training sessions ever presented to teach the newly called disciples how to fulfill their stewardships. It continues to testify of

Jesus' divinity, godly wisdom, and unsurpassed teaching skills. Truly, it is a discourse given by God Himself.

A New Dispensation

Ancient Israel, as a whole, lived life in the throes of apostasy from the time of Moses until the coming of Jesus Christ. As a result of unadulterated rebellion at the very time Jehovah desired to sanctify His people so they might behold His face following their release from Egyptian captivity, the nation of Israel forfeited that unparalleled opportunity while encamped at Mount Sinai. Therefore, "the Lord in his wrath, for his anger was kindled against them, swore that they should not enter into his rest while in the wilderness, which rest is the fulness of his glory. Therefore, he took Moses out of their midst, and the Holy Priesthood also; and the lesser priesthood continued, which priesthood holdeth the key of the ministering of angels and the preparatory gospel" (Doctrine and Covenants 84:24–26).

For more than a thousand years after Moses was taken away, the people of Israel, as a whole, lived without the Melchizedek Priesthood and the higher law, including the ordinances associated with the endowment (see JST Exodus 34:1–2). Only the lesser law and lesser priesthood, including the law of Moses, continued among the general population. All of that changed with the coming of Jesus Christ. He was the Elias who would restore all things (JST John 1:24–28). He restored to Israel the Melchizedek Priesthood and the higher law. His ministry of restoration followed a long period of apostasy, just as did Joseph Smith's ministry eighteen hundred years later.

Thus, by delivering the Sermon on the Mount, Jesus, first and foremost, signaled the restoration of doctrines, ordinances, and powers long withheld from the children of men. The Sermon on the Mount constituted, as it were, the keynote address of restoration in the meridian dispensation. Second, in delivering the Sermon on the Mount, Jesus announced that His restoration of higher principles was a fulfillment of what had gone before. "Think not that I am come to destroy the law, or the prophets," He said. "I am not come to destroy, but to fulfil" (Matthew 5:17). The Greek term, *plērōsai*, from which the English word "fulfill" is derived, means "to fill completely, to make complete, to render perfect, to complement, to make up a deficiency." In Matthew 5:17 specifically, and in the entire sermon generally, Jesus was, among other things, affirming His mission of restoration. The doctrines, principles, and ordinances He was teaching, as reflected in the Sermon on the Mount, completed or made whole the lesser law by bringing back what had been lost centuries earlier (which loss and restoration we understand so much more clearly through the revelations of the Prophet Joseph Smith).

In support of this view, it is important to note that almost immediately following Jesus' announcement of His mission of "fulfillment" or restoration, He listed several significant examples of the way in which His higher-order teachings rounded out, completed, or made whole the principles and requirements of the old order. One of the best known or most graphic examples of this higher law, as taught by Jesus, demonstrates the Savior's increased emphasis on spiritual and mental behavior above and beyond mere physical or corporeal compliance with the outward signs of the law. "Ye have heard that it was said by them of old time, Thou shalt not commit adultery: But I say unto you, That whosoever looketh on a woman to lust after her hath committed adultery with her already in his heart" (Matthew 5:27–28). A higher standard of behavior and elevated level of thought were now restored to Israel's consciousness.

The Sermon on the Mount, then, causes us to reflect on two preeminent symbolic mountains in Israel's theological history—Mount Sinai, where the higher law was suspended and the law of Moses was revealed, and Mount Eremos (the traditional site of the Beatitudes and great Sermon), where the restoration of the higher law was announced. The Sermon on the Mount symbolically parallels the giving of the law at Mount Sinai (Exodus 19:1ff).[1] But one mountain

---

[1] Though the learned W. D. Davies argues against seeing too much in such a parallel, he still admits there is something to it. "At first sight it might be argued that the location of the delivery on 'the Mountain' in v. I is very deliberate, and designed to

represents apostasy and the old law, whereas the other represents restoration and the new law. The Sermon on the Mount is a discourse both of contrasts as well as parallels.

The Master Teacher at Work

The opening verses of Matthew 5 disclose the setting for the Sermon: "And seeing the multitudes, he went up into a mountain: and when he was set, his disciples came unto him: And he opened his mouth, and taught them" (Matthew 5:1–2).

Great crowds had been following Jesus because of His spreading fame, owing to the many miracles He performed. People from all over the Holy Land—Galilee, Decapolis, Jerusalem and all Judea, and the area east of the Jordan River called Transjordan—had become part of the entourage (see Matthew 4:24–25). Matthew 5:1 is a continuation of the report in the previous verses, a fact sometimes obscured by the chapter break. However, unlike those commentators who see the language in Matthew 5:1 as merely "a literary link with the foregoing . . . for the Sermon was apparently intended only for the disciples,"[2] we believe that it describes what actually occurred on that occasion and was not simply editorial transitioning.[3] It is true that the Sermon was meant "only for the disciples," but precisely because great crowds were following him, including the disciples, Jesus chose that moment to instruct those who would be responsible for leading the Church and teaching the unconverted multitudes in the future.

In fact, as the Joseph Smith Translation of the Bible indicates, the whole of the Sermon was not specifically intended for all disciples; rather, important portions were pointedly directed at the Twelve

---

suggest a counterpart to Sinai, because in Q, as is clear from Luke vi. 17, the Sermon was 'delivered' after Jesus had descended from the mountain and 'stood on a level place.' . . . Taken in isolation, the circumstances described in v. 1 ff. cannot be made too much to suggest a New Sinai, a suggestion which, as we noted above, only acquires force from other elements in the Gospel which point to this." See W. D. Davies, *The Setting of the Sermon on the Mount* (Atlanta: Scholars Press, 1989), 99. Others see a stronger parallel.

[2] Samuel Tobias Lachs, *A Rabbinic Commentary on the New Testament* (Hoboken, New Jersey: KTAV Publishing House, 1987), 67.

[3] In support of this view, see Davies, *The Setting of the Sermon on the Mount*, 8.

Apostles and Seventy (see JST Matthew 5:3–4; 6:25–39; 7:6–17). Elder Bruce R. McConkie confirms this view:

> With some major additions, corrections, and improvements, the Sermon on the Mount as preserved by Matthew was given over again by Christ to the Nephites (3 Nephi 12; 13; 14), showing that the material recorded in Matt. 5; 6; 7 is all one continuous discourse. The Nephite version was given after the call of the Nephite Twelve, and portions of the sermon are addressed expressly to those apostolic ministers rather than to the multitude in general (3 Nephi 13:25). In Matthew's account, as found in the Inspired Version, the Prophet [Joseph Smith] adds a considerable amount of material that applies to those called to the Twelve rather than to people in general.[4]

As the Master Teacher, Jesus chose that time and place to provide an important training session for His Church leaders and disciples. Others, many others, may have been listening to the Sermon on the Mount, but Jesus was teaching the Twelve and the Seventy, giving them a kind of Missionary Training Center experience, as it were.

To those who might object to this idea on the grounds that the mission of the Twelve Apostles is not discussed until a later chapter, Matthew 10, I emphasize the following: Matthew does not describe the call and ordination of the Twelve or Seventy at all. Neither does he present the events of this part of Jesus' ministry in any kind of purposeful, chronological sequence. However, Luke does, placing the call of the Twelve (Luke 6:12–16) just prior to his version of the Sermon on the Mount, the so-called Sermon on the Plain (Luke 6:17–49). In Luke, the Twelve are sent forth later (Luke 9:1–5), as they are in Matthew, after they have been given some training, which includes the Sermon on the Mount (Plain).

For didactic and symbolic purposes, Matthew presents material according to patterns recapitulating the life and ministry of Moses.[5]

---

[4] McConkie, *DNTC*, 1:214.
[5] See, for example, discussions in Dale C. Allison, *The New Moses* (Minneapolis:

Rather than present the Savior's life in strict sequential order, Matthew is trying to show that Jesus is the "new Moses," such as was prophesied in Deuteronomy 18:15–18. Finally, as mentioned by Elder McConkie, the Book of Mormon provides a helpful model: the Nephite version of the Sermon on the Mount was given *after* the call of the Nephite Twelve, and portions were addressed expressly to them. This is an important parallel to help us understand both the intended audience of certain portions of the Sermon on the Mount in the Old World and the relative timing of its delivery. It came after the Twelve had been called, and Luke's relative chronology is correct.

There is much to learn from Matthew's description of the setting of the Sermon. Jesus was in charge. Circumstances did not dictate to Him. Rather, He began to teach only when "he was set" (Matthew 5:1); He "opened his mouth, and taught them" (Matthew 5:2) when He was ready. Jesus was ever the perfect example of the Master Teacher.

Jesus chose an open-air setting for His instruction, which differed from the usual rabbinic practice of choosing an indoor venue for significant instruction, such as the synagogue or academy.[6] Notable exceptions to this rule are presented in rabbinic literature, but they usually involve the greatest of the rabbis: "It was related of R. Johanan ben Zakkai that he was sitting in the shadow of the Temple and teaching all day" (Babylonian Talmud Pesachim 26a).[7]

Jesus purposely chose to be seated when He began his teaching. This also contradicted rabbinic norms for the way in which major instruction was to be delivered, at least in the first half of the first century. From the Babylonian Talmud, we read, "Our Rabbis taught: From the days of Moses up to Rabban Gamaliel, the Torah was learned only standing" (Babylonian Talmud Megillah 21a).[8] Maybe this is one more reason why Matthew makes a special point of noting,

---

Fortress Press, 1993).

[6] Lachs, *A Rabbinic Commentary on the New Testament*, 67.

[7] Translation in Lachs, *A Rabbinic Commentary on the New Testament*, 67.

[8] Translation in Lachs, *A Rabbinic Commentary on the New Testament*, 67–68.

at the end of the Sermon, that Jesus "taught them as one having authority, and not as the scribes" (Matthew 7:29). Not only was His doctrine different but also His method of teaching and manner of delivery were different.

Jesus did not teach after the manner of rabbis. He did not say the things the rabbis usually said. The scribal or rabbinic method of teaching was based on precedent. One always cited previous rabbinic authority to lay the foundation for subsequent instruction—"Rabbi so-and-so used to say . . ." Jesus, on the other hand, specifically overturned and dismissed this method of referring to previous rabbinic or scribal authority.

Jesus made oblique reference to this way of teaching by acknowledging that His audience had heard it before, but He then spoke as though He was the sole authority to be reckoned with: "You have heard that it was said by them of old time . . . But *I say* unto you . . ." Jesus spoke this way by divine right. He *was* the sole authority of instruction. He was Jehovah who gave the law (3 Nephi 15:5). He alone was the Judge of correct principle, doctrine, and behavior. He spoke as God. No wonder that when He "ended these sayings, the people were astonished at his doctrine: for he taught them as one having authority, and not as the scribes" (Matthew 7:28–29).

Beatitudes

The first, and perhaps most famous, section of the Sermon on the Mount comprises the Beatitudes, long regarded by many as a hallmark of Christian teaching. However, the Beatitudes were not simply nice, ethical exhortations to the world at large. Nor were they expressions of "attitudes" that people should cultivate, not "be-attitudes" as is occasionally said, not samples of Jesus saying, "You should *be* this or *be* that."

The Beatitudes are both characteristics of, and conditions enjoyed by, the exalted—those who are or will be recipients of eternal life. The word "beatitude" is derived from the Latin *beatus*, meaning, "to be happy, prosperous, abundant, rich, or blessed," which is the equivalent of the Greek *makarioi* and the Hebrew *'ashrē*. The latter is found in some of Israel's ancient psalms: "*Blessed* is the man that walketh not in the counsel of the ungodly, nor standeth in the way of sinners, nor sitteth in the seat of the scornful" (Psalm 1:1). In one sense, Jesus was adopting the language of ancient Israel's great lyric prophet-kings and inspired poets to teach His profound message. Beatitudes, as a literary form, are also found in intertestamental and rabbinic literature.[9] But Jesus put a different twist on them.

We can immediately see the irony in some of Jesus' statements in the Sermon on the Mount precisely because several of the attributes He lists—"the *poor* in spirit," "they that *mourn*," "the *meek*," and "they which do *hunger* and *thirst*"—do not immediately connote happiness, prosperity, richness, or blessedness as the world measures such conditions. Our Lord is talking about the happy, blessed, rich condition that pervades, permeates, and exists eternally in the celestial kingdom—God's kingdom. All worldly characteristics and conditions must be totally and completely eradicated in God's environment and exalted state. And God's perfect, righteous, exalted status is the ultimate goal to which the Beatitudes and the whole Sermon point us: "Be ye therefore perfect, even as your Father which is in heaven is perfect," said Jesus (Matthew 5:48). These are not idealistic, isolated words; they hark back to the Beatitudes.

The characteristics or attributes that must be possessed by each individual who desires to obtain the condition of blessedness,

---

[9] Some examples of beatitudes in rabbinic literature include the following: ". . . and R. Johanan b. Zakkai said . . . 'Happy [blessed] are you, our father Abraham, that Eleazar b. Arakh came forth from your loins'" (Tosefta, Hagigah 2.1).

"R. Jose the priest went and told what had happened before R. Johanan b. Zakkai, and the latter said, 'Happy [blessed] are you, happy is she who bore you, happy are my eyes that I have seen this'" (Babylonian Talmud, Hagigah 14b).

"Happy [blessed] is the king who is praised in his house! Woe to the father who had to banish his children, and woe to the children who had to be banished from the table of their father" (Babylonian Talmud, Berakhot 3a).

All of the foregoing are translated in Lachs, *A Rabbinic Commentary on the New Testament*, 70. For examples of beatitudes in intertestamental literature, see Psalms of Solomon 5:18; 6:1; 10:1, and Ben Sira 14:1; 25:8,9.

happiness, and abundance of which Jesus speaks are, in fact, a reflection of Jesus' own character and personality. President Harold B. Lee taught:

> Christ came not only into the world to make an atonement for the sins of mankind but to set an example before the world of the standard of perfection of God's law and of obedience to the Father. In his Sermon on the Mount the Master has given us somewhat of a revelation of his own character, which was perfect, or what might be said to be "an autobiography, every syllable of which he had written down in deeds," and in so doing has given us a blueprint for our own lives.[10]

Hence, the Beatitudes embody "the constitution for a perfect life."[11] This view of the Beatitudes makes it impossible to regard the attributes described therein (poor in spirit, mournful, meek, and so forth) as anything but the most profound expressions of discipleship, ones that cannot be arrived at in a moment. Rather, these characteristics are developed after a person is baptized and receives the gift of the Holy Ghost, after a significant price has been paid, and after a period of loyalty to the Lord and service in His Church have been offered. In fact, the more complete expression of the Beatitudes, as found in 3 Nephi 12:1–12, makes it clear to this writer that the Beatitudes pronounced by Jesus in the Old World were intended for those who had or would participate in the first principles and ordinances of the gospel and who heeded the words of the prophets. After calling the Twelve,

> he stretched forth his hand unto the multitude, and cried unto them, saying: Blessed are ye if ye shall give heed unto the words of these twelve whom I have chosen from among you to minister unto you, and to be your servants; and unto them I have given power that they may baptize you with water; and after that ye are baptized with water,

---

[10] Harold B. Lee, *Decisions for Successful Living* (Salt Lake City: Deseret Book, 1973), 55–56.

[11] Lee, *Decisions for Successful Living*, 56.

behold, I will baptize you with fire and with the Holy Ghost; therefore blessed are ye if ye shall believe in me and be baptized, after that ye have seen me and know that I am.

And again, more blessed are they who shall believe in your words because that ye shall testify that ye have seen me, and that ye know that I am. Yea, blessed are they who shall believe in your words, and come down into the depths of humility and be baptized, for they shall be visited with fire and with the Holy Ghost, and shall receive a remission of their sins. (3 Nephi 12:1–2)

That the King James and earlier biblical versions of the Beatitudes, as well as the entire Sermon itself, are deficient in many particulars should not really surprise us. All accounts of the Sermon—whether Matthew, Luke, 3 Nephi, or the Joseph Smith Translation—"are abridgements only, and the same truths were not abridged in every particular into each of the accounts."[12] Elder Bruce R. McConkie feels that "the most comprehensive and complete report" of the Sermon as a whole is the JST Matthew account.[13]

Characteristics and Rewards

The first essential characteristic possessed by the blessed or exalted, according to Matthew's version, is "poor in spirit" (Matthew 5:3). This expression is not found in either the Massoretic Text or rabbinic literature. Presumably, it means those who are "poor in pride," those who are devoid of pride, or those who are "poor in the spirit of the world." The Greek term for "poor" used here by Matthew, *ptōchoi*, originally denoted "begging," but in this passage the term means "dependent on others for support" or even "those who are poor in the world's estimation."[14] This fits perfectly with the fuller accounts of this beatitude in 3 Nephi and in the Joseph Smith Translation, wherein the poor in spirit are blessed or happy if they

---

[12] McConkie, *DNTC*, 1:214–15.
[13] McConkie, *DNTC*, 1:215.
[14] Arndt and Gingrich, *GEL*, "ptōchoi," 728.

come unto Christ (3 Nephi 12:3; JST Matthew 5:5), on whom all of us are dependent. In fact, all of the Beatitudes may be read more profitably by inserting the phrase "who come unto me," for, in truth, that is the implication in all of them. We are dependent on Jesus for exaltation and lasting happiness.

Those who follow Him are often judged as "poor" or misguided in the world's estimation. Through another Book of Mormon prophet, Moroni, the Lord promises to those who will come unto Him that He "will show unto them their weakness," explaining, "I give unto men weakness that they may be humble; and my grace is sufficient for all men that humble themselves before me; for if they humble themselves before me, and have faith in me, then will I make weak things become strong unto them" (Ether 12:27). The natural and expected reward of those who are poor in the spirit of the world and come unto Christ is nothing less than the riches of the kingdom of heaven.

The second essential characteristic of those who are blessed or happy has to do with mourning. "Blessed are they that mourn: for they shall be comforted" (Matthew 5:4). Of all the Beatitudes, this one may appear to be the most difficult to comprehend at first glance. It seems completely contradictory to a state of happiness or blessedness. To mourn is to show grief or pain at the loss of something precious, whether the death of a loved one or the loss of the Spirit of the Lord because of transgression. However, the Lord promised His disciples on another occasion that He would give rest and comfort to all who labored and were heavy laden if, again, they came unto Him (Matthew 11:28–30). As Elder Robert E. Wells has noted:

> It may be that pain and suffering at the death of loved ones is an essential part of our mortal experience that obliges us to face the question of the reality of the spirit world and the hope of the Resurrection. It is through suffering that we discover what is eternally important.
>
> It might be that it is a blessing for us to become more fully aware that God's ways are not always our ways, and that we must trust him

when things don't go as we believe they should. When we can see the Lord's purposes fulfilled in our sorrowful moments, the Holy Ghost can console us and the Atonement and Resurrection can become the cornerstones of our faith.[15]

What is true about mourning for the loss of a loved one is also true about mourning over our sinful actions. "Godly sorrow," says Paul, "worketh repentance to salvation" (2 Corinthians 7:10). In other words, when we come unto Christ, we will become more sensitive to, and feel godly sorrow for, sin. His atonement becomes the cornerstone of our faith, and we continue to become more like Him as we repent.

The third characteristic of those who will enjoy the state or condition of true blessedness is meekness. The meek are not weak, for Jesus was the meekest of men. This quality might be defined as poise under pressure, patience in the face of provocation. Peter's first epistle tells us that though Jesus was reviled, He did not revile in return (1 Peter 2:23). Meekness is one of the clearest reflections of how closely a disciple's personality or makeup, or even reactions, mirror those of the Savior.

The reward for meekness is possession of the earth. Thus, meekness is a celestial attribute, a sanctifying attribute, and it will be found in rich abundance among those who inhabit the celestial kingdom. For, as we learn, the location of the celestial kingdom, at least for those who have lived on this earth, is, in fact, this earth. As the Lord revealed to Joseph Smith:

> The redemption of the soul is through him that quickeneth all things, in whose bosom it is decreed that the poor and the meek of the earth shall inherit it. Therefore, it must needs be sanctified from all unrighteousness, that it may be prepared for the celestial glory; for after it hath filled the measure of its creation, it shall be crowned with glory, even with the presence of God the Father; that bodies who are of the

---

[15] Robert E. Wells, "Pattern for Coming unto Christ," *Ensign* (December 1987): 9.

celestial kingdom may possess it forever and ever; for, for this intent was it made and created, and for this intent are they sanctified. (Doctrine and Covenants 88:17–20)

Our understanding of the fourth characteristic of those who enjoy an eternal condition of blessedness is greatly enhanced by Restoration scripture. Matthew reports that Jesus said, "Blessed are they which do hunger and thirst after righteousness: for they shall be filled" (Matthew 5:6). Both 3 Nephi and the Joseph Smith Translation add that intense seekers of righteousness will be filled "with the Holy Ghost" (3 Nephi 12:6; JST Matthew 5:8).

The Holy Ghost is the great comforter and testator and is only one of three who can really satisfy our emotional and mental hunger and quench our spiritual thirst (John 14:16–18, 26). He operates under the direction of Jesus Christ (John 16:13–16). The Greek word used by Matthew that is translated as "filled" originally meant "to feed or fatten an animal in a stall" and carries the notion of eating till completely full, "to eat one's fill, be satisfied, to gorge."[16] Such is the Lord's promise to those who hunger and thirst after righteousness. He will feed us more than we can possibly imagine or desire initially.

Beatitudes five through eight describe characteristics that seem to be the essence of Jesus' personality. "Blessed are the merciful" (Matthew 5:7). Jesus is filled with mercy. He does not merely extend mercy through His atoning sacrifice. He is mercy personified. We know from His statement in the fifth beatitude that He understands that those of like minds and actions will associate with each other. The merciful will obtain mercy because "intelligence cleaveth unto intelligence; wisdom receiveth wisdom; truth embraceth truth; virtue loveth virtue; light cleaveth unto light; mercy hath compassion on mercy and claimeth her own; justice continueth its course and claimeth its own; judgment goeth before the face of him who sitteth upon the throne and governeth and executeth all things" (Doctrine and Covenants 88:40).

---

[16] Arndt and Gingrich, GEL, "chortazō," 883–84.

In describing the condition or state of blessedness that flows from having a pure heart, the sixth beatitude, Jesus makes the explicit connection to God's presence (Matthew 5:8). The environment in which God resides, the celestial glory, is devoid of any impure person or thing. The resurrected Jesus declared to the Nephites, "No unclean thing can enter into his [God's] kingdom; therefore nothing entereth into his rest save it be those who have washed their garments in my blood" (3 Nephi 27:19). Thus, obtaining the mercy of Jesus referred to in the previous beatitude is a prerequisite for becoming pure in heart, which then allows a person to enter God's kingdom and literally see Him.

The Prophet Joseph Smith was told, "It shall come to pass that every soul who forsaketh his sins and cometh unto me, and calleth on my name, and obeyeth my voice, and keepeth my commandments, shall see my face and know that I am" (Doctrine and Covenants 93:1). Thus, the pure in heart are also those who forsake their sins, call on the Savior's name, obey His voice, and keep His commandments.

It is obvious to most readers that when Jesus singled out, in the last two beatitudes, the peacemakers and those persecuted for righteousness' sake, He was speaking out of personal experience. He was the prince of peace in the face of persecution. When He promised, "Blessed are the peacemakers, for they shall be called the children of God" (Matthew 5:9), He was teaching unique doctrine for that time and place. "Peacemakers . . . are nowhere in rabbinic literature called 'the children of God,'" though they were called blessed by some of the intertestamental writers.[17] Hillel, an older contemporary of Jesus, on the other hand, referred to peacemakers as the "disciples of Aaron." Hillel said, "Be of the disciples of Aaron, loving peace and pursuing peace; be one who loves his fellow men and draws them near the Torah."[18]

---

[17] Lachs, *A Rabbinic Commentary on the New Testament*, 76.

[18] *Pirqe Avot* 1:12, in Philip Birnbaum, trans., *Daily Prayer Book* (New York: Hebrew Publishing Company, 1977), 482.

Many of Jesus' statements make it clear that He intently desires peace (see, for example, 3 Nephi 11:29; Doctrine and Covenants 98:34). Paul admonished disciples to follow after "the things which make for peace" (Romans 14:19). As disciples try their best to emulate their Master, proclaiming peace and living as advocates and makers of peace, they take on His name and countenance and become His sons and His daughters. They have their natures changed and desire no more to do evil (see Mosiah 5:2, 7; 27:24–26; Alma 5:14). As this happens, they become a likeness of Him who presented an outline of His own nature in the form of the Beatitudes.

It has been suggested that when Jesus extolled the blessed state of those who were persecuted for righteousness' sake (Matthew 5:10), He was really saying "for the sake of the Righteous One"—meaning Himself.[19] In Hebrew, the difference between *zedeq* (righteousness) and *zadiq* (righteous one) is very small. Either way, disciples are bid to follow Jesus because He is both the Righteous One and the embodiment of righteousness.

A Knowledge of the Father

The Sermon on the Mount speaks much about our Father in Heaven. The expression "Father in heaven" is characteristic of Matthew's Gospel as a whole and is found throughout the Sermon. A profound and critical aspect of Jesus' role as the Elias of Restoration was His restitution of the knowledge of God the Father, His character, attributes, and concerns. Through centuries of apostasy, this had dimmed. In the Sermon on the Mount, Jesus brought God the Father back into focus through a series of parables, commands, and explanations.

The first example of Jesus' desire to have His disciples understand and know God the Father comes immediately after Jesus finished laying out the Beatitudes. He began by emphasizing to the disciples their responsibility to live so righteously and present such fine

---

[19] Lachs, *A Rabbinic Commentary on the New Testament*, 77.

examples of righteousness that others would see their good words and glorify their Father in heaven (Matthew 5:16). The kind of examples Jesus said He wanted His followers to become were symbolized by salt and light: "Ye are the salt of the earth," He said (Matthew 5:13), and "Ye are the light of the world" (Matthew 5:14).

Salt and light immediately and unmistakably influence whatever environment they are placed in. It is important to note that salt was a preservative in the ancient world, but it was also a token of Israel's covenant with God and part of their sacrificial system (see Leviticus 2:13; Numbers 18:19). The sacrificial system was a type, shadow, and symbol of the great and last sacrifice that Jesus Himself would offer (see Hebrews 9 and 10). Salt ultimately points to Jesus.

Light is also a stunning choice for a symbol of discipleship and exemplary behavior. It, too, is ultimately a reference to Jesus Himself. Later in His ministry, Jesus openly declared that He was "the light of the world" and that whoever followed Him would "not walk in darkness" (John 8:12). To the Nephites, He was even more pointed and encompassing: "I am the law, and the light" (3 Nephi 15:9).

It would seem that in pointing His listeners to an increased knowledge and understanding of God the Father, Jesus also pointed them to Himself. In many ways, Jesus taught His students the close connection between the Father and the Son. He seemed to be saying, "When you become like salt and light, you become like me; you will influence your environment, which is the Father's desire."

Perhaps the greatest attribute of God the Father is love. The Apostle John wrote, "God is love" (1 John 4:8). We can assume He meant by this that perfect love and fairness shape, mediate, and influence all of God's other attributes, "for with all the other excellencies of his character, without this one to influence them, they could not have such powerful dominion over the minds of men."[20] Thus, in the Sermon on the Mount, Jesus commands His audience to love their enemies, bless those who hurl curses at them, and pray for those who despitefully use them. The reason given: "That you may be

---

[20] *Lectures on Faith*, 3:24.

the children of your Father which is in heaven" (Matthew 5:45). This is unique in the New Testament, although it picks up the refrain of Deuteronomy 14:1, "Ye are the children of the Lord your God."

The Greek wording of Matthew 5:45 connotes a rebirth of sorts: "so that you may become [be born] (*genēsthe*) sons of your Father in heaven." This idea parallels the doctrine of being spiritually born of God and receiving His image in one's countenance, as found in the Book of Mormon (Alma 5:14). Disciples must reflect in their lives, in their behaviors, and in their countenances the distinguishing trait of the great Parent of the universe in order to truly become His children and His heirs in every way and to pass the tests of mortality.

After all, God the Father loves all His children, even those who forsake or ignore Him. God the Father is patient and long-suffering. "He maketh his sun to rise on the evil and on the good" (Matthew 5:45), meaning that righteousness and wickedness are not, cannot be, immediately and constantly rewarded or punished. Such constant interference in the lives of men and women would thwart the plan of salvation and the purposes for which earth life was designed—to allow individuals to walk by faith and be tested. It is no accident that Jesus concludes this section of the Sermon by commanding His listeners to be perfect, as their Father in heaven is perfect (Matthew 5:48). Patient love and tolerant restraint are the great hallmarks of God's perfection.

Jesus' command to His disciples given in the Sermon that they love their enemies and pray for those who despitefully use them (Matthew 5:44) may, in fact, be a direct response to a contemporary belief circulating among the Essenes living at Qumran and elsewhere (even in Jerusalem). This sectarian group of Jews is associated with the Dead Sea Scrolls (being their authors, editors, and/or preservers).

It is from the document known as the Rule of the Community that we learn much about the Qumran covenantors' beliefs and practices, including the very view that Jesus contradicts in the Sermon on the Mount. That document declared, "Love all that He [God] has chosen and hate all that He has rejected" and "These are the rules of conduct for the Master in those times with respect to his loving and hating. Everlasting hatred in a spirit of secrecy for the men of perdition!"[21] Thus, it seems clear that some points of Jesus' doctrine were an intentional rebuttal of Essene teaching.

The Instruction in Matthew 6

Jesus spent a good deal of the next portion of His Sermon teaching about the nature of our Father in heaven by discussing private daily devotions. Do not, He said, make a public show of doing that which is better done in private—almsgiving, welfare relief, and personal prayer (Matthew 6:1–6)—for "thy Father which seeth in secret shall reward thee openly" (Matthew 6:6). Those who "sound a trumpet" or give alms to be seen of men are "hypocrites," an epithet favored by Matthew to describe those Pharisees who sought prestige above all else. One of the most strident denunciations of the Pharisees as hypocrites is found in another sermon to a multitude congregated during the last week of Jesus' mortal ministry (see Matthew 23:1–39).

Significantly, this sermon recapitulates some of the teachings in the Sermon on the Mount and ends with a beatitude: "Blessed is he that cometh in the name of the Lord" (Matthew 23:39). Because of Jesus' use of vocabulary such as "hypocrite" (Greek, literally "play actor, pretender, dissembler"), some authorities see this as evidence to connect Jesus with visits to theatre towns such as Sepphoris, only a few miles north of Nazareth.[22]

As the Sermon progressed, Jesus continued to emphasize that God the Father cares about proper decorum. His is a kingdom of quiet dignity, and He honors those who behave in like manner. He prefers brevity, sincerity, and intensity in prayer, unlike the "heathen" (Greek, *ethnikoi*, literally "Gentiles") who use "vain repetitions"

---

[21] *Rule of Community* (1QS) I and IX, quoted in Andrew C. Skinner, "The Ancient People of Qumran: An Introduction to the Dead Sea Scrolls," in Donald Parry and Dana Pike, eds., *LDS Perspectives on the Dead Sea Scrolls* (Provo: Foundation for Ancient Research and Mormon Studies, 1997), 37.

[22] Richard A. Batey, *Jesus and the Forgotten City: New Light on Sepphoris and the Urban World of Jesus* (Grand Rapids: Baker, 1991), 83–103.

(Greek, *battalogēsēte*, literally "babble," or "speaking without thinking") and "think that they shall be heard for their much speaking" (Matthew 6:7).

Such ideas as Jesus presented correspond, in a remarkable way, to the ideas on prayer as expressed in rabbinic thought. Rabbi Simeon said, "Be careful in reading the Shema [the Jewish confession of faith found in Deuteronomy 6:4–7].... [For] when you pray, do not regard your prayer as a perfunctory act (or fixed form), but as a plea for mercy and grace before God, as it is said: 'For he is gracious and merciful, slow to anger, abounding in kindness, and relenting of evil.'"[23]

Jesus teaches two profound truths about prayer in the Sermon on the Mount. First, God the Father knows what things any of us need before we supplicate Him (see Matthew 6:8 and 32). The Father knows all things, which is one reason we may have complete confidence in Him, but it is also why we cannot deceive Him. President Spencer W. Kimball elaborated on this in our day:

> In our prayers, there must be no glossing over, no hypocrisy, since there can here be no deception. The Lord knows our true condition. Do we tell the Lord how good we are, or how weak? We stand naked before him. Do we offer our supplications in modesty, sincerity, and with a "broken heart and contrite spirit," or like the Pharisee who prided himself on how well he adhered to the law of Moses? Do we offer a few trite words and worn-out phrases, or do we talk intimately to the Lord for as long as the occasion requires? Do we pray occasionally when we should be praying regularly, often, constantly? Do we pay the price to get answers to our prayers?[24]

The second great matter to which Jesus gives considerable attention in the Sermon is the true order or pattern of prayer (see Matthew

---

[23] *Pirqe Avot* 2:18 in Birnbaum, *Daily Prayer Book*, 490.

[24] Spencer W. Kimball, *Faith Precedes the Miracle* (Salt Lake City: Deseret Book, 1972), 207.

6:9–13). That He intended His sample prayer, what has come to be known as the "Lord's Prayer," only as a sample and not as recitation is clear from His instruction, "*After this manner* therefore pray ye" (Matthew 6:9; emphasis added). Jesus instructed His disciples to pray to the Father, teaching them that the Father's name is to be hallowed or sanctified ("let all men beware how they take my name [the Lord] in their lips" [Doctrine and Covenants 63:61]) and that God presides over His kingdom and possesses *all* power (Matthew 6:9, 13).

Following His instruction on prayer, Jesus presented a series of doctrinal statements that tell His disciples much more about our Heavenly Father's personality and desires for His sons and daughters. For example, God is forgiving, but He requires that individuals forgive each other or His divine mercy will be held in abeyance (Matthew 6:14–15).

God rewards those who fast with dignity, not with outward showiness and not seeking sympathy (Matthew 6:16–18). Ultimately, said Jesus, if one's eye—one's attitudes, priorities, and motives—were "single" (Greek, *aplous*, literally "sound, healthy, simple, sincere"), his or her whole body would be full of light. Joseph Smith reminds us that Jesus really said, "If therefore thine eye be single *to the glory of God,* thy whole body will be full of light" (JST Matthew 6:22; emphasis added). In a revelation given in 1832, the Lord expanded our understanding of the implication of this verse, saying, "The word of the Lord is truth, and whatsoever is truth is *light,* and whatsoever is *light* is Spirit, even the Spirit of Jesus Christ" (Doctrine and Covenants 84:45; emphasis added). Through single-minded focus on God's will and God's glory, Jesus' disciples could reap an incredible reward—being filled with light, truth, and the Spirit of Jesus Christ. But anything other than single-minded focus on God would dissipate the light and increase the darkness (Matthew 6:23).

Training His Servants

Jesus changed the focus of His instruction, as well as His audience, for the concluding section of his great Sermon (Matthew 6:24–7:27).

He turned His attention to the Twelve and, probably, the Seventy, whose calling was also to go out two by two to teach and testify (see Luke 10:1).

Jesus began this instruction by declaring in stark fashion the necessity of choosing only one master, exclusively. Any thought of devoting time to the acquisition of mammon (Aramaic, literally, "riches") was not acceptable. Service to God and the pursuit of worldly wealth were mutually exclusive (see Matthew 6:24). Rather, the Twelve and Seventy were told to "trust the Father for what they needed, taking no thought of food, drink, clothing, or even of life itself, for all these were to be supplied by means above their power to control."[25] Jesus cited the lessons of nature to illustrate His truths. If all creation was in God's hands, how much more so the leaders of His kingdom! They were to seek first the welfare of the kingdom, and all things would be added to them (see Matthew 6:33).

What followed next might well be summarized as a dialogue in which Jesus provided help to the Twelve on how to teach the people and overcome the challenges or objections they would present. This is made clear only in the Joseph Smith Translation: "Now these are the words Jesus taught his disciples that they should say unto the people" (JST Matthew 7:1).

The counsel the Master provided included such things as judging with righteous judgment, calling into question blatant hypocrisy, and cautioning against revealing sacred things or even teaching too much to those who would trample sacred truths underfoot. Here the words of Jesus as reported in the Joseph Smith Translation are quite strong:

> Go ye into the world, saying unto all, Repent, for the kingdom of heaven has come nigh unto you.
>
> And the mysteries of the kingdom ye shall keep within yourselves; for it is not meet to give that which is holy unto the dogs; neither cast ye your pearls unto swine, lest they trample them under their feet.
>
> For the world cannot receive that which ye, yourselves, are not

---

[25] Talmage, JTC, 243.

able to bear; wherefore ye shall not give your pearls unto them, lest they turn again and rend you. (JST Matthew 7:9–11)

The corresponding Greek text of these verses indicates that Jesus was probably using a proverbial saying, in vogue at the time, when He referred to dogs and swine. The Greek term translated as "dog," *kusin*, can also mean an "unclean animal" or even a "reprobate." The Greek term, *choirōn*, refers to a young pig and may imply a combination of immaturity and impurity.[26]

The Joseph Smith Translation of Matthew 7 is much more pronounced in its castigation of Jewish leadership than the King James Version or the Greek text. At one point in the Sermon, Jesus says to His apostolic leaders: "Beholdest thou the Scribes, and the Pharisees, and the Priests, and the Levites? They teach in their synagogues, but do not observe the law, nor the commandments; and all have gone out of the way, and are under sin. Go thou and say unto them, Why teach ye men the law and the commandments, when ye yourselves are the children of corruption?" (JST Matthew 7:6–7). At another point, the Twelve voiced concerns in extremely blunt language about the response of certain Jews to their new, Christ-centered message. Here, the Sermon on the Mount turned into the Dialogue on the Mount:

> And then said his disciples unto him, they will say unto us, We ourselves are righteous, and need not that any man should teach us. God, we know, heard Moses and some of the prophets; but us he will not hear.
>
> And they will say, We have the law for our salvation, and that is sufficient for us.
>
> Then Jesus answered, and said unto his disciples, thus shall ye say unto them,
>
> What man among you, having a son, and he shall be standing out, and shall say, Father, open thy house that I may come in and sup with

---

[26] Arndt and Gingrich, *GEL*, "choirōn," 883.

thee, will not say, Come in, my son; for mine is thine, and thine is mine? (JST Matthew 7:14–17)

This is extremely insightful. Nowhere else except in the Joseph Smith Translation do we get the information that Jesus was so careful in helping His apostolic ministers craft their teaching points. And nowhere else do we receive such insightful but disheartening data about the social and religious atmosphere in which the Apostles had to carry out their ministry. The attitudes held in certain quarters of Judaism toward the doctrines of continuing revelation, salvation, and Jesus as Messiah indicate that Judaism was in much sadder condition than might be supposed from evidence in the other versions of the text of the Sermon on the Mount.

For some Jews, revelation had completely ceased; and even when it was alive, not all the prophets were heard by God. For some, there was no hope that God would listen to them, let alone answer. For some, there was no humility but rather a pitiful attitude of self-sufficiency. With the coming of Jesus and His apostolic ministers, however, the ax had begun to be laid to the root, and, unfortunately, the tree (Israel in the meridian dispensation) would not survive intact. As Jesus said near the end of the Sermon, "A good tree cannot bring forth evil fruit, neither [can] a corrupt tree bring forth good fruit. Every tree that bringeth not forth good fruit is hewn down, and cast into the fire" (Matthew 7:18–19).

It is possible that in this last statement, Jesus was playing off a well-known rabbinic chastisement that used the image of a tree. "He [Rabbi Eliezer ben Azarya] used to say: One whose wisdom exceeds his deeds, to what is he like? To a tree that has many branches and few roots, so that when the wind comes, it plucks it up and turns it over."[27] This saying also reminds us of a similar concept expressed much earlier by the ancient prophet Jacob and seems to corroborate the authenticity and antiquity of such images in the prophetic teaching of the Book of Mormon: "And it came to pass that the

---

[27] *Pirqe Avot* 3:22 in Birnbaum, *Daily Prayer Book*, 502.

servant said unto his master: Is it not the loftiness of thy vineyard—have not the branches thereof overcome the roots which are good? And because the branches have overcome the roots thereof, behold they grew faster than the strength of the roots, taking strength unto themselves. Behold, I say, is not this the cause that the trees of thy vineyard have become corrupted?" (Jacob 5:48).

Jesus concluded the Sermon on the Mount with a graphic illustration about the need to build our lives upon a solid foundation or "rock" (Matthew 7:24), meaning the Rock of the Redeemer (see Helaman 5:12). If our lives and faith are not built upon this solid foundation, as authorized by Deity, both will fall apart, no matter how many miraculous works we have accomplished (see Matthew 7:22–27).

Concluding Thoughts

Here Jesus ends the Sermon on the Mount. Elder James E. Talmage believed that no discourse delivered since that time can match it: "The Sermon on the Mount has stood through all the years since its delivery without another to be compared with it. No mortal man has ever since preached a discourse of its kind."[28]

The Sermon is filled with doctrine that leads to, and speaks of, exaltation. It both alludes to and speaks explicitly of restoration. It provides a window into the challenges faced by the primitive Church in the context of first-century Judea. It is filled with allusions to the culture and language of its time, but it also shows that that time was not completely different from our own. When Jesus says, for example, "Whosoever shall say to his brother, Raca, shall be in danger" (Matthew 5:22), He is warning against our proclivity toward anger against our fellowman. Calling someone a fool or "empty head" (*Raca* literally means "empty" in Aramaic and may, in modern parlance, be analogous to calling someone an "idiot") is the outward expression of an inner emotion that Jesus is seeking to change.

---

[28] Talmage, JTC, 246.

For much of what Jesus preached, we can find parallels in rabbinic teaching or intertestamental literature. But Jesus always gave fresh insight or provided new perspective. And, of course, some things were simply unique to Him. There was not then, nor is there now, any question about the significance of all that He proclaimed. He could speak with such power because He lived what He taught, every syllable. The day the Sermon on the Mount was preached was the day God Himself gave a discourse.

XIII.
THE SERMON ON THE PLAIN

THOMAS A. WAYMENT

And he came down with them, and stood in the plain, and the company of his disciples, and a great multitude of people out of all Judea and Jerusalem, and from the sea coast of Tyre and Sidon, which came to hear him, and to be healed of their diseases.

LUKE 6:17

The Sermon on the Mount in Matthew has almost always overshadowed its lesser-known cousin in Luke, the Sermon on the Plain. Tradition does not distinguish a separate location for the Sermon on the Mount; instead, most scholars have felt and continue to feel that the Sermon on the Mount and the Sermon on the Plain are the same discourse and were therefore delivered in the same location. The region near Capernaum is suggested by Matthew 8:5 as the area where Jesus delivered the Sermon before entering Capernaum. The location of the Sermon on the Mount is well attested in literature and has been located between Capernaum and Tabgha on a broad hill. The modern hill, known as the Mount of Beatitudes, once housed a Byzantine church commemorating the delivering of the Sermon on the Mount. It was at one time known as Mount Eremos and currently houses a Catholic church built in 1939.[1]

---

[1] Catholic tradition ascribes the location of the Sermon on the Mount to the "Horns

The early Church fathers apparently did not know of any certain locations for the Sermon on the Mount or the Sermon on the Plain, but the traditions now attested appear to date from the crusader period.

For many, the Sermon on the Plain in Luke is unwittingly viewed as a less complete version of the sermon recorded by Matthew. In fact, in describing Luke's sermon, scholars often like to explain it in terms of the Sermon on the Mount so that a known point of reference may inform our understanding. Several different approaches to the Sermon on the Plain have been employed so scholars can interpret its meaning both within the context of the first century A.D. and for our day. The first approach is that the Sermon on the Mount and the Sermon on the Plain represent two different sermons that were delivered on two separate occasions, much as a modern speaker will deliver a presentation on numerous occasions, making alterations each time it is delivered. A second approach is that the two sermons are ultimately the same sermon in two different yet stylistically similar accounts. The third approach treats both sermons as creations by the evangelists themselves who copied from an original sermon or sermons to which they had access and which they altered heavily.[2] The first approach seems to be a response to the last approach, seeking to avoid the implications of having the evangelists appear to be creators of tradition rather than communicators of tradition.

It is theoretically impossible, without further information, to prove absolutely that the Sermon in Matthew and the Sermon in Luke were the same sermon delivered on two separate occasions or whether they are two different accounts of the same sermon. Knowing the tendencies of the Gospel of Luke, we ought to consider whether it is possible that the two sermons are different accounts of

---

of Hattin," a mountainous outcropping northeast of Capernaum. The mountain is much steeper than the Mount of Beatitudes but is in the near vicinity. Napoleon's men located the Mount of Beatitudes on Mount Arbel in the nineteenth century.

[2] Hans D. Betz, *The Sermon on the Mount: A Commentary on the Sermon on the Mount, Including the Sermon on the Plain (Matthew 5:3–7:27 and Luke 6:20–49)*, ed. Adela Yarbro Collins (Minneapolis: Fortress Press, 1995), 18–50.

the same sermon. Although we cannot exclude the possibility that Luke's version is a second version of the same sermon delivered on a later occasion by Jesus, it is equally possible that the accounts represent two different viewpoints on what was both said and felt on that day in Galilee.[3] As with all eyewitness accounts, discrepancies exist; and, in fact, those very discrepancies are a signature feature of authentic eyewitness reports. Harmonization of the accounts and exact verbatim overlap lead to the suspicion that the accounts have been altered to complement the views of the persons giving the accounts. The two similar, yet markedly different, accounts attest to their authenticity and provide a glimpse into the earliest years of Jesus' ministry and the ways in which the first generation of converts attempted to understand the teachings of the Master.

We might take a lesson from the numerous accounts recorded of the First Vision in this dispensation. The story was written or published no fewer than six times during Joseph Smith's lifetime, and it was subsequently reported by those who had heard the Prophet relate the story on at least four separate occasions.[4] Although several

---

[3] Talmage, JTC, 229, states that Luke's Sermon on the Plain is a summary of the Sermon on the Mount. Robert J. Matthews, *Behold the Messiah* (Salt Lake City: Bookcraft, 1994), 110, holds that the Sermon on the Mount was the version delivered to the Twelve Apostles, whereas the Sermon on the Plain was the public version of the same sermon. In the same year, Richard Lloyd Anderson raised the possibility that Luke intentionally gave a more concise version of the Sermon on the Mount that was crafted specifically for his audience (Richard Lloyd Anderson, "Paul's Witness to the Early History of Jesus' Ministry," in *The Apostle Paul: His Life and His Testimony*, ed. Paul Y. Hoskisson [Salt Lake City: Deseret Book, 1994], 18–19). Bruce R. McConkie concluded that "the Sermon on the Mount and the Sermon on the Plain are one and the same" (McConkie, DNTC, 214).

[4] The early versions are the 1838 version, which is recorded in the Pearl of Great Price; the Wentworth letter version (published in *Times and Seasons* 3, no. 9 [March 1, 1842], 706–10); Orson Pratt's 1840 version (published in a pamphlet entitled *Interesting Account of Several Remarkable Visions, and of the Late Discovery of Ancient American Records* [Edinburgh: Ballantyne and Hughes, 1840]); Orson Hyde's 1842 German version (*Ein Ruf aus der Wüste* [Frankfurt, 1842]); The *Pittsburg Gazette* version (*Pittsburg Weekly Gazette* 58, September 15, 1843); Alexander Neibaur's journal version (May 24, 1844); Edward Stevenson's versions (*The Life and History, Elder Edward Stevenson*, 19–23 [Church Historian's Office] and *Reminiscences of Joseph, The Prophet, and the Coming Forth of the Book of Mormon* [Salt Lake City, 1893], 4); John Taylor's version (*Journal of Discourses*

accounts of the First Vision circulated in the Prophet's lifetime, we have little evidence that the individual accounts relied on one another for information. The majority of the accounts appear to have originated with the Prophet himself but were each related by him personally on separate occasions. In reading these early independent accounts, we find little agreement in their exact wording, although we find a significant degree of similarity in content.[5] However, in the Orson Pratt and Orson Hyde versions of 1840 and 1842, respectively, we see instances where the wording is quite similar.[6] In writing his 1842 account, Orson Hyde apparently had access to the Wentworth letter version that was subsequently published in the *Times and Seasons*.[7] Orson Hyde may also have been familiar with Orson Pratt's 1840 version.

Both of these authors appear to have borrowed heavily from the biographical sketch published in the *Times and Seasons* on the early life of Joseph Smith, and each created his own account using written sources and unwritten early accounts. Looking at the two accounts side by side, we are left with the impression that these two authors made use of a similar account of the First Vision. Each author has his own unique manner of telling the story, but the similarity in wording and overall content suggests a common background. In looking at the two accounts, we can obviously see that each author has emphasized different portions of the story, thus leading to the suggestion that each author found meaning in different sections of the story. The literary connection between these early accounts is compounded by the fact that the Prophet Joseph Smith continued to tell the story

---

[London, 1881], 21:161–63), and the Welch version (Ronald D. Dennis, trans., *History of the Latter-day Saints* [Rhydybont: J. Jones], 14–16).

[5] Milton V. Backman, *Joseph Smith's First Vision: Confirming Evidences and Contemporary Accounts*, 2nd ed. (Salt Lake City: Bookcraft, 1980), 112–37.

[6] We should keep in mind that these two accounts were written in English and German respectively; therefore, the similarity in language can also be attributed to the tendencies of the translator. The two accounts, however, are structurally quite similar.

[7] March 15, 1842. See Paul R. Cheesman, "An Analysis of the Accounts Relating Joseph Smith's Early Visions" (Master's thesis, Brigham Young University, 1965), 64–65.

and thus added a continuing stream of information available to these early authors. In many respects, this situation mirrors the environment of the evangelists and their use of traditions in composing their Gospel accounts.

Are the Sermon on the Plain and the Sermon on the Mount the Same Sermon?

Several important stylistic similarities suggest that the Sermon on the Plain and the Sermon on the Mount are ultimately the same sermon. The Sermon on the Plain follows the order of the Sermon on the Mount almost identically for verses that the two discourses have in common. Of the thirty verses contained in the Sermon on the Plain, only three of them appear in a different order than they are found in the Gospel of Matthew (Luke 6:29–31); five verses do not appear in Matthew's Sermon on the Mount but are found elsewhere in the Gospel (Luke 6:34–35, 39–40, 45); and three do not appear in any other location (Luke 6:24–26).[8] Structurally, the two sermons contain a remarkable degree of similarity, literally paralleling one another in order of content. The Sermon on the Plain, however, does not contain any verses from the sixth chapter of the Gospel of Matthew, the central section of the Sermon, but literally skips that chapter in its entirety.[9] The evidence of shared order strongly suggests that the two sermons have a common heritage, although it does not force the conclusion that these two discourses are the same sermons delivered on the same occasion.

A discussion of the shared order of the sermons leads naturally into a discussion of shared wording. Although the two outlines may bear significant parallels, the absence of shared wording suggests that the original author significantly altered the wording of the original

---

[8] The word counts exclude the introductory accounts because these passages were obviously not spoken by Jesus but were likely original to the two different accounts.

[9] The Gospel of Luke does contain many of the passages from Matthew 6—although in different order and scattered throughout its account. See Matthew 6:7–15/Luke 11:1–4; Matthew 6:19–21/Luke 12:33–34; Matthew 6:22 23/Luke 11:34–36; Matthew 6:24/Luke 16:13; Matthew 6:25–34/Luke 12:22–32.

discourse (the Sermon on the Mount) but retained its original outline (the Sermon on the Plain), a feature that is common in edited works. The issue of a shared outline may also overemphasize the commonalities of the two discourses because two similar discourses can share a common structure but have little verbal similarity. This is not the case with the Sermon on the Plain and the Sermon on the Mount. The two sermons share a remarkable degree of verbal similarity, in some instances so strong that the conclusion has been made that both Matthew and Luke referred to an earlier written account.[10] Although some scholars have supposed that the evangelists composed the sermons themselves and altered an original account to fit their own needs, their similarity is also a hallmark feature of independent eyewitness accounts. It would be more disconcerting if the Gospels shared nothing between them—a sign that they were not themselves eyewitnesses or that they had used contradictory accounts. Modern court proceedings have made it painstakingly clear that eyewitness accounts do not always agree.

The Sermon on the Mount and the Sermon on the Plain contain a great deal of shared wording. Unfortunately, some of the similarities are lost in translation, and others may yet remain hidden because of textual difficulties with the Greek text. A few short examples may be sufficient to demonstrate the point.

Matthew:	Luke:
And why beholdest thou the mote that is in thy brother's eye, but considerest not the beam that is in thine own eye? (7:3)	And why beholdest thou the mote that is in thy brother's eye, but perceivest not the beam that is in thine own eye? (6:41)[11]

---

[10] Robert H. Stein, *The Synoptic Problem* (Grand Rapids: Baker Books, 1987), 95–104; John S. Kloppenborg Verbin, *Excavating Q: The History and Setting of the Sayings Gospel* (Minneapolis: Fortress Press, 2000), 90, 106.

[11] The KJV uses the words "perceivest" and "thine." The wording is identical in the Greek. The translators obviously were working either from a traditional translation or did not carefully compare their translations of these two verbatim passages.

Blessed are ye, when men shall revile you, and persecute you, and shall say all manner of evil against you falsely, for my sake. Rejoice and be exceeding glad: for great is your reward in heaven: for so persecuted they the prophets which were before you (5:11–12).	Blessed are ye, when men shall hate you, and when they shall separate you from their company, and shall reproach you, and cast out your name as evil, for the Son of man's sake. Rejoice ye in that day, and leap for joy: for, behold, your reward is great in heaven: for in the like manner did their fathers unto the prophets (6:22–23).

Such a high degree of verbal similarity, in many cases verbatim similarity, suggests a common origin for the two sermons. Although it is theoretically possible that they still represent two different sermons, that is highly unlikely. We would have to suppose that Matthew and Luke, or their earlier sources, each heard the two different sermons and were able to record, in many instances, verbatim parallels in the same order independently of one another. In an oral society where notebooks and writing instruments were not as portable as they are today, this situation seems highly improbable.

The Sermon on the Plain contains 573 words in Greek.[12] Of those, 170 have a verbatim parallel somewhere in Matthew, and 150 have a verbatim parallel in Matthew's Sermon on the Mount. Therefore, 30 percent of the Sermon on the Plain has a verbatim parallel in Matthew, and 26 percent has a parallel in the Sermon on the Mount. It is nearly impossible to imagine that Matthew and Luke both recorded these sermons entirely independent of one another and then were subsequently able to replicate almost identically the

---

[12] This number is subject to the decision of which textual variants to include and therefore may vary slightly if different variants are chosen or excluded. There are no fewer than fifty-eight variant readings for Luke's Sermon on the Plain.

other's outline.[13] Furthermore, one-fourth of their language is identical. These findings reveal a common origin or source for these two important sermons.

Luke's Clarifying Tendency

Another detail that may help to clarify whether the Sermon on the Plain and the Sermon on the Mount are indeed two separate discourses can be seen in Luke's corrective or clarifying tendencies. In the Sermon on the Mount, Matthew implies that the discourse was delivered to a group of disciples; however, if we look to the period before the sermon, only four disciples had been called. The Gospel of Matthew also refers briefly to the fact that Jesus had garnered a large following from Galilee, Decapolis, Jerusalem, Judea, and beyond Jordan, a list that includes several places Jesus had not yet visited (Matthew 4:18–21, 25). Matthew goes so far as to mention the fame of Jesus spreading beyond the boundaries of Galilee into Syria (Matthew 4:24). The Gospel of Matthew does not relate the call of the disciple Matthew until after the Sermon on the Mount, whereas the calling of the Twelve is only implied when Jesus prepares to send the Twelve on their first mission (Matthew 9:9; 10:1–5).

Luke, probably aware of the Gospel of Matthew, sought to clarify some of these difficulties. For example, in Matthew, Jesus did very little before delivering the Sermon on the Mount, and His miracles were limited to a brief and general description of actions that took place in Galilee but concerning which the author knew few details. Luke, on the other hand, recorded that Jesus had taught powerfully in Capernaum, Nazareth, Judea, and on the Sea of Galilee and had already had encounters with Pharisees in Galilee. In Luke, Jesus had gained enough of a following to catch the attention of Jewish authorities and also had become popular enough so that, as Matthew records, "his fame went throughout all Syria" (Matthew 4:24). Luke

---

[13] Robert K. McIver and Marie Carroll, "Experiments to Develop Criteria for Determining the Existence of Written Sources, and Their Potential Implication for the Synoptic Problem," *Journal of Biblical Literature* 121 (2002): 667–87.

clarifies this even further by showing that Jesus' fame had spread not only into all of Syria, and hence Damascus, but also into the bordering cities of Tyre and Sidon (Luke 6:17). There appears to be an intentional effort to clarify ambiguity in Matthew.

Luke also remedies the problem of whether the Twelve had been called prior to the sermon. In Luke 6:13–16, the author expressly states that the Twelve had been called and organized prior to the sermon, and therefore it could more logically function as missionary training for the newly called Twelve. Matthew, on the other hand, delays mentioning the Twelve until after the sermon. This strong corrective tendency, which is also seen elsewhere in Luke, is not a suggestion that one author is correct and the other incorrect. Instead, it is likely that as firsthand accounts, like Matthew, were read by second-generation Christians, there was a need to clarify and polish the newness and unrefined first-generation witnesses. This is often the case with firsthand and secondhand accounts. Luke's corrective tendency also suggests that he was working on the same sermon as recorded in Matthew; but, at the same time, he intended to make the story less ambiguous in historical detail.

Two Different Viewpoints

One of the most intriguing facets of the Sermon on the Plain and the Sermon on the Mount is the possibility that they represent two different vantage points for a single sermon delivered by Jesus during His mortal ministry. These two sermons most likely represent how Matthew and Luke, or their sources, felt about and understood this important discourse of the Savior. We recognize that all listeners come away with different vantage points, different perceptions, and independent inspiration. These different viewpoints do not alter what was originally spoken but instead reveal the thoughts, needs, and heart of the individual who left us the account. This is the case with the Sermon on the Mount and the Sermon on the Plain. We can naturally suppose that the Sermon on the Mount, which is highly focused on the future of the Church, issues of sin and righteousness within the Church, and current Church government, would be passed on in the name of one of Jesus' earthly Apostles. An Apostle, like Matthew, would have a much different vantage point than would one of Paul's traveling companions, namely Luke.[14]

An Emphasis on Poverty

When comparing these two great sermons in detail, we immediately recognize that Matthew and Luke understood "poverty" in a slightly different sense:

Matthew:	Luke:
Blessed are the poor in spirit: for theirs is the kingdom of heaven. . . . Blessed are the meek: for they shall inherit the earth[15] (Matthew 5:3, 5).	Blessed be ye poor: for yours is the kingdom of God. . . . Woe unto you that are rich! for ye have received your consolation (Luke 6:20, 24).

We can see that the inclusion of the phrase "in spirit" clarifies that economic poverty does not guarantee blessing, whereas Luke's open-ended "blessed are the poor" raises the question of who the poor are. Did Jesus' teachings in the sermon indicate that the poor "in spirit" and therefore the humble were the object of his discourse (Matthew), or did he mean "blessed are the poor" and therefore "woe unto you rich" (Luke)? Because both Matthew's and Luke's versions are translations from Jesus' spoken Aramaic, it is difficult to know the

---

[14] The complex issue of authorship cannot be resolved in a few short sentences. Few scholars today advocate the position that Matthew wrote Matthew and that Luke wrote Luke. Scholars tend to speak of traditions going back "to the time of Matthew" or to the "milieu of the early Church." Authorship is, in reality, a minute issue compared with the larger issue of whether a certain saying originated with Jesus. Although we cannot prove who wrote each Gospel account, we have sufficient evidence that they do accurately preserve the words spoken by Jesus Christ.

[15] Many scholars think that the same Aramaic word (the language of Jesus) stands behind these two beatitudes, *anawim*. See Ernst Bammel, "ptochos" in Kittel and Friedrich, *TDNT*, 6:904. The two different beatitudes may express the resultant hope associated with poverty—namely vindication in the present and glory in the hereafter. Therefore, each beatitude defines one aspect of hope associated with poverty.

exact words that were said. The second half of each beatitude, however, clearly directs the interpretation of the parable. Both versions promise that the poor will receive the kingdom of heaven. The present tense of the verb should not confuse the issue because the two phrases, "kingdom of heaven" and "kingdom of God," both refer to the future place of the poor in God's eternal kingdom.[16] Physical poverty is rarely remedied in earthly circumstances, whereas poverty is not an issue of the eternities unless we are to understand that future glory may be determined in part by the humble acceptance of earthly poverty.

The Gospel of Luke maintains a constant perspective on the reality of actual poverty and its relationship to the earthly kingdom or church. Much of what Luke felt and of how he understood poverty may have been a result of his experiences in the early Church and as a missionary companion of Paul.[17] Poverty was a persistent problem in the early Church, as evidenced by the neglect of the Greek widows (Acts 6:1), the collection for the poor Saints of Judea (Galatians 2:10), and the predominance of teachings on taking care of the poor within the Church (for example, James 1:27; 1 Corinthians 13:3; 1 John 3:17). Did Luke learn from experience that the need to supply temporal matters in the Church was a great concern and was intricately connected to the preaching of the gospel? Paul had made it abundantly clear that he had not required the Saints to provide temporally for him while he worked among them (1 Corinthians 9:18; 2 Corinthians 11:9). Paul's teachings often focused on the fact

---

[16] The verb "to be" should be understood as a proleptic present, referring to the future vindication of the poor in heaven. See F. Blass and A. Debrunner, *A Greek Grammar of the New Testament and Other Early Christian Literature*, rev. and trans. Robert W. Funk (Chicago: University of Chicago Press, 1961), 168.

[17] Linguistically, we have sufficient evidence to substantiate the claim that Luke and Acts were written by the same author. The author of Acts includes himself as a personal witness to some of the events of the second and third missionary journeys of Paul (Acts 16:10). According to the author's own account in Acts, he joined Paul in Troas as Paul was preparing for the mission into Macedonia. Regardless of the current skepticism concerning the connection to the Luke of the Pauline mission, the author clearly had valuable firsthand experience in the early Church.

that requiring the Saints to provide for him created a stumbling block to their acceptance of the Lord's teachings.

If the story of Lazarus and the rich man can be taken as indicative of what teachings held special importance for Luke, then we can see that riches can lead to neglect of weightier matters (Luke 16:19–31).[18] Although no special goodness is ascribed to Lazarus in the story nor any particular sin to the rich man, an underlying assumption is that Lazarus was worthy to enter the kingdom, whereas the rich man was not only excluded from the kingdom but also would not have accepted the word "though one rose from the dead" to deliver it (Luke 16:31). Luke's unique combination of the beatitude for the poor and the woe to the rich express a sentiment born of experience. Unlike Matthew, Luke may have been looking for teachings from the Lord that clarified the status of the rich in the kingdom. In Matthew, on the other hand, we see a greater emphasis on the role of Christ as the fulfillment of scripture, a teaching that held greater import to a newly converted disciple.[19]

Luke's beatitudes carry another nuance not felt in the beatitudes of the Sermon on the Mount. The beatitudes in the Sermon on the Mount are written in the third person plural (they), whereas the beatitudes of the Sermon on the Plain are all written in the second person plural (you). This vividness makes Luke's reporting of these teachings more direct in scope and personal in approach. Although both constructions achieve nearly identical results, Luke's is more direct. The Gospel of Luke emphasizes this point with the inclusion of the adverb "now." The inclusion of the temporal adverb creates a direct correspondence between earthly experiences and rewards in the hereafter.

Two of Luke's three beatitudes make the correspondence between what is experienced "now" with blessings that will reconcile

---

[18] Other instances of the Gospel of Luke's emphasis on the poor are 4:18; 7:22; 14:13, 21; 16:20, 22; 18:22; 19:8; 21:3.

[19] See Thomas A. Wayment, "Jesus' Use of the Psalms in Matthew," in *Covenants, Prophecies, and Hymns of the Old Testament*, ed. Victor L. Ludlow et al. (Salt Lake City: Deseret Book, 2001), 277–81.

these present discrepancies. The first beatitude lacks the adverb "now," but it is unnecessary since poverty is not a condition of eternity and must therefore already be part of present reality. It is also interesting that Luke's three beatitudes focus more particularly on present temporal concerns.[20] The three beatitudes of the Sermon on the Plain are "blessed be ye poor," "blessed are ye that hunger now," and "blessed are ye that weep now" (Luke 6:20–21). All three beatitudes share the common thread of present suffering. Two of the beatitudes focus particularly on conditions caused by poverty, and the third beatitude could be a result of those conditions. Did Luke's experience in the early Church expose him to poverty, hunger, and sadness? The outlook in the Sermon on the Plain emphasizes these teachings when viewed against the background of the Sermon on the Mount.

Love Thy Enemies

Both the Sermon on the Plain and the Sermon on the Mount include directives to love those who do not love us. In the Sermon on the Mount, these sayings are given in light of the law of Moses and stand as a corrective to the attitude of "an eye for an eye, and a tooth for a tooth" (Matthew 5:38). The context of the teaching on loving those who would traditionally be considered enemies suggests that a higher law was being given against the background of the law of retaliation (the *lex talionis*). The new law of Christianity is easily identifiable in this context. The Sermon on the Plain, however, does not refer to the law of Moses as the background for these teachings but instead presupposes the background of Christians who have been mistreated and marginalized in their own towns and cities. Luke included the unique verses, "Love your enemies, do good to them

---

[20] Luke's focus on present realities can also be seen in the saying, "Why call ye me Lord, Lord, and do not the things which I say?" (Luke 6:46). Both Matthew and Luke record this saying in a similar form, yet Matthew's focuses on rewards in the hereafter, whereas Luke's is aimed at those who appear to be Christians now but, in reality, are not living the gospel. See Matthew 7:21–23.

which hate you, bless them that curse you, and pray for them which despitefully use you" (Luke 6:27–28).

The Sermon on the Plain also refines the subject of two clauses that both sermons have in common. In Matthew, the two phrases, "but whosoever shall smite thee" and "if any man will sue thee," both appear to refer to the future fate of Christians who will go out into the world after the death and resurrection of Jesus and face opposition (Matthew 5:39–40). The indefiniteness of the subject of the verb directs the interpretation toward the future instead of the present realities of the disciples' world.

Luke, on the other hand, has interpreted or heard these passages differently, understanding them as present circumstances rather than future realities. Luke refines the subject of each verb, "unto him that strikes you" and "give to every man that begs of you," thereby focusing the listeners' attention on the "he" who is striking them on the cheek and the "beggar" who is asking help from them (Luke 6:29–30).[21] The Sermon on the Plain carries the sense of the present situation of Christians. Instead of placing these teachings in the context of the law of Moses, as does the Sermon on the Mount, Luke includes the saying, "As ye would that men should do to you, do ye also to them likewise" (Luke 6:31).

The Golden Rule, as many have called it, is also included in the Sermon on the Mount, but in that context, it appears toward the end of the sermon as a conclusion to the entire discourse. Luke, however, includes this statement in the context of getting along with those not of the faith and those who might mistreat them for their beliefs. It could be referred to as a statement on community behavior and inter-Christian relations; in Matthew it seems to focus more on behavior that will permit entrance into the kingdom as well as a prophecy of future persecutions. A first-generation Christian convert who had seen the struggles of the Church would be more apt to be inspired by those teachings that helped bring about harmony in the Church.

---

[21] The KJV reads, "unto him that smiteth thee" and "give to every man that asketh of thee."

Be Ye Therefore Perfect

Although we cannot be certain of the exact Hebrew adjective underlying the adjective "perfect" as it used in the statement "Be ye therefore perfect" (Matthew 5:48), we can be relatively certain of the sense of the word as it was employed by the evangelists Matthew and Luke.[22] In the Gospel of Matthew, the command comes at the end of the first chapter of the Sermon on the Mount and functions as a natural summary of the preceding contents. Matthew 5 contains a series of instructions that require absolute perfection. For example, in the command on adultery, how can anything more be required than casting out all impure thoughts and intentions? It is no longer enough to remove ourselves from impure actions; instead, we must not even think unchaste thoughts.

Likewise, in the commandment to love one's enemies, Jesus taught that if we love only those who love us in return, then we are no better off than the world. Instead, He said, we should also love our enemies and pray for those who would do us harm. If we love our friends already and if we expand that love to include those who despise us, then whom is left to love? Both requirements are absolute, requiring perfect obedience and discipleship. At the end of these instructions given in Matthew 5, it is, therefore, logical to point to our Father in Heaven who is perfect in this sense. The logical progression of Matthew 5 suggests that we can achieve the perfected position that the Father now enjoys.

The Gospel of Luke has a different perspective on this same issue. For Luke, the saying likewise comes at the conclusion of the materials from Matthew 5; but being a much shorter version of the same discourse, it appears that the saying comes in the middle of a rather short sermon. The wording is also quite different. Luke records the saying as "Be ye therefore merciful, as your Father in heaven is merciful" (Luke 6:36). Luke's account directs our attention to the

---

[22] The two likely candidates are "šalēm" or "tāmîm," which signify "unblemished" or "complete." See Genesis 6:9; Exodus 12:5.

practice of religion rather than to the result. Unlike the Sermon on the Mount in Matthew, Luke does not record the references that Jesus made to the law of Moses and how the new law changed it. Instead, the law of Moses and popular perceptions of it are clearly in the background of Luke—but are left unstated. The Sermon on the Mount develops as a series of opposites and uses logic to direct obedience. It is Luke, however, who recorded the famous reasoning of Jesus as "If ye do good to them which do good to you, what thank have ye?" or "if ye lend to them of whom ye hope to receive, what thank have ye?" (Luke 6:33–34). The context of the Sermon on the Plain is in the purity requirements of the law of Moses, whereas Luke's context is that of the early church.

The practical approach of the Sermon on the Plain focuses on daily events and daily life in the Church. The outlook, on the other hand, appears to have in mind the difficulties in organizing, administering to, and doing missionary work in a small branch. If only the members would love their enemies, the missionary work could proceed with vigor; or if the members could show true Christian love, fewer squabbles would take place in the branch. Luke seems to have been influenced by these practical concerns. Therefore, when including this summary statement that Matthew included as the summary of chapter 5, Luke gives the wording as, "Be ye therefore merciful, as your Father also is merciful" (Luke 6:36). Perhaps perfection was too lofty a goal when pragmatic concerns had influenced what the Spirit could teach. The reality of the matter is a matter of perspective. Do we look at the ideal or the present reality?

Much as in the Sermon on the Mount, where Jesus' saying on perfection functioned as a logical summary to chapter 5, even so in the Gospel of Luke, the saying on being merciful is a more logical summary to the everyday-life concerns of the Sermon on the Plain.[23] Both Matthew and Luke used the saying on the Father's perfection or

---

[23] The word for "mercy" in Luke 6:36 derives from the Greek *oiktos* and is used to describe the emotions of pity, mercy, and lamentation. Clearly, the author of the Gospel of Luke did not confuse this word for "perfect," which is recorded by Matthew.

mercy to conclude the first portion of their sermons. No real confusion between the terms in Greek or Aramaic is evident; therefore, it is highly unlikely that the authors of Matthew and Luke confused the original terminology when they recorded their Gospels. Instead, the two sayings are likely more interpretive than exact, or one of them may reveal the original wording whereas the other is more interpretive. On the basis of the Sermon to the Nephites in 3 Nephi 12–14, it would seem that Matthew has recorded the most accurate wording as it was originally delivered. Verse 48 in 3 Nephi 12 records the same saying as, "Therefore I would that ye should be perfect even as I, or your Father who is in heaven is perfect." This is not to say that Luke mistook what was said or inaccurately recorded what was taught.

More likely, the change from "perfect" to "merciful" reveals the same tendencies as seen elsewhere in the Sermon on the Plain. Luke's emphasis has been directed toward the more practical aspects of living together in harmony and the need for love and forgiveness in human relationships. Is Luke here interpreting Matthew's "perfect" in terminology that describes what makes God perfect? This possibility strongly suggests that it is God's mercy that makes Him perfect and therefore that the Sermon on the Plain refers to the Son instead of the Father as in Matthew. Matthew clearly intends the Father, as does the Sermon to the Nephites, but it is probably the Son whom Luke has in mind.

In 2 Corinthians 1:3, a grammatically difficult passage may provide a window into Luke's thinking. Paul taught, "Blessed be God, Father of our Lord Jesus Christ, who is the Father of mercies and God of all comfort."[24] The issue is whether the second clause refers to the Father or the Son. Did Paul mean to say that the Father is the God of comfort and mercy, or did he mean to say that the Son is the God of mercy and comfort? The KJV translators appear to have understood

---

[24] The KJV translates this passage as "Blessed be God, even the Father of our Lord Jesus Christ, the Father of mercies, and the God of all comfort." The NRSV translates it as, "Blessed be the God and Father of our Lord Jesus Christ, the Father of mercies and the God of all consolation."

it to mean the Son, whereas the above translation forces that interpretation.[25] If the Father is meant, then the passage can be understood to mean that God the Father is the author of the plan of mercy, but if the Son is meant, then He is understood as the Father of mercy and hence the Atonement of mankind.

Clearly, Jesus' most defining act was the Atonement, a fact that both Matthew and the Nephite Sermon point out. In Matthew's Sermon on the Mount, the Savior does not include Himself in the statement to be perfect, yet in the Nephite Sermon, the Savior states plainly, "even as I, or your Father who is in heaven is perfect" (3 Nephi 12:48). The physical difference between Matthew and 3 Nephi is that the Savior has completed the Atonement and has been resurrected. Luke became a Christian after the Atonement had been wrought; therefore, his perspective may fall more in line with 3 Nephi instead of the living Savior of the Sermon on the Mount. For Luke, the most accurate way to express the perfection of the Savior was to describe His mercy.

The Blessing of Persecution

Both Luke and Matthew record a beatitude that promises blessings to those whose faith engenders persecution. Each author includes this beatitude as a logical corollary to the directives on discipleship given in the opening lines of their sermons. Matthew's is probably more logically connected to the preceding beatitudes because, in his account, the seven preceding beatitudes set forth the requirements of how a disciple can be *in* the world but not *of* the world. The logical connection in Matthew is that those who live the law of discipleship set forth in the sermon can expect persecution. This sign, Jesus taught, should be interpreted positively because the prophets have regularly been persecuted. Although the account of the Sermon on the Plain carries many of the same connotations, a slight difference in viewpoint is evident.

---

[25] I believe that the repetition of the noun "Father" in the second clause forces a change of subject from the Father to the Son.

The Sermon on the Plain includes a fourth expression (*misēsōsin*) of hating as well as a more vivid expression of rejoicing. Luke 6:22–23 points to the nature of persecution more precisely than does the Sermon on the Mount. In its description of the persecution that will follow the righteous, the Gospel of Luke includes a direct connection between the name of Christians being slandered on account of "the Son of man." The historical reality behind this prophecy of Jesus may have been the eventual excommunication of Christians from the synagogues in the mid-fourth century A.D.[26] During the latter half of the first century A.D., as Jewish relations with the Roman government became increasingly strained, the Jewish leaders exerted increased efforts to strengthen solidarity among Jews and to exclude dissenters and outsiders. In this era, a document that has been passed down, the *Shemoneh Esreh* or the Eighteen Benedictions, was initiated. Various prayers are canonized in the document, but it is the twelfth "prayer" that has received so much attention. The twelfth prayer, known as the Birkhat ha-minim or "Blessing against the Heretics," contains a phrase that appears to curse Jews who had converted to Christianity but who still attended synagogue services.[27] During the late fourth century A.D., this benediction or prayer mandated the excommunication of Christians or Christian sympathizers from the synagogue.[28]

Although the author of the Gospel of Matthew would certainly have been interested in Jewish Christian relations in the first century, because the majority of early missionary work took place in the synagogues, the Gospel of Luke focuses more precisely on this issue. The phrase recorded in the Sermon on the Plain, "and cast out your

---

[26] Pieter W. van der Horst, "The Birkhat Ha-minim in Recent Research," in *Hellenism-Judaism-Christianity: Essays on Their Interaction*, ed. T. Baarda, et al. (Kampen, The Netherlands: Kok Pharos, 1994), 99–111. Van der Horst argues that the distinct addition of gentile Christians to this list took place in the anti-Jewish environment of the late fourth century A.D. Before that time, the prayer excluded all Jews whose views were contrary to orthodox Jewish beliefs, including Jewish Christians and Jewish Gnostics.

[27] The term "blessing of the heretics" is a euphemism for a cursing.

[28] Van der Horst, "The Birkhat Ha-minim," 110–11.

name as evil, for the Son of man's sake" (Luke 6:22), almost certainly has some direct connection to those early Jewish formulations that sought to define Judaism more precisely and to defend itself from what they viewed as heretical beliefs—that is, Christianity. Luke appears to have not only a later perspective, one engendered from the late first century A.D., but also one born in an environment of hostility to the faith. The Gospel of Luke also records the early opposition to Jesus in the Nazareth synagogue (Luke 4:28–29).

The Sermon on the Plain also specifies the origin of the persecution that will follow active believers. Matthew states simply, "For so persecuted they the prophets which were before you" (Matthew 5:12). The account in Luke adds the finger-pointing detail, "For in the like manner did their fathers unto the prophets" (Luke 6:23). Without trying to pinpoint blame for early Christian opposition, Luke is clearly making a direct genealogical connection between those who persecuted the prophets in the past (their fathers) and those who persecute Christians now (their children). The Sermon on the Plain makes the connection not only between the wicked and evil of the Old Testament but also between the prophets of the Old Testament and Christians. For the Sermon on the Plain, the children of the prophets are unmistakably associated with the Christians. Such sentiments may indeed have been born out of the opposition that Paul faced in his early missionary labors by the Judaizers.[29]

Two Sermons or One?

Did Jesus give two sermons or only one sermon? In connection with that question, another question that may legitimately be asked is, What difference does the answer make in our understanding of the Sermon on the Mount and the Sermon on the Plain? The following list outlines the key reasons for considering the Sermon on the Mount and the Sermon on the Plain to be different accounts of the same sermon delivered by Jesus.

---

[29] *Judaizers* is the generic term to describe the opposition that Paul faced from those who wanted to mire the early Church in Jewish controversies.

1. The similarity of structure, content, wording, and placement in the public ministry of Jesus all suggest a common background. Although the similarity does not rule out the possibility that Jesus gave two very similar sermons on different occasions, it does convincingly suggest that the two sermons derive from a very similar source. Scholars suggest that the two sermons derive from two disparate sources, Matthew and Luke; but internal evidence reveals that they share a common ancestry.

2. Both Matthew and Luke include their respective sermons prior to the first mission of the disciples in Galilee and toward the beginning of the public ministry (Matthew 10; Luke 9). If the sermons derive from a similar source, then we have two different accounts of what the early disciples understood and recorded of Jesus' earliest teachings. The accounts are different, not inaccurate, and tell us something of what was understood and felt on that day.

3. Neither Matthew nor Luke was called to be a disciple when the Sermon on the Mount or the Sermon on the Plain was delivered. Matthew records his own call two chapters after the conclusion of the Sermon on the Mount, and Luke likely converted in the fifties or early sixties (Matthew 9:9; Acts 16:10; Colossians 4:14; 1 Timothy 4:11).[30] Therefore, both of these disciples must have relied on earlier sources and accounts for their respective sermons and may have easily misunderstood that these two sermons were simply different accounts of the same sermon delivered months, or even decades, prior to their call.

4. Given Luke's tendency to permit his situation in the Church to dictate what he saw, felt, and understood, we are likely justified in thinking that the Sermon on the Plain represents a more-missionary-minded and new-convert-oriented version of the Sermon on the Mount. The early Church was faced with the

---

[30]The first of the so-called "we" passages occurs in Acts 16:10. Beginning with Acts 16, the author includes himself in many of the travels and events from Paul's life. Before that time, he reports the work of the early brethren in the third person singular. The suggestion is that Acts 16:10 corresponds to Luke's conversion date or the date for joining Paul on his second mission.

challenges of poverty, young and untrained leadership, and a need to organize the kingdom. The Sermon on the Plain provides answers to these very questions in the words of Jesus. The Sermon on the Mount is more directly focused on training the first group of disciples.

5. Luke's Sermon on the Plain provides an interesting glimpse into the struggles of the early Church and the ways in which its leaders and missionaries, such as Luke, administered the gospel. It reveals a profound devotion to the sacred words of the Lord and at the same time reveals that the men serving the Church were deeply influenced by the weight of their callings. Even though some of them had known the Lord personally, they still struggled with issues similar to those of our day.

6. We have no compelling reason to consider them to be different sermons, even though they are not verbatim accounts. In the modern world of computers, tape recorders, and media, we forget that there was no way to record every single word that Jesus spoke exactly as He said it. Authors went home and reconstructed what they heard and felt; and for many authors, they were inspired to remember the truths that were spoken (John 14:26). Granting that the ancients had superior memory to our own does not mean that they could hear a two-hour sermon and then return home and record every word that was spoken. The Sermon on the Mount and the Sermon on the Plain were delivered in such a society, where different individuals felt and heard what was most important to them. Their accounts reflect those differences.

Summary and Conclusions

The debate over whether the Sermon on the Plain and the Sermon on the Mount are the same sermon has created a wide rift among New Testament scholars. The results of this discussion have led to a variety of theories, some compatible with and some contrary to Latter-day Saint beliefs. Scholars have used the Sermon on the Mount and the Sermon on the Plain to discuss how the evangelists have altered, changed, and shaped the traditions they received. For many scholars today, Matthew is the sole author of the Sermon on the Mount, and Luke is likewise responsible for composing much of the Sermon on the Plain. Some scholars concede that a few verses may originate with the Savior but claim that, for the most part, the two sermons are the product of the early first-century Christian Church. These conclusions seem to make war against our faith and undermine our acceptance of the accuracy of the New Testament Gospels. These findings have forced a shift in more conservative scholarship, where it is now often claimed that the two sermons are really independent of one another and were delivered by Jesus on two separate occasions. Therefore, they cannot be used as easily to assert that Matthew and Luke both created their respective sermons. The various arguments used to support these claims are complex and difficult to appreciate. But are these sufficient reasons not to consider the possibility that these two sermons are really one and the same?

In nearly all eyewitness accounts, we find variations, disagreements, and ambiguities because no single author can comprehend all facets of existence. These variations, disagreements, and ambiguities are what lend credence to the accuracy of the Gospel accounts. We should also not be suspicious that later Christian authors would try to correct the difficulties in their firsthand accounts. Like our own accounts of the First Vision, we tend to favor one of the many different accounts, but we can still learn from the perspectives given in the other accounts. It may very well be that the account in the Pearl of Great Price is the most historically accurate, but that does not mean that the other accounts are not accurate. Their beauty lies in the fact that they reveal something of their author, setting, and time of composition. Luke and Matthew share a similar relationship. Luke's perspective, gained from his experiences in the cities of Paul's mission, helped him see things in a slightly different light. His emphasis was on the teachings of Jesus that helped remedy the problems the churches were facing in the latter half of the first century as Gentiles and Jews came together under the single banner of Christianity.

Surely there were difficulties associated with the cosmopolitan nature of early Christianity. The need for answers to these difficulties can still be seen in Luke.

It was Luke's generation that sought to answer the issue of poverty in the Church and take the Church from its humble beginnings to a well-structured and organized institution. Welfare must have been a major concern to the early Church members, especially as more affluent members joined their ranks. Luke's focus seems particularly aimed at helping members feel the need to share with one another and take care of others in need.

There is also a great concern in Luke over with the issue of persecution. Persecution must have been a significant part of Church life, and nearly all of Paul's epistles deal with the issue of persecution and enemies within the Church. Without persecution, the Church could not grow strong, but with persecution, it was difficult for the Church to grow large. Luke seems to have been particularly touched by the teachings of Jesus on faithful endurance of persecution. It may have helped him make sense of his own experiences as well as offer solace to those who were suffering in the churches. Clearly, the account that has been passed down to us as the Sermon on the Plain is born out of the experience of the somewhat hostile missionary setting of the early Church.

CONCLUSION

A JOURNEY THROUGH A SACRED STORY

RICHARD NEITZEL HOLZAPFEL AND THOMAS A. WAYMENT

We planned our venture into the Holy Land and the life of the Savior as if we were pursuing a journey through a sacred story, which indeed it is. Our plan from the beginning has been to tell the story in three segments—three volumes. If you have read this volume, you have experienced the second segment of the series.

We have intentionally pursued this project with the approach that "the last will be first." That is, the third segment of our journey, which is the first volume that was written in the series, is *From the Last Supper through the Resurrection: The Savior's Final Hours* (2003). For a season, we now end the first segment of our journey through the sacred story with this volume, *From Bethlehem through the Sermon on the Mount* (2005), and we have already made preparations to continue on to complete the third and final segment of this journey of discovery with the forthcoming volume, *From the Mount of Transfiguration through the Triumphal Entry* (2006).

This period of the third segment of our series, spanning from the time Jesus delivered His Sermon on the Mount through His final and fateful journey to the Holy City, just a week before the crowning events of His life, is a focus of the four Gospel authors. In our next volume, as we slip on our sandals, put on our cloaks, and pick up our walking staffs to continue this journey through a land made holy by the presence of God's own Son, we will ascend the Mount of Transfiguration and witness the majesty from on high. Next, we will listen attentively as Jesus teaches the multitudes and unfolds His message through parables. Finally, our travels will lead us to Galilee and Judea, where we will meet and become acquainted with Jesus' family and His faithful and loving disciples like Lazarus, Martha, and Mary.

We will pause for a season to paint a word-picture of Galilee and of Capernaum, the town where Jesus lived for nearly three years on the shore of a beautiful freshwater lake. Taking up our travels again, we will join the crowd gathered to hear Jesus and witness the feeding of thousands. Finally, nearly at journey's end, we will head south to Jerusalem and ascend from the Rift Valley to higher and higher elevations as we go up to Jerusalem to prepare ourselves for the final week of Jesus' ministry as described by the Gospel writers—some of whom were eyewitnesses of the events.

Though Matthew, Mark, Luke, and John may never have imagined that someone would carefully examine their unique and precious writings in the twenty-first century and treasure them more than any priceless gem, they nevertheless did record for all time the most important events that occurred in their lifetimes when John the Baptist startled his countrymen, announcing that the time had at long last arrived—the "Lamb of God, which taketh away the sin of the world" was already among them (John 1:29).

For Jesus, John the Baptist symbolized the final transition from the Old Testament (covenant) and the beginning of the New Testament (covenant). The time of the law and the prophets had passed, and the time of the Messiah had arrived. John the Baptist, the last legal administrator of the Mosaic covenant, had one foot in each dispensation. Jesus, like John, lived the fullness of two complementary covenants—the law of Moses and the higher law. They were both faithful Jews and Christians who taught the way to higher obedience. In fact, for the earliest followers of Jesus, the truths that Jesus taught were not described as Christian, nor were Jesus' followers called Christians while He traveled on His journey during His mortal ministry. His teachings were simply referred to as "the way" (Acts 11:26).

To say that the period from the birth of Jesus in Bethlehem until His death in Jerusalem is the most important epoch in world history is to say too little. No human's birth, life, and death have influenced the human race and all creation as much as His birth, life, and death, and they continue to do so today.

For the faithful, of course, the story of Jesus' mortal ministry, which ended in rejection, suffering, and death, does not close with His burial in a new tomb on a fateful Friday afternoon or with His resurrection on the first day of the week—Sunday morning. Reaching the end of a sacred journey in the final chapters of the Gospels, therefore, is not the end but is the beginning: "He is not here: for he is risen" (Matthew 28:6).

APPENDIX

THE BIRTH AND DEATH DATES OF JESUS CHRIST

THOMAS A. WAYMENT

To assume that there is anything like a consensus on the birth date of the Savior would be to underestimate the complexity of the issue. Outside of the Church of Jesus Christ, a lively discussion on this topic has been ongoing, a discussion that has certainly influenced the way in which Latter-day Saint commentators have made reference to the birth date of the Lord. To begin with, Elder James E. Talmage taught that "we believe Christ to have been born in the year known to us as B.C. 1 . . . in an early month of that year."[1] Further, Elder Talmage clearly understood Doctrine and Covenants 20:1 as an endorsement of April 6, 1 B.C. for the birth date of the Savior.[2] Shortly after the publication of *Jesus the Christ*, Elder Hyrum Smith of the Quorum of the Twelve Apostles wrote, "The organization of the Church in the year 1830 is hardly to be regarded as giving divine authority to the commonly accepted calendar. . . . All that this Revelation means to say is that the Church was organized in the year commonly accepted as 1830, A.D."[3] A generation later, Elder

---

[1] Talmage, *JTC*, 97–98.
[2] Talmage, *JTC*, 98.
[3] Hyrum M. Smith, *The Doctrine and Covenants Containing Revelations Given to Joseph Smith Jr., the Prophet with an Introduction and Historical and Exegetical Notes* (Salt Lake City:

J. Reuben Clark Jr. entered the discussion, saying, "I am not proposing any date as the true date. . . . I have taken as the date of the Savior's birth the date now accepted by many scholars—late 5 B.C., or early 4 B.C."[4]

To the historian, the question and answer are of vital importance because the result allows scholars to converse in a common language and make reference to an established reconstruction of the Savior's life that is fixed in time. Doctrinally, the question has little bearing on belief and practice and therefore has often been seen as a purely academic pursuit. Regarding the birth and death dates of the Savior, two different methods of answering the issue have been pursued, both of them underlined with questions. Did the Lord intend to reveal His own birth date in Doctrine and Covenants 20:1, or was it a recognition of the date of the organization of the Church using recognizable terminology? On the other hand, do we have enough data to accurately fix the birth and death dates?

We can learn important facts from an accurate reconstruction of the Savior's life—such as the date of Paul's conversion (which can be fixed in time in relation to the Savior's death), the expansion of the early Church out of Judea, and the impending influences of apostasy that subsequently entered the Church. These are just a few of the important things that can be ascertained if we understand accurately the birth date and therefore the death date of Jesus Christ.

This appendix will reconstruct the birth and death dates of Jesus Christ using our most accurate historical sources and methods. This approach does not mean that the dates given are fixed with certainty but means only that today these conclusions are based on the best information we have. We realize that the reconstructed dates will differ significantly from those of the Doctrine and Covenants, but we also realize that we should be conversant in both. Many do not realize that the writing of Doctrine and Covenants 20 was begun as early as

---

Deseret Book, 1919), 138.

[4] J. Reuben Clark Jr., *Our Lord of the Gospels: A Harmony of the Gospels* (Salt Lake City: Deseret Book, 1954), vi.

1829 and was authored by Joseph Smith and Oliver Cowdery. Therefore, the language of section 20 is based on the inspiration of the Prophet Joseph Smith and Oliver Cowdery, but the wording was not dictated directly by the Lord, as evidenced by an earlier draft of the section that was written in 1829.[5] The wording of Doctrine and covenants 20:1 likely reflects standard dating conventions of the day rather than the Lord's revealed endorsement of His birth date.

Several important historical considerations must be made if we are to establish firmly the dates of the birth and death of Jesus. First, the Gospel of Matthew informs us that Jesus was born during the reign of Herod (the Great) (Matthew 2:1). The Gospel of Matthew also records that Herod slew the infants in Bethlehem of two years of age and younger (Matthew 2:16). The Gospel of Luke relates that John the Baptist began his ministry in the fifteenth year of Tiberius, during the tetrarchy of Herod, Philip, and Lysanias (Luke 3:1–3). The Gospel of Luke notes that Jesus was about thirty years old at the beginning of His public ministry (Luke 3:23), and the Gospel of John says that Jesus taught for approximately three years.[6] John also records that the Jews, at the beginning of Jesus' public ministry, stated that their temple had been under construction for forty-six years (John 2:20). All four Gospels relate that Pontius Pilate was the Roman governor of Judea when Jesus was executed.

The date of Herod's reign has been firmly established by scholars, and both Josephus and Roman sources agree that he was proclaimed king of Judea in Rome in 40 B.C. and that he died in 4 B.C.[7] Josephus

---

[5] Lyndon W. Cook, *The Revelations of the Prophet Joseph Smith: A Historical and Biographical Commentary on the Doctrine and Covenants* (Salt Lake City: Deseret Book, 1985), 31–32, 125.

[6] It is a well-known fact that the synoptic Gospels depict Jesus' ministry as a one-year event and that the Gospel of John uses the framework of a three-year ministry. John speaks of three Passover festivals during Jesus' ministry (John 2:13; 6:4; 12:1). Another unnamed festival is spoken of in John 5:1 and may have indeed been another Passover. In the miracle of the feeding of the five thousand, the Gospel of Mark refers to "green grass," which is a definite springtime occurrence in Galilee, implying that Jesus' ministry did last beyond the assumed one-year period (Mark 6:39).

[7] Josephus, *War*, 1.14.4; *AJ*, 17.8.1

records that Herod ruled for thirty-seven years after being appointed by Antony in Rome and thirty-four years after the death of Antigonus I. Sometime during 40 B.C., after Antony had returned to Rome from the eastern empire, he conferred the title of king upon Herod after the latter had escaped Judea during the Parthian invasion of his homeland.[8] Although the exact season or month of 40 B.C. cannot be ascertained, if years are counted inclusively, we arrive at the year 4 B.C. for the death of Herod.[9] Josephus associates the death of Herod with a lunar eclipse that can be dated astronomically to either September 15–16, 5 B.C. or March 13–14, 4 B.C.[10] The difficulty with the date of 5 B.C. is that it cannot be easily reconciled with either the thirty-seven-year reign of Herod or the thirty-four-year period from the death of Antigonus I.

The mention that Herod slew the infants in Bethlehem has been taken to be either a historical inaccuracy of the Gospel of Matthew (a reason to alter the dates of Herod's reign so that he died up to two years after Jesus' birth) or a means of showing that Jesus was born as early as 6 B.C. Because Herod's dates can be fixed with confidence, we can wisely begin with them and work forward. The phrase in question, "*kata ton kronon on ēkribōsen para tōn magōn*," is rendered in the King James Version as "according to the time which he had diligently inquired of the wise men," or, in the New Revise Standard Version, as, "according to the time that he had learned from the wise men" (Matthew 2:16). The sense of the verb, *ēkribōsen*, an aorist indicative,

---

[8] Tacitus, *Histories* 5.9; Appian, *Historia Romana*, 5.7.75, *Bella Civilia*, 5.75; Dio Cassius, *Histories* 49.22.

[9] Cf. T. D. Barnes, "The Date of Herod's Death," *Journal of Theological Studies* 19 (1968): 204–9, who is followed by S. Kent Brown, C. Wilfred Griggs, and H. Kimball Hansen, Book Review of John C. Lefgren, "April Sixth," *BYU Studies* (1982): 376–67. Both argue for a possible death date of Herod in November/December 5 B.C. to allow sufficient time for the final acts of Herod's reign to be completed before the Passover in 4 B.C. The difficulty of 5 B.C. is that it does not allow for a thirty-seven-year reign from Antony's appointment of Herod, although placing the death of Herod only a few months prior than the traditional March 4 B.C. definitely decreases the issue. Scholarship has not followed T. D. Barnes in his proposed dating of September 15–16, 5 B.C. for the death of Herod.

[10] Josephus, *AJ*, 17.6.4.

is to ascertain exactly or precisely and describes Herod's intense interest to know the date previously established by the wise men.[11]

The dating provided by the wise men led Herod to believe that he could kill the infant Jesus if he were to kill all infants two and under. This thinking appears to suggest that Jesus may have been born up to two years previously; however, this dating places more weight on the evidence than it can support. First, Matthew records that the wise men were aware of Herod's intentions (Matthew 2:12), and therefore the possibility that they would have intentionally deceived him is considerable. Second, Herod's mental condition in his last few years of life was significantly compromised. Josephus records that Herod had become something of a madman during his last few years, and it is not beyond reason that he would have added a year or more to their calculations to be "safe," especially given that Bethlehem was such a small town.[12] Third, there are two ways to calculate the date based on the appearance of the star. The time of the star could indicate the date of the birth or conception of Jesus, a fact that may have been painfully obvious to Herod, who clearly lacked concrete information on the birth and whereabouts of the Messiah. Herod's attempt to kill the infants two years old and under may, therefore, be a simple calculation on this fact alone and may have had nothing to do with a sign of the birth that was given two years in the past.[13] By the time the wise men arrived, the sign of the conception could already have been a year in the past; therefore, Herod's calculation may be an attempt to catch all infants that were conceived about one year in the past. Therefore, this evidence should be used only with caution.

Based on the calendrical and Gospels evidence available to us today, the following chronology of Jesus' early days in Bethlehem appears to be correct. Jesus must have been born in the spring or

---

[11] Cf. Philo, *De Opificio Mundi*, 77; Josephus, *War*, 1.33.1.

[12] Josephus, *AJ*, 17.8.1–2; *War*, 1.33.7–8. Although from an earlier period, Old Testament references to Bethlehem consistently mention its small size; see Micah 5:2; Nehemiah 7:26; Ezra 2:21.

[13] Gerard Mussies, "The Date of Jesus' Birth in Jewish and Samaritan Sources," *Journal for the Study of Judaism* 29 (1998): 417.

winter of 5 B.C., during the final year of Herod the Great's reign in Judea and Galilee. Joseph and Mary stayed in Bethlehem for at least the forty-day period of Mary's purification and Jesus' circumcision, naming, and presentation at the temple. While the family was still in Bethlehem, they learned of Herod's edict to slay the infants of Bethlehem, and the young family fled to Egypt. Whether Jesus was born in spring or winter of 5 B.C., the family would have stayed in Egypt no longer than ten months and possibly less than a month. At the death of Herod in March, 4 B.C., the family of Joseph returned to Judea and intended to go back to Bethlehem but instead went to Joseph's hometown of Nazareth because Herod's son, Archelaeus, ruled in Judea.

The logical sequence of events is that the family of Jesus waited in Bethlehem until Mary could complete her days of purification and the young Jesus could be both circumcised and presented at the temple (Luke 2:21–24; Leviticus 12:1–8). The Gospel of Matthew records that the wise men visited Jesus sometime early in His life. This visit appears to have taken place in the city of Bethlehem, although the evidence is not conclusive (Matthew 2:8, 16). Herod's attempt to slay the infants in Bethlehem implies he was under the impression that the infant Jesus was still there. Matthew does not indicate that Jesus was still in the manger, but the family had probably made more accommodating arrangements (Matthew 2:11; Luke 2:16). Matthew uses the term "house" to describe the living quarters of Jesus' family when the wise men arrive, whereas Luke uses the term "manger" in reference to the visit of the shepherds. While in Bethlehem, and still within close proximity of Jerusalem and the temple, Mary and Joseph could easily travel back and forth to the temple to take care of important ordinances. It may even have been while they were at the Jerusalem temple that the actual act of slaying the infants was carried out, and that may explain why none of the Gospel writers recorded a miraculous delivery of Jesus. His family may have simply been at Jerusalem doing what Mosaic law required. After a short stay in Egypt, the young family of Joseph would have returned to their home in Nazareth, where Luke implies that they lived prior to Jesus' birth (Luke 2:4).

The reference to the fifteenth year of the reign of Tiberius as the starting point for the ministry of John is also helpful. The death of Augustus is known precisely: August 19, 14 A.D. We also know that the Senate subsequently proclaimed Tiberius emperor on September 17 of the same year. If we simply add fifteen years to the reign of Tiberius, then a date of A.D. 29 is the logical starting point for John's ministry and also the baptism of Jesus. This date implies that Jesus began His ministry in the same year and subsequently died in A.D. 32 or 33. One of the difficulties of this reconstruction is that Luke also records that Jesus was about thirty years old at the beginning of His ministry. If the date of A.D. 29 is used as the date for the beginning of the public ministry and if we work backward thirty years, then Jesus would have had to be born in 1 or 2 B.C.—dates that do not coincide with the death of Herod. To remedy this inconsistency, scholars have been overly hasty to conclude that Luke is not a historically reliable source. This conclusion, however, is clearly not the case.

After returning from a self-imposed exile in Rhodes in 4 B.C., Tiberius was granted tribunican powers from the Senate for a ten-year period.[14] The extent of Tiberius's *imperium* can be appreciated by the Senate's approving a term of ten years, as opposed to the normal five years, a grant to command the Roman legions in Germany, and Augustus's adoption of Tiberius.[15] The extent of Tiberius's power and command was likely limited at this time to Gaul and the provinces. This situation continued until Tiberius's proconsular power was extended in A.D. 13.[16] Previous to A.D. 13, it is questionable

---

[14] The granting of tribunican powers gave to Tiberius essentially the same powers as the emperor. It was an act of goodwill toward Tiberius by the Senate, and it confirmed their choice of a replacement for Augustus after the death of his grandsons Gaius and Lucius.

[15] The events can be dated to June 26, 4 B.C., and Tiberius's popularity is confirmed by his reluctance to accept such titular honors. See Velleius, 2.104; Suetonius, *Tiberius*, 16.1; Tacitus, *Annals*, l.3.3.

[16] Barbara Levick, *Tiberius the Politician* (London: Thames and Hudson, 1976), 63.

whether Tiberius could exert his powers in the Roman capital, and they were likely limited strictly to his areas of command. After a series of impressive military victories, all limitations on Tiberius's *imperium* were removed on October 23, 13 A.D.[17] The question that arises is whether those living in Greek-speaking communities (like Luke) or the colonies would recognize the date in A.D. 13 as the beginning of Tiberius's reign, or would it be counted only from the point after Augustus had died in A.D. 14? Although considerably later than the period in question, there is strong evidence in the third century that the date of the emperor's actual exercise of power was used to calculate their reigns and not the beginning of their titular rule.[18]

We also know that Augustus counted the years of his own reign from the date when he was granted tribunican powers (the *tribunicia potestas*, the same powers granted to Tiberius in A.D. 13).[19]

If this method of calculating the reign of Tiberius in the Gospel of Luke was used, then we arrive at the date of A.D. 27 for the beginning of John the Baptist's ministry—if the years are counted inclusively. Assuming that Jesus began his public ministry shortly after John's and calculating backward thirty years (Luke 3:23), we arrive at a birth year of Jesus in 4 B.C., corresponding exactly to the reign of Herod.

Another important piece of information comes from John 2:20 where the Jews say that "forty and six years was this temple in building, and wilt thou rear it up in three days?" The statement in John refers to the expansion and enlargement of the temple that took place under Herod and continued in Jesus' day. Assuming this to be a

---

[17] Levick, *Tiberius*, 63; Victor Ehrenberg and A. H. M. Jones, *Documents Illustrating the Reigns of Augustus and Tiberius*, 2d ed. (Oxford: Clarendon Press, 1955), 54; Suetonius, *Tiberius*, 20.1; 21.1; Velleius, 2.121; Ovid, *Epistulae ex Ponto*, 2.1; 2.2; 3.3, 85.

[18] Clearly, Tertullian has calculated a date in the reign of Tiberius using the hegemony of Tiberius as the starting point; see Tertullian, *Against Marcion* 1.15. See Rainer Riesner, *Paul's Early Period: Chronology, Mission Strategy, Theology*, trans. D. Stott (Grand Rapids: Eerdmans, 1998), 39–40.

[19] P. A. Brunt and J. M. Moore, eds., *Res Gestae Divi Augusti: The Achievements of the Divine Augustus* (Oxford: Oxford University Press, 1967), 10; Ronald Syme, *The Roman Revolution* (Oxford and New York: Oxford University Press, 1939), 336; Dio Cassius, *History*, 56.28.

statement that represents the first year of Jesus' mission as it is depicted in the Gospel of John and by calculating forward from the date of the beginning of the Herodian temple, we should be able to arrive at a date for the first year of Jesus' public ministry. Josephus records two different dates for the beginning of the construction on the Jerusalem temple, 23–22 B.C. and 20–19 B.C.[20] Scholars have generally assumed that the earlier reference to 23–22 B.C. is either inaccurate or refers to the date when planning began for the temple lot.[21] The earlier date would also point to a date of 23 A.D. for the beginning of Jesus' public ministry, an impossibly early date. However, when the latter date is used, a date of 26–27 A.D. emerges as the first year of Jesus' ministry, a date that coincides well with our previous calculations.

The final piece of evidence comes from the last week of the Savior's life when He was crucified during the Passover. The Last Supper, by all accounts, occurred during the day(s) prior to the Passover in Jerusalem.[22] All four Gospels also agree that the Crucifixion took place on Friday and that Jesus was buried on that same day.[23] The four Gospels agree that the day of the execution was the preparation day for the Sabbath.[24] The synoptics and John, however, differ on some important aspects of the dating of the Last Supper. According to the synoptic accounts, the Last Supper would have taken place on Thursday, the 15th of Nisan (the first month of the Jewish calendar) and was a Passover meal (Matthew 26:17; Mark 14:2; Luke 22:7–8, 15). John, however, relates that the Last Supper, not a Passover meal, took place on the day of preparation and the day that the sacrificial lambs were slaughtered in the temple—therefore, the 14th of Nisan (John 18:28, 39). Jewish tradition mandated that the Passover

---

[20] Josephus, *War*, 1.21.1; *AJ*, 15.11.1.
[21] Karl P. Donfried, "Chronology," in Freedman, *ABD*, 1:1014.
[22] See John 13:1; Matthew 26:2; Mark 14:1; Luke 22:1.
[23] See John 19:31, 38–42; Matthew 27:50, 57–62; Mark 15:37, 42–46; Luke 23:46–54.
[24] John 19:31, 42; Matthew 27:62; Mark 15:42; Luke 23: 54–56.

sacrifice be made on the 14th day of the first month.[25] The day following was to be the day of the Passover meal—after sundown on the 15th of Nisan. The Passover celebration would then continue for another seven days. The discrepancy between the synoptics and John has proven to be a nearly insurmountable obstacle, and no simple solution to this problem exists.[26]

For several important reasons, the chronology of the Gospel of John should be preferred to that of the synoptics. First, the tradition that Jesus became the new Passover Lamb for Christians is already found in the writings of Paul (1 Corinthians 5:7). Second, Pilate's granting of amnesty to a prisoner on the eve of Passover can make sense only before the actual Passover festival had begun.[27] Third, many scholars have suggested that Pilate's presence in Jerusalem would have been part of his judiciary assignment in the city, and any hearings or trials must have taken place before the Passover had begun.[28] Therefore, Pilate would have tried Jesus before the feast had actually started. Fourth, a later Talmudic tradition from the second century dates the execution of Jesus to the day prior to the Passover and thus on 14 Nisan.[29] Finally, the Gospel of Peter, a late second-century Christian apocrypha, dates the crucifixion of Jesus to the day before the Passover.[30] Although the lateness of this pseudepigraphical work causes some reservations, it clearly bears witness that by the second century, Christians were already following the chronology of the Gospel of John instead of that of the synoptics, a fairly strong argument that the early Church felt John's account to be more accurate in this matter.

---

[25] Exodus 12:19; Leviticus 23:5; Numbers 9:1–5; 28:16.

[26] For a thorough discussion of the various solutions that have been offered, see David R. Seely, "The Last Supper According to Matthew, Mark, and Luke," in Richard Neitzel Holzapfel and Thomas A. Wayment, eds., *From the Last Supper through the Resurrection: The Savior's Final Hours* (Salt Lake City: Deseret Book, 2003), 64–74.

[27] Riesner, *Paul's Early Period*, 48–49.

[28] Riesner, *Paul's Early Period*, 49.

[29] Hermann L. Strack and Paul Billerbeck, *Kommentar Zum Neuen Testamentum aus Talmud und Midrasch*, 6 vols. (Munchen: Oscar Beck, 1926), 2:812n1; 834–35.

[30] *Gospel of Peter*, 5.3

APPENDIX: THE BIRTH AND DEATH DATES OF JESUS CHRIST

Modern advances in astronomy also permit us to make some calculations to determine the days on which the Passover fell during the period in question and how those dates correspond to the new moon that was seen during the last week of Jesus' life. The most logical range of dates would be those Passover festivals that occurred during the governorship of Pilate in Judea (A.D. 26–36).

We must consider the fact that Passover takes place during the rainy season of the year and that any society dependent upon an actual sighting of the new moon to calculate their months will always produce discrepancies because of inclement weather. Therefore, any astronomical calculations used to determine a late winter or early spring date in Judea should be viewed with caution. From the period of Pilate's tenure in Judea, two likely dates emerge as possibilities for the date of the crucifixion, April 7, 30, and April 3, 33, based on astronomical calculations of when the Passover festival fell on a Friday, the day of Jesus' death, during the reign of Pilate (A.D. 26–36).[31]

From the foregoing discussion, we can immediately see that the date in April 33 can be excluded for several reasons. It cannot account for a birth date during the reign of Herod, Jesus' age of thirty at the beginning of His ministry, and a subsequent three-year public ministry. According to all of the data, if April 33 is accepted, then Jesus must have been about thirty-seven years old when he died. This date also seems to conflict with the dating offered in the Book of Mormon. The evidence provided by the Book of Mormon reveals that the time period between the sign of Jesus' birth and the signs of His death was thirty-four years (thirty-three if counted inclusively).[32] Unfortunately, we do not know whether the Book of Mormon peoples used a solar or a lunar calendar or exactly how their years correspond to our Julian calendar. We do know that in either method of calculation, lunar or solar, a period of thirty-seven years can be ruled out.

---

[31] Riesner, *Paul's Early Period*, 50.
[32] 3 Nephi 8:5.

APPENDIX: THE BIRTH AND DEATH DATES OF JESUS CHRIST

The most likely date for the death of the Savior is A.D. April 7, 30.[33] This date coincides with the majority of other date-specific references in the Gospels and elsewhere. It can account for a birth date under the reign of Herod and a subsequent life span for Jesus of about thirty-three to thirty-four years. It also agrees with the dating provided by Josephus and Roman sources for the reigns of important historical figures. The early Christian author Clement of Alexandria also refers to this date.[34] The Montanists, an early Christian splinter group, also recognized April 6 or 7 as the date of Jesus' crucifixion.[35] After considering all the historical accounts, we maintain that the first weekend of April A.D. 30 is the most likely time of the death of Jesus. His birth took place between spring and winter of 5 B.C.

---

[33] This would mean that when comparing Book of Mormon date references to our modern Gregorian calendars, we should subtract four years to give us the modern date. Unfortunately, using this method does not yield a date that corresponds with the known dates of Zedekiah's reign.

[34] *Stromateis* 1.21.146.

[35] Riesner, *Paul's Early Period*, 51.

CONTRIBUTORS

Richard Neitzel Holzapfel
Director, Religious Studies Center—Publications
Associate Professor of Church History and Doctrine, Brigham Young University
Ph.D. from University of California at Irvine in Ancient History
From the Last Supper through the Resurrection: The Savior's Final Hours (Salt Lake City: Deseret Book, 2003).

Thomas A. Wayment
Assistant Professor of Ancient Scripture, Brigham Young University
Ph.D. from Claremont Graduate School in New Testament Studies
From the Last Supper through the Resurrection: The Savior's Final Hours (Salt Lake City: Deseret Book, 2003).

Kent P. Jackson
Professor of Ancient Scripture, Brigham Young University
Ph.D. from University of Michigan in Old Testament and Ancient Near Eastern Studies
The Book of Moses and the Joseph Smith Translation Manuscripts (Provo, Utah: Religious Studies Center, Brigham Young University, 2005).

Jeffrey R. Chadwick
Associate Professor of Church History and Doctrine, Brigham Young University
Ph.D. from University of Utah in Middle East Archeology
"Lehi's House at Jerusalem and the Land of His Inheritance," in Glimpses of Lehi's Jerusalem, ed. John Welch, David Rolph Seely, and Jo Ann Seely (Provo, Utah: Foundation for Ancient Research and Mormon Studies, 2004).

CONTRIBUTORS

S. Kent Brown
Professor of Ancient Scripture and Director of Ancient Studies, Brigham Young University
Ph.D. from Brown University in Religious Studies with and emphasis in New Testament and Early Christian Studies
Voices from the Dust: Insights from the Book of Mormon (American Fork, Utah: Covenant Communications, 2004).

Richard D. Draper
Professor of Ancient Scripture and Associate Dean of Religious Education, Brigham Young University
Ph.D. from Brigham Young University in Ancient History
"The First Coming of the Lord to the Jews: A Book of Mormon Perspective," in *A Book of Mormon Treasury: Gospel Insights from General Authorities and Religious Educators* (Salt Lake City, Deseret Book, 2003).

Eric D. Huntsman
Assistant Professor of Ancient Scripture, Brigham Young University
Ph.D. from University of Pennsylvania in Ancient History
"Before the Romans," in *From the Last Supper through the Resurrection: The Savior's Final Hours* (Salt Lake City: Deseret Book, 2003).

Gaye Strathearn
Assistant Professor of Ancient Scripture, Brigham Young University
Ph.D. from Claremont Graduate School in New Testament Studies
"Simon and the Woman Who Anointed Jesus' Feet," *Religious Educator* 5:(2004).

Cecilia M. Peek
Assistant Professor of Classics and Comparative Literature, Brigham Young University
Ph.D. from University of California at Berkeley in Ancient History and Mediterranean Archaeology
"The Burial," in *From the Last Supper through the Resurrection: The Savior's Final Hours* (Salt Lake City: Deseret Book, 2003).

Frank F. Judd Jr.
Assistant Professor of Ancient Scripture, Brigham Young University
Ph.D. from University of North Carolina at Chapel Hill in New Testament and Early Christianity
"The Priceless Parables," *Ensign*, 33 no. 1 (January 2003).

Andrew C. Skinner
Professor of Ancient Scripture and Dean of Religious Education, Brigham Young University
Ph.D. from University of Denver in European and Near Eastern History
Golgotha (Salt Lake City: Deseret Book, 2004).

SCRIPTURE INDEX

Genesis
1:1, pp. 160, 183
1:3, p. 303
4:12, p. 189
6:9, p. 369
6:18, p. 270
12:3, p. 124
17, p. xxii
18:9, p. 176
22:1, p. 175
22:1–10, p. 71
22:1–18, p. 10
22:2, p. 169
22:2, 12, 16, p. 175
22:2,012, p. 10
24:65, p. 109
48:7, p. 136
49:10, p. 126

Exodus
1, p. 124
3:1, p. 189
3:11, 13, p. 112
3:11,013, p. 93
3:11–14, p. 265
4:1, p. 93
4:1, p. 112
5:1, 10:9, p. 151
6:23, p. 101
12.1, p. 175
12:3–10, p. 180

12:5, p. 369
12:19, p. 392
13:2, 11–15, p. 117
13:21, p. 190
15:20–21, p. 101
16:29, p. 320
16:35, p. 270
19, pp. xxii, 174
19:1, p. 332
20:8–10, p. 320
20:12, p. 320
20:13, p. 328
22:16–17, p. 104
23:14, p. 151
23:14–17, p. 106
23:20, p. 164
23:20, pp. xix, 164, 190
24, p. 243
24:1, p. 54
24:18, p. 270
34:1–2 (JST), p. 331
34:19, p. 175
34:19–20, p. 117
34:21, p. 321
34:27–28, p. 270
34:28, p. 186

Leviticus
1:14, p. 141
4:7, p. 141

12, p. 80
12:1, p. 388
12:2, p. 141
12:2–8, p. 116
12:8, p. 81
13, p. 324
15:11, p. 64
18:13–16, p. 200
19:18, p. 321
20:21, p. 200
21:13–14, p. 100
23:5, p. 392

Numbers
9:1, p. 392
9:12, p. 8
10:33, p. 190
11:16, p. 54
13:26–30, p. 198
14:33–35, p. 270
18:15–16, p. 117
18:19, p. 345
20:5, p. 189
21:8, p. 10
24:17, p. 145
30:3–5, 16, p. 104
35:5, p. 320

Deuteronomy
4:2, p. xxvii
6, p. 186

SCRIPTURE INDEX

6:4, p. 185
6:4–7, p. 348
6:13, p. 186
6:16, pp. 185, 187
8, p. 186
8:1–5, p. 186
8:2, p. 186
8:3, pp. 185, 186, 190
8:25, p. 189
9:9, 18, p. 186
11:29, p. 256
14:1, p. 346
16:16, p. 151
18:15, p. 124
18:15, 18, p. 11
18:15–18, pp. 262, 335
18:18, p. 255
18:18–19, p. 263
21:10–13, p. 104
21:22, p. 57
22:13, p. 133
22:15, p. 104
22:21, p. 107
22:22, p. 133
22:23, p. 129
27, p. 256
27:4–8, p. 256
27:11–12, p. 256
32:10, p. 189

Joshua
3:15, p. 167
8:33, p. 256

Ruth
1:22, p. 136

1 Samuel
16:11, p. 94

2 Samuel
7:4, p. 127
7:8, p. 130
7:12, p. 127
12:1–12, p. 165

1 Kings
2:35, p. 50
7:51, p. 71
12:1–16, p. 250
14:6, p. 230
17, p. 298
19, p. 189
19:8, p. 186

2 Kings
1:8, pp. 165, 199
5, p. 298
15:29, p. 288
15:30, p. 108
16:9, p. 108
17, pp. 251, 253
17:24, pp. 249, 252
17:32–33, p. 252
18:26, p. 22

1 Chronicles
3, p. 127
24, p. 51

2 Chronicles
3:1, p. 71
34:9, p. 253
36:15, p. 230

Ezra
2:21, p. 387
4, pp. 251, 253, 254
4:2, 10, p. 249
4:3, p. 254
4:4–6, p. 254
5, p. 254
7:14, p. 231

Nehemiah
7:26, p. 387
13:23–28, p. 257
13:28–31, p. 257

Job
30:3, p. 189
38:26, p. 189

Psalms
1:1, p. 337
2, pp. 11, 177
2:7, pp. 11, 169, 177
14:2–3 (JST), p. 8
22, p. 12
22:1, p. 12
22:1, 7–8, 18, p. 12
22:6–8, p. 12
22:16, p. 12
22:18, p. 12
23, p. 87
69:25, p. 13
72:10, p. 145
72:10, 11, 15, p. 147
91, p. 83
91:11–12, p. 185
107:4, p. 189

Proverbs
21:19, p. 189
23:7, p. 326

Isaiah
1, p. 111
1:4–5, p. 8
2:2, pp. 69, 71
7:11, 14, p. 109
7:14, pp. 13, 108, 129, 135, 150
7:14–16, p. 111
7:15, pp. 108, 156
7:16, p. 108
7–8, p. 14
8:1–4, p. 13
9, 40, p. 17
9:1, p. 290
9:1–7, p. 14
9:2, p. 289
9:6, p. 130
9:6–7, p. 14
9:7, p. 289
13:21, p. 189
18:1–2, p. 232
21:1, p. 189
34:14, p. 189
40:1–5, p. 15

SCRIPTURE INDEX

40:3, p. 35
40:3, pp. 14, 164
42:1, p. 169
42:1, 6–7, p. 15
42:1–4, p. 15
42:1–7, p. 15
42:6, p. 15
42:7, p. 15
43:2, p. 174
43:11, p. 9
49:6, p. 142
49:7, p. 145
52:10, p. 142
53, pp. 16, 18
53:2, p. 156
53:3–5, p. 16
53:7–12, p. 180
60:6, p. 147
60:16, p. 9
61:1–2, pp. 17, 278, 295
61:1–11, p. 17
63:7, p. 174
63:11, p. 175
63:14, p. 175
63:16, p. 175
64:1, p. 175
64:12, p. 175

Jeremiah
1:6, pp. 93, 112
2:2, p. 190
6:6–7, p. 8
18:11, p. 165
21–22, p. 165
31:6–7, p. 150
31:15, p. 148
31:31, p. xxii
41:17, p. 136
49:14, p. 230

Ezekiel
22:2–4,008–13, p. 8
23:40, p. 230

Daniel
5:24, p. 231

6:16, p. 183
7:14, p. 130

Hosea
2:15, p. 190
4:1–2, 11–18, p. 8
11:1, pp. 13, 149
11:1–12, p. 13
13:15, p. 189

Joel
2:28–29, p. 167

Amos
2:4, 6–8, p. 8

Micah
5:2, pp. 146, 148
5:2, p. 387
6:10–13, 16, p. 8

Habakkuk
1:2–4, p. 8

Zephaniah
1:4–6, p. 8

Zechariah
9:9, p. 17
9:11, p. 18
13:4, p. 199

Malachi
3:1, pp. 35, 164

Matthew
1, pp. xviii, 126
1:1, p. 32
1:18, pp. 113, 128, 129, 133
1:18–19, p. 105
1:18–25, p. 175
1:19, pp. 133, 134
1:20, pp. 105, 113, 127, 134
1:20–21, p. 106
1:20–25, p. 273

1:21, p. 134
1:22–23, p. 275
1:23, pp. 13, 109
1:25, p. 129
1:33 (JST), p. 166
1–2, p. 217
1–7, p. 306
1–13, p. 311
2:1, pp. 145, 385
2:1–8, p. 17
2:4 (JST), p. 146
2:8, 16, p. 388
2:9, p. 147
2:11, pp. 114, 118, 144, 388
2:12, pp. 273, 387
2:13, pp. 106, 118
2:13–15, 19–21, p. 273
2:15, p. 13
2:15,017–18, 23, p. 275
2:16, pp. 118, 144, 385, 386
2:19–20, p. 119
2:20, p. 149
2:22, pp. 272, 273
2:23, p. 273
2:24, 26 (JST), p. 169
3:1–12, p. 166
3:1–7:29, p. 238
3:3, pp. 15, 274
3:4, p. 199
3:5, pp. 173, 190
3:7, pp. 67, 198
3:7–10, pp. 173, 207
3:13–17, p. 172
3:14, p. 173
3:15, p. 173
3:16, pp. 162, 168, 191
3:16–4:11, p. 204
3:17, pp. 162, 175
3:24–25 (JST), p. 157
3:43 (JST), p. 172
3:45 (JST), p. 162
3:46, p. 162

SCRIPTURE INDEX

4:1 (JST), pp. 39, 182
4:1, pp. 38, 39, 182, 184
4:1, 8, p. 184
4:1,003, 10, p. 186
4:1–2 (JST), p. 182
4:1–11, pp. 186, 202, 269, 274
4:1–11, pp. 162, 191
4:2, p. 187
4:3, pp. 182, 184
4:3–9, p. 181
4:3–10, p. 202
4:4, p. 186
4:5 (JST), p. 82
4:5, p. 82
4:5, 8 (JST), p. 186
4:5–7, pp. 76, 83
4:6, p. 184
4:8–9, p. 184
4:11 (JST), p. 187
4:11, p. 187
4:12, pp. 150, 272, 276, 308
4:12–13, 18–22, p. 203
4:12–16, p. 275
4:13–14, p. 276
4:13–17, p. 289
4:13–22, p. 222
4:15, p. 290
4:17, pp. 270, 289, 290, 291
4:18, p. 362
4:18, 21, p. 313
4:18–22, p. 218
4:18–23, p. 308
4:23, p. 291
4:23–25, p. 292
4:24, p. 362
4:24–25, p. 333
5, pp. 333, 334, 369
5:1, pp. 308, 312, 333
5:1–2, p. 333
5:1–7:29, pp. 238–39
5:2 (JST), p. 310
5:2, p. 335

5:3 (JST), p. 310
5:3, p. 356
5:3, 5, p. 364
5:3–4 (JST), p. 334
5:4, p. 340
5:5 (JST), p. 340
5:6, p. 342
5:7, p. 342
5:8 (JST), p. 342
5:8, p. 343
5:9, p. 343
5:10, p. 344
5:11–12, p. 361
5:13, p. 345
5:14, p. 345
5:16, p. 345
5:17, pp. 323, 325, 326, 332
5:18, 26, p. 23
5:18–19, p. 324
5:22, pp. 23, 353
5:31 (JST), p. 325
5:38, p. 367
5:39, p. 368
5:43, p. 321
5:44, pp. 322, 346
5:45, p. 346
5:48, pp. 337, 369
5–7, pp. 309, 322
6, pp. 334, 347, 359
6:1 (JST), p. 309
6:1–6, p. 347
6:6, p. 347
6:7, pp. 348, 359
6:8, p. 348
6:9, pp. 36, 349
6:9, 13, p. 349
6:14–15, p. 349
6:16–18, p. 349
6:19, p. 359
6:22 (JST), p. 349
6:22, p. 359
6:23, p. 349
6:24, pp. 349, 350
6:25, p. 359
6:25–34, p. 315
6:25–39 (JST), p. 334

6:33, p. 350
7, pp. 334, 351
7:1 (JST), p. 350
7:1, p. 239
7:1, 4, 7, 9 (JST), p. 310
7:3, p. 360
7:6–7 (JST), p. 351
7:6–17 (JST), p. 334
7:9 (JST), p. 239
7:9, p. 310
7:9–11 (JST), p. 351
7:12, p. 61
7:14–17 (JST), p. 352
7:18–19, p. 352
7:21, p. 367
7:24, p. 353
7:28, p. 309
7:28, p. 309
7:28–29, pp. 319, 336
7:29, p. 336
7:36 (JST), pp. 309, 316
7:37, p. 323
8:1–10:42, p. 238
8:5, p. 355
8:5–13, p. 239
8:17, p. 16
8:28–9:1, p. 240
9:1–2, p. 203
9:1–8, p. 285
9:9, pp. xxvi, 172, 313, 362, 375
9:14, p. 312
9:18–19, 23–26, p. 240
9:20–22, p. 240
9:27–34, p. 240
10, pp. 217, 334, 375
10:1, pp. 312, 362
10:1, 5, p. 234
10:1–2, p. 311
10:1–42, p. 238
10:2, p. 232
10:2–4, pp. 225, 312
10:3, p. 224
10:3, 38, p. 226

10:5, pp. 240, 248, 266
10:7–8, p. 240
10:8, p. 262
11:1, pp. 39, 234, 311, 312
11:2, p. 312
11:11, p. 212
11:14, p. 165
11:28–30, p. 340
12:1–21, p. 225
12:14–15, p. 272
12:28, p. 189
13:1–43, p. 239
13:53–58, p. 294
13:54, p. 317
13:54–58, p. 277
13:55, pp. 105, 156
13:58, p. 28
14:1–13, p. 200
14:3–12, p. 276
14:14–21, p. 240
14:27, p. 240
15:1–6, p. 62
15:1–6, p. 64
15:2, p. 319
15:20, p. 64
15:33, p. 202
16, p. 67
16:13, p. 241
16:14, p. 165
16:16, p. 241
16:17, p. 218
16:18, p. 242
16:19, p. 242
16:21–23, p. 243
16:23, p. 186
17:1–13, p. 243
17:5, p. 171
17:9, p. 244
17:10–13, p. 165
17:14–21, p. 285
17:22–23, pp. 243, 276
18:1–35, p. 244
18:18, p. 244
19:25, p. 317

20:1–12, p. 74
20:17, pp. 234, 311
20:17–19, p. 243
20:18–19, p. 276
20:20–28, p. 224
21:1–11, p. 87
21:4–5, pp. 18, 275
21:12, p. 78
21:12–16, p. 49
21:12–17, p. 87
21:23–25, p. 67
21:23–27, p. 87
21:33–46, p. 49
21:43, p. 290
22:15–17, p. 68
22:15–25, p. 88
22:16, p. xv
22:23, p. 57
22:23–33, p. 88
22:32 (JST), p. 317
22:33, p. 317
22:34–40, p. 88
23, p. 64
23:1–3, p. 64
23:1–39, pp. 88, 347
23:13–33, p. 173
23:35, pp. 96, 97
23:39, p. 347
24:1, p. 88
24:5, p. 32
24:20, p. 320
26:2, pp. 196, 391
26:2, 14–16, 48, p. 276
26:14, 20, 47, p. 234
26:17, p. 391
26:26, p. xxii
26:36, p. 28
26:39, p. 275
26:53–54, p. 275
27:20–22, p. 57
27:35, pp. 12, 275
27:39–43, p. 12
27:50, 57, p. 391
27:55–56, p. 218
27:62, p. 391
28:6, p. 381

28:19, p. 290
6:2, p. 23

Mark
1: 23–26, p. 297
1:1, pp. xxv, 160, 161, 166, 171
1:2, pp. xix, 35, 164, 166
1:2–3, pp. 15, 164
1:2–8, pp. 163, 166
1:3, pp. 181, 274
1:3, 5, p. 166
1:4 (JST), p. 166
1:4, pp. xix, 161, 165
1:4, 6:16–29, p. 165
1:5, p. 168
1:6 (JST), p. 167
1:6, p. 165
1:7, pp. xxix, 163, 164
1:9 (JST), p. 162
1:9, p. 168
1:9–10, p. 191
1:9–11, p. 168
1:9–15, p. 166
1:10 (JST), p. 182
1:10, pp. 162, 168
1:10–11, p. 168
1:11 (JST), p. 184
1:11, pp. 168, 169, 189
1:12–13, pp. 181, 269, 274
1:12–13, p. 202
1:13, pp. 162, 182, 183, 189, 191
1:14, pp. 202, 281
1:14, p. 276
1:14–15, pp. 270, 279, 286
1:15, p. 161
1:16–20, pp. 218, 222, 280
1:21–28, p. 281
1:22, pp. 281, 317
1:23–26, p. 282

401

1:23–28, p. 162
1:24, p. 284
1:24–26, p. 286
1:27, pp. 287, 318
1:33–34, p. 162
1:44, p. 324
2:14, pp. xxvi, 223, 224
2:14, p. 172
2:18–20, p. 321
2:23, p. 321
2:23–3:12, p. 225
2:24, p. 321
3:6, pp. 66, 67
3:11, p. 171
3:13–14, p. 238
3:13–35, p. 228
3:14, pp. 232, 234, 238
3:16–19, p. 225
3:18, p. xxvi
3:19–21, p. 228
3:22, p. 228
3:31, p. 228
3:32–35, p. 228
4:1–34, p. 239
4:10, p. 234
4:35–41, p. 240
5:1–21, p. 240
5:7, p. 171
5:22–24, 35–43, p. 240
5:25–34, p. 240
5:41, p. 23
6:1–6, pp. 277, 294
6:2 (JST), p. 317
6:2, p. 317
6:3, pp. 105, 138, 156
6:5, p. 28
6:7, pp. 234, 238
6:15, p. 11
6:15, p. 165
6:17–19, p. 200
6:30, p. 240
6:34–44, p. 240
6:39, pp. 197, 385
6:50, p. 240

7:1–13, pp. 62, 64
7:3, 5, p. 319
7:5, p. 321
7:10–13, p. 320
7:11, p. 64
7:34, p. 23
7:37, p. 317
8:4, p. 202
8:11–15, p. 67
8:15, pp. 65, 67
8:27, p. 241
8:31 (JST), p. 241
8:31–9:1, 30–37, p. 243
9:2–13, p. 243
9:3 (JST), p. 163
9:7, p. 171
9:9, p. 244
9:29, p. 285
9:35, p. 234
10:3–5, p. 243
10:26, p. 317
10:32, p. 234
11:1–11, p. 87
11:11, p. 234
11:15–19, p. 87
11:17–33, p. 87
11:27, p. 68
11:27–28, p. 170
12:6, p. 171
12:13, p. 68
12:13–17, p. 88
12:14, p. 69
12:18, p. 57
12:18–27, p. 88
12:28–34, p. 88
12:38–40, p. 88
13:1, p. 88
14:1, p. 391
14:1, p. 196
14:2, p. 391
14:10,017, 20, 43, p. 234
14:32, p. 28
14:36, pp. xv, 23
14:51–52, p. 25
14:62, p. 171

15:11–13, p. 57
15:34, p. 23
15:37, 42, p. 391
15:39, p. 171
15:40, pp. 218, 224
15:42, p. 391
16:6, p. 161
16:15, p. 290
6:17–29, p. 276
9:11–12, p. 165
11:18, p. 317

Luke
1, pp. xviii, 52, 163
1:1, pp. xxiii, xxvi, 123
1:3, p. 38
1:3, p. 39
1:5, pp. xvii, 82, 98, 199
1:5, 36, pp. 101, 126
1:5–23, 39–44, 57–80, p. 177
1:6, p. 98
1:7, 18, p. 98
1:9, 11, p. 92
1:12, p. 111
1:13, pp. 92, 98
1:15, p. 98
1:18, pp. 92, 98
1:20, 22, 62, p. 95
1:24, p. 99
1:25, p. 98
1:27, pp. 128, 129
1:28, pp. 110, 129
1:29, pp. 111, 129
1:30, pp. 111, 130
1:31, p. 130
1:31, 34, p. 111
1:31–32, p. 99
1:32, pp. 127, 130
1:33, p. 130
1:34, pp. 129, 130
1:34–35, p. 113
1:35, pp. 113, 130, 131
1:36, pp. 94, 100, 112, 132, 217

1:39, p. 198
1:39–56, p. 197
1:40, p. 132
1:41, p. 99
1:42, p. 100
1:42–43, p. 99
1:44, pp. 100, 132
1:45, p. 99
1:46–55, p. 101
1:56, pp. 105, 110
1:57–79, p. 95
1:61–64, p. 95
1:67, 76–79, p. 96
1:67–79, p. 95
1:80, p. 161
1–2, p. 217
2:4, p. 389
2:5, p. 135
2:7 (JST), pp. 114, 115
2:7, p. 115
2:7, pp. 114, 115, 116, 138
2:7–8, p. 114
2:8, pp. 94, 112
2:9, p. 138
2:10, pp. 138, 139
2:11, pp. 138, 170
2:12 (JST), p. 139
2:12, p. 139
2:14, p. 139
2:15, p. 139
2:18, p. 140
2:21, pp. 80, 106, 388
2:22, p. 116
2:22–23, p. 117
2:23, p. 106
2:24, p. 116
2:25, p. 142
2:25–38, p. 81
2:26, p. 142
2:29, p. 142
2:32, p. 142
2:33, p. 144
2:34, p. 143
2:35, pp. 117, 143
2:38, p. 143

2:39, p. 117
2:41, pp. 106, 196
2:41–51, p. 107
2:43, pp. 38, 178
2:46 (JST), pp. 154, 316
2:46, pp. 61, 153, 154
2:46–47, p. 82
2:47, p. 316
2:48, p. 154
2:48–49, p. 297
2:49, p. 154
2:51, p. 155
2:52, p. 157
3:1, pp. 308, 385
3:1–2, p. 176
3:1–14, p. 176
3:1–19, p. 176
3:1–20, p. 166
3:2, p. 201
3:3, p. 201
3:4, p. 274
3:4–6, p. 15
3:5 (JST), p. 176
3:7, p. 198
3:7–9, p. 207
3:9, p. 161
3:12 (JST), p. 166
3:13 (JST), p. 165
3:18, p. 168
3:19–20, pp. 165, 200, 276
3:21, p. 177
3:21–22, pp. 162, 191, 204
3:22, pp. 177, 178
3:23, pp. 107, 169, 176, 198, 385, 390
3:28 (JST), p. 177
4:1, pp. 182, 188
4:1–13, pp. 162, 188, 191, 202, 204, 274
4:1–14, p. 269
4:2 (JST), p. 184
4:3, p. 184
4:3–11, p. 181
4:3–12, p. 202

4:5, 9 (JST), p. 186
4:5–7, p. 184
4:8, p. 187
4:9, p. 82
4:9–11, p. 184
4:9–12, p. 83
4:13, p. 188
4:14, pp. 162, 191, 202
4:14–16, p. 203
4:14–30, p. 277
4:16, p. 110
4:16–30, pp. 222, 295, 298
4:17, p. 22
4:18, pp. 189, 191
4:18–21, p. 296
4:21, p. 17
4:22, p. 297
4:24, p. 297
4:25–27, p. 298
4:28, p. 374
4:28–30, p. 17
4:29, pp. 278, 295
4:30, p. 298
4:31–32, p. 162
4:31–37, p. 298
4:32 (JST), p. 317
4:32, p. 317
4:33, p. 317
4:33–37, p. 162
5:1–11, pp. 218, 222
5:10, p. 218
5:16, p. 189
5:27, p. 223
6:1–5, p. 62
6:1–11, p. 225
6:12–13, p. 214
6:12–16, p. 334
6:13, pp. 214, 228, 230, 233, 311, 363
6:13–49, p. 313
6:14–16, p. 225
6:17, p. 363
6:17–49, p. 239
6:20, pp. 356, 367
6:20, 24, p. 364

6:22, pp. 373, 374
6:22–23, p. 361
6:23, p. 374
6:24, p. 359
6:27, p. 368
6:29, p. 359
6:31, p. 368
6:33, p. 370
6:34, p. 359
6:36, pp. 369, 370
6:41, p. 360
6:46, p. 367
7:1–10, p. 239
7:11–17, p. 240
7:19, p. 39
7:28, p. 212
7:28, 33–34, p. 163
8:1 (JST), p. 239
8:1, p. 236
8:2–3, p. 223
8:4, p. 239
8:22–25, p. 240
8:26–40, p. 240
8:41–42, 49–56, p. 240
8:43–48, p. 240
9, p. 375
9:1, p. 236
9:1–2, p. 238
9:1–5, p. 334
9:10, pp. 233, 240
9:11–17, p. 240
9:20 (JST), p. 241
9:28–37, p. 243
9:35, p. 171
9:36, p. 244
9:43, p. 317
9:51–53, p. 268
9:51–56, p. 251
10:1, pp. 237, 350
10:25–37, p. 267
10:34, p. 137
11:2, p. 36
11:34, p. 359
11:49, p. 233
11:51, pp. 96, 97
12:22, p. 359

12:33, p. 359
15:4, p. 202
16:13, p. 359
16:31, p. 366
17:5, p. 233
17:11–19, p. 267
19:1–10, p. 223
19:29–44, p. 87
20, p. 69
20:19–22, p. 69
20:20–26, p. 88
20:27, p. 57
20:27–39, p. 88
20:45–47, p. 88
22:1, pp. 196, 391
22:3, 28, 31, p. 188
22:7, p. 391
22:11, pp. 115, 137
22:14, p. 233
22:31, p. 183
22:37, p. 16
22:42, p. 155
23: 54, p. 391
23:13–23, p. 57
24:10, p. 233
24:18, p. 224
24:27, p. 18
24:39, p. 12
24:44–45, p. 19

John
1, p. 206
1:1, pp. xxvii, xxviii, 160, 180
1:1, 14, p. 264
1:1–2, p. 170
1:3, p. 303
1:6–28, p. 166
1:14, p. 109
1:19, pp. 201, 207
1:19, 23, p. 204
1:19, 24, p. 52
1:19–25, p. 165
1:19–28, p. 201
1:20–29 (JST), p. 11
1:21, pp. 124, 199
1:23, p. 274

1:24–28 (JST), p. 331
1:25, p. 11
1:27, pp. 38, 39
1:28, p. 166
1:29, pp. 20, 180, 278, 380
1:29–33, p. 179
1:29–34, p. 201
1:30, p. 180
1:31, p. 180
1:31, 33, p. 198
1:32, pp. 162, 191
1:32–34, p. 179
1:33, p. 201
1:33–34, p. 167
1:34, p. 278
1:35, p. 204
1:35–42, pp. 219, 278
1:35–44, p. 204
1:35–51, p. 216
1:36, pp. 208, 217
1:37, 40, p. 204
1:37–40, p. 201
1:38–39, p. 217
1:40–42, p. 217
1:41, p. 218
1:42, p. 218
1:43, pp. 204, 299
1:43, 50, p. 278
1:44, p. 219
1:45, pp. 107, 220, 299
1:46, pp. 150, 220, 278
1:47–48, p. 220
1:49, p. 299
1:50, p. 300
2, p. 83
2,001–12, p. 301
2:1, p. 104
2:1–10, p. 120
2:1–11, pp. 279, 300, 302
2:1–11, p. 221
2:4, pp. 277, 301
2:5, pp. 301, 303
2:6, pp. xv, 52

2:6–10, p. 301
2:11, pp. 221, 300, 304
2:13, pp. 196, 197, 205, 385
2:13–4:42, p. 205
2:13–17, p. 48
2:13–25, p. 222
2:14–16, p. 205
2:15, pp. 52, 78
2:16, pp. 49, 83
2:18, p. 207
2:18, 20, p. 83
2:19, p. 83
2:20, pp. 385, 390
2:22, p. 205
2:23, p. 83
3, p. 260
3:1, pp. 84, 206
3:1–12, p. 222
3:2, pp. 62, 206, 207
3:3–13, p. 208
3:14–15, p. 10
3:16, p. xx
3:16–17, p. 185
3:17, p. 365
3:22, p. 162
3:23, pp. 166, 201
3:23–26, p. 167
3:30, p. 209
3:31, pp. 248, 260
3:31–4:3, p. 247
4, pp. 249, 267
4:1–3, pp. 202, 207, 209
4:1–4 (JST), p. 167
4:4, p. 247
4:4–42, p. 222
4:5–6, p. 247
4:6, p. 261
4:8, pp. 205, 248, 260
4:10, p. 261
4:11, p. 261
4:14, p. 261
4:15, p. 261
4:16–18, p. 262
4:19, p. 262

4:19–20, p. 251
4:20, p. 263
4:20, p. 263
4:21, p. 264
4:22, p. 264
4:24, p. 264
4:25, pp. 255, 265
4:26 (JST), p. 265
4:26, p. 265
4:27, p. 266
4:28, p. 265
4:34, p. 266
4:35, p. 266
4:38, p. 266
4:39, p. 267
4:41, p. 267
4:42, pp. 259, 267
4:43–54, p. 222
5, pp. 45, 57, 84, 85
5:1, pp. 45, 84, 196, 224, 385
5:1–16, p. 57
5:1–18, p. 225
5:2–9, p. 74
5:16, p. 84
5:17–47, p. 225
5:28–29, p. 85
5:35, p. 163
6, p. 260
6:1, p. 45
6:1–15, p. 302
6:4, pp. 196, 385
6:14, p. 11
6:15, 26–34, p. 181
6:20, p. 240
6:35–58, p. 241
6:67–69, p. 241
6:69, p. 241
6:71, p. 227
7, p. 85
7:1, p. 85
7:5, p. 143
7:10, p. 85
7:14, 31–32, p. 85
7:15, p. 22
7:19, p. 85
7:20, p. 85

7:21, p. 85
7:22–24, p. 86
7:25, p. 85
7:30, p. 277
7:32, p. 86
7:45–52, p. 78
7:50–51, p. 86
8, p. 260
8:12, p. 345
8:19, p. 114
8:19, 41, p. 136
8:20, pp. 79, 277
8:23, p. 260
8:33–58, p. 86
8:41, p. 114
8:48, p. 86
8:48–52, p. 267
8:52–53, p. 86
8:56–57, p. 180
9, p. 62
9:1, p. 86
9:1–7, p. 79
9:6–7, p. 86
9:14–16, p. 86
9:16, p. 62
9:18, p. 86
9:22, p. 87
9:35–41, p. 87
10, p. 87
10:22–23, p. 87
10:23, p. 74
10:31, p. 87
10:41, p. 168
11, p. 260
11:16, p. 226
11:47–57, p. 78
11:54, p. 189
11:55, p. 196
12, p. 87
12:1, p. 385
12:12–50, p. 87
12:16, p. 18
12:20–22, p. 220
12:20–36, p. 243
12:23, 27, p. 277
12:28, p. 171
12:38, p. 16

SCRIPTURE INDEX

13, p. 260
13:1, pp. 277, 391
13:16, p. 233
14:5, p. 226
14:6–14, p. 264
14:16–18, 26, p. 342
14:26, p. 376
16:13–16, p. 342
17:1, p. 277
17:18, pp. 245, 246
18:3, pp. 54, 65
18:5, p. 317
18:6, p. 317
18:12, p. 176
18:28, 39, p. 391
18:31, pp. 23, 29
19:6, p. 57
19:12,015, p. 58
19:24, p. 12
19:25, pp. 218, 224
19:31, 38, p. 391
19:31, 42, p. 391
19:36, p. 8
20: 31, p. 179
20:19–23, p. 246
20:21–23, p. 244
20:27–28, p. 226
20:31, pp. xiii, 47
21:2, p. 220
21:15, p. 180
21:20–24, p. 216
21:25, p. xxix
7:1–4, p. 181
21:2, p. 221

Acts
1:1, p. xxiii
1:2, 26, p. 233
1:5, p. 167
1:8, pp. 266, 290
1:12, p. 320
1:13, p. 225
1:20, p. 13
1:21–22, pp. 191, 215, 234
2, p. 167
2:36, p. 170

2:37, 42, p. 236
2:37, 42, 43, p. 233
3:11, p. 74
3:18, 24, p. 20
4:1, p. 93
4:3, p. 75
4:33, 35, 36, p. 236
4:33, 35, 36, p. 233
5, p. 63
5:2, 12, 18, 29, 40, p. 236
5:12, p. 74
5:17–18, p. 63
5:21, p. 63
5:24, p. 93
5:27–39, p. 55
5:33–40, p. 63
6:1, p. 365
6:6, pp. 233, 236
6:11–14, p. 323
6:14, p. 323
8, p. 267
8:1, 14, 18, p. 236
8:1,014,018, p. 233
8:30–31, p. 18
8:32–33, p. 16
9:27, pp. 233, 236
10:37, p. 161
10:37–38, p. 170
10:37–43, pp. xxv, 172
10:38, pp. 162, 191
11:1, pp. 233, 236
11:1–2, p. 323
12:12, p. xxv
12:25, p. xxv
13:12, p. 318
13:33, p. 11
14, p. 238
14:4, p. 234
14:14, p. 233
14:14, p. 236
15:1–2, p. 323
15:2, 4, 6, 23, p. 233
16:4, pp. 233, 236
16:10, pp. xxvi, 25, 375

17:2–3, p. 18
18:24, p. 39
19:1, p. 168
20:29, p. 32
21:37–40, p. 75
22:24, p. 75
5:2, 12, 18, 29, 40, p. 233
5:18, p. 75
15:2, 4, 6, 23, p. 236

Romans
1:1, p. 233
1:3, pp. 101, 126
4:25, p. 31
6:3, p. 171
8:32, p. 10
11:13, p. 233
14:19, p. 344
16:7, pp. 233, 235
5:8, p. 31

1 Corinthians
1, p. 365
1:1, p. 233
1:23, p. 31
2:8, p. 31
4:9, pp. 233, 236
5:7, pp. 8, 31, 180, 392
9:1, 2, 5, p. 233
9:5, p. 236
10:13, p. 182
11:23, p. 31
12:28, 29, p. 233
12:28–29, p. 236
13:3, p. 365
15:7, p. 236
15:7, 9, p. 233
15:54, p. 34
15:9, p. 236

2 Corinthians
1:1, p. 233
1:3, p. 371
7:10, p. 341
8:23, p. 233

8:23, p. 235
11:5, p. 235
11:5,013, p. 233
11:9, p. 365
11:13, pp. 235, 236
13:5, p. 182

Galatians
1:1, p. 232
1:1, 17, 19, p. 233
1:15, p. 31
1:17, p. 236
1:19, p. 236
2:20, p. 236
3:5, p. 236
4:1, p. 236

Ephesians
1:1, p. 233
2:2, p. 181
2:20, p. 242
3:5, p. 233
4:11, p. 233
18, p. 126
2:20, p. 233

Philippians
2:5, p. xxviii
2:8, p. 31
2:25, pp. 233, 235
3:10, p. 31

Colossians
1, p. 375
1:1, p. 233
2:14, p. 31
4:14, pp. xxvi, 375
1, p. 31

1 Thessalonians
2:6, p. 233
3:5, p. 182

2 Thessalonians
2:6, p. 236

1 Timothy
1:1, p. 233
2:7, p. 233
6:13, p. 31
6:20, p. 41

2 Timothy
1:1, 11, p. 233

Titus
1:1, p. 233

Hebrews
2:14, p. 189
2:16, p. 158
2:17, p. 158
2:17–18, p. 181
3:1, pp. 213, 233
5:2, p. 181
5:8, p. 158
5:8–9, p. 174
9, p. 345
9:15, p. 270
9:28, p. 16
4:15–16, p. 181

James
1, p. 109
1:27, p. 365
2, p. 126
2:8, p. 31
9, p. 102
18, p. 115

1 Peter
1:1, p. 233
1:19, p. 8
5:13, p. xxv

2 Peter
1:1, p. 233
1:16, p. 171
1:17, p. 31
1:19, p. 244
2:13, p. 34
3:2, p. 233

1 John
4:8, p. 345
5:7, p. 40

Jude
1:17, p. 233

Revelation
1:1, p. xxiv
1:5, p. 181
4:1, p. 168
5:6, p. 180
11:19, p. 168
19:11, p. 168
22:18, p. xxvi
22:19, p. 30

1 Nephi
1:9, p. 4
1:19, p. 4
4:10–18, p. 328
4:18, p. 328
10, p. 216
10:4, p. 4
10:6, p. 5
10:7–9, p. 5
10:9, p. 166
10:11, p. 5
10:14, p. 5
10:17, p. 5
11:13, p. 123
11:13, 15, p. 109
11:16, p. 123
11:18, p. 129
11:18–20, p. 112
11:19, p. 131
11:20–21, p. 109
11:27, p. 178
11:34, p. 214
14:18–27, p. 216
22:20, p. 124
22:21, p. 11
3, p. 11

2 Nephi
10:3, p. 5
10:5, p. 53
11:4, p. 8

SCRIPTURE INDEX

25:4, 7, p. 4
25:19, p. 5
31:5–13, p. 174
31:8, p. 178

Jacob
4:4, p. 20
4:5, pp. 10, 169
5:48, p. 353

Mosiah
2:1, 6, p. 92
3:5, p. 5
3:5–6, p. 5
3:7, p. 6
3:8, pp. 107, 111, 129
3:9, p. 6
3:10, p. 6
3:13, p. 3
3:15, p. 4
5:2, 7, p. 344
12:31–32, p. 318
13:27, p. 327
13:33, p. 20
14–16, p. 16
15:1, p. 6
15:7–9, p. 6
16:7, p. 6
27:24–26, p. 344

Alma
5:14, pp. 344, 346
7:10, pp. 107, 113, 129
7:11, p. 182
12:9, p. 4
19:13, p. 111
25:15, p. 324
29:8, p. 4
32:4–12, p. 264
34:8, p. 6
34:13–14, p. 324
34:14, p. 8

39:15, p. 6

Helaman
5:12, pp. 242, 353
8:14–15, p. 10
8:16, 18, p. 20
14:2, p. 121
14:5, p. 147

3 Nephi
1:6, p. 122
1:7, p. 122
1:11, p. 121
1:12, p. 122
1:15, p. 122
1:16, p. 122
1:18, p. 122
1:21, p. 147
1:24, p. 323
1:25, p. 323
7:26, p. 314
8:5, p. 393
9:13, p. 314
9:17, 19, p. 325
11:1, p. 92
11:1–2, p. 314
11:29, p. 344
12, pp. 334, 371
12:1, p. 314
12:1–2, p. 339
12:1–12, p. 338
12:3, p. 340
12:6, p. 342
12:29, p. 325
12:48, p. 372
12–14, pp. 309, 313
13, p. 334
13:25, p. 334
13:25–34, p. 315
14, p. 334
14:1, p. 315
15:5, pp. 323, 336
15:9, p. 345

19:1–3, p. 314
20:24, p. 20
27:19, p. 343
28:6, pp. 29, 31

Ether
4:16, p. 216
12:27, p. 340

Doctrine and Covenants
1:38, p. 329
4, p. 266
7:1, p. 29
7, p. 216
20, p. 384
20:1, p. 384
33:1, p. 143
63:61, p. 349
84:24–26, p. 331
84:45, p. 349
88:17–20, p. 342
88:40, p. 342
88:141, p. 216
93:13, p. 157
93:29–30, p. 280
107:23, 35, p. 311
127, p. 97
131:5, p. 244
138, p. 16
77:1–15, p. 216

Moses
1:39, p. 304
6:31, pp. 93, 112

Abraham
3:21–22, p. 280
3:22, p. 129

Articles of Faith
1:9, p. xx

SUBJECT INDEX

Aaronic priest(s): temple and, 51–52; build Temple of Herod, 71; Jesus Christ as, 82
Accuracy, perspective and, 376–78
Action, thoughts lead to, 325–26
Adoptionism, 37–38, 170, 177–78
Aenon, 201
Age: of brides and grooms, 102–3; relativity of, 176; of Jesus Christ during ministry, 198; of Jesus Christ at death, 391–93
Alexander the Great, xvii
Alteration of texts: apostasy and, 31–32; adoptionism and, 177–79. *See also* Corruption, Textual variants, Scribal errors
Andrew: background of, 216–17, 217–19; called as apostle, 226; becomes disciple, 307–8
Angel: appears to Zacharias, 92–97; appears to Joseph, 106, 118, 134; appears to Mary, 111–12, 128–32; appears to shepherds, 138–40
Animals, wild, 183
Anna, 142
Annas, house of, 53
Annunciation, 128–32
Anointing, of Jesus Christ, 170
Antiochus Epiphanes IV, 258
Antipas, xviii
Antonia fortress, 75
Apostasy: alteration of texts and, 31–32; new dispensation and, 331
Apostles: called from disciples, 213–14; definition of term, 214, 311; backgrounds of, 215–25; calling of, 225–28, 246; definition, history, and usage of term, 228–38; J. A. Baker on term, 231 given authority, 237–40; miracles performed by, 239–40; preparation of, 244–46; Brigham Young on calling of, 311; versus disciples, 311–12; Joseph Fielding Smith on Nephite, 313; Sermon on the Mount directed at, 333–34; trained for missions, 349–53
Aramaic, 21–22
Aristobulus, 101–2
Ashton, Marvin J., on astonishment at Jesus Christ, 316
Assyria, Samaritans and, 251–52
Astonishment: Marvin J. Ashton on, 316; at Sermon on the Mount, 316–18
Atonement: prophecies on, 5–6, 16
Attributes, beatitudes as desired, 338–39. *See also* Characteristics
Audience: of New Testament, xxv–xxvi; of gospel of Matthew, 173–76; of Sermon on the Mount, 308–15, 333–36; Catherine Thomas on Sermon on the Mount's, 312
Authority: of Jesus Christ, 170; apostles given, 238–41; teaching with, 318–23; Francis Wright Beare on scribes', 319; Herman Hendrickx on teaching with, 322
Authors, of New Testament, xxv–xxvi

SUBJECT INDEX

Babies, slaughter of, 147–48, 147–48
Baker, J. A., on term apostle, 231
Balas, Alexander, 259
Ballard, M. Russell, on being disciples, 311
Baptism, 163–66; of Jesus Christ, 166–72, 201–4; Mark's account of, 172–73; Matthew's account of, 173–76; Luke's account of, 176–79; John's account of, 179–80; Joseph Fielding Smith on Nephites', 314
Barclay's Gate, 76–77
Bartholomew, called as apostle, 226
Beare, Francis Wright, on authority of scribes, 319
Beasts, 183
Beatitudes, 336–39; in gospel of Luke, 366–67; on blessings and persecution, 372–74
Benson, Ezra Taft, on Sermon on the Mount, 306
Bethabara, 201
Bethlehem: prophecy on, 17; Joseph and Mary stay in, 117–18, 136–38; slaughter of babies in, 147–48
Betrothal, 103–5, 128; of Mary, 110
Bias, xxviii
Biblical narratives, Glenn A. Koch on, 174
Birds: sacrificed at Temple of Herod, 80–81; Mary and Joseph offer sacrifice of, 116–17, 141–42
Birth of Jesus Christ, 115–16, 137–38; Nephi has vision of, 122–23; gospels testify of, 123–25; annunciation of, 128–32; witnesses to, 147; date of, 383–94
Blessed, characteristics of, 339–44
Blessings, persecution and, 372–74
Boethus, house of, 53
Book of Mormon, prophecies of Jesus Christ in, 4–6
Bride price, 104–5

Caesar, tribute to, 68–69
Caiaphas, Joseph, 53
Cana: wedding at, 221, 300–303
Canaanite, definition of term, 226–27
Canonization, of New Testament, 41–44
Capernaum. *See* Galilee

Carpenter, Joseph as, 105–6
Cave, 137
Change, repentance as, 279–80
Characteristics: beatitudes as desired, 337–38; of blessed, 338–43; of Father in Heaven, 343–46. *See also* Personality
Chief priests, Sadducees and, 49–58
Childhood, of Jesus Christ, 155–57
Children, measuring worth by, 98
Choice, Sadducees' view on, 56–57
Circumcision, of Jesus Christ, 140–41
Clark, J. Reuben, on date of Jesus Christ's birth, 383–84
Clopas, 224
Cloward, Robert: on Sermon on the Mount, 310, 315; on disciples, 312
Comma Johanneum, 40
Communion, in wilderness, 189–90
Conception, of Jesus Christ, 130–32
Condescension, 123, 156
Corruption: of New Testament texts, xvi; of New Testament, 31–32. *See also* Alteration of texts, Textual variants, Scribal errors
Covenants, of Old and New Testaments, xxii
Crucifixion, Sadducees' view on, 57

Dating: of New Testament, xxvi–xxviii; of gospel of John, 28–31
Davies, W. D.: on fulfillment of law of Moses, 325; on location of Sermon on the Mount, 332–33
Dead Sea Scrolls, 65–66
Death: of Zacharias, 96–97; of Joseph, 107; of Jesus Christ, 383–94
Declaration, of Peter, 241–42
Deliverance, prophecy of, 13–14
Demon, casting out of, 282–87
Development, of New Testament canon, 41–44
Disciples: Jesus Christ calls, 203–4; early Judean ministry and, 204–5; apostles called from, 213–14; definition of term, 215–16, 310–11; John the Baptist prepares, 217–19; Samaritans and, 266–67; at Sermon on the Mount, 308–15, 333–36; M. Russell Ballard on being, 311; versus apostles, 311–12; Robert Cloward on, 312

410

SUBJECT INDEX

Dispensation, new, 331–33
Division(s): of New Testament, xxii–xxiv; of Israel, 142–43
Divorce, 133–34
Doctrine: Sadducean, 55–58; of Pharisees, 63–64
Donkey, prophecy of Messiah on, 18
Dreams: 118–19, 147–49, 272–74

Eastern Wall, of Temple of Herod, 74
Egypt, flight to, 118–19, 148–49
Eighteen benedictions, 373
Elijah, John the Baptist and, 199
Elisabeth, 97–101, 112
Enemies, commandment to love, 321–22, 345–47, 367–68
Enthronement poem, 11–12
Ephraem the Syrian, on Jesus Christ at Jacob's well, 267
Epistles, xxiii–xxiv
Erasmus, Textus Receptus and, 35–36
Essenes, 57, 64–69
Eusebius, development of New Testament canon and, 43
Exorcism, 282–87

Families, Sadducean, 53
Father in Heaven, characteristics of, 344–47. *See also* God
Fear, ministry in Galilee and, 274–75
Feast of Tabernacles, Jesus Christ at temple during, 85–86
Fiery serpent, as symbol of Jesus Christ, 10
First vision, similarities in accounts of, 357–59
Fishing, disciples and, 219–20
Forty days, 186, 270

Galilee: Jesus Christ departs to, 209–10, 307–8; Jesus Christ's early ministry in, 271–79, 279–88
Gamaliel, 62–63
Genealogy, of Jesus Christ, 125–28
Gifts, of wise men, 147
God: of Old Testament, 7; knowledge of, through Sermon on the Mount, 344–47; personality of, 349
Golden rule, 60, 368
Good news, beginning of, 160–61
Gospel(s), xxii–xxiii; translated to Greek, 25–26; sources of, 25–31;

of John, 28–31; testify of Jesus Christ's birth, 123–25
Government, Roman, 53–54, 58
Grace, 157
Grain: Jesus Christ picks, 320–21; Bruce R. McConkie on harvesting, 321
Greek: interpretation of, xv–xvi; New Testament translated in, 21–26; in gospel of Mark, 26–28. *See also* Hellenization
Grooms, age of, 102–3
Guelich, Robert A., on Jesus Christ's teaching with authority, 322

Hanukkah, 87
Happiness, in kingdom of heaven, 337
Hasmonean family, 49–51
Healing, on Sabbath, 61–62
Heart, pure in, 343
Hebrews, xxiii
Hellenization: of Jerusalem, xvii–xviii; Sadducees and, 49–50
Hendrickx, Herman, on Jesus Christ's teaching with authority, 322
Herod Antipas: John the Baptist rebukes, 199–200; threatened by Jesus Christ and John the Baptist, early ministry and, 274–75
Herodians, 64–69
Herod the Great, xvii–xviii; builds temple, 71; end of reign of, 91–92; orders murder of children, 118–19, 147–48, 385–86; wise men and, 144–46; Jesus Christ's birth measured by reign of, 384–85
Hiding, Elisabeth and, 98–99
Higher law, restoration of, 331–32
High priests, at time of Zacharias, 93
Hill, David, on term disciples, 312
Hillel, 59–63
Hinckley, Gordon B., on thoughts leading to action, 325–26
Holland, Jeffrey R., on Jesus Christ's showing nature of Heavenly Father, 264
Holy Ghost, conception of Jesus Christ and, 130–32
Hypocrisy, 347, 350–51
Hyrcanus, John, 258

Identity: of Jesus Christ, 259–67;

SUBJECT INDEX

demon knows Christ's, 282–87
Immanuel, prophecies on, 108–9
Immediately, definition of term, 168–69
Inn, 114–15
Intercessory Prayer, 245–46
Interpretation, corruption of New Testament through, xvi
Isaac, as prophecy of Jesus Christ, 10
Iscariot, definition of term, 227–28. *See also* Judas
Ishmael ben Phiabi, house of, 53
Israel: division of, 142–43; higher priesthood restored to, 331

Jacob's well, 259–67
James: background of, 217–19; called as apostle, 226; transfiguration of, 242–44; becomes follower of Jesus Christ, 307–8
Jealousy, Elisabeth and, 100
Jehovah, 7
Jerusalem: Hellenization of, xvii–xviii; Jesus Christ visits, as child, 151–55
Jerusalem temple, Samaritans and, 253–54
Jesus Christ: prophecies about, in Book of Mormon, 4–6; prophecies about, in Old Testament, 7–10; D. Kelly Ogden on walking as, xiv; as salvation, 18–20; language of, 21–22; adoptionism and, 37–38; geneaology of, 37–38; casts money changers from temple, 52, 205–6; trial of, 55; Pharisees and, 62; heals on Sabbath, 67; asked about tribute to Caesar, 68–69; at Temple of Herod, 79–88; as Aaronic priest, 82; Sadducees seek, to arrest and kill, 85–86; Elisabeth prophesies coming of, 99–100; prophecies on, 108–9; birth of, 115–16, 137–38; Nephites await coming of, 121–22; Nephi has vision of birth of, 122–23; gospels testify of birth of, 123–25; genealogy of, 125–28; conception of, 130–32; naming of, 134–35; circumcision and naming of, 140–41; presentation of, at Temple of Herod, 141–44; wise men visit, 144–47; witnesses to birth of, 147; taken to Egypt, 148–49; Moses and, 149, 270; grows up in Nazareth, 149–51; visits Jerusalem as child, 151–55; teaches in Temple of Herod, 153–55; young adulthood of, 155–58; condescension of, 156; John the Baptist preaches of, 163–66; baptism of, 166–72, 201–4; as Son of God, 169–70; anointing and authority of, 170; begins ministry, 170–71; as lamb, 180; temptations of, 181–89, 202; communes in wilderness, 189–90; length of ministry of, 195–97; age of, 198; calls disciples, 203–4; early ministry of, in Judea, 204–11; Herod Antipas threatened by, 207–8; departs to Galilee, 209–10; calls apostles, 225–28; gives apostles authority, 238–41; walks on Sea of Galilee, 240–41; identity of, 259–67; teaches Samaritan woman at Jacob's well, 259–67; as prophet, 262–63; early ministry of, 271–79; early ministry of, in gospel of Mark, 279–88; preaches in synagogue, 280–82; casts out demon, 282–87; early ministry of, in gospel of Matthew, 288–93; early ministry of, in gospel of Luke, 293–99; early ministry of, in gospel of John, 299–304; at wedding at Cana, 300–303; goes to Galilee, 307–8; Marvin J. Ashton on astonishment at, 316; Robert J. Matthews on, teaching doctors, 316; astonishment at, 316–18; teaching with authority and, 318–23; picks grain, 320–21; Herman Hendrickx on, teaching with authority, 322; as fulfillment of law of Moses, 323–27; restores higher priesthood to Israel, 331–33; as master teacher, 333–36; teaches about prayer, 347–49; teaches of God's personality, 349; birth and death dates of, 383–94
Jews: Babylonian, 144–45; John the Baptist preaches repentance to, 163–66; as Matthew's audience, 173–76

412

SUBJECT INDEX

Joanna, 223
Johannine Comma, 40
John: gospel of, xxvi–xxviii; dating and gospel of, 28–31; alterations in gospel of, 38–39; account of Jesus Christ's baptism, 179–80; background of, 216–17, 217–19; called as apostle, 226; transfi transfiguration of, 242–44; Jesus Christ's early ministry in gospel of, 278–79, 299–304; becomes follower of Jesus Christ, 307–8
John the Baptist, 163–66; naming of, 95–96; baptizes Jesus Christ, 166–72, 201–4; beginning of ministry of, 197–99, 389–90; rebukes Herod Antipas, 199–200; public ministry of, 199–201; Herod Antipas threatened by, 207–8; prepares disciples, 217–19; Jesus Christ's early ministry and, 271–79
Joseph, 101–7; angel appears to, 118; reaction of, to Mary's pregnancy, 132–36; goes to Bethlehem, 136–38; flees to Egypt, 148–49; returns to Nazareth, 149–51; departs into Galilee, 273–74
Josephus: on Solomon's Porch, 74; on Western Wall of Temple of Herod, 75; on Royal Stoa, 77–78
Judaism: in Old and New Testaments, xviii; versus religion of Samaritans, 255–59
Judas: replacement for, 190–91; called as apostle, 227–28. *See also* Iscariot
Jude, called as apostle, 226
Judea, ministry in, 204–11
Judgment, righteous, 350–51

Kathros, house of, 53
Kearl, James, on childhood of Jesus Christ, 156
Keys: fiery serpent and, 10; prophesies of Jesus Christ's ministry, 11; Jesus Christ and, 149, 270. *See* Priesthood keys
Kimball, Spencer W., on prayer, 348
King, enthronement poem for, 11–12
Kingdom of heaven, 337, 364–67
King Herod. *See* Herod
Koch, Glenn A., on biblical narratives, 174

Lamb: sacrificed at Passover, 81; Jesus Christ as, 180
Language: of Old and New Testaments, xvii; of Jesus Christ, 21–22
Last Supper: Intercessory Prayer at, 245–46; determining Jesus Christ's death date by, 391–93
Law of Moses, 7–8; Hillel, Shammai, and, 60; oral and written, 318–23;fulfillment of, 323–27; Nephites and, 327–28
Lazarus, rich man and, 366
Lee, Harold B.: on conception of Mary, 113; on Jesus Christ's character, 338
Lehi, receives revelation on Jesus Christ, 4–5
Lesser law, 331
Levites, 223
Liberation, in gospel of Luke, 293–99
Light, 345
Lineage, of Mary and Elisabeth, 100–101
Lord's prayer, variants in, 35–36
Love, for enemies, 321–22, 345–47, 367–68
Luke: gospel of, xxvi; alterations in gospel of, 39; foretells birth of Jesus Christ, 124–25; account of Jesus Christ's baptism in gospel of, 176–79; account of temptations in, 183–89; Jesus Christ's early ministry in gospel of, 277–78, 293–99; rejection and liberation in gospel of, 293–99; clarifications in sermons of, 362–63; beatitudes in gospel of, 366–67; golden rule and, 368; commandment to be perfect and, 369–70

Magic, versus miracles, 282–87
Manuscripts, 23–24
Marcion, development of New Testament canon and, 41–42
Mark: gospel of, xxv, 26–28; as Peter's scribe, 27–28; account of Christ's baptism in gospel of, 172–73; account of temptations in gospel of, 181–83; early ministry in gospel of, 271–72, 279–88
Marriage: of Joseph and Mary, 114,

135; Jewish, 128; of Herod Antipas, 199–200
Mary: Elisabeth and, 99–101; parents of, 103; prophecies on, 107–9, 107–9, 110–11; influence of parents on, 109–10; betrothal of, 110; angel appears to, 111–12, 128–32; visits Elisabeth, 112; pregnancy of, 112–14; marriage of, 114, 135; stays at inn, 114–15; gives birth, 115–16; takes Jesus Christ to Temple of Herod, 116–17; stays in Bethlehem, 117–18; flees to Egypt, 118–19, 148–49; goes to Bethlehem, 136–38; purification of, 141; returns to Nazareth, 149–51
Mary Magdalene, 223
Mary, wife of Clopas, 224
Master, commandment to serve one, 350
Matthew: gospel of, xxv–xxvi; foretells birth of Jesus Christ, 124; account of Jesus Christ's baptism in gospel of, 173–76; account of temptations in gospel of, 183–89; background of, 223; Jesus Christ's early ministry in gospel of, 272–74, 288–93; Sermon on the Mount in gospel of, 307–8, 333–36
Matthews, Robert J., on Jesus Christ's teaching doctors, 316
McConkie, Bruce R.: on wedding at Cana, 221; on prophets as rivers of living water, 261; on harvesting grain on Sabbath, 321; on salvation, 328; on Sermon on the Mount, 334
Meekness, as characteristic of blessed, 341–42
Melchizedek priesthood, restored to Israel, 331–33
Mercy: as characteristic of blessed, 342; perfection and, 369–72
Messiah: prophecy on, 17–18; Sadducees' view on, 57–58; Elisabeth prophesies coming of, 99–100
Messianic prophecies, 10–18
Millennium, prophecy on, 14–15, 16–17, 17–18
Ministry: of Jesus Christ, 170–71; length of Jesus Christ's, 195–97; beginning of John the Baptist's, 197–99, 389–90; John the Baptist's public, 199–201; Jesus Christ's Judean, 204–11; location of Jesus Christ's early, 271–79; Jesus Christ's early, according to Mark, 279–88; Jesus Christ's early, according to Matthew, 288–93; Jesus Christ's early, according to Luke, 293–99; Jesus Christ's early, according to John, 299–304
Miracle(s): performed by Apostles, 239–40; of casting out demon, 282–87; of water turned to wine, 300–303; astonishment at, 317
Missions: of Jesus Christ, 170–71; of apostles, 238–39; apostles trained for, 349–53
Money changers, 52, 205–6
Montanists, development of New Testament canon and, 42
Moses. See also Law of Moses
Mount Eremos, 332–33
Mount Gerizim, 256–59
Mount Moriah, 69–71
Mount Sinai, 332–33
Mourning, as characteristic of blessed, 340–41
Murder, Catherine Thomas on, 325

Names, of Old and New Testaments, xvii
Naming: of Jesus Christ, 134–35, 140–41; of Peter, 242
Nathaniel: background of, 219–21; called as apostle, 226; in gospel of John, 299–300
Nephi: receives revelation on Jesus Christ, 4–5; has vision of Jesus Christ's birth, 122–23
Nephites: await coming of Jesus Christ, 121–22; Joseph Fielding Smith on apostles among, 313; Sermon at the Temple and, 313–15; Joseph Fielding Smith on baptism of, 314; law of Moses and, 327–28
New Testament: questions for writers of, xiv–xv; corruption of, xvi, 31–32; difference between Old Testament and, xvi–xix; 22–23; divisions of, xxii–xxiv; authors and

SUBJECT INDEX

audience of, xxv–xxvi; dating of, xxvi–xxviii; translated into Greek, 22–23; manuscripts of, 23–24; textual variants of, 33; development and canonization of, 41–44; on Sadducees, 56–57
Nicodemus, 62–63; visits Jesus Christ, 206, 208–9

Oaks, Dallin H., on personal revelation, 328–29
Ogden, D. Kelly, on walking as Jesus Christ walked, xiv
Old Testament: prophecies of Jesus Christ in, 7–10; differences between New Testament and, xvi–xix
Oral Law, 318–23
Ordination, of apostles, 238–39
Origen, development of New Testament canon and, 43

Pagan priests, wise men as, 144–45
Papias, on Mark's writing for Peter, 27–28
Papyrus, xxv
Parentage: of Jesus Christ, 37–38; of Joseph and Mary, 103
Passover: Jesus Christ at temple during, 81–82, 83, 87–88; Jesus Christ in Jerusalem during, 151–55; Jesus Christ's ministry measured by, 195–97; determining Jesus Christ's death date by, 391–93
Pauline letters, xxiii
Peacemakers, 343–44
Pentateuch, 255–56
Perfect, commandment to be, 369–72
Persecution: in beatitudes, 344; blessings and, 372–74
Personality, of God, 349. *See also* Characteristics
Perspective, accuracy and, 376–78
Peter: gospel of Mark and, 172; background of, 217–19; called as apostle, 226; declaration of, 241–42; definition of name, 242; receives priesthood keys, 242–44; becomes follower of Jesus Christ, 307–8
Pharisees, 58–64

Philip: background of, 219–21; in gospel of John, 299–300
Pinnacle: of Temple of Herod, 76; Jesus Christ on, 82–83
Pirke Aboth, 319
Poem: enthronement, 11–12; prophesying of abuse, 12
Pools, at Temple of Herod, 74
Poverty: as characteristic of blessed, 339–40; in two sermons, 364–67
Pratt, Parley P., on getting keys, 245
Prayer, 347–49; intercessory, 245–46; twelfth, 373
Preachers, 307
Pregnancy: of Mary, 112–14; Joseph's reaction to, 132–36
Priestcraft, of Sadducees, 52–54
Priesthood keys: Peter receives, 242–44; Joseph Smith gives apostles, 245
Prophecies: about Jesus Christ in Book of Mormon, 4–6; about Jesus Christ in Old Testament, 7–10; messianic, 10–18; of deliverance, 13–14; millennial, 14–18; on Mary, 110–11
Prophet: John the Baptist as, 163–66; Bruce R. McConkie on, 261; Jesus Christ as, 262–63
Protevangelium of James, 96
Pure in heart, 343
Purification, of Mary, 141

Q, gospel of, 45–47
Questions, for New Testament writers, xiv–xv

Rabbis, teaching methods of, 335–36
Rain, during temple construction, 71
Rejection, in gospel of Luke, 293–99
Religion, of Samaritans, 255–59
Repent, definition of term, 279–80
Repentance, John the Baptist preaches, 163–66
Restoration, of higher law, 331–32
Resurrection, Sadducees' view on, 56–57
Revelation: scripture and, 3–4; understanding prophecies through, 19; as rock, 242; John Taylor on, 327; Dallin H. Oaks on, 328–29
Rich man, Lazarus and, 366

SUBJECT INDEX

Righteousness, searching after, 342
Robinson, Stephen E., on fulfillment of Law of Moses, 326–27
Rock, Peter as, 242
Roman government, 53–54; Sadducees and, 58
Rosh HaShanna, Jesus Christ at temple during, 84–85
Royal Stoa, 77–79
Running script, 33–34

Sabbath: Sadducees' view on, 57, 84–85; Hillel and Shammai's views on, 61–62; Jesus Christ heals on, 67; oral and written laws on, 319–21; Bruce R. McConkie on harvesting grain on, 321
Sacrifice: birds as, 80–81; Mary and Joseph offer, 116–17, 141–42
Sadducees: Chief priests and, 49–58; ask about tribute to Caesar, 68–69; Jesus Christ sends, from temple, 83; views on Sabbath of, 84–85; seek to arrest and kill Jesus Christ, 85–86. *See also* Essenes, Herodians
Salome, as disciple, 223–24
Salt, 345
Salvation: Book of Mormon prophecies on, 5–6; temporal, 9–10; Jesus Christ is, 18–20; Bruce R. McConkie on, 328
Samarians, versus Samaritans, 250
Samaritans: origin of, 249–59; religion of, 255–59; at Jacob's well, 259–67
Samuel, prophecy of, 121–22
Sanhedrin, 54–55
Sargon, 251–52
Schiffman, Lawrence, 65–66
Scribal errors: inadvertent, 33–35; intentional, 35–40. *See also* Alteration of texts, Corruption, Textual variants
Scribes, Francis Wright Beare on authority of, 319
Scriptures: temptation of Jesus Christ and, 187; Brigham Young on, 306–7, 329
Sea of Galilee, Jesus Christ walks on, 240–41
Second Coming, Old Testament prophecies of, 8–9

Separatists, Pharisees as, 59
Sepphoris, 105–6
Sermon at the Temple, 313–15
Sermon on the Mount, 239: Ezra Taft Benson on, 306; social setting of, 307–8; audience of, 308–15; Robert Cloward on, 310; Catherine Thomas on audience of, 312; Robert Cloward on, as missionary training, 315; astonishment at, 316–18; taught with authority, 318–23; as beginning of new dispensation, 331–33; W. D. Davies on location of, 332–33; as means of teaching disciples, 333–36; beatitudes and, 336–39; knowledge of Father through, 344–47; prayer and, 347–49; apostles trained for missions during, 349–53; location of, 355–56; identified with Sermon on the Plain, 374–76. *See also* Sermons
Sermon on the Plain, identified with Sermon on the Mount, 374–76. *See also* Sermons
Sermons: similarities in accounts of, 356–62; Luke's clarifications in, 362–63; perspective in, 363–64; poverty in, 364; commandment to love enemies in, 367–68; commandment to be perfect in, 369–72; beatitude on persecution in, 372–74; on mount and plain as same sermons, 374–76; accuracy and perspective in, 376–78. *See also* Sermon on the Mount, Sermon on the Plain
Serpent, 10
Service, of Aaronic priests, 51–52
Shammai, 60–63
Shepherds, angel appears to, 138–40
Sign, Sadducees and Pharisees request, 66–67
Simeon, Rabbi, 142–43; on prayer, 348
Simon, called as apostle, 227
Slaughter, of babies in Bethlehem, 147–48, 386–87
Smith, Hyrum, on date of Jesus Christ's birth, 383
Smith, Joseph: on Sadducees, 56; on Temple of Herod, 72; on

416

SUBJECT INDEX

revelation, 242; gives apostles keys, 245
Smith, Joseph Fielding: on transfer of priesthood keys, 244–45; on calling of apostles, 246; on Nephite apostles, 313; on baptism of Nephites, 314
Solomon, Temple of, 71
Solomon's porch, 74
Son of David, 127
Son of God, Jesus Christ as, 153–55, 169–70
Sources, of gospels, 45–47
Southern wall, of Temple of Herod, 79
Spacing, in translations, 33–34
Spirit, temptation of Jesus Christ and, 186
Star, 146–47
Strecker, Georg, on Jesus Christ's teaching with authority, 319
Suffering, prophecy on Jesus Christ's, 16
Susanna, 223
Synagogue: Jesus Christ preaches in, 280–82; demon cast out in, 282–87
Synoptic, definition of term, xxii

Taheb, 255, 265
Talmage, James E.: on apostles as witnesses, 242; on astonishment at Jesus Christ, 318; on Sermon on the Mount, 353; on date of Jesus Christ's birth, 383
Talmud, on Sadducees, 56
Taylor, John, on revelation, 327
Teaching with authority, 318–23
Temple: Aaronic priests and, 51–52; Sadducees' priestcraft in, 52–54; Samaritans and, 253–54; on Mount Gerizim, 256–59
Temple of Herod: history and physical attributes of, 69–79; diagram of, 70; Jesus Christ at, 79–88; Mary and Joseph take Jesus to, 116–17; Jesus Christ's presentation at, 141–44; Jesus Christ teaches in, 153–55; Jesus Christ casts money changers out of, 205–6; determining Jesus Christ's birth date by, 390–91

Temple of Solomon, 71
Temple of Zerubbabel, 71
Temptations: on pinnacle of Temple of Herod, 82–83; of Jesus Christ, 181–89, 202
Testament, definition of term, xxii
Testing, versus tempting, 182–83
Textual variants, in New Testament, 33, 34. *See also* Alteration of texts, Corruption, Scribal errors
Textus Receptus, 35–36
Thaddeus, called as apostle, 226
Thomas, called as apostle, 226
Thomas, Catherine: on audience of Sermon on the Mount, 312; on murder, 325
Thoughts, lead to action, 325–26
Tiberius, birth of Jesus Christ and, 389–90
Times and Seasons, 96
Tormenters, poem prophesying of, 12
Transfiguration, of Peter, James, and John, 242–44
Translation: corruption of New Testament through, xvi; of New Testament, 22–23, 24; inadvertent scribal errors in, 33–35
Trial of Jesus Christ, 55
Tribute to Caesar, 68–69
Trinity, alteration of text and, 40
True worship, 264–65
Twelfth prayer, 373

Understanding, revelation and, 3–4

Versions. *See* Translation
Virgin, prophecy on, 108

Warren's gate, 76
Water: as commodity, 260–61; prophets as living, 261; turned to wine, 300–303
Wedding at Cana, 221, 300–303; Bruce R. McConkie on, 221
Well, Jacob's, 259–67
Wells, Robert E., on suffering, 340–41
Western wall, of Temple of Herod, 75–76
Wild beasts, 183
Wilderness: temptations in, 181–89, 202; communication and communion in, 189–90

Wine, water turned to, 300–303
Wirthlin, Joseph B., on thoughts leading to action, 326
Wise men, 144–47
Witnesses: to birth of Jesus Christ, 147; apostles as, 213–14
Woodruff, Wilford, on getting keys, 245
Worship, true, 264–65
Worth, children as measure of, 98
Writing utensils, xxiv–xxv
Written Law, 318–23

Yadin, Yigael, 65
Young, Brigham: on reading scriptures, 306–7, 329; on calling of apostles, 311

Zacharias, 92–97
Zadokites, 49–50
Zerubbabel, temple of, 71